Telecommunications and Networking

Udo W. Pooch
Texas A&M University

Denis Machuel
Telecommunications Consultant

John McCahn
Networking Consultant

CRC Press
Boca Raton   Ann Arbor   London   Tokyo

Library of Congress Cataloging-in-Publication Data

Catalog information available from the Library of Congress.

ISBN 0-8493-7172-4

International Standard Book Number 0-8493-7172-4

Printed in the United States of America
4 5 6 7 8 9
Printed on acid-free paper

TABLE OF CONTENTS

PART I   BASICS OF TELECOMMUNICATIONS

Chapter 1   Basics of Telecommunications

Chapter 2   The Signal and Information

PART II   TRANSMISSION SYSTEMS

Chapter 3   Basic Transmission Systems

Chapter 4   Telecommunications Transmission Media

Chapter 5   Analog Versus Digital Communications

Chapter 12 Local Area Network Standards

Chapter 13 Wide Area Network

PART III NETWORKING

Chapter 6 Computer Networks and the User

Chapter 7 Switching Techniques

Chapter 8 Network Topologies

Chapter 9 Routing Algorithms and Flow Control

Chapter 10 Layered Network Services

Chapter 11 Protocols and Example Networks

PREFACE

The purpose of this book is threefold. First, the book is designed to provide to both the practitioner and the student of computing science a familiarity with the basic vocabulary and concepts of telecommunications. Second, it presents an overview of the interaction and relationship between telecommunications and data processing. And third, it addresses in a single volume the widest spectrum of the new environment, computer communications.

The majority of the changes in the data processing environment in the last two decades have been both dynamic and obvious. Even to the casual observer the significant changes in software capabilities coupled with the explosive advances in hardware technology have demanded reexamination and new approaches. Systems analysts and programmers are faced, almost daily, with tradeoffs between the hardware and software elements of their systems. Moreover, curriculums and the published literature stress ever-widening ranges of subjects dealing with both hardware and software. Yet with all this activity and concern, one central trend seems to have developed without attracting the attention it deserves--or at least it developed in such a way that the members of the data processing community have not been properly prepared to deal with it. That trend is the increasing importance of telecommunications in the data processing arena.

No longer can system designers and programmers be effective simply by understanding the tradeoffs between hardware and software. With the advent of the new system designs and concepts, such as networking and distributed processing, data processors must develop a basic understanding of telecommunications. This need is not limited to the complex systems. Even the most elementary data system design involving I/O requires a familiarity with the rudiments of telecommunications principles. Moreover, as the complexity of the data processing system increases, the need for understanding takes on increased importance. In fact, the dividing line between traditional computing science and telecommunications quickly becomes blurred or disappears in today's environment.

Surveys of both graduate and undergraduate computing science majors demonstrate that students are not prepared to deal with this trend. Further, it appears that the same conclusion can be drawn about people who work in both the government and the private sectors of the computer industry. It is our opinion that this situation need not exist.

We readily admit that expecting any individual to be able to deal with the entire spectrum of telecommunications and computing science is unrealistic. However, we hold that given a basic overview of telecommunications and some closely related areas (for example, queueing theory and information theory), and additional reading that provides depth and more vigorous mathematical approaches to specific problems or areas, the majority of the computing science community can be adequately prepared to function in the new environment. It is to this end that our book is designed. Our approach does not require a rigorous background in either mathematics or electronics. On the other hand, it does assume a familiarity with the computing science discipline.

The early chapters of the book present the basic vocabulary and concepts of telecommunications for computer science majors. Besides providing the building blocks for understanding later chapters, these early chapters emphasize and discuss the major limitations and constraints of the common telecommunications services from the data processing viewpoint. In fact, after reading Part I and Part II, the reader should be able to deal with or at least be conversant with the majority of the telecommunications concerns inherent in typical applications. More specifically, the reader should understand why the basic analog services (local telephone and leased-line service) are adequate for voice, but require attention and/or modification to be acceptable for data transmission. The important relationships among coding, error detection and correction, and noise are covered in detail. In addition, the reader should have a basic vocabulary, a familiarity with common nomenclature, and a background in telecommunications fundamentals that will allow him or her to attack the major issues covered in Part III.

It was our intention to make the book useful both as a ready reference tool for data processors in their everyday environment and as a textbook for both graduate and undergraduate computing science majors. Therefore, we have provided practical discussions and problems that deal with "real-world" situations, and detailed references. This approach should allow readers to study any area in the depth demanded by their interest or by the problem on which they are working.

The later chapters provide an overview of computer communications. More specifically, after outlining a classification scheme for computer communications and the networking concept, the book presents specific discussions of such topics as switching, timing, topological structures, and routing algorithms. It then turns to the concept of teleprocessing, and to the ever-increasing overlap between computer science and telecommunications. The impact of changes in hardware technology and the increasing use of minis and micros as front-end processors, multiplexers, concentrators, and terminals is used in illustrating the developing trends.

Specific concerns inherent in computer communications, such as protocols, error detection and correction, network monitoring and security, and validation of the system are reserved for the last chapters. Discussion of these areas provides the opportunity to tie the concepts of networking and computer communications together.

It is our hope that this book will motivate and assist the reader in adequately preparing to function as a member of today's computer industry.

We have tried to reference all the material carefully so that the reader can pursue some area in more detail, to obtain a different point of view, and that proper credit is given to the source of each technique, procedure, method and idea. We sincerely regret any errors or omissions in the latter. All references are collected at the end of the book and are cited in the text.

We take great pleasure in closing this Preface by acknowledging those individuals that make this book possible. Many people have contributed to this book, and we wish space were available to acknowledge and thank all of them. However, special mention must be made to acknowledge Tom Boyd, John Shieh, Richard Wong, Kent Johnson, Ancelin Shaw, Kevin Stroud, Robert Hafernick, Joseph Turner, Eric Nelson, Walter Stolleis, and Peter Schiavi who all read drafts and made valuable comments, Mike Jaffe, who supplied numerous suggestions and corrected several technical errors, Nicole Peed, David Cook and James Wall who provided text processing, editing, formatting and graphics, and David Safford, Robert Diersing and Madhwesh Arun who have read the text more times than we can count and made extensive suggestions.

The Department of Computer Science, Texas A&M University is to be acknowledged for its implicit support and for a stimulating environment in which to write this book. This book evolved from the networks classes in the CS Department; we thank the many students who have passed through these classes for their stimulation, curiosity, good humor and enthusiasm. Our final acknowledgements go to the many researchers and practitioners who have contributed to the development of the fields of telecommunications and networking.

PART 1

Basics of Telecommunications

1

BASICS OF TELECOMMUNICATIONS

1.1 Introduction

During the past few years several dramatic and often rapid changes in hardware and software have occurred. The result to the user of these technologies has been rapid change and improvement in the quality of these systems. Stand-alone and networked microcomputers have become the dominant force in end-user computing. This dominance has resulted in more users coming into direct contact with computers. And, hence, a greater reliance on computers and their systems has taken place.

New skills must be mastered to keep current with the rapidly evolving technology. New systems and the lack of support has made it necessary for these users to become their own mentors. Unfortunately some system's concepts and skills are not grasped by some users. In these cases, experts or those who know are turned to, by the user, for help. One rapidly expanding technology is that of telecommunications and networking.

Telecommunications is frequently defined as "the art and science of communicating at a distance, especially by means of electromagnetic impulses, as in radio, radar, television, telegraphy, telephony, etc." [20].

For the majority of end-users the means of telecommunications and networking are not familiar and will most likely never be familiar. There are, however, the managers or super users of these systems. These users must be familiar with the concepts needed for telecommunications and networking.

Unfortunately, the telecommunications expert was often prepared to provide only a limited degree of support. The existing systems were designed almost exclusively to move voice communication or messages via analog facilities. Furthermore, the telecommunications expert was often unfamiliar with the nuances of transmitting digital data. As a result, telecommunications support for data processing applications was

3

provided by existing common user systems (e.g., telephone lines) or by leased or specially designed user-owned dedicated resources.

The first approach, the use of common user systems, was often unreliable and accompanied by high error and low data rates. The second approach, the use of leased or user-owned dedicated facilities, improved the error and data rates, unfortunately at a much higher cost. The most important concern, however, was that future development in these computer systems would be based on existing telecommunications capabilities. Yet most professionals in the telecommunications industry believed that their systems, with perhaps minor modifications, would be adequate to support the newer developments in future computer system configurations. It appeared that the professionals in neither discipline, the computer sciences nor the telecommunications field, seemed to realize that the trade-offs between the telecommunications subsystem and the computer subsystem were as important as the trade-offs between the hardware and software elements within a single computer system itself. As a direct consequence of this trade-off, system designs often produced complex configurations that failed entirely or that required very costly modifications for only moderate levels of performance.

These early design efforts produced a realization in the unavoidable intertwining of telecommunications and computer processing concepts as far as the design of computer systems is concerned. In fact, the current realization is that whenever computer systems involve internetting, shared resources, or remote users, these systems are then collectively referred to as *computer communications systems*. Thus it appears that some degree of telecommunications skills will be required by most computer systems users.

1.2 Terminology

Fundamental to the understanding of telecommunications is the notion of the signal. It is the signal that contains the information that is moved between two points within the telecommunications system.

1.2.1 Signals

The signal can be most easily discussed by considering a basic sine wave, as illustrated in Figure 1.1. Yet even in this basic form a signal has characteristics that can be discussed in various ways. A signal can be classified as either continuous or discrete, periodic or aperiodic. A signal is said to be *continuous* (also *analog*) if as it passes through its range of values it can assume all of the values within its spectrum. A *discrete*, or *digital*, signal can only assume certain specific values within its range. A *periodic* signal assumes repeated forms of its shape. For example, the sine wave of Figure 1.1 is a periodic signal in that its basic shape is repeated again and again. *Aperiodic* signals, on the other hand, are signals in which the shape is not identically duplicated. Examples of such aperiodic signals are illustrated in Figure 1.2, for both aperiodic analog as well as aperiodic digital signals.

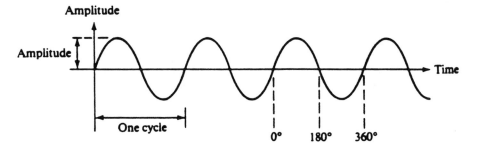

Figure 1.1. Sine wave representation of a signal.

A signal can further be described in terms of three fundamental attributes, frequency, amplitude, and phase. *Frequency* refers to the number of repetitions or appearances of the signal in a given period of time. For example, if the simple sine wave occurs three times within a time period of 1 second, the signal would have a frequency of 3 cycles per second (see Figure 1.3). Cycles per second can be abbreviated as either cps or as hertz, where 1 hertz (Hz) is defined to be 1 cps.

The *amplitude* of the signal represents the instantaneous value of the signal during a cycle (see Figure 1.4). Consider for example the periodic signal illustrated in Figure 1.5, which represents a continuous plot of the instantaneous amplitudes versus 1 second of time.

All of the signals to be used in these examples will be sinusoidal, and can therefore be completely described using the following equation.

$$v(t) = A \sin(2\pi ft + \theta) \tag{1.1}$$

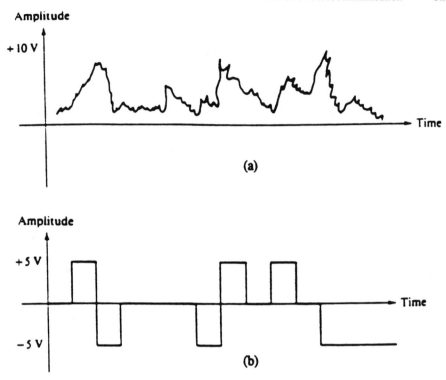

Figure 1.2. Representation of Aperiodic Signal. (a) Aperiodic analog signal (e.g., human voice); (b) Aperiodic discrete signal.

It is easy to see that the signal has an amplitude of zero at time T_0 , and then moves through a range of high values before it returns to zero at point B at time T_2 . The maximum or peak value of +3 V was reached at time T_1 . Once the signal has reached point B, it then takes on negative amplitude values and returns to zero at point C at time T_4 . During one complete cycle the periodic signal's amplitude values assume a complete range, returning to its starting position. For example, in Figure 1.5 the signal moves from point A to point B, returning to zero at T_2 . However, the amplitude of the signal has not yet assumed the complete and full range of values and therefore has not completed a full cycle. The cycle of the signal is from point A to point C. Furthermore, at points C, E, and G this signal has completed one, two, and three cycles, respectively. In the given time period of 1 second the signal has completed three cycles, and thus has a frequency of 3 cps or 3 hz. In addition, the signal is continuous, assuming all values between +3 V to

-3 V during the cycle, and furthermore is periodic, because it repeats itself exactly cycle after cycle.

If the signal could only assume the three discrete values of +3 V, 0, and -3 V, its amplitudes and shape might appear as in Figure 1.5(b). This signal is discrete and periodic. The individual cycles still end at points C, E, and G, and the fundamental frequency is also 3 Hz. It is more important to notice that the continuous signals assume all values between 0 V and +3 V during the period from T_0 to T_2. During this same time period $(T_0 - T_1)$ the discrete signal remains at an amplitude value of 0.

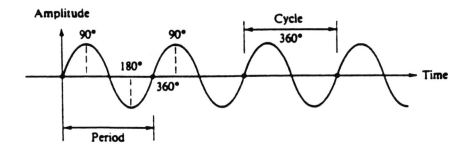

1. A period represents one full cycle
2. A cycle represents 360^0 or 2π radians
3. Angular velocity of the wave = the number of radians that the wave completes in a second.
$$\omega = 2\pi f; \quad f = cps; \quad period = 1/f$$
4. Total angle a sine wave completes in time T is
$$\theta = \omega T = 2\pi f T$$

Figure 1.3. Definitions for frequency and cycles.

The third descriptor of a signal is called a *phase*. When the signal is sinusoidal or consisting of sinusoidal components (i.e., all signals can be decomposed into sine and cosine components), then a cycle represents 360^0 or 2π radians. Thus if a signal has a frequency of 3 Hz, it has passed through $3(2\pi) = 3(360^0) = 1080^0$. Phase therefore represents the part of a cycle that the signal has passed when it is measured. Phase is illustrated in Figure 1.6. Phase can also be viewed as a signal that has advanced a certain number of degrees past the reference point of 0 (see Figure 1.7). Consider the two identical sinusoidal signals, A and B, except that signal A leads signal B by 90^0 or $\pi/2$

radians. Thus, at time T_1 signal A will be at $5\pi/2$, while signal B will be at 2π radians. In other words, signal A will always have traveled further from its starting point and will always lead signal B by $\pi/2$ radians.

In equation 1.1, A represents the maximum amplitude, f is the frequency, t is the instant of time, θ is the phase angle that the signal is ahead of or behind a starting reference point, and v(t) represents the instantaneous values of amplitude. Using this equation it is possible to construct the signal by plotting the individual amplitudes [v(t)] versus time. The signal can be described using amplitude, frequency, or period, and the phase angle can be used to position the signal relative to a specific origin. The phase angle can also be used as a common reference point, and thus will permit the comparison of two or more signals.

Although the signal shapes so far have been sinusoidal or square wave, a wide variety of other waveforms exist. Figure 1.8 illustrates some of the more common waveforms.

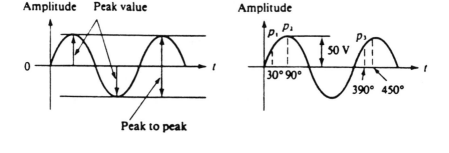

(a) Maximum Values

(b) Instantaneous Values

$$E_p = E_{max} \cdot \sin \theta$$
$$E_{p1} = 50V \cdot \sin(30^0) = 25V$$
$$E_{p1} = 50V \cdot \sin(90^0) = 55V$$
$$E_{p1} = 50V \cdot \sin(390^0) = 25V$$

Figure 1.4. Definition of Amplitude.

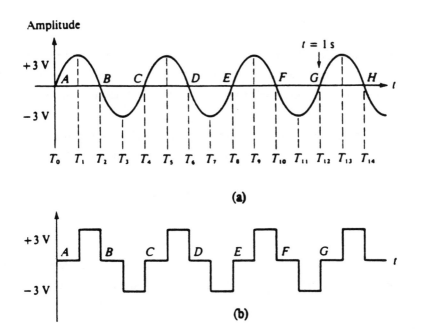

Figure 1.5. Example of frequency and cycles for continuous and discrete signals. (a) Continuous signal; (b) Discrete signal (digital representation of sine wave).

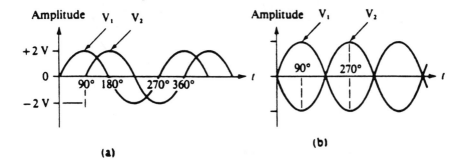

Figure 1.6. Representation of Phase. (a) 90^0 out of phase (V_1 leads V_2 by 90^0); (b) 180^0 out of phase. Phase difference exists when two signals do not pass through the maximum and minimum points at the exact same instant of time

1.2.2 Signals and Time

Although signals can take on many shapes or waveforms, most can be described or derived from simple mathematical models. In fact, most waveforms can be represented by the step function, the exponential function, and the sinusoidal function [1,2,8,10,11, 15,18,19].

The *unit step function* is a discrete function which assumes only on/off or zero/nonzero values. Thus the unit step function can be represented as follows.

$$v(t) = u(t) = \begin{cases} 0 \text{ for } t < 0 \\ 1 \text{ for } t \geq 0 \end{cases} \tag{1.2}$$

This function does not describe what happens at the discontinuity (i.e., during the time intervals where the value of the function changes), where the transition between the two values is instantaneous.

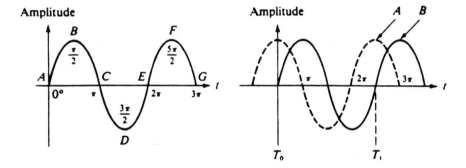

Figure 1.7. Phase Difference between two Signals.

Let us consider how we can manipulate the unit step function. First the amplitude can be changed by multiplying the unit step function (equation 1.2) by a constant A.

$$v(t) = A \cdot u(t) = \begin{cases} 0 \text{ for } t < 0 \\ A \text{ for } t \geq 0 \end{cases} \tag{1.3}$$

Next, the instant at which the step function is discontinuous can be modified in equation 1.3 by replacing t with t - T_0. Thus the value of the function can be rewritten.

$$v(t)= A{\cdot}u(t{-}T_0) = \begin{cases} 0 \text{ for } t < T_0 \\ A \text{ for } t \geq T_0 \end{cases} \tag{1.4}$$

To build a rectangular pulse train, a pair of step functions can be used to express both the amplitude of the state as well as the time when the state changes. Thus, the rectangular pulse can be expressed as the difference of two step functions:

$$v(t) = A{\cdot}u(t - T_x) - A{\cdot}u(t - T_y) \tag{1.5}$$

This formula represents a rectangular pulse of amplitude A, whose value becomes A at T_x and becomes 0 at T_y. A rectangular pulse train which is nonzero for $t \geq 0$ is given by

$$A\sum_{k=0}^{\infty} u(t - KT) - u(t - kT - \tau)$$

where T is the period and τ is the pulse width.

The *sinusoidal function* was already given as

$$v(t) = A \sin(2\pi ft+\theta) \tag{1.1}$$

where f represents the frequency, t the instant of time, A the peak amplitude, and θ the phase angle.

The signal can obviously be changed by varying the amplitude, the frequency or period, and the phase angle.

A function of the type

$$v(t) = u(t) = a^t \tag{1.6}$$

in which the base a is a constant and the exponent t is a variable is called an *exponential function*. It is convenient to express exponential functions with the base e,

$$v(t) = u(t) = e^{t \log a} \tag{1.7}$$

If a > 1, then

$$v(t) = e^{\alpha t} \tag{1.8}$$

where α is $0 \leq \alpha < \infty$, while if a < 1, then

$$v(t) = e^{-\beta t} \tag{1.9}$$

where β is $0 \leq \beta < \infty$.

Again, the amplitude of the signal can be changed by multiplying the exponential function by a constant A.

$$v(t) = A \cdot u(t) = A \cdot e^{\alpha t} \qquad a > 1 \tag{1.10}$$

or

$$v(t) = A \cdot e^{-\beta} \qquad a < 1 \tag{1.11}$$

where $0 \leq \alpha < \infty$ and $0 \leq \beta < \infty$.

Finally, to change the state time we need only replace t by t - T_0 or t + T_0 [i.e., u(t) by u(t $\pm$ T_0)].

It should be obvious that most of the waveforms can now be represented by combinations or products of these three functions.

Amplitude

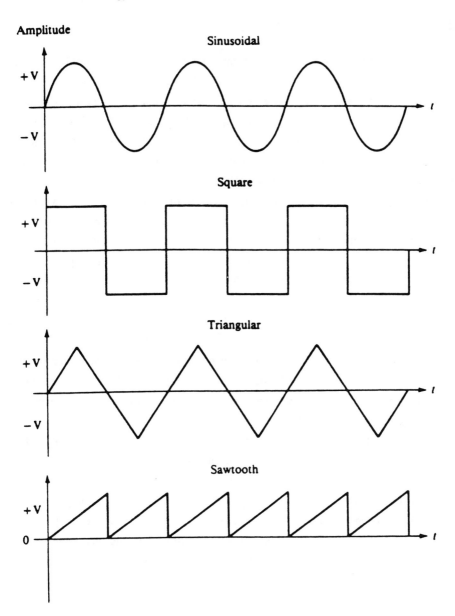

Figure 1.8. Examples of Common Waveforms.

1.2.3 Signals and Frequency

The examples thus far have all represented signals in terms of amplitudes versus time. Systems and devices are usually characterized either by their responses to a signal that contains all frequency components (such as a step function or impulse) or specified by their spectral response. Indeed, time domain and frequency domain characterizations are both used to specify signals and systems. Using both the time and the frequency representations, the impact of signals on the telecommunications systems and their behavior under varying conditions can be analyzed.

Elementary physics provides the actual structure of light. Light can be viewed as consisting of photons (where photons are elementary packets of energy) and thus as a color spectrum, or light can be viewed to consist of electromagnetic waves and thus as a frequency spectrum. This spectrum can be represented in terms of frequency (f) or wavelength (λ), with the following relationship.

$$c = f \lambda \qquad (1.12)$$

Here, the velocity of light ($c = 3 \times 10^8$ m/s) or magnetic wave is constant in a vacuum and is independent of frequency. Using this relationship, the following generalization results. High-frequency waves have short wavelengths, while low-frequency waves have long wavelengths (see Figure 1.9).

Once all these frequencies and wavelengths are plotted, multiple versions of the light spectrum result (see Figure 1.10). The resulting spectrum has been subdivided into arbitrary bands by the telecommunications industry. This has been done for two principal reasons. First, telecommunications systems are classified into types according to the band in which these systems operate. A common classification of these frequency bands is given in Table 1.1. Secondly, systems operating within these defined bands can be described using their operational parameters. The corresponding classification of wavelength bands is given in Table 1.2.

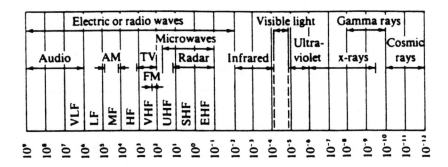

Wavelength (in cm)

Figure 1.9. Light viewed as electromagnetic waves measured in centimeters results in the Electromagnetic Spectrum.

Table 1.1 Common Frequency Bands and Associated Names [2,12-13, 15,17]

Frequency range	Band name
0-30 kilohertz (kHz)	Very low frequency (VLF)
30-300 kHz	Low frequency (LF)
0.3-3 megahertz (MHz)	Medium frequency (MF)
3-30 MHz	High frequency (HF)
30-300 MHz	Very high frequency (VHF)
0.3-3 gigahertz (GHz)	Ultra high frequency (UHF)
3 - 30 GHz	Super high frequency (SHF)
30-300 GHz	Extremely high frequency (EHF)

Table 1.2 The Frequency Range of Various Communication Services

Frequency (cycles per second)	Frequency Range	Communication Service
10^2	Extremely low frequency (ELF) Hertz	Telegraph, teletypewriter
10^3	Voice frequency (VF) 300 Hz to 3 kHz	Telephone circuit
10^4	Very low frequency (VLF) 3 to 30 kHz	High fidelity
10^5	Low frequency 30 to 300 kHz	Fixed, maritime mobile, navigational radio broadcasts
10^6	Medium Frequency 300 kHz to 3 Mhz	Land and maritime mobile radio, radio broadcasts
10^7	High Frequency 3 to 30 MHz	Fixed, mobile, maritime and aeronautical mobile, radio broadcast, amateur radio
10^8	Very high frequency (VHF) 30 to 300 MHz	Fixed, mobile, maritime and aeronautical mobile, amateur radio, television broadcast, radio location and navigation, meteorological communications
10^9	Ultrahigh frequency (UHF) 300 MHz to 3 GHZ	Television, military, long-range radar
10^{10}	Superhigh frequency (SHF) 3 to 30 GHz	Fixed, mobile, radio location and navigation, space and satellite communications, microwave systems
10^{11}	Extremely high frequency (EHF) 30 to 300 GHz	Waveguides, radio astronomy, radar, radiometry
10^{12}	Far infared region 300 GHZ to 3 THz	
10^{13}	Mid-infared region 3 to 30 THz	
10^{14}	Near infared region 30 to 400 THz	Optical Fibers
10^{15}	Visible	Heliograph, signal flags

1 kilohertz = 1000 hertz; 1 megahertz = 1,000,000(10^6) hertz;
1 gigahertz = 1,000,000,000 (10^9) hertz; 1 terahertz = 1,000,000,000,000 (10^{12}) hertz

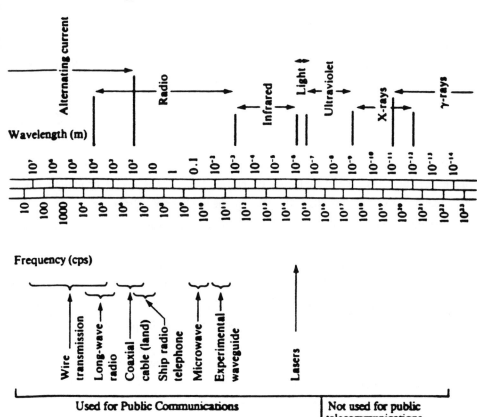

Figure 1.10. The electromagnetic spectrum from the viewpoint of frequency and wavelength.

1.3 Fourier Transforms*

Fourier transforms are a mathematical technique that maps a representation of a waveform (signal) from the time domain to the frequency domain or vice versa (see Figure 1.11). These mathematical transforms are used in widely varying applications including antenna radiations, radio wave propagations, and circuit analysis problems.

---

* see references 3–8 and 14–17

When the transforms are applied to a signal they produce a spectrum of the frequencies that are composites of the signal.

If the signal or waveform is periodic in nature, then the Fourier series that transform between the time and the frequency domains can be represented by

$$v(t) = A_0 + \sum_{n=1}^{\infty} A_n \cos(2\pi nf_0 + \theta_n) \tag{1.13}$$

where f_0 is the fundamental frequency or the first harmonic. A_0 is the dc component of the signal or zero frequency, θ_n is the phase at the nth harmonic frequency.

Periodic signals can therefore be broken into their frequency components by simply expanding the Fourier series. However, in most cases solutions can be obtained by consulting tables (see Appendix I, and also [2,6,15,17,21]) that list the expansions for A_0, the dc component, and the A_n, the harmonic amplitudes, for the most common signals. As an example, consider the waveform illustrated in Figure 1.12. Since the waveform is periodic, the Fourier series will produce the basic frequency components.

P = Period = 100 ms

T = Time pulse = 50

A = Amplitude of cycle = 10 V

D = Duty cycle = T/P = $50\mu s/100\mu s$ = 0.5

f_0 = 1/P = $1/100\mu s$ = 10 kHz

A = A•D = (10 V)(0.5) = 5 V; F = 0

$A_n = \left(\dfrac{2A}{n\pi}\right)$ sin (AπD); $F_n = nF_0$

The expansions are straightforward:

n = 1, $A_1 = \left(\dfrac{20V}{\pi}\right)$•sin (0.5$\pi$) = 6.37; $f_0 = f_1$ = 10 kHz

n = 2, $A_2 = \left(\dfrac{20V}{2\pi}\right)$•sin ($\pi$) = 0; f_2 = 20 kHz

n = 3, $A_3 = \left(\dfrac{20V}{3\pi}\right)$•sin $\left(\dfrac{3\pi}{2}\right)$ = 2.12; f_3 = 30 kHz

n = 10, $A_{10} = \left(\dfrac{20V}{10\pi}\right)$•sin (5$\pi$) = 0; f_{10} = 100 kHz

As can be seen, once the information has been plotted, as in Figure 1.12, the nulls occur whenever sin(nπD) is equal to 0, or at all even n values (corresponding to even frequencies). From the resulting amplitude-versus-frequency plot, it can be seen that only a few of the harmonics are required to obtain a reasonable reproduction of the signal.

Correspondingly, it follows that the more of the spectrum that is included, the closer the original signal or waveform is reproduced. This is illustrated with the next example (see Figure 1.13).

T = Time pulse = 10µs

P = 100µs

D = Duty cycle = T/P = 10µs /100µs   = 0.1

f_0 = Fundamental frequency = $1/P$ = 10 kHz

$A_0 = A \cdot D = (10\ V)(0.5) = 5\ V;\ \ F = 0$

$A_n = \left(\dfrac{2A}{n\pi}\right) \cdot \sin{(A\pi D)};$ $F_n = nF_0$

Again, to show the calculations involved, several amplitude values will be calculated.

$n = 1,\ A_1 = \left(\dfrac{6mV}{2\pi}\right) \cdot \sin(0.1\pi) = 0.59\ mV;$ $f_0 = f_1 = 10\ kHz$

$n = 2,\ A_2 = \left(\dfrac{6mV}{2\pi}\right) \cdot \sin(0.2\pi) = 0.56\ mV;$ $f_2 = 20\ kHz$

$n = 3,\ A_3 = \left(\dfrac{6mV}{3\pi}\right) \cdot \sin(0.3\pi) = 0.51\ mV;$ $f_3 = 30\ kHz$

Another conclusion that can be drawn from this analysis is that a system that detects, constructs, or "reconstructs" the signal need not recognize the entire frequencies but rather only a portion of the frequencies. This characteristic of periodic waveforms will prove to be very useful in the design of telecommunications systems.

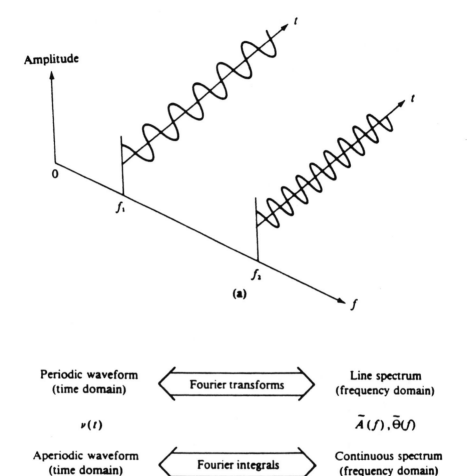

(a)

Periodic waveform   Fourier transforms   Line spectrum
(time domain)   (frequency domain)

$v(t)$ $\tilde{A}(f), \tilde{\theta}(f)$

Aperiodic waveform   Fourier integrals   Continuous spectrum
(time domain)   (frequency domain)

(b)

Figure 1.11. (a) Relationship between time and frequency Domain.; (b) Fourier
transformations between time and frequency domain.

Just as for periodic signals, aperiodic signals can be transformed from the time
domain to the frequency domain by the use of Fourier integrals. The result of the integral
is not a discrete line spectrum as produced by the Fourier series. Instead, the result is a
continuous spectrum of frequencies under a series of envelopes. Thus the aperiodic
waveform in the time domain [v(t)] is mapped using Fourier integrals into the continuous
spectrum of the frequency domain [$\tilde{A}(f), \tilde{\theta}(f)$]. Once again tables have been tabulated (see
Appendix II) for a number of aperiodic signals that allow the analysis of waveforms

without actually performing the integration process. An example of such a process is illustrated in Figure 1.14.

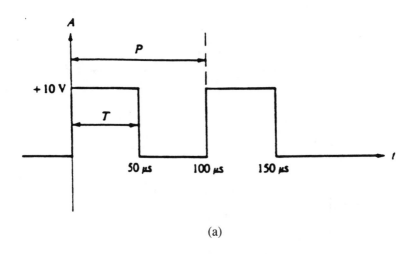

(a)

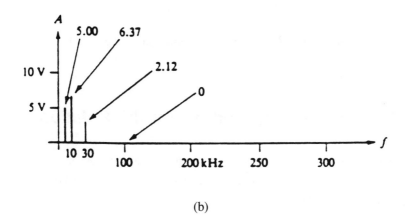

(b)

Figure 1.12. Example of fourier series approximation comparing (a)the time domain; and (b) the frequency domain.

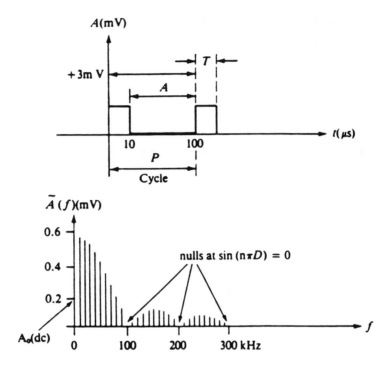

Figure 1.13. Example 2 of fourier series application.

1.4 Time, Frequency, and Bandwidth Relationships

Before describing the time, frequency, and bandwidth relationships, it is convenient to discuss the partial signal descriptions that describe four parameters: Amplitude (A), frequency (f), phase (θ), and time (t).

1.4.1 Amplitude

The *peak value* (V_p) of the amplitude is the maximum absolute value, while the *peak-to-peak value* (V_{pp}) represents the difference between the maximum and the minimum value (see Figure 1.4). The *average value* (V_{av}) represents the area under the waveform divided by the period and is also called the dc value, the constant value, or the zero frequency value. It essentially measures the offset from the amplitude value of V =

0. The *root-mean square value* (V_{rms}) or the *effective value* (V_{eff}) are an indication of the energy contained in the signal and can be used to compare signals.

Waveforms   Amplitude Spectrum

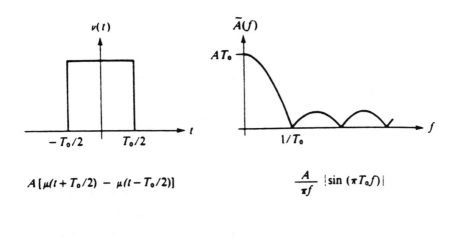

$$A[\mu(t + T_0/2) - \mu(t - T_0/2)]$$

$$\frac{A}{\pi f} |\sin(\pi T_0 f)|$$

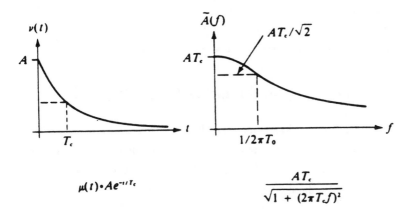

$$\mu(t) \cdot A e^{-t/T_c}$$

$$\frac{AT_c}{\sqrt{1 + (2\pi T_c f)^2}}$$

Figure 1.14. Fourier Integral Waveform-Spectrum Pair.

1.4.2 Frequency

The *lower cut-off frequency* (F_l) is the frequency below which the spectrum is negligible, while the *upper cut-off frequency* (F_u) is the frequency above which again the spectrum is negligible. The *bandwidth* is then defined as (F_u - F_l), and whenever F_u is large while F_l is small, it can be approximated by F_u (i.e., BW $\approx$ F_u).

1.4.3 Phase

Two sinusoidal waveforms that go through the maximum and the minimum value at the same instant are in phase, while if they do not, then the two signals are out of phase with a corresponding phase difference (see Figure 1.15).

1.4.4 Time

A *period* (T_p) is the measure or interval of repetition of a periodic signal. The *rise time* of a pulse (T_R) is the time required for the signal to increase from 10 percent of its peak value to 90 percent of its peak value (see Figure 1.16). The *fall time* (T_F) of a pulse is the time required for the signal to decrease from 90 percent to 10 percent of its peak value. The *duration* of a signal (T_D) is the total elapsed time from the beginning to the end of its excursion measured at 50 percent points of its peak value.

1.4.5 Time, Frequency, and Bandwidth relationships

For both periodic and aperiodic pulse signals the *reciprocal spreading property* states that if signals spread out in the time domain, the corresponding shape will be compact in the frequency domain and vice versa (see Figure 1.17). As a general rule, the bandwidth of a signal times the pulse duration approximates 1. That is,

$$BW \cdot T_D \approx 1.$$

For example, with $T_D \approx 0.1$ ms, BW = 10 kHz.

The signal spreads out farther in the time domain, with a larger T_D, with a corresponding compaction in the frequency domain (i.e., F_u is lower). This implies that shorter duration pulses require greater bandwidths. As a result we have more pulses at greater speed but with greater bandwidths (see Figure 1.18). For example, if T_D = 0.2 ms, F_u = 5 kHz while on the other hand if T_D = 1 ms, F_u = 1 kHz. Thus a pulse with five times smaller pulse duration requires five times the bandwidth.

Periodic pulse signals can be broken into their frequency components using Fourier series, where the amplitude spectrum need not include all frequency harmonics to have a good approximation of the original signal (see Figures 1.19 and 1.20). As can be seen from Figure 1.21 and the preceding two diagrams, the exact values of F_l and F_u are a matter of choosing the components which provide the closeness of representation needed for the desired application.

It should also be fairly obvious that for some signals, certain harmonic components can be eliminated from the signal's spectrum without grossly distorting the signal waveform.

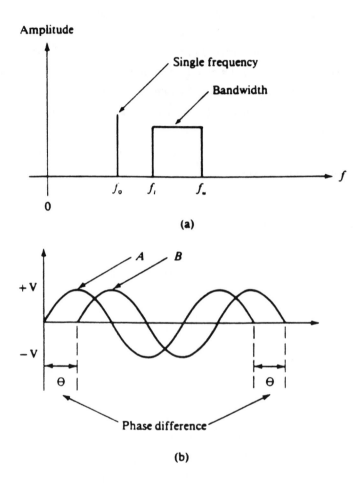

Figure 1.15. (a) Representation of Single Frequencies and Bandwidth; (b) Phase Difference between two Waveforms.

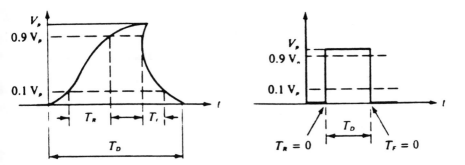

Figure 1.16. Rise time (T_R), fall time (T_F), and duration (T_D) of a Signal.

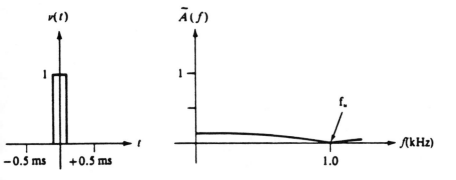

Figure 1.17. Illustration of the reciprocal spreading property of pulse signals.

Note: F_U can be considered to be $1/T_D$. (BW) = F_U - F_L

But when $F_L \approx 0$, (BW) $\approx F_U = 1/T_D$

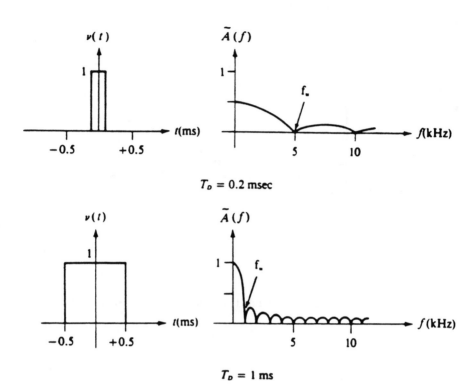

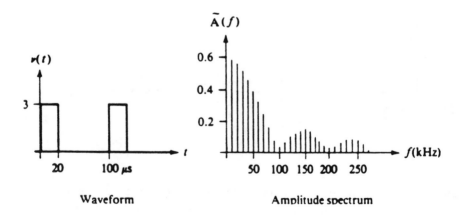

Figure 1.18. Bandwidth-Pulse Duration Relationship BW•T_D≈1.

Figure 1.19. Waveform-Spectrum Correspondence.

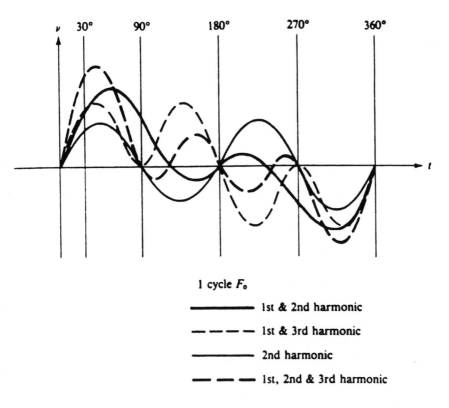

1 cycle F_o

—————————— 1st & 2nd harmonic

— — — — — 1st & 3rd harmonic

—————————— 2nd harmonic

— — — — 1st, 2nd & 3rd harmonic

Figure 1.20. Amplitude Spectrum made using various Harmonics.

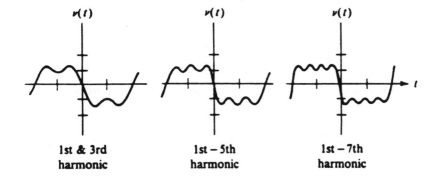

1st & 3rd
harmonic

1st – 5th
harmonic

1st – 7th
harmonic

Figure 1.21. Effect of Spectral Components on a Square Waveform [9].

1.5 Exercises

1.1   What is meant by each of the following terms:

        carrier

        sidebands

        modulation

        harmonics

1.2   What is the purpose for using the Fourier series? What are the coefficients of the Fourier series?

1.3   Prove, by integration, the Fourier coefficient given below for the cosine function of a sawtooth waveform yields zero:

$$a_n = \frac{1}{\pi} \int_0^{2\pi} \omega t \, \cos(n\omega t) \, d(\omega t)$$

1.4   Explain in general terms how Fourier series are related to data communications.

1.5   How does an analog signal differ from a digital signal?

1.6   Find the Fourier transforms and plot the amplitude and phase spectra of the following exponential signals ($\alpha > 0$):

        (a) $x(t) = Ae^{-\alpha t}u(t)$

        (b) $x(t) = Ae^{-\alpha|t|}$

1.7   If a single rectangular pulse is the input to a PM system, the modulated signal will be of the form

$$x(t) = \begin{cases} A \cdot \cos 2\pi(f_c + \Delta f)t & |t| < \frac{1}{2}\tau \\ A \cdot \cos 2\pi f_c t & \text{otherwise} \end{cases}$$

Find the Fourier transform of x(t) and plot the amplitude spectrum.

1.8   Given the Fourier transform $X(f)$ of $x(t)$, how would you obtain the Fourier transform of $x^2(t)$?

1.9   Why is code translation required in communication networks?

1.10   Describe each of the following terms as completely as possible:

        analog signal

        digital signal

        continuous signal

        discrete signal

> periodic signal
> aperiodic signal

1.11 What relationship exists between the time and the frequency representation of a signal?

1.12 What is the relationship between time, frequency, and bandwidth?

1.13 Discuss the reciprocal spreading property for both periodic and aperiodic signals in the time and the frequency domain.

1.14 What is meant by a telecommunications system? Does it differ from a data communications system?

1.15 How is a signal described? How is it possible to transmit information by way of these signals? Does any one description have advantages over the other?

1.6 References

1   Beckenbach, E. F. (ed.), *Modern Mathematics for the Engineer*. New York, NY: McGraw-Hill, 1961.

2   Black, U., *Data Networks: Concepts, Theory, and Practice*. Englewood Cliffs, NJ: Prentice-Hall, 1989.

3   Bracewell, R., *The Fourier Transform and Its Applications*. New York, NY: McGraw-Hill, 1965.

4   Campbell, J., *The RS-232 Solution*. Berkeley, CA: Sybex, Inc., 1984.

5   Churchill, R. V., *Fourier Series and Boundary Value Problems*. New York, NY: McGraw-Hill, 1963.

6   Couch, L. W., *Digital and Analog Communications Systems*. New York, NY: MacMillan Publishing Company, 1983.

7   Couch, L. W., *Digital and Analog Communications Systems* (2nd edition). New York, NY: Macmillan Publishing Company, 1987.

8   Hammond, J. L., and O'Reilly, J. P., *Performance Analysis of Local Computer Networks*. Reading, MA: Addison-Wesley, 1986.

9   Heath Company, *Electronic Communications*. Benton Harbor, MI, 1981.

10   Kaplan, W., *Advanced Calculus*. Reading, MA: Addison-Wesley, 1952.

11   Kennedy, G., *Electronics Communication Systems*. New York, NY: McGraw-Hill, 1970.

12   Martin, J., *Telecommunications and the Computer*. Englewood Cliffs, NJ: Prentice-Hall, 1977.

13   Martin, J., *Future Developments in Telecommunications*. Englewood Cliffs, NJ: Prentice-Hall, 1977.

14   Papoulis, A., *The Fourier Integral and Its Applications*. New York, NY: McGraw-Hill, 1962.

15   Pooch, U. W.; Greene, W. H.; and Moss, G. G., *Telecommunications and Networking*. Boston, MA: Little, Brown and Company, 1983.

16   Sneddon, I. A., *Fourier Transforms*. New York, NY: McGraw-Hill, 1951.

17   Stallings, W., *Data and Computer Communications*. New York, NY: MacMillan Publishing Company, 1985.

18   Tanenbaum, A. S., *Computer Networks*. Englewood Cliffs, NJ: Prentice-Hall, 1981.

19   Tanenbaum, A. S., *Computer Networks* (2nd edition). Englewood Cliffs, NJ: Prentice-Hall, 1988.

20   *Webster's New Collegiate Dictionary* (8th edition). Springfield, MA: G. and C. Merriam Company, 1977.

21   Ziemer, R.; Trauter, W.; and Fannin, D., *Signals and Systems: Continuous and Discrete*. New York, NY: MacMillan Publishing Company, 1983.

2

THE SIGNAL AND INFORMATION

2.1 Information and Coding

Information, derived from the Latin word *informatio*, means a representation, an outline, or a sketch. *Webster's New Collegiate Dictionary* [28] includes such definitions as "1. the communication or reception of knowledge or intelligence; 2. knowledge obtained from investigation, study, or instruction; 3. a numerical quantity that measures the uncertainty in the outcome of an experiment to be performed; 4. intelligence, news, facts, data..." From these definitions it appears that information has two aspects, a quantitative characteristic and a qualitative characteristic. The qualitative aspect of information, corresponding to the value of the data, is of utmost importance to the user who understands its meaning. This aspect of information is of no interest to the telecommunications expert, nor to the telecommunications system. It is the quantitative aspect of information that is important to the communications system. The user of a communications system is concerned only with the knowledge the system provides with each new input.

Information theory can be used to choose codes and correct modulation techniques, to predict the effect of noise and error rates, and also to relate channel capacity and the noise penalty incurred in using multiple-level codes. The idea is to choose a coding scheme that will allow the average number of bits per character to equal H. Brown and Glazier have shown that the binary Huffman coding technique is a useful procedure in optimizing codes [4] (i.e., optimal in the sense of minimizing the average code length). In fact, using these coding schemes it is possible to generate all the states that a telecommunications system must be able to recognize [3,4,13,26,27].

System designers must specify levels of signal strength such that the system, in an environment with noise, can identify each of the particular code levels. If the noise level is relatively low there is no identification problem; but as the levels are bunched closer together or as the noise power approaches the signal power, other methods must be used to identify these weak or multilevel signals. One solution to this problem is to increase the range between distinguishable signal levels, or, for lower information rates, to allow for a longer period for detection to determine which of the particular signal levels was transmitted.

Shannon has given a relationship between the signal rate, bandwidth, and noise [3,14,15,18,20,23,24,26].

$$C = B \log_2(1 + S/N) \tag{2.1}$$

where C is the signaling rate, B the bandwidth of the channel, S the power of the signal, and N the power of the noise. The signal-to-noise ratio (S/N) also requires an appropriate adjustment as the levels of code increase, if the probability of correctly detecting the signal is to be maintained [1,2,5,8,15].

From the foregoing discussion it can be seen that it is necessary to determine the proper coding scheme, for then the requirements of the system can be determined in terms of S/N, C, and the bandwidth. These theoretical values only provide bounds on the design and requirements of the system.

2.2 Modulation*

Information can be superimposed on a carrier signal by a technique called *modulation* and then removed at the receiving end in a reverse process called *demodulation*. In other words, if the tone or carrier signal is represented by

$$f(t) = A \cdot \cos(2\pi f_c + \theta) \tag{2.2}$$

where A is the amplitude, f_c is the carrier frequency, and θ the phase angle, modulation will occur if any one of the three variables varies in accordance with the input signal waveform. The objective of any of these various modulation schemes is to translate the frequency band of the input signal to another band centered around the carrier frequency.

---

* see references 3, 10, 13, 15, 16, 19–21 and 27.

For example, in order to multiplex two signals and allow them to share one channel, we modulate one of them so that their frequency spectra become disjoint. This includes matching the signal or waveform to the channel characteristics while at the same time minimizing the alteration, distortion, and noise effects on the signal.

The three basic forms of modulation, illustrated in Figure 2.1, are amplitude modulation (AM), frequency modulation (FM), and phase modulation (PM). From these three, additional modulation techniques have been developed (e.g., delta modulation or pulse code modulation). Each form of modulation can be further subdivided into three subtypes depending on the format of the input signal (i.e., analog input, binary input, or M-ary(groups of binary input).

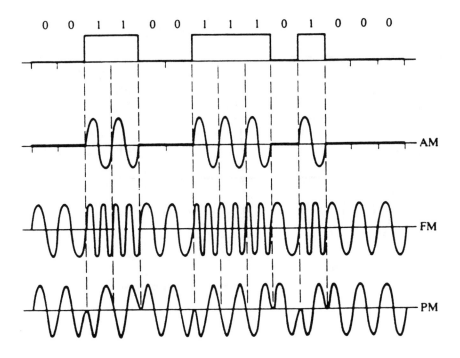

Figure 2.1. Three Fundamental Modulation Techniques.

2.2.1 Amplitude modulation

Amplitude modulation (AM) is derived from early carrier telegraph systems as an outgrowth of the dc telegraph system. The most basic AM system consists of on/off keying of a tone generator, as illustrated in Figure 2.2. The system was used for simple binary data where ones (tone on) or zeros (tone off) were used to denote the information content. AM systems (especially, the on/off keying systems) employ 100 percent modulation, i.e., tone full on or full off. This represents, in general, the optimum signal-to-noise ratio.

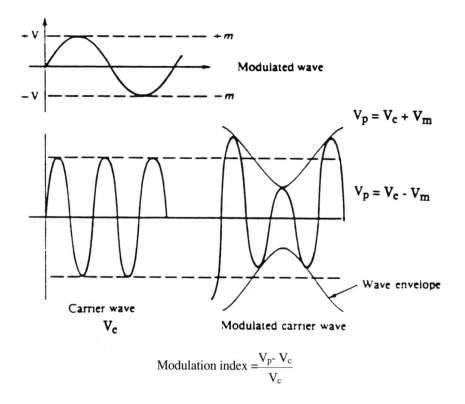

Figure 2.2. In amplitude modulation, the amplitude of the carrier wave is controlled by the modulated wave (information-carrying wave).

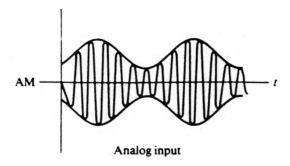

Analog input

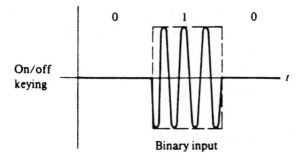

Binary input

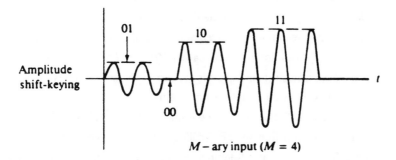

M – ary input (M = 4)

Figure 2.3. Amplitude modulation with three types of input signals.

In *AM modulation*, the amplitude and the power of the carrier change in accordance with the input signal (see Figure 2.3). In the first case, the analog input signal causes the power of the carrier to vary smoothly as the signal changes (e.g., used in commercial radio broadcasts). On/off keying imposes a binary condition onto the carrier. The power or amplitude varies between two values in accordance with the input signal. The last form of input uses M-ary signaling. This procedure collects the binary input data into groups and converts them into a signal, where each signal represents modulo 2 information. The resultant output signal becomes a mix between true binary and true analog data. The still-discrete data are packed modulo 2 into a signal. In the case illustrated in Figure 2.3, the data bits are gathered in groups of two, and since four permutations of two data groups are present, the keying technique transmits one of four amplitude levels. When these amplitude levels are detected at the receiving end, the generation of corresponding two data bits is produced.

In AM, media attenuation, delay distortion, and echo will change the shape of the signal output. In addition, since there are places in the pulse train when and where there are no signals present, the receiver will then see an idle line and is therefore extremely susceptible to noise peaks, intermodulation products, and crosstalk from adjacent channels. The problems of varying signal level often necessitate the use of AGC (automatic gain control) circuits in the receiver.

2.2.2 Frequency modulation

Frequency modulation (FM) is a technique in which the frequency of the signal is varied at a rate equivalent to the value of the modulating signal (see Figure 2.4). Analog input signals will shift the frequency of the signal about a nominal center frequency, called the carrier frequency, at the rate of the frequency of the input signal.

The next modulation technique uses frequency shift keying (FSK) to transmit binary data. These frequency states are generally called *Mark and Space*. Mark is the carrier frequency plus the described shift and Space is the carrier frequency minus the shift.

FSK, like AM, has its origin in the carrier telegraph system. Unlike AM, where the carrier is turned on and off, FSK uses a continuous carrier and therefore permits the receiver to employ limiting action and also makes FSK insensitive to amplitude changes. For this reason, FSK has a greater tolerance to signal fades, impulse noise, and other disturbances which affect amplitude.

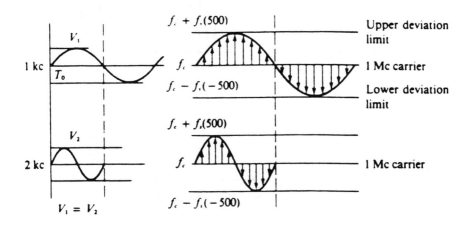

Figure 2.4. Frequency modulation. If a carrier of 1 megacycle is modulated by a 1000 cycle sinusoidal signal, the frequency swing (amount of change) will depend on the amplitude of the 1000-cycle modulated wave. If frequency swing is 500 cycles for amplitude V_1, the carrier will swing between 1,000,500 and 999,500 cycles at the rate of 1000 Hz. If a 2000-cycle modulating signal is used with $V_2 = V_1$, then the frequency swing is still ±500 cycles but the rate of change will be 2000 Hz. The deviation rate is the rate at which the carrier frequency is shifted.

M-ary signaling, called *multitone* in frequency signaling, provides higher data throughput. Similar to FSK, this technique gathers the input, data stream into groups and supplies an output signal of a discrete number of frequencies. In general, forms of M-ary signaling diminish the given signal bandwidth and make the system more susceptible to noise and drift.

2.2.3 Phase modulation

Although *phase modulation* (PM) is the most complex to generate and detect, this technique provides the best performance under noisy conditions. With analog inputs, the instantaneous carrier phase deviates in proportion to the amplitude of the data, while the rate of deviation depends on the frequency of the incoming information. The phasor swings back and forth about the origin in accordance with the analog data (see Figure 2.1). It should also be noted that a phase modulated signal is frequency modulated because the instantaneous frequency is the derivative of the phase.

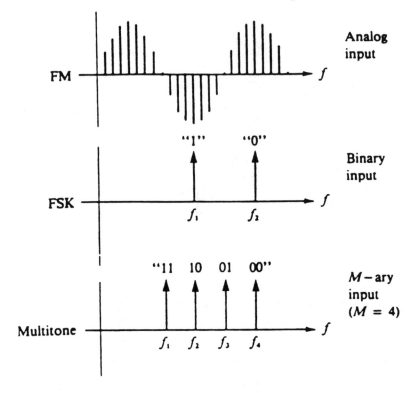

Figure 2.5. Frequency modulation with three types of input signals.

As in FSK, *phase-shift-keying* (PSK) is a form of angle modulation and the PM signal does not have amplitude variations. A simple binary modulating signal would cause the generation of the 0^0 and 180^0 phases of a carrier to represent Mark and Space (or binary one and zero), respectively. The receiver recognizes these shifts and the data are presented to the receiving destination. Note that both phase angles are referenced to a defined phase angle, recognized by both the transmitter and the receiver.

For higher data rates, phase shifts of 90^0 and 45^0 might be used, each corresponding to a binary bit in the transmitter data. Since 90^0 (or 45^0) phase shifts represent discrete bits, it follows that as the shifts become smaller a larger number of data bits may be accommodated. These four-and eight-phase systems are widely used, since they reduce the required channel bandwidths.

The proper reception of data depends on the accurate detection of the phase changes with respect to some starting point, thus an accurate, stable reference phase is required at the receiver to distinguish between various phases. The need for the precise phase-reference signal is avoided by using what is called a *differentially coherent PSK* (DPSK). In DPSK, the data are encoded in terms of phase changes, rather than absolute phases, and are detected by comparing the phases of adjacent bits.   This technique uses M-ary signaling to increase throughput when noise permits.   Note that in Figure 2.6 data bit groups cause one of a discrete group of phasors to be transmitted.   At the receiving end, the appearance of this phasor causes two logical data bits to appear at the output of the receiver.   Also note that the multiphase technique diminishes the signal bandwidth and therefore requires greater stability in transmit and receive references.

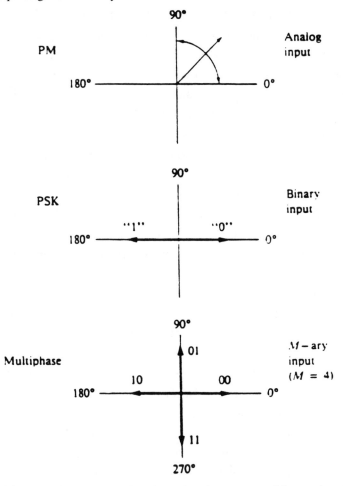

Figure 2.6. Phase modulation with three types of input signals.

PSK or DPSK provides the best tolerance to noise of any system thus far discussed, but when differential detection is used, it is limited to synchronous systems. Differential coherent four-phase modulation is generally used at data rates of 2400 bps. It does not require complex detection circuitry and results in low system operating costs. Differential coherent eight-phase modulation is used for synchronous operation at 4800 bps.

2.2.4 Pulse modulation

In all of the three previous modulation techniques the information/data (the condition of zero or one) was used to modify either amplitude, frequency, or phase. For example, when the frequency was varied, the amplitude and the phase remained constant, and when the phase changed the amplitude and the frequency remained constant. From the concepts of coding and information theory we know that increasing the possible states also increases the complexity of the decoding as well as the possibility of noise and distortion. A coding scheme involves a trade-off between the data/information that can be packed into a signal and the probability of a correct identification of the signal in the presence of the noise and distortion in a given bandwidth. The same trade-offs are inherent in the modulation procedure which is tied directly to the coding approach.

The basic *pulse modulation* techniques, illustrated in Figure 2.7, correspond to the three basic modulation approaches. The sampling of the signal occurs at specified intervals. The value for each sample is then converted into a pulse, which is then transmitted.

In *pulse amplitude modulation* (PAM) each of the sampled pulses that is transmitted varies in height to reflect the measured value, but remains constant in width and time position. In *pulse width modulation* (PWM) or *pulse duration modulation* (PDM) the width of the transmitted pulse is changed to reflect the value that was measured. The time position and the amplitude of the pulse remain constant. Finally, in *pulse position modulation* (PPM) the position of the pulse relative to a fixed time position varies, while the other two values are held constant [17].

Pulse code modulation (PCM) is a special variation of PAM and, as in PAM, the signal is sampled at specific intervals. However, unlike PAM, the sample is only allowed to take on discrete and not continuous values. The procedure that places the sample into one of the discrete values is called *quantizing*. The quantized values or samples are then converted into a pulse pattern of constant amplitude and width by a device called an *encoder*. At the receiving end, a device called a *decoder* breaks the pattern

back into pulses. The pulses contain representations of the periodic sampled values of the
original signal.

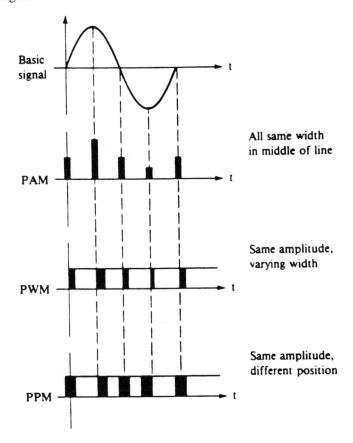

Figure 2.7. Three basic pulse-modulation techniques.

The restructured signal is generated which approximates the input signal (see Figure
2.8). The three basic operations for PCM are sampling, quantizing, and encoding. Basic
sampling theory indicates that an analog signal can be reproduced with very little
distortion if the sampling frequency is at least twice as high as the highest frequency to be
transmitted. The number of steps used to represent the sample (or to quantize it)
determines the quality of the recovered signal at the receiver. The number of binary bits
necessary to give a digital code representation is of course dependent on the quantization
steps. For example, in the T1 carrier, 24 voice channels are TDM multiplexed in an
overall frame of 193 bits. To each 7-bit sample from each of the constituent channels is

added an eighth bit, a "one," for timing purposes. This last bit of the frame is used to maintain frame synchronization. With 193 bits and a frame rate of 8000 frames/s, the overall bit rate of the carrier is 1.544 Mbps.

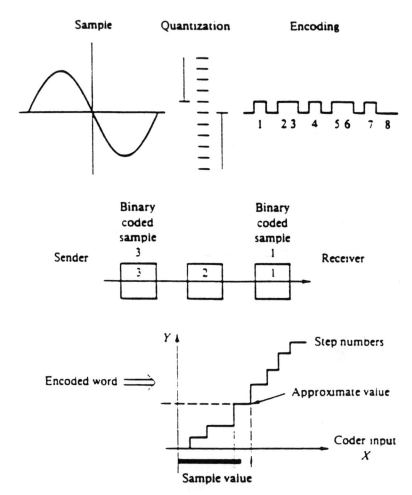

Figure 2.8. Pulse-coded modulation.

The advantage of this approach is that information is transmitted in digital form, which is less likely to be misinterpreted or interfered with. The sender and the receiver in effect just see patterns of zeros and ones. The transmission system periodically examines the signal, recognizing the presence or absence of pulses. These pulses can be regenerated periodically. Any attenuation or distortion is removed by the regeneration of the pulse.

When the pattern arrives at the decoder, the pulse pattern is most likely to be distorted. The majority of error is found in the quantizing of the original signal and the approximating of the regenerated signal at the receiver. This error is referred to as the *quantizing error* and can be minimized by using nonuniform quantization/regeneration steps. That is, low-level samples at the input of the coder are compared against (quantized by) small steps, whereas high-level samples are quantized by large steps. This is a compression technique which maintains relatively constant quantizing distortion over the range of samples. The quantizing error can also be related directly to acceptable noise levels, and trade-offs can be made in codes, recognizable sample levels, and the S/N ratio.

Once the voice signal has been digitized, it is tempting to try to use statistical techniques to reduce the number of bits needed per channel. These techniques are appropriate not only to encoding speech, but to any digitization of an analog signal. All of the compaction methods are based on the principle that the signal changes relatively slowly compared to the sampling frequency, so that much of the information in the 7-or 8-bit digital level is redundant.

One method, called *differential pulse-code modulation*, consists of not outputting the digitized amplitude, but the difference between the current value and the previous one. Since jumps of 32 or more on a scale of 128 are unlikely, 5 bits should suffice instead of 7. If the signal does occasionally jump wildly, the encoding logic may require several sampling periods to catch up. For speech, the error introduced can be ignored.

A variation of this compaction method requires each sampled value to differ from its predecessor by either +1 or -1. A single bit is transmitted, telling whether the new sample is above or below the previous one. This technique is called *delta modulation*. Like all compaction techniques that assume small-level changes between consecutive samples, delta encoding can misrepresent the signal if it changes too fast.

An improvement to differential PCM is to extrapolate the previous few values to predict the next value and then to encode the difference between the actual signal and the predicted one. The transmitter and receiver must use the same prediction algorithm, of course. Such schemes are called *predictive encoding*. They are useful because they reduce the size of the numbers to be encoded, hence the number of bits to be sent.

2.2.5 Comparison among the types of modulation

The various modulation techniques have distinct advantages and disadvantages in terms of cost and noise susceptibility. In the broadest sense, noise is any interference with the telecommunications signal (more detail is given in Ch. 3). Resistance, thermal, johnson, or *white noise* is due to thermal agitation or radiation. This type of noise is relatively constant and uniformly distributed in terms of energy across the frequency spectrum (see Figure 2.9). *Impulse noise*, on the other hand, is sporadic, occurs in nonuniform bursts, and is caused either by nature (e.g., lightning, aurora borealis) or, more often, by humans (e.g., ignition, power lines, switching systems).

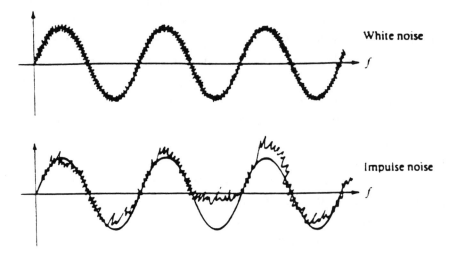

Figure 2.9. White and impulse noise.

Amplitude modulation is widely used in radio communications and is simple to implement, easy to maintain, relatively low in cost, and less susceptible to delay distortion. On the other hand, AM is very susceptible to impulse noise and susceptible to changes in transmission levels.

Frequency modulation, when above S/N threshold, is more effective in terms of noise resistance and the reproduction of frequencies (i.e., insensitive to level variations), relatively inexpensive, and can be used easily in medium-speed applications (up to 2400 bps). On the other hand, the shifting of frequency to transmit data reaches a practical limit at approximately 2400 bps, while frequency modulation, in general, is suitable for all data rates. A new and growing application of FM is in the area of data communications.

Phase modulation is by far the most complex and most costly approach. However, it is insensitive to level variations, can transmit low modulating frequencies including zero, and theoretically makes the best use of bandwidth for a given transmission speed. All systems are subject to some phase drift and phase ambiguity, i.e., if a disturbance destroys a preceding pulse, then the receiver must guess at a zero or a one. If the guess is wrong, then all the following data are wrong. This can be corrected by the use of a reference or *pilot tone*.

Phase modulation and hybrids of phase and amplitude modulation are increasingly being used in data communications applications.

2.3 Multiplexing*

Multiplexing is a technique whereby a number of independently generated signals can be combined and transmitted on a single physical circuit. The justification for the use of multiplexing is more effective utilization of systems resources. Multiplexing is usually divided into two categories, time multiplexing and frequency multiplexing.

A discussion dealing with the simultaneous transmission of several messages over the same channel would be impossible without the use of filter circuits, which are designed to accept certain frequencies and reject all others. These filters are commonly called *bandpass filters* and consist of resistors, capacitors, and inductors whose values determine the frequency that the filter will accept or reject. Thus, when a signal is transmitted through a filter, only the frequencies within the passband will be transmitted over the communications channel. A filter for the same frequency at the destination will permit only the desired frequencies to be received. Thus, when several frequencies are transmitted on the same channel, filters are used at both the transmitting and receiving stations to "separate" one frequency from another. This is one of the basic functions of a frequency-division multiplexing system. Frequency translations of the different signals into disjoint frequency bands is another basic function.

Frequency division multiplexing (FDM) consists of dividing a high-capacity circuit into compartments on the basis of frequency bands (see Figure 2.10). When a number of different low-bandwidth signals are combined and transmitted simultaneously over a higher-bandwidth circuit, either amplitude, frequency, or phase modulation can be used to multiplex the signals.

---

* see references 1–3, 6, 9–12, 16, 21, 22 and 25

Major inefficiencies exist in the use of FDM techniques. These inefficiencies are primarily reflected in the limited number of low-bandwidth channels that can be multiplexed. For example, a voice-grade circuit having an effective bandwidth of 3000 Hz (from 350 to 3350 Hz) can be theoretically divided into ten 300-Hz channels. Guard bands are used with FDM to prevent interference from adjacent channels (see Figure 2.11). The primary disadvantage of FDM is therefore the limited number of low-bandwidth signals that can be multiplexed to share a high-bandwidth circuit (sometimes called high-speed trunk). If the low-bandwidth signals are to be used at yet a lower transmission rate, additional low-speed circuits could be realized by filtering each low-speed channel (300 Hz) into yet narrower channels.

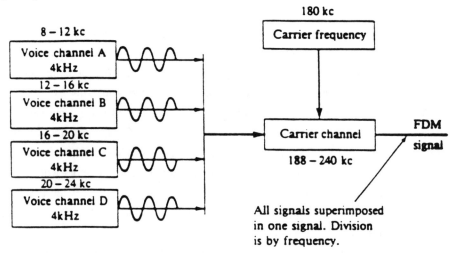

Figure 2.10. Frequency-division multiplexing.

Some advantages of FDM are reliability, simplicity of the equipment, and lack of bit-level synchronization. Each low-speed channel before and after the multiplexing function operates as an independent transmission circuit. Thus the timing technique is indicated entirely by the termination equipment on each low-speed channel. Between the FDMs there is no timing or synchronization activity required. For example, once the low-bandwidth channel of the FDM is set to carry 300 Hz, any channel operating up to and including the capacity of the channel can be supported regardless of code format. This characteristic of FDM is known as *code transparency*. The multiplexers are transparent transmission elements with respect to the information and data transmission activity.

In practice, FDM systems are arranged so that the widest bandwidth-derived channels are assigned to the center of the band, with slower channels on the sides. This approach minimizes the effects of line nonlinearities.

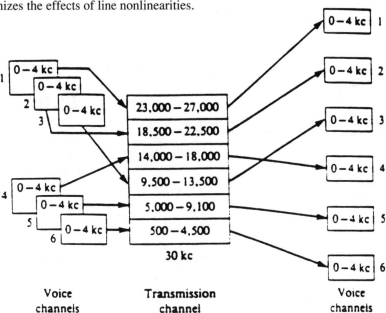

Figure 2.11. FDM example illustrating multiplexed bandwidths.

Time division multiplexing (TDM) operates by apportioning the entire bandwidth of the high-capacity channel to a character or bit from one of the low-speed signals for a small segment of time (see Figure 2.12). TDM divides the channel into discrete time slots, where each time slot can take an individual input. In this way, many low-bandwidth signals can be accommodated over the same high-capacity channel by interleaving them in the time domain. This full use of the bandwidth for a low-speed signal in TDM differs from FDM, where each source signal is transmitted simultaneously over a derived channel. In effect, the TDM takes signals from a number of low-speed circuits and concentrates the signals into a single long high-speed stream for transmission.

Each low-speed channel is assigned a register in the TDM, in which the character bits generated by the low-speed channel are accumulated. The logic of the TDM scans each register in a predetermined time sequence. The character bits from the various low-speed channels are packed into a continuous stream that is transmitted over the high-speed trunk line to be demultiplexed at the receiving end.

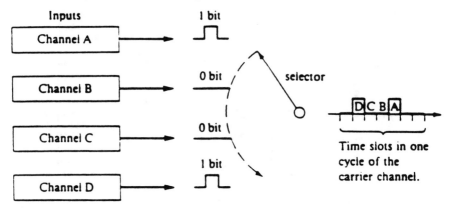

Figure 2.12. Time-division multiplexing.

The determination of the theoretical multiplexer capacity, using frequency division, is achieved by dividing the bandwidth of the low-speed channels into the bandwidth of the trunk circuit. With TDM the theoretical capacity of the multiplexer system is calculated by dividing the rate of a low-speed channel into the rate to be used on the high-speed trunk circuit.

The most important consideration, however, in the design of a TDM is the synchronization necessary over the trunk circuit. The TDM operates on a cyclical basis, such that a cycle must be completed within the transmission time of a unit of information on the low-speed circuits. A complete cycle or scan of all low-speed circuits is called a *frame*. Each frame transmitted over the trunk circuit is divided into a number of bytes, where a byte is a unit of information that can consist of a data bit or a full data character, depending on the multiplexer.

Again, consider the Bell Telephone T1 carrier system with 24 TDM channels, a sampling rate of 8000 periods/s, 8 pulses/sample (7 standard levels plus one for synchronization), and a pulse allocation width of 0.625µs. This means that the interval between samples is $10^6/8000 = 125µs$, and the period of time required for each pulse group is 0.625 x 8 = 5µs. If only a single channel were sent (instead of multiplexing), the transmission would consist of 8000 periods/s, each made up of significant activity during the first 5µs, and nothing at all during the remaining 120µs. This would be quite wasteful, since PCM systems are more complex to generate and demodulate than continuous systems, and using any form of pulse modulation for just one channel would be uneconomical. With TDM, however, each 125-µs period is subdivided into 25 periods of 5-µs duration; the first 24 are used for an equal number of separate channels, and the remaining one is employed for signaling and synchronization.

The resulting train of pulses would consist of successive 5-µs periods used by a different channel, the process repeated 8000 times every second, and 24 separate transmissions interleaved to create a TDM signal. If transmission is by wire, this is the signal sent, but if radio communication is used, the pulse train modulates the carrier with AM or FM.

The major advantages of TDM is the high-multiplexing capacity, adaptive speed control (by using the synchronization character within the frame), and a significant amount of common electronics used by all low-speed channels.

The final decision as to the use of FDM or TDM is based solely on the associated systems considerations. The choice is dictated by the total equipment costs, line capacity, and line configurations. These two multiplexing techniques should be considered as complementary rather than opposing techniques.

2.4 The Difference Between Analog and Digital Transmission*

Communications systems utilize many combinations of modulating and multiplexing schemes to produce the desired services. For example, a series of PCM inputs from several users could be multiplexed using a TDM scheme. Voice systems have combined FDM with AM and FM schemes. Digital systems often revert to PM techniques combined with TDM schemes.

Digital communication involves the transmission of discrete coded symbols over a transmission channel that has a potential for a high noise level. A digital receiver must be capable of correlating the received signal with this finite set of digital values and, if necessary, converting to an analog signal. In general, if the S/N ratio is above a certain threshold, the reproduced digital signal will be free of errors. With an analog signal, the noise, regardless of its level, will distort the signal proportionately to the S/N ratio. If there are any signal regenerators (or repeaters) in the transmission system, the digital

---

* see references 3, 7, 13, 15, 16, 20, 22, 26 and 27

signal will be regenerated, free of any noise, at each repeater, while the noise associated with an analog signal accumulates at each repeater. Since there are only two states that need to be distinguished in binary data, the noise level in the transmission system can be quite high before it causes errors in the reception of the message. Expressed in terms of voltage levels, a binary data bit requires only two discrete voltage levels. The greater the difference between these two levels, the greater can be the noise in the system before any errors are introduced.

An analog signal is simply a signal that is continuously variable within a range of values. In an analog system, data are represented by measurements on a continuous scale, usually represented as a voltage, phase, current, or frequency.

As long as the digital signal being transmitted is within the analog spectrum (whether frequency or amplitude), there is no difficulty in transmitting it on the analog channel.

The reverse is not true without some additional steps. An analog signal cannot be transmitted and received on digital equipment unless the analog signal is first sampled, quantized, and then coded according to some predetermined standards. Then at the receiving end, the digitized signal is restored (restructured) to its analog signal (e.g., PCM).

Data modems are generally used when transmitting a digital signal over an analog channel. The modem is responsible for making sure the digital signal is in the proper part of the spectrum for transmission and also for making sure that both ends of the transmission system are properly synchronized so that the data received correspond with the data sent.

By recognizing the differences between analog and digital transmission the communications designer can make the best possible use of such commodities as money, bandwidth, and time, and best satisfy any accuracy needs. There are definite trade-offs that can be made between digital and analog transmission when considering bandwidth and data rates. For example, if it is desired to digitize analog voice signals for a band-limited system using PCM, a standard sampling rate of 8000 bps and an 8-bit code are used to convert each analog sample into its PCM equivalent, the transmission rate required would be 64 kbps [17]. On the other hand, the theoretical capacity of a standard voice-channel phone circuit, with 3-kHz bandwidth and S/N = 30 dB, is 30 kbps. Phenomena such as intersymbol interference and envelope delay distortion lower this theoretical capacity to a maximum practical data rate of 9.6 kbps. Even this is achieved only if channel conditioning and differential two-phase, two-level modulation are used [17]. Also, the age and condition of the typical local-loop plant sometimes limit systems to lower data rates [17]. This indicates that maximum digital transmission rates of 9.6 kbps are practical over voice-grade lines.

2.5 Exercises

2.1 Describe the three general classifications of modulation? What are their respective advantages/disadvantages? How does modulation differ from multiplexing? Name and describe two kinds of multiplexing.

2.2 Describe how phase-shift keying permits an increase in the packing density of a relatively low-bandwidth carrier over frequency-shift keying. Can this packing density be increased forever? If not, why not?

2.3 What is meant by each of the following:
> sideband frequency
> differential coherent PSK
> quantization
> white noise

2.4 What are frequency and phase modulation? In what respect do they differ from amplitude modulation? Show how similar phase modulation is to frequency modulation.

2.5 What are the major advantages of frequency modulation over amplitude modulation? What are the advantages of amplitude modulation?

2.6 What advantages, if any, does frequency modulation have over phase modulation from the standpoint of noise? On the basis of best possible noise performance, compare and contrast amplitude and phase modulation.

2.7 What is meant by single-sideband modulation? What are its advantages with respect to ordinary AM? What are the advantages/disadvantages when compared to FM?

2.8 Briefly discuss each of the following concepts:
> frequency-shift keying
> two-tone modulation
> code transparency
> phase-shift keying

2.9   Define and explain what is meant by information and information theory. Why
           is meaning separated from information? What is the mathematical definition of
           information?

2.10   Describe the various forms of pulse-time modulation. What advantages do they
           have over PAM?   What are the advantages/disadvantages of PWM when
           compared to pulse-position modulation?

2.11   Explain what pulse-code modulation is and how it differs from all other
           modulation systems. Draw one complete cycle of some irregular waveform, and
           show how it is quantized using eight standard levels.

2.12   Discuss time-division multiplexing, including how interleaving of channels
           takes place.   Specifically, how does it differ from frequency-division
           multiplexing.

2.13   What is meant by quantizing noise? Explain why PCM is more noise resistant
           than the other forms of pulse modulation. In fact, under what conditions is
           PCM not affected by noise at all?

2.14   Show diagrammatically how channels are combined into groups, then into
           supergroups, and supergroups into the baseband when FDM is used in a practical
           system.

2.15   Define each of the following terms as fully as you can:
                    frequency
                    wavelength
                    harmonic component
                    signal amplitude
                    phase angle
                    interference
                    impulse noise
                    trunk

2.16   (a) Under what conditions will a modulated wave contain sidebands instead of
           side frequencies?
           (b) How many sidebands are there?
           (c) What determines the maximum extent of the sidebands?

2.17   In a frequency-modulated signal
           (a) What property of the wave is changed by the modulation?
           (b) What is the unmodulated value of this property called?
           (c) What determines the amount and rate of this change?

2.18 In an amplitude-modulated signal (a) What is the maximum limit of this modulation? (b) Over what range does the amplitude of the modulated wave vary?

2.19 Explain why the total energy in an FM wave cannot increase in the modulated level.

2.20 (a) For a given modulated-signal frequency, what determines the deviation of an FM wave?

(b) Is there any limitation imposed on this deviation? Explain.

2.21 As the modulation level is increased what happens to

(a) the carrier power in an AM wave?

(b) the carrier power in an FM wave?

(c) the sideband power in an AM wave? (d) the sideband power in an FM wave?

(e) the total power in an AM and/or FM wave?

2.22 If a carrier is phase-modulated

(a) What characteristic of the carrier is varied?

(b) What determines the magnitude of this variation?

(c) What determines the rate of this variation?

2.23 When two signals of different frequencies are mixed

(a) Describe the effect (if any) on the amplitude of the resultant.

(b) Describe the effect (if any) on the phase of the resultant with respect to either original signal.

(c) What is meant by "beat frequencies"?

2.24 Delta modulation (DM) is an easily implemented form of digital pulse modulation. In DM the message signal is encoded into a sequence of binary symbols. The binary symbols are represented by the polarity of the impulse functions at the modulator output. How is demodulation done?

2.25 Compare the various modulation techniques discussed in this chapter. Be sure to include cost, complexity of both transmitter and receiver, the bandwidth requirements, compatibility with existing systems, and performance, especially in the presence of noise.

2.26 Quadrature modulation (QM) results when two message signals are translated, using linear modulation with quadrature carriers, to the same special locations. Demodulation is accomplished coherently using quadrature demodulation carriers. Discuss the problem of distortion, especially how it results from phase errors.

2.27 Select a suitable modulation scheme (explain the reasons for your choice) for the following applications:

(a) Data transmission from a satellite over a noisy radio link; satellite has limited power capability.

(b) Point-to-point voice communication over a twisted pair of wires.

(c) Multiplexed voice transmission over coaxial cable;the primary objective is to transmit as many signals as possible over a single cable.

2.28 If a 1,500 kHz radio wave is modulated by a 2 kHz sine-wave tone, what frequencies are contained in the modulated wave (the actual AM signal)?

2.29 What is meant by low-level and high-level modulation? Explain the relative merits of high- and low-level modulation schemes.

2.30 Describe a means of generating and detecting each of the following:

PAM

PDM

PPM

2.31 Briefly describe four different methods for handling voice transmissions. Explain why PCM is strictly the only true digital system of the four.

2.32 Describe the meaning and importance of quantizing error in a PCM system. Why does a PCM TV transmission require more quantizing levels than a PCM voice transmission?

2.33 Discuss the advantages of PCM systems. Explain why PCM is adaptable to systems requiring many repeaters and TDM.

2.34 A continuous data signal is quantized and transmitted through a PCM system. If each sample at the receiving end of the system must be known to within 1 percent of the peak-to-peak full scale value, how many bits must each digital word contain?

2.35 If a PM signal is demodulated using an FM demodulator, what can be done to retrieve the modulating signal from the demodulator output?

2.36 Sketch a channel-interleaving scheme for time-division multiplexing the following PAM channels: five 4 kHz telephone channels and one 20 kHz music channel. Find the pulse repetition rate of the multiplexed signal. Estimate the minimum system bandwidth required.

2.37 Two voice signals (3 kHz upper frequency) are transmitted using PCM with eight levels of quantization. How many pulses per second are required to be transmitted and what is the minimum bandwidth of the channel?

2.38   Explain why a PPM system would require some form of time synchronization while PAM and PWM do not require any additional information. We are considering a single channel without TDM.

2.6 References

1   Bellamy, John, *Digital Telephony*. New York, NY: John Wiley and Sons, 1982.

2   Bell Laboratories, *Transmission Systems for Communications*, Number 500-036. Holmdel, NJ, 1982.

3   Black, U., *Data Networks: Concepts, Theory, and Practice*. Englewood Cliffs, NJ: Prentice-Hall, 1989.

4   Brown, J., and Glazier, E. V. D., *Telecommunications*. London: Chapman and Hall, 1974.

5   Brugger, R. D., "Information: Its Measure and Communications." *Computer Design*, 8, 11, 1970.

6   Chou, W. (ed.), *Computer Communications, Vol II: Systems and Applications*. Englewood Cliffs, NJ: Prentice-Hall, 1985.

7   Couch, L. W., *Digital and Analog Communications Systems*. New York, NY: MacMillan Publishing Company, 1983.

8   Davenport, W. P., *Modern Data Communication*. New York, NY: Hayden, 1971.

9   Doll, D. R., *Data Communications: Facilities, Networks, and System Design*. New York, NY: John Wiley and Sons, 1978.

10   Faro, R. M., *The Transmission of Information*. New York, NY: John Wiley and Sons, 1961.

11   Freeman, R., *Telecommunication Transmission Handbook*. New York, NY: Wiley - Interscience, 1975.

12   Freeman, R., *Telecommunication Transmission Handbook*. New York, NY: John Wiley and Sons, 1981.

13   Halsall, F., *Data Communications, Computer Networks, and OSI* (2nd edition). Reading, MA: Addison-Wesley, 1988.

14   Hamming, R. W., *Coding and Information Theory*. Englewood Cliffs, NJ: Prentice-Hall, 1980.

15   Hammond, J. L., and O'Reilly, J. P., *Performance Analysis of Local Computer Networks*. Reading, MA: Addison-Wesley, 1986.

16   Heath Company, *Electronic Communications*. Benton Harbor, MI, 1981.

17   International Telephone and Telegraph Corp., *Reference Data for Radio Engineers*. Indianapolis, IN: Howard W. Sams, 1975.

18   Jayant, N. S., and Noll, P., *Digital Coding of Waveforms: Principles and Applications to Speech and Video*. Englewood Cliffs, NJ: Prentice-Hall, 1984.

19   Kennedy, G., *Electronics Communication Systems*. New York, NY: McGraw-Hill, 1970.

20   Martin, J., *Telecommunications and the Computer*. Englewood Cliffs, NJ: Prentice-Hall, 1977.

21   Pooch, U. W.; Greene, W. H.; and Moss, G. G., *Telecommunications and Networking*. Boston, MA: Little, Brown and Company, 1983.

22   Rey, R. F. (ed.), *Engineering and Operations in the Bell Systems* (2nd edition). Murray Hill, NJ: AT&T Laboratories, 1983.

23   Shannon, C. E., "Communication in the Presence of Noise." *Proceedings of the IRE*, January 1949.

24   Shannon, C. E., and Weaver, W., *The Mathematical Theory of Communication*. Urbana, IL: University of Illinois Press, 1949.

25   Sherman, K., *Data Communications: A User's Guide*. Reston, VA: Reston Publishing Company, Inc., 1985.

26   Stallings, W., *Data and Computer Communications*. New York, NY: MacMillan Publishing Company, 1985.

27   Tanenbaum, A. S., *Computer Networks*. Englewood Cliffs, NJ: Prentice-Hall, 1981.

28   *Webster's New Collegiate Dictionary* (8th edition). Springfield, MA: G. and C. Merriam Company, 1977.

PART 2

Transmission Systems

3

BASIC TRANSMISSION SYSTEMS

3.1 Introduction

A telecommunications system is designed to convey information from a point of origin to a point of destination. In almost every case, the information content of the signal is not used by the telecommunications system itself. The system is designed to accept the input data and structure these data into a format that can be moved quickly, economically, and accurately to specified destinations. This structuring of data into a form suitable for transmission often involves the addition of control characters, routing or processing instructions, recording, or even reformatting of the data. The essential notion is that the system accepts the original input data in whatever format, structures the data for transmission, transmits the data to the specified destination, restructures the data back into their original format, and finally makes the data available at the appropriate destinations (i.e., the system is *information transparent*).

The information transmitted over telecommunications systems ranges from voice, telemetry, and facsimile data to simple or complex data messages. Furthermore, telecommunications systems vary considerably in their designs and components with regard to technology, electrical components, and methodologies or procedures. Most existing telecommunications systems were designed to deal with specific applications but then were modified or expanded to incorporate additional or changed requirements. This approach is exemplified by the use of voice (analog) systems to support data-processing users. More details about the voice communications systems will be given in the next chapter.

Despite the fact that there is such a wide range of input data and a large diversity in the design of telecommunications systems, they have a significant amount in common. All telecommunications systems exist to transmit information from point to point.

Moreover, when viewed functionally, these systems have common structures and problems.

3.2 The Basic Telecommunications System*

The basic functional components of a telecommunications system and two specific examples are given in Figure 3.1. The first component, the *transmitter*, accepts the input signal, matches this signal to the communications channel or medium, and then provides the carrier signal or power required to transmit over the communications channel or the medium. The second component, the *channel*, provides the path over which the signal travels. Examples of such communications channels or media include the atmosphere, wires, coaxial cable, lasers, and special waveguides. The last component, or the *receiver*, extracts the signal from the channel, restructures the original input data, and delivers this signal to the output device. Frequently, the input device and the output device are combined with the transmitter or receiver, respectively.

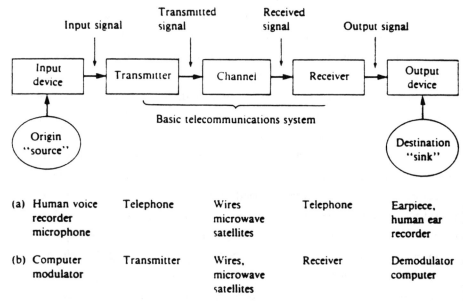

Figure 3.1. Conceptual telecommunications network.

---

* see references 11, 15, 16, 20, 27, 35, 40 and 41.

Designers of telecommunications systems attempt to optimize the design of each of the system's components and their respective interfaces. Otherwise, each component can significantly detract from the signal's accuracy and the system's reliability.

3.3 Telecommunications Media Problems*

In real telecommunications systems all of the "electrical" components detract from the quality of the signal because they are resistive, inductive, or capacitive in nature. As a result, these components amplify, attenuate, or distort the signal as the signal passes through the communications system (see Figure 3.2).

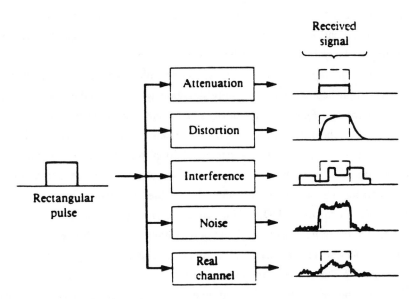

Figure 3.2. Impairments in channels.

---

* see references 6, 7, 9, 11, 17, 18, 21, 23, 27, 31, 35, 36 and 39.

3.3.1 Distortion

Attenuation distortion is the alteration of the signal because the channel does not respond perfectly. In other words, the system fails to react identically to all frequency components in the signal. Any signal that carries information is made up of a complex array of frequencies called a *spectrum*. Associated with these frequencies are specific amplitudes. Any disturbance in either the frequency components of a signal will cause a reduction in the quality of the transmission. From the amplitude point of view, a transmission medium should have a perfectly flat amplitude-versus-frequency characteristic; however, real systems do not have this characteristic because of the distributed inductance, capacitance, and resistance exhibited by transmission media. The nonideal amplitude-gain-versus-frequency characteristic is commonly referred to as *frequency response*. A transmission media that is ideal has a flat frequency response over the range of frequencies in which the spectrum of the signal is nonzero.

Attenuation distortion is much less a problem in voice transmission than in data transmission because of the redundant nature and low information content of speech. Data transmission has little if any redundancy and usually attempts to maximize the data rate (information content) in the allocated voiceband. The loss or altering of a symbol alters the meaning of the code word in which the symbol was contained.

Because of the rapid rates normally associated with data transmission, compensation must be accomplished to remove not only signal delays, but also the frequency selective amplitude distortion. *Equalizers* are devices that attempt to equalize the delays as well as to compensate for the different components that make up the amplitude distortion.

A signal that carries information has, in addition to frequency and amplitude, also a phase component. Any relative change between the phases of the frequency components in the spectrum will affect the detectability of the composite signal [this is called *envelope delay distortion* (EDD)]. Thus, from the viewpoint of an undistorted signal, it is required that the transmission medium not only have a flat amplitude-versus-frequency characteristic but also a linear phase-versus-frequency characteristic.

Again, as in the case of attenuation distortion, real transmission systems do not exhibit ideal response because of the distributed inductances, capacitances, and resistances (see Figure 3.3).

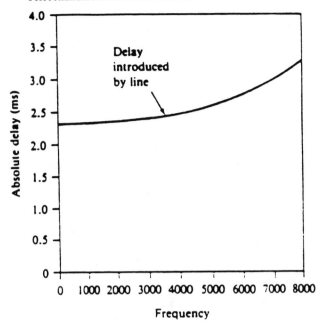

Figure 3.3. Delay distortion.

The nonideal phase-versus-frequency characteristic causes the various frequency components of a complex spectrum to propagate through the transmission medium at different velocities, causing the composite signal arriving at the receiving end to be distorted. If the distortion is sufficiently great, the late-arriving energy from one pulse can interfere with the start of a following pulse. This phenomena is often called *intersymbol interference* (see Figure 3.4).

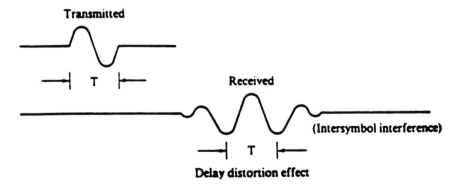

Figure 3.4. Intersymbol interference.

The direct measurement of phase delay is not practical because of the need to establish an absolute phase reference and to devise a method of conveniently keeping track of phase excursions over multiples of 360 . Instead, a measurement of envelope delay has been devised from which a very close approximation of phase-versus-frequency curve at any point along the curve.

Typical sources for EDD are bandpass filters and the lowpass, highpass, and/or bandpass characteristics exhibited to some extent by all transmission media. Line phase equalizers are designed to provide the opposite distortion of the transmission medium and thus cancellation occurs and equalization is achieved (see Figure 3.5).

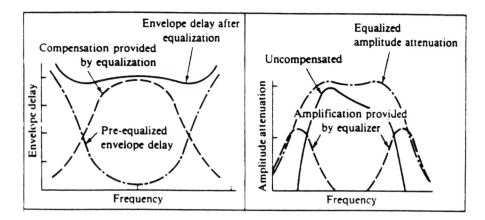

Figure 3.5. Effects of delay equalization [28].

Frequency errors can occur in any part of the signal spectrum that has undergone a frequency translation. Frequency errors can be especially troublesome for systems that transmit a frequency-division multiplexed signal. This type of system relies heavily on channel filters in the modulation-demodulation process. Frequency errors cause a shift in the desired energy spectrum for which the system was designed. The spectrum shift causes some of the desired information energy to encounter the undesirable amplitude and phase distortion characteristics found at the band edges of filters (see Figure 3.6).

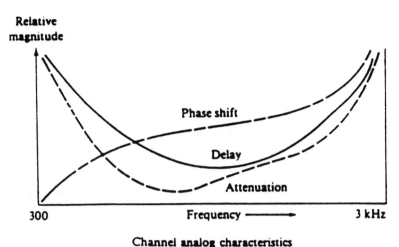

Channel analog characteristics

Figure 3.6. Distortion characteristics of voice-grade channel [28].

If the frequency error is sufficiently large, the system will be seriously degraded, especially for high-rate data transmission. This is because many data modems use carriers or subcarriers that are synchronized between the receiving and transmitting ends, and frequency errors in the media appear as errors in modems.

Frequency errors can be measured by using multiple tones whose frequency relationship is precisely known. When frequency offsets occur, this relationship is altered and the degree of alteration is proportional to frequency.

3.3.2 Noise*

Interference and noise are additions of inputs to the system (see Figure 3.7) that make the identification of the signal more complex. *Interference* usually refers to the inclusion of man made disturbances that produce inputs similar in shape and/or strength to the real signal. Examples are equipment and cross talk. *Noise* is usually used to refer to the disturbances caused by the system itself, or from natural causes such as sunspots, electrical storms, and magnetic formations or fields. Although noise and interference are differentiated as to origin, noise is sometimes also referred to as white noise or impulse noise. *White* or *random (background) noise* (including *Gaussian noise*) is the somewhat constant background noise that exists at all times in the system. It is usually weak in

---

* see references 9, 11, 21, 23, 25, 28, 31, 35, 36, 38, 39 and 41.

telephone lines (this is not true for satellite links) and recognized in the system design, thus causing only minimal problems. Designers seem to be of the opinion that the inherent white noise can be reduced but not eliminated from communications systems (see Figure 3.8).

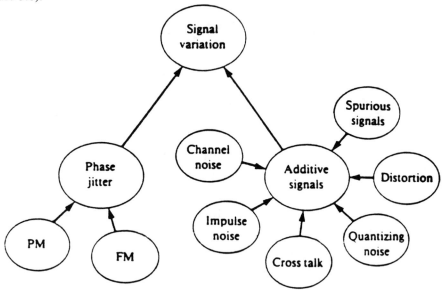

Figure 3.7. Sources of signal variations [28].

Impulse noise, on the other hand, caused by lightning, switching equipment, etc., consists of short spikes of high energy. The impulse noise exhibits an approximately flat spectrum over the frequencies of interest because of its short duration and high amplitude (i.e., impulsive characteristic).

Both impulse noise and steady-state noise are present in any transmission system. The important difference between impulse noise and steady-state noise is the short duration of impulse noise. Receiving systems are designed to handle steady-state noise with relative ease, but impulse noise of high amplitude duration "shocks" the system. The system has a response time constant predominantly determined by its steady-state requirements. If an amplitude spike occurs which the automatic gain control (AGC) cannot follow, the spike continues on unhibited.

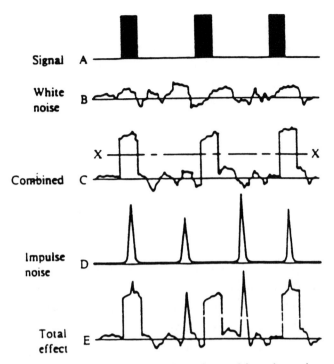

Figure 3.8. Effects of white noise and impulse noise.

The amplitude impulse noise is troublesome not because of its short duration (on the order of milliseconds), but because of its high peak strength. Therefore, as long as the noise is kept below a level which could damage hearing (in voice communication), it is little more than an annoyance. The situation is entirely different, however, for systems used for data communication.

Data communication is normally coded and the loss or the alteration of a portion of that code usually changes the meaning of the communication. Therefore the level of impulse noise is an important measurement on data systems. Figures 3.8 and 3.9 show the effect an impulse can have on data transmission. The receiver system only looks for the presence or absence of energy in a time slot to determine whether a one or a zero is present. The impulse in Figure 3.9 had sufficient energy to be treated as a one by the receiver, and thus a transmission error occurred.

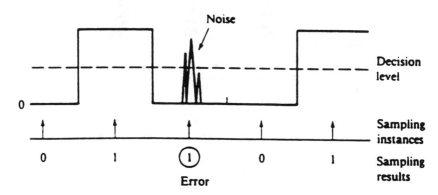

Figure 3.9. Effect of impulse noise on data transmission.

Because impulses are of short duration, their presence does not have as much effect in systems that support a low data rate than they have in systems supporting high data rates. In low-data-rate systems, the width of the data pulse is much greater than the width of the impulse noise pulse. Therefore, it is easy for the receiving system to distinguish a data pulse from an impulse noise pulse, and few errors due to impulse noise occur. As the data rate of a system increases, the width of each data pulse becomes shorter and approaches the width of an impulse noise pulse. It becomes clear that as the data rate increases, it becomes increasingly difficult for the device to distinguish between a data pulse and an (impulse) noise pulse, and the errors due to impulse noise will increase.

Phase jitter (or incidental FM) appears as a low-index-frequency modulation on a carrier, subcarrier, or baseband in a communications system. The phase jitter is normally introduced by noise or undesired discrete signal interference caused by jitters in clocks.

Phase jitter is of little consequence in voice transmission because the ear is relatively insensitive to phase information. Phase jitter, however, can seriously affect data transmission. Phase jitter causes the zero crossing of the data pulses to vary. If large variations occur, one data pulse may try to occupy the time slot of another pulse, causing an error. In addition, data synchronization can be difficult to maintain without degrading the detected bit error rate (see Figure 3.10).

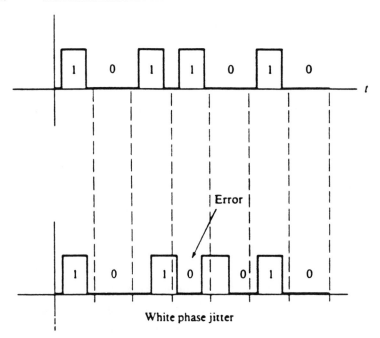

Figure 3.10. The effect of phase jitter.

3.3.3 Transmission Measurements[*]

The combination of all the effects of distortion and noise on the signal is often referred to as the *effects of the real channel*. Communications systems are designed to minimize these effects. In the area of attenuation and distortion, communications systems are designed to maximum power outputs and to respond equally to all frequencies by conditioning the channel and constraining the bandwidth in which the signal can exist. Moreover, attenuation and distortion vary with the system's resistance, capacitance, and inductance. Attenuation and distortion often will vary with temperature, pressure, and other weather conditions. Therefore, to have a flat (constant or equal) frequency response, some channels (transmission media) are "loaded" with inductance coils to offset the inherent capacitance. Much attention is also given to matching the characteristics or impedance of component interfaces to prevent standing waves or reflections of energy. In many systems, periodic repeaters are installed to minimize the effect of the channel (i.e., resistance) by regenerating new signals. This approach works much better in digital

---

[*] see references 6, 7, 9, 11, 12, 17, 18, 21, 23, 24, 31, 35, 36, 39 and 41.

systems than in analog systems because changes in the analog signal are cumulative and not removed by regeneration.

Systems designed to offset the effects of interference and noise have used a variety of procedures. Laws have been instituted to prevent or minimize the effects of interference created by humans and their machinery. The use of filters and special circuit designs has helped to eliminate man made interference. Noise, as defined above, is usually dealt with in the system design, and in most cases is only an irritation.

Nonetheless, the cumulative effects of the channel and system problems can lead to errors. It is possible that a signal is so distorted and attenuated that it cannot be restructured at the receiver. This possibility continues to be a major concern to system designers and users.

Bandwidth of a transmission medium is defined as the effective frequency (i.e., the range over which the frequency response is relatively flat) spectrum of a communications channel. Typically, a frequency system is considered effective as a function of its attenuation, that is, the loss of signal gain or input energy level. In a practical communications channel, the bandwidth is not detected by sharp cutoff frequencies. As the bandwidth's upper and lower limits are approached, a higher attenuation or loss of those frequency components is measurable, until, for all practical purposes, no signal or energy can be passed or transmitted. Since there are no two exact frequencies at which this total loss of energy occurs, bandwidth limits must be specified at some point on the attenuation curve or plot. By convention, bandwidth is defined as being effective between those two upper and lower frequency points on the curve. These points are generally selected as the upper and lower frequencies, at which only one-half the power of energy found within the bandwidth is measured, and are called *half-power points*.

The power gain of an amplifier or attenuator, measured in decibels (dB), is defined as:

$$\text{Power Gain} = 10 \log_{10}\left(\frac{P_o}{P_i}\right) \tag{3.1}$$

where P_o is the measured output power level, and P_i is the measured input power level. If both power measurements are equal, i.e., the channel has no attenuation, the result is 0 dB. If there were some attenuation, P_o would be less than P_i and the result would be negative. The half-power points, which define the limits of a particular bandwidth, can be expressed in terms of decibels at relative energy levels.

$$10 \log_{10}\left(\frac{0.5}{1}\right) = -3 \text{ dB} \qquad (3.2)$$

The effective bandwidth is therefore defined as the frequency spectrum between the measured -3 dB points and is referred to as the *passband* of the channel (see Figure 3.11).

Loss is defined between the signal transmitted and the signal received, expressed in dB; or the ratio of the power transmitted to the power received. Loss occurs for such reasons as absorption, radiation, improper adjustment, and media imperfections or discontinuities. Measurement of loss is normally referenced to relative power in decibels and measured at a standard test frequency.

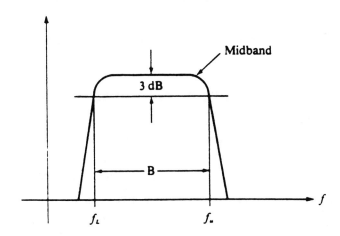

Figure 3.11.   3 dB below midband is the point at which one-half of transmitted power is lost in channel.

The measurement is a key factor for determining repeater spacing. If the transmission medium were noise-free, losses would be unimportant because the signal could simply be reamplified to the desired level. But because all transmission media have noise, each time loss occurs, a degradation in signal-to-noise ratio also occurs. Thus, for any given transmission system configuration there is a finite amount of total loss that can occur before the received signal becomes useless for the transmission of information. Some simple examples follow.

dB change	Change in power
+ 3	double power
- 3	half-power
+ 6	4 times the power
+10	increased the power by 10
+ 1	power increase by 1 1/4

Most power losses in voice systems are designed to be constant around a loss of 30 dB. Using the above rule-of-thumb, 30 dB = 10 dB + 10 dB, or $10 \cdot 10 \cdot 10 = 1000$ times. In short, typical voice systems are designed to put out 1 W of power, realizing that the signal received will be about one-thousandth the size of the original signal (or 1 mW).

3.4 Characterizing Communications Channels

As we have seen, data transmission systems generally consist of three basic elements, a transmitter or source of information, a transmission channel (or carrier or data link), and a receiver of the transmitted information. The channel or data link is a transmission path between two or more points and may be a single wire, a group of wires, or a special part of the radio-frequency spectrum. A communications channel is the logical type of communications medium without regard for the technique or the signaling method used.

3.4.1 Transmission direction

Communications channels are referred to as simplex, half-duplex, and full-duplex (Figure 3.12). *Simplex* channels can only send data in one direction and therefore are rarely used in data communications where a return path for control and error checking is essential. *Half-duplex* can send data in both directions, but only in one direction at a time. In other words, this type of channel provides "nonsimultaneous" two-way communication. *Full-duplex* channels provide for complete two-way simultaneous transmission. In half- or full-duplex modes, the data may be transmitted over either two-

or four-wire facilities. A *two-wire* channel can support transmission in one direction only (except when special parallel tone modems are used). It can, however, support transmission alternately in either direction. A *four-wire* channel can support transmission simultaneously in both directions at considerably less than twice the cost of a two-wire facility. The two- or four-wire selection is the common carrier's responsibility, unless terminal specifications indicate differently.

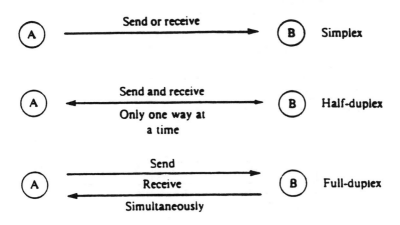

Figure 3.12.   Types of channels.

One full-duplex line is equivalent to two simplex lines with reduced transmission capabilities. The transmission paths are separated in frequency. Although in most cases full-duplex channels are four-wire and half-duplex channels are two-wire, full-duplex service can be provided by the use of only two wires by using part of the bandwidth for a reverse channel.

3.4.2   Bandwidth classification

Channels are sometimes classified according to their bandwiths: wideband, narrowband, or voiceband (see Figure 3.13). In commercial terms, *narrowband* channels are usually reserved for teletype or extremely low rate services (up to 300 bps), capable of handling manual keyboard devices. *Voiceband* channels are the 4-kHz services provided by most of the common carriers (see Table 3.1). *Wideband* or *broadband* channels are above the upper limit of the voiceband channels and are frequently conditioned to allow higher data speeds. For low speeds (0 to 2400 bps), FSK is used up to about 2400 bps,

while AM is used up to 1800 bps. For speeds above 2400 bps, PSK, Dibit AM, and
Dibit PM are used.

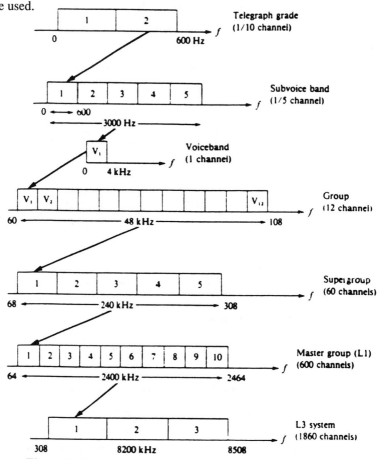

Figure 3.13. Creation of carrier systems by FDM.

An ideal channel should have flat amplitude and linear phase as a function of
frequency. Instead, among other things, telephone lines introduce amplitude variations
and phase variations. The amplitude response tends to drop sharply at the upper and lower
edges of the band and the delay (derivative of phase with frequency) has a parabolic shape.

For data rates of 2000 bps and above, the channel requires correction or the modems
often cannot overcome the resultant intersymbol interference. That is, successive pulses
interfere with one another at the sample times. At the maximum voice-grade rate, 56
kbps, nonlinear distortions and harmonic and signal-dependent noise subvert
communications. Phone lines often show an increase in ambient noise when a signal is

present because of the compandors on the line. Thus, at higher transmission speeds, *circuit conditioning* is mandatory.

Table 3.1 Summary of telephone carrier systems [14]

Carrier system	Transmission medium	Line frequency band	Equivalent telephone circuits	Long or short haul[*]	Data rate
	Wire or cable, 1 pair	300-3300 Hz	1	Short	1 voice channel
C	Open Wire,1 pair	4.6-30.7 Hz	1	Short	500 voice channels
J	Open wire, 1 pair	36-143 Khz	12	Short	800 voice channels
N	Cable, 2 pairs	44-260 Khz	12	Short	200 voice channels
N3	Twisted Pair	172-268 Khz	24	Long	24 voice channels
T1	Twisted Pair	varies	24	Long	1.544 Mbps
T2	Twisted Pair	36-268 Khz	96	Long	6.312 Mbps
L1	Coaxial Cable	68-2788 Khz	60	Long	60 voice channels
L3	Coaxial Cable	312-8248 Khz	600	Long	600 voice channels
L4	Coaxial Cable	564-17,548 Khz	3600	Long	3600 voice channels
L5	Coaxial Cable	3120-60500 Khz	10800	Long	10800 voice channels
	Optical Fiber	1310[**]	≈14000	Long	up to 878 Mbps
TD3	Microwave	3700-4200 MHz	1200	Long	19800 voice channels
TH1	Microwave	5925-6425 MHz	1800	Long	42000 voice channels
TN1	Microwave	10700-11700 MHz	1800	Long	25200 voice channels
IntelSat V	Microwave	4/6 and 11/14 GHz	14500	Long	14500 voice channels

[*] Short-haul systems usually vary from 25-800 miles, but usually about 100-200 miles.
[**] This represents the wavelength of the light source in nanometers

Bandwidths, information capacity, and signaling speeds are all closely related. The arbitrary classifications of high- and low-speed circuits or channels are often used in lieu of wideband and narrowband classifications. Examples of common service provided by various carriers is given in Figure 3.14.

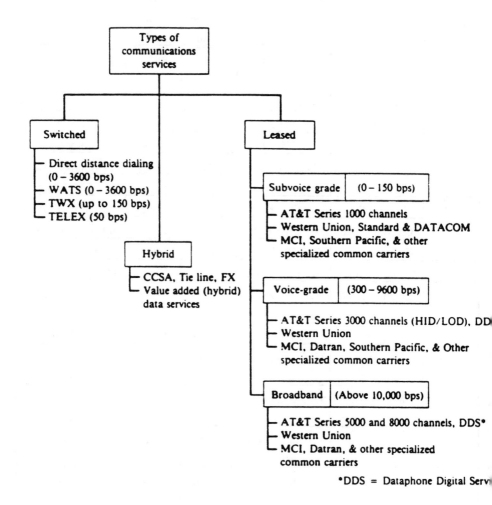

Figure 3.14. Types of communications services [11,22,35,41,42].

3.4.3 Transmission modes

Transmission systems can also be classified as being serial or parallel, and synchronous or asynchronous. *Serial* transmission can be serial-by-bit or serial-by-character (see Figure 3.15) on a single wire. *Parallel* transmission uses a separate communications path for each signal or utilizes FDM to transmit signals over a single line using separate frequencies for each signal. The most common form of parallel transmission is serial-by-character, parallel-by-bit, usually adding one line for timing or reference (see Figure 3.15). Parallel transmission, inefficient in terms of line utilization, is commonly used with inexpensive terminals, and implant on private lines. Except for very short distances (up to a few thousand feet) serial transmission is more efficient and therefore more prevalent.

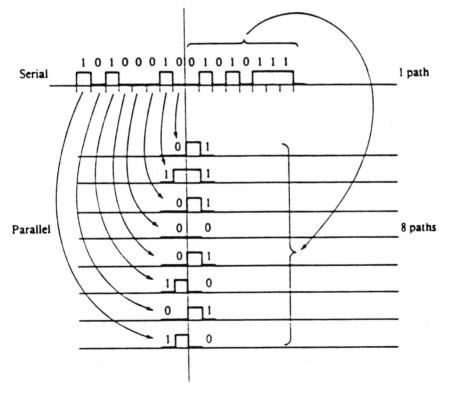

Figure 3.15. Serial versus parallel transmission modes.

3.4.4 Transmission speeds

For the receiving unit to decode the receiving signal properly, the unit must operate at the same "speed" as the transmitting unit and be synchronized with it. *Asynchronous* transmission requires special start and stop bits called start and stop signals (see Figure 3.16). By convention, the line rests at logic one. The first bit is a zero, then the code bits come, which are followed by one or two stop bits (both logic one). The first transition trips the receive controller and additional circuitry allows examination of the line state at the proper bit time. The receive terminal also knows the number of information bits. The stop bits frame the end-of-character and are compatible with the idle or wait state.

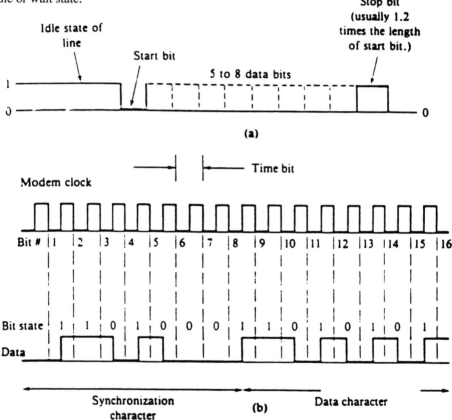

Figure 3.16 Transmission speeds. (a) asynchronous data character format; (b) synchronous data character format.

Baudot code uses five information bits; ASCII seven, and EBCDIC eight. The total bits sent per character also depends on the necessary stop time (number of stop bits). The asynchronous systems were developed and used for early teletype applications, low-speed devices, and devices without buffers. Today, they often are used in systems that utilize keyboard inputs, operating at variable speeds with an upper limit of 1800 to 2000 bps.

Synchronous transmissions (Figure 3.16) depend on a timing mechanism or procedure to keep the transmitter and the receiver in phase. Synchronous transmission consists of a steady stream of bits with no start and stop bits or pauses between characters. Characters are sent in a continuous stream (continuous transmission). Before synchronous transmission begins, the transmitting and receiving units (usually modems) are synchronized in phase usually by sending a synchronization pattern or character at the start of each "block," which then puts the system oscillators or clocks in phase. The two ends, the transmitter and the receiver, remain synchronized until the end of the block (which usually is an error-checking pattern.)

Synchronous modems are more complex and costly (due to the timing and synchronization procedures) than asynchronous modems and are used in applications where characters are serial at fixed intervals (with a fixed transmission rate). Synchronous transmission permits increased data speeds and multilevel signaling and provides for better protection from errors by using the error-checking pattern at the end of the block. The checking of the error pattern can be performed by the terminal, line controllers, or modem, but essentially the receiver generates its own pattern from the received data and then compares this pattern against the received error pattern.

Synchronous transmission allows faster transmission of data (there are no start/stop characters), higher-speed modulation techniques, and better and more elaborate error-checking and correction techniques than does asynchronous transmission.

Advantages and disadvantages for both of these timing procedures are given in Table 3.2. It is important to remember that the continuous data transmission demands three levels of synchronization. First, the receiver must know when the bit starts and ends. Second, the receiver must determine the individual bit positions within each character, and thirdly, must decide which characters or patterns start and end messages. Error correction and detection procedures are given in Appendix IV.

Table 3.2 Advantages and disadvantages of various timing procedures

| | Serial | | Parallel |
	Start/Stop	Synchronous	
Advantages	Little, if any, data lost through lack of synchronization, as each character is individually synchronized	Good ration of data to control bits (low redundancy)	Low-cost transmitter
Disadvantages	Hight rate of control information to data information (high redundancy)	Much data can be lost between synch pattern if devices become "unsynched"	High-cost receiver may waste bandwidth

3.4.5 Bauds versus bits

A *bit* is defined as the smallest unit of digital information, while a *baud* represents the rate of transmitted information. The terms are not interchangeable. Depending on the modulation scheme used, the information rate in bits per second may have the same or different values in different systems (see Figure 3.17).

When a data terminal or digital computer generates information to be transmitted, it forms that information into coded binary digits, or bits, which are sequentially transmitted to the communications channel. The rate of that transmission is expressed in terms of bits per second. This serial stream (bits) must first be converted from the dc digital signal environment of the data processing equipment into the signal environment of the communications channel.

In terms of transmitting a digital signal, modulation must be performed by a modem. When the digital bit stream is ready to be modulated, it is converted into the compatible analog form required by the communications channel and transmitted to the line. The speed at which this converted information flow is transmitted to the communications channel is the baud rate of the system.

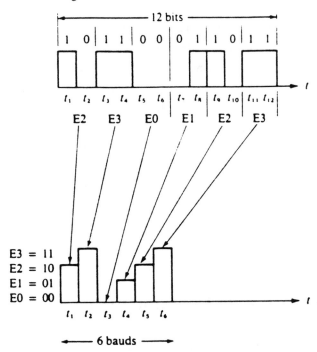

Figure 3.17. Comparison between baud and bit.

In a low-speed data transmission application, the digital bit per second and transmitted baud rates may have the same value. For each unit of information on the digital side of the modem there is a corresponding unit on the analog side. Such a system might use a modem that is essentially passive and generates a unit of analog information for each unit of digital information presented to the digital interface.

With higher-speed systems, modems perform functions other than simple modulation and demodulation. Due to the limitations of available communications channel bandwidths or passbands, the digital data must be compressed to reduce the number of actual units of information transmitted. This is accomplished by transmitting a single unit of information representative of a number of digital bits of information generated at the interface between the data processing equipment and the modem. Such data transmission systems are referred to as *multilevel modulation systems* and are most common at the higher transmission rates.

If a transmitted unit of information can be used to recover more than one digital bit, the number of digital bits that can be transmitted in a given period of time may be greater than the transmission rate (baud) of the communications channel. For example, a system using AM may employ two discrete signal levels to represent the different binary values. The maximum number of bits that can be transmitted in 1 s is equal to the baud rate of the communications channel. Assume that an AM system actually had four discrete amplitude levels that could be transmitted and detected. Two digital bits would be represented for each signal unit transmitted. In such a system the baud rate would be half the bit rate. Other modulation schemes also use this technique. By using four different frequencies in an FM system or four distinct phases (45^0, 135^0, 225^0, and 315^0) in a PM system, the same type of bit-rate compression can be achieved. This concept has been carried further with eight discrete steps, where three consecutive bits are transmitted in a single unit of transmitted information. With these techniques, commercially available modems are able to transmit 4800, 7200, and 9600 bps on a communications channel with less than 3 kHz effective bandwidth.

3.5 Modulators and Demodulators*

A device typically found in data communications systems is the *modem*. A modem is a combination modulator and demodulator, often also referred to as data set, line adapter, modulator, or subset. Regardless of the name, the purpose of each of these components is to convert digital pulses into a form compatible and suitable for transmission over a communications system. Figure 3.18 illustrates the position of the modems in a data link and the signals into and out of each element of that link.

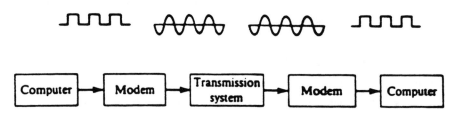

Figure 3.18. Basic elements of a communications system.

The rectangular digital pulses that represent computer-related data are highly distorted and attenuated or weakened by telephone-line characteristics. This is because rectangular

---

* see references 1–8, 10, 11, 13, 15, 19, 21, 23, 26, 29–34, 49 and 41.

pulses contain both dc and VHF components, whereas telephone channels are only geared to transmit frequencies from about 500 Hz to 3500 Hz.

In the modem, the square-edged pulse train from the computer or terminal is tailored electronically to fit between the telephone channel frequencies by a process called *modulation*. With the appropriate modulation technique, data can be sent by telephone at high speeds without undue distortion.   At the receiving end, the data are recovered from the transmitted signal by a process called *demodulation*, whereby the transmitted analog signals are reconverted to digital data compatible with the receiving data-handling equipment.   Figure 3.19 summarizes the modem function.

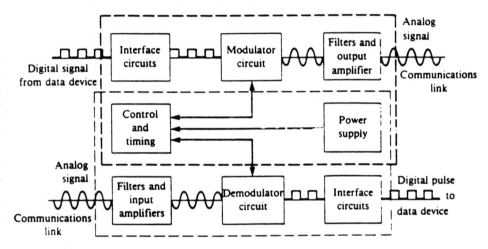

Figure 3.19. Functions of a modulator/demodulator [8,10,26,32,41].

In the process of carrying out this primary function, the modem must be compatible with the data communications equipment at its digital interface as well as with the transmission medium at its analog interface.   Inside the United States, data interface standards are set by the Electronic Industries Association (EIA).   Data transmission standards are only broadly defined by the Federal Communications Commission (FCC), so that considerable user choice is possible.   In practice, users tend to adhere to telephone company standards.   Outside the United States, data transmission standards are set by the International Telegraph & Telephone Consultative Committee (CCITT), which is a part of the International Telecommunications Union in Geneva (Table 3.3).

Table 3.3 Common International Telegraph and Telephone Consultative
Committee Standards (CCITT)

V.21	0 to 200 (300) bps (similar to Bell 103). Defined for full-duplex (FDX) switched network operation
V.23	600 to 1200 bps (Similar to Bell 202). Defined for half-duplex (HDX) switched network operation. 75 bps channel optional
V.24	Definition of interchange circuits (similar to EIA RS-232-C).
V.25	Automatic calling units (similar to Bell 801).
V.26	2400 bps (identical to Bell 201B). Defined for four-wire leased circuits.
V.26bbls	1200 to 2400 bps (similar to Bell 201C). Defined for switched network.
V.27	4800 bps (similar to Bell 208A). Defined for leased circuits using manual equalizers.
V.28	Electrical characteristics for interchange circuits (similar to TS-232-C).

Since most data communications systems transmit and receive on the same pair of wires, the modulator and demodulator circuits are usually combined within the same package, called a modem. The Bell Telephone company gives the name *data set* to its modems, but the two expressions are synonymous (see Figure 3.20).

Aside from its basic function as an interface, a modem may perform many peripheral functions. For example, a voice communication between two terminal locations might be useful at times, even if the primary mode of use is for digital data transmission. With a suitable adaptor, a transmission channel may alternate between both uses. Commonly incorporated modem functions are summarized in Table 3.4.

Modems in communications networks can be checked either at the modem or from the central host computer when problems occur. The technique used for diagnosing problems involves *looping* signals back toward their origins at various sites in the system. However, this technique works only when the system is capable of full-duplex operation. Since loopbacks of both analog (operating on the analog side of the media) and digital (operating on the modem's digital side) forms can occur either toward or away from the modem, four potential loopbacks exist at each end. Therefore, in any operating communications system with two ends, eight loopbacks are possible. Utilizing *local loopback* and *remote loopback* provides for convenient self-check features with rapid, unassisted fault isolation within a system, so that transmitted and received patterns can be pinpointed at all locations.

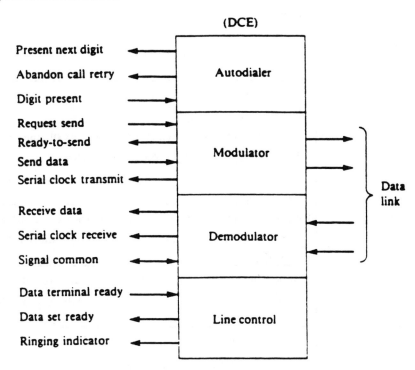

Figure 3.20. Typical data set interface configuration.

The modem and the communications line can be connected directly (hard-wired) or indirectly (acoustic or inductive coupling). Acoustically coupled modems are portable since they can be used with any available telephone. With *acoustic coupling*, the dc data signals are converted to audible sounds which are then picked up by the transmitter in an ordinary telephone handset. The audible signal is converted to electrical signals and transmitted over the telephone network. The process is reversed at the receiving end.

Inductive coupling, like acoustic coupling, requires no direct connection. With inductive coupling a data signal passes to the telephone through an electromagnetic field by way of a hybrid coil.

Acoustic-inductive couplers generally do not operate as reliably as direct electrically connected modems, because they involve an extra conversion step (e.g., digital to audible to electrical), where noise and distortions may be introduced. For this reason acoustic-inductive modems are limited to transmission speeds below 1200 bps. A direct connection to the communications channel is preferable, since it is less error-prone and not limited to low-speed transmission.

Table 3.4 Commonly used optional modem features [3,4,10,26,32,41]

Voice adapter	Permits oral communication between terminal locations whose main function is data transmission.
Reverse or sideband channel	A secondary low-speed channel (5 bps) for use of control & acknowledgement signals on voice-grade channel.
Dial-up capability	Permits dialing a line, even where normal operation is on a fixed private line.
Self-test features	Built-in test signal pattern and local loopback connections. Modem may include all test indicators required for diagnostics.
Remote testing	Can be manual or automatic. Automatic means that it may be used for looping back at key points within a system without operator assistance.
Multiporting	Allows servicing of lower-speed terminals from a signal, higher-speed modem.
Automatic answering	Used in modems on DDD lines and allows a modem to answer ringing signals, pass information on to the interfaced terminal, and notify caller that it has received the signal. The modem will automatically answer incoming calls. This feature allows you to use your computer for unattended remote access, whereby someone can access your computer's information from a remote location. Auto-answer also enables you to run bulletin board programs on your computer.
Automatic, adaptive equalization	Allows high-speed, voiceband modems to operate on minimally conditioned or unconditioned voice-grade lines.
Multistate modulation	Complex, high-speed modems that implement a signal-scrambling technique to equalize state density independent of the customer's data code.

Table 3.4 Commonly used optional modem features (cont.)

System expandability	May be an important requirement based on anticipated future needs. Includes adding or modifying channels and permits adding features.
Auto-dial	The modem can automatically make outgoing calls under computer control. This feature, coupled with auto-dial software, allows you to dial telephone numbers with just a few keystrokes. Auto-dial also enables you to program your computer so that it will make unattended outgoing calls. With this feature you can have your computer call a data service late at night, and retrieve information at the lowest rates, all while you're asleep.
On-board call progress speaker with volume control	The on-board call progress speaker allows you to listen in while your modem is making outgoing calls. This enables you to easily determine whether the modem is successful in reaching a dialed number. The loudness of the speaker can be easily adjusted via the modem's volume control knob.
1A2 mechanical key system light control	When used with a 1A2 mechanical key telephone system, your modem can properly control the line-in-use indicator lights.
Call progress detection and demon dialing	the modem to Demon Dial the number. The modem would immediately dial the number and, if busy, would hang up and try again. This would be repeated over and over again - automatically. When the modem finally gets through, it plays a chime through the speaker to notify you that the call is ringing.Your modem's dialtone detection can also be used to improve security in auto-callback situations.
True computer tone detection	Your modem can detect the computer tones used by many alternate long distance services. True computer tone detection is faster and more reliable than the "pause" approach used by many modems.

Table 3.4 Commonly used optional modem features (cont.)

Audio input interface	Your modem provides an audio input interface which allows you to couple audio signals from an outside source, such as a voice synthesizer, onto the telephone line. This feature, along with the optional touchtone decoder and the proper software, enables you to use your computer as a touchtone activated remote access system, whereby someone can call your computer from a touchtone telephone and retrieve spoken information.
Audio output port	Your modem provides an audio output interface which allows you to connect an external speaker to the modem phone line monitor. This will then take the place of the onboard speaker already present on the modem, since the on-board speaker is then disconnected from the amplifier circuit which drives the speakers. You can also record phone sessions with this port by using this output signal to drive an external recording device.
Touchtone decoder with auto-answer touchtone password (optional)	A central-office-quality touchtone decoder can decode all 16 touchtones. The 16 touchtones are comprised of the 12 standard tones plus the four "fourth column" tones. When in auto-answer mode, your modem can be programmed to require a touchtone password of up to three digits before carrier tone is sent to a caller, to protect your computer from unauthorized callers.

Because modems are considered as subsystems, they come in an array of shapes, sizes, and forms. An *acoustic modem* combines the functions of a modulator-demodulator with an acoustic coupler, into which a telephone handset is placed to connect to dial-up lines. These types of modems are built into such equipment as time-sharing terminals or telecopiers. *Integral modems* do not use acoustic coupling because only portable equipment requires that flexibility. For example, TWX/Telex machines contain integral, nonacoustic modems hard-wired to the telephone lines. *Packaged modems*, usually separate from the data terminal equipment, are self-contained. *Stand-alone modems* come in rack-mount packages, in modem cards that fit into a card file rack, and in chip modems.

Modems can be characterized by the modulation technique used, by operating speed and mode (i.e., simplex, half-duplex, full-duplex, serial or parallel, and synchronous or asynchronous), and by error performance and the various options included. The modulation technique is important since it not only tailors the data to the line characteristics, but the modulation techniques determine the speed with which the data can be sent and with what protection from line noise and distortion. In fact, there is a trade-off between noise detection and speed, as well as reliability and cost.

Although modems are classified into three speed groups, little consensus on the range of these groups exists. *Low-speed* modems are loosely defined as those which operate up to 1200 or 1800 bps. *Medium-speed* modems operate up to 4800 bps, and *high-speed* modems up to 9600 bps. All of these modems essentially operate on voice-grade telephone circuits, either dial-up or leased lines from the common carrier, and fall into two broad categories: asynchronous and synchronous. Asynchronous data are transmitted over the transmission line one character at a time and typically are produced by low-speed terminals. Asynchronous transmission is advantageous when transmission is irregular and is cheaper because of the simpler terminal interface logic and circuitry. Synchronous transmission makes for better use of the transmission facility and allows for higher transmission speeds. Because of the more complex circuitry, synchronous transmission is far more costly.

Asynchronous modems are generally low-speed, with speeds up to 1200 bps over dial-up telephone facilities, or up to 1800 bps using a conditioned leased line. Use of the modem in conjunction with the dial-up facilities (direct distance dialing or DDD) requires that the user interface the modem to the carrier line with a direct access arrangement (DAA). This device limits the signaling power of the attached modem so that it does not exceed the power-level restrictions of the network (excessive power surges cause cross talk).

Modems obtained from the telephone companies (called data sets) on lines leased from AT&T do not require DAAs. Acoustic couplers, low-speed asynchronous modems, also do not require DAAs. While their speed is limited (up to about 600 bps), these devices offer the user the advantage of low cost and portability. Higher-speed modems generally require higher-grade transmission lines, usually requiring conditioning and equalization. A great deal depends on such features as modulation techniques, use of multilevel encoding, and utilization of means within the modem itself for compensating for deficiencies in the line's transmission characteristics.

In addition to the voice-grade modems, there are *hard-wired modems* capable of speeds up to 1 Mbps (1 million bps) that are used mostly for short-range transmission (e.g., in-house systems). *Wideband modems* capable of speeds up to 200 kbps are used principally for computer-to-computer communications, or in large-volume multiplexing applications (see Table 3.5).

Table 3.5 Categories of available modems

Modem Type	Communication channel	Data rates (kbps)	Applications
Short distance	Private leased line	19.2, 1 mbps	Limited distance (10 miles maximum)
Wideband			
Half-group	8803	19.2	Large-volume telephone lines, multiplexing
Group	8801	40.8, 50	(same as above)
Supergroup	5700 (TELPAK C)	2304.4	Computer-to-computer links
Voice grade			
High-speed synchronous	Leased lines	4.8, 7.2, 9.6	Computer terminal, data acquisition, process control, data collection
Medium-speed synchronous	Leased lines, dial-up	2, 2.4, 3.6, 4.8	(same as above)
Low-speed asynchronous	Dial-up, leased lines	1.2, 1.8	(same as above)

Digital data may be sent over a communications system in either series or parallel mode. If the stream of data is divided into characters, each composed of bits, it then is possible to send the stream serial-by-character, serial-by-bit (see Figures 3.21 and 3.22).

For parallel transmission, separate communications paths for each bit are required, or FDM techniques must be used to transmit the bits over a single line, using separate frequencies for each bit.

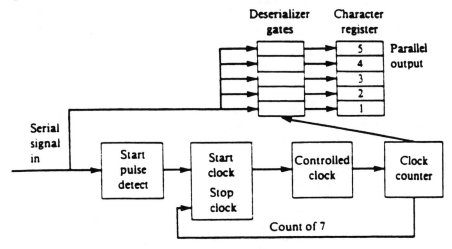

Figure 3.21. Serial-to-parallel adapter.

Parallel transmission is inefficient in terms of line utilization, but inexpensive for terminals. Thus, parallel-wire transmission is often used in private lines and in-house systems. Non-common-carrier lines within a plant or system are called *in-plant* to distinguish from the conventional common-carrier lines or *out-plant*. With parallel transmission systems, the operating speed is often expressed in terms of characters per second (cps), while serial systems use bits per second (bps).

Modems may operate in three different modes: simplex, half- duplex, and full-duplex. Simplex transmission is rarely used for data since normally control or error signals are required, even if data are only transmitted in one direction. Most data communications system users have half-duplex systems, even though full-duplex lines would considerably improve transmission efficiency for little extra line costs. One reason is that most terminals that use full-duplex lines are more expensive than those operating with half-duplex lines. Another reason is that local loops of dial-up lines are two-wire facilities which are easier to operate in half-duplex than full-duplex mode.

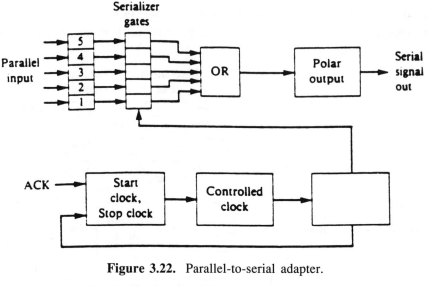

Figure 3.22. Parallel-to-serial adapter.

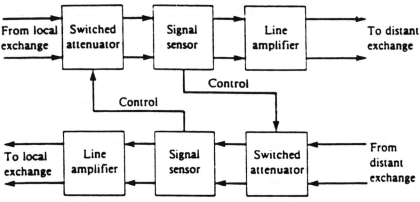

Figure 3.23. Echo-Suppressor Configuration.

Modems that operate full-duplex over dial-up lines use two separate frequency bands to transmit in two directions simultaneously. Here the modem generally transmits data in one direction and receives control signals in the other. The modem will utilize most of the line's capacity for data transmission, reserving a narrowband (called *reserve channel*) for the control signals.

The deleterious influence of delay distortion on data transmission increases with rising transmission rate. To achieve high rates, circuitry is added to the transmission channel to equalize the delay and compensate for amplitude distortion within the passband.

This improvement in line characteristics is called *conditioning* or *equalization*. Dedicated telephone lines may incorporate various grades of conditioning with prescribed distortion limits, in contrast with dialed lines which vary more widely with each dial-up between the same locations.

In addition to conditioning, which is available from the common carriers, equalization is frequently added within the modem so that the line's delay and amplitude distortion characteristics may be substantially improved, increasing its transmission capacity. Although fixed equalizers matching average line conditions are used with dial-up lines, equalization within a modem is more effective with dedicated lines whose characteristics are relatively fixed or at least predictable. Periodic readjustments are required only to compensate for long-term drift.

Many higher-speed modems use automatic equalization, which, during the first few seconds of an initial connection, continuously compensates for any changing line conditions. Automatic equalization must be used with discretion in applications requiring constant switching among terminals where varying line conditions require constant, time-consuming reequalization.

Another criterion that the user must be concerned with is the selection and type of phone lines to be used in the system. The type of phone lines determines the type of modem, asynchronous or synchronous, the speed of the modem, and the effective data throughput.

Dial-up lines are half-duplex lines with a maximum transmission rate of 1200 bps asynchronously, and 4800 bps synchronously. The advantages of using the common carrier's switched network are that the user can communicate with any point on the network and that the user pays only for the actual time usage of the line.

However, there are four major disadvantages. First, the line may be noisy and data may be misinterpreted. Second, because of delay distortion data at the receiving end may be lost or misread. Third, the switched transmission network consists of half-duplex lines. This is sufficient to transmit data, but elaborate error-checking must be performed at the receiving end. The line must then be turned around (so as to transmit in the opposite direction) each time to reverse the *echo suppressors* (these are one-way attenuators to remove echoes from the voice-grade line) so that control messages can be returned to acknowledge the data (see Figure 3.23). Failure to reverse the echo suppressors also can result in erroneous messages. The last disadvantage is that sometimes no connection or dial tone is even present on the dial-up network.

The basic advantages of private, leased data lines are ready availability and freedom from busy signals, fixed cost, and the availability of conditioned lines, which results in better data rates and higher transmission rates and throughput. Leased lines are generally four-wire or full-duplex lines, permitting simultaneous transmission and reception. Thus control signals can be transmitted and received at the same time as data. Their basic disadvantages are higher cost and single fixed connections. However, if the user's telecommunications demands call for high-volume, high-quality, high-speed transfer between two points, leased lines are one of the best alternatives.

It is important to remember that whether or not to use the dial-up network (DDD) or to obtain private leased lines is to a great extent dependent on how the modem modulates the data before those data are sent over the communications link. Certain modulation techniques, as we have seen, are limited in the speed at which they can transmit data. Other modulation techniques permit higher speeds. All modulation techniques are directly related to the bandwidth required and to the error performance, and, consequently, to the data throughput.

For the reader's convenience, a summary of the more common modem application considerations is given in Table 3.6. It should be noted that the economic aspects of modem selection are more important than for most computer system packages because they relate to the continuously receiving costs of leasing telephone lines. Modem selection must therefore emphasize efficient line usage.

Table 3.6 Application factors [cont.]

Table 3.6 Application factors [3,4,10,26,32,41]

Factor	Description
Economic consideration	Minimizing system cost means initial cost of the modem against recurring costs of the common carrier transmission lines and system throughput. Multiplexers, modem-sharing devices, and auxiliary items can contribute to cost reduction.
Interface compatibility	A principle selection factor, since a modem's primary function is to serve as an interface. Inputs and outputs must conform to applicable specifications.
Transmision rate	Bps of digital data transmission must be compatible for transmitting and receiving modems, analog transmission line capacity, and other system elements as applicable. In general, synchronous transmission provides higher data rates. Multilevel encoding permits higher data rates for a fixed line capacity but adds complexity and increases line noise sensitivity.
Number of channels	Determined in overall system design. To conserve bandwidth, channel capacities must match individual transmission requirements. Flexibility in expanding the number of channels, or modifying the manner in which separate channels share a transmission band, is a frequently used option.
Transmission line	Principal selection factors relate to line capacity and degree of line conditioning required for proper modem performance. Mode of operation determines the need for a two- or four-wire line. Since modems vary in quality of transmission line they require, line rental costs must be checked.

Table 3.6 Application factors [cont.]

Noise immunity	Varies with modem design, particularly with modulation means. In general, it is greater for FM than for AM and better yet for PM. Nevertheless, multilevel modulation is more sensitive to line noise than simple two-level modulation. On provate lines having relatively uniform and identifiable noise characteristics, a modem should be evaluated for its immunity to this specific noise.
Equalization	In most modems, some is included to compensate for transmission-line distortion. Equalization may be fixed to match average line conditions or may be manually or automatically adjustable. Modem may include meters and indicators required to carry out equalization functions.
Error rate	Determined by the application. An adequate error rate specification must define line characteristics, including S/N specification and noise bandwidth, and transmission rate.
Reliability and servicing	Reliability must be consistent with application requirements. Modular packaging, use of plug-in elements, self-checking procedures, and availability of key test points simplify fault isolation. Manufacturer's capability for fast response to servicing requirements is essential for minimizing downtime.
Packaging	Functional modularity is desirable for purposes of flexibility of modification as well as for ease of servicing. Individual boards versus a stand-alone package must be viewed in terms of overall system requirements.

3.6 Exercises

3.1   What is the relationship between bandwidth and transmission speed? bandwidth and cost?

3.2   Show how bauds can be converted to bits per second, and/or words per minute.

3.3   Discuss the differences and/or distinctions between base-band, bandwidth, and voice channel.

3.4 A baseband signal of 0 to 5 kHz amplitude modulates a 2.37 MHz carrier (DSB). What is the spectrum of the transmitted signal?

3.5 Discuss the relationship between speed of transmission, channel bandwidth, and modulation.

3.6 Define each of the following terms: baseband, attenuation, filter, repeater, amplifier, signal, ac, dc, signal distortion, baseband distortion, intersymbol interference.

3.7 What are some of the reasons for the various different baseband waveforms? Discuss the advantages/disadvantages of some of these waveforms.

3.8 Discuss what causes signal distortion, and what can be done about this distortion. What are the effects of delay distortion, delay equalization, impulse noise, white noise, and frequency distortion on the transmission signal?

3.9 What kind of devices can be placed on a transmission line to overcome the distortion effects and thereby increase the transmission distance?

3.10 Discuss and relate each of the following terms:
> bandwidth
> passband
> power loss
> return loss
> signal-to-noise ratio (S/N)

3.11 Compare and contrast acoustic couplers to modems. Are there any advantages that are inherent to acoustic couplers? How do they differ from a data set?

3.12 A friend of yours says that she can design a system for transmitting the output of a microcomputer to a line printer operating at a speed of 30 lines/min over a voice-grade line with a bandwidth of 3.5 kHz, and S/N = 30 dB. Assume that the line printer needs 8 bits of data per character and prints out 80 characters per line. Would you believe your friend?

3.13 Discuss the problem of distortion, including such topics as attenuation, frequency distortion, envelope delay distortion, and intersymbol interference. What effects do equalizers and filters have on these problems?

3.14 Differentiate between interference and noise. What relation does phase jitter have to each?

3.15 Systems must be designed to offset the cumulative effects of interference and noise. Discuss the relevant design factors as they apply to this problem.

3.16   How is the spacing of repeaters determined to minimize the degradation of transmission signals? What measures can be used to determine a mismatch of impedance from the source to the load and then along the transmission path?

3.17   What specifically does the signal-to-noise (S/N) ratio measure? How can this measurement be used?

3.18   Categorize the various bandwidth classifications, including transmission rates, channel groupings, and other special characteristics.

3.19   Discuss the relationship that exists between bandwidth, information capacity, and signaling speeds.

3.20   Compare and contrast the various types of conditioning available for private lines. Be sure to include a discussion of the types of problems each conditioning is designed to overcome.

3.21   What is the purpose of the modem in the data communications system? Are modems used in digital transmission systems? How does the role of the modem differ from that of an acoustic coupler?

3.22   What is meant by adaptive equalization? Where is it used? For what purpose is it used?

3.23   What is meant by the baud rate of channel? What determines the number of signal levels that can be carried by each baud?

3.24   Discuss the interrelationship of message block sizes to communications channel error rates, especially for half-duplex and full-duplex channels.

3.25   When should asynchronous transmission systems be used instead of a synchronous system? Describe each method and give advantages/disadvantages for each.

3.26   Discuss how it is possible to transmit rates of up to 9600 bps on a communications channel with only a 3-kHz effective bandwidth. Is this transmission speed the upper limit? If not, what factors affect the transmission speed?

3.27   Discuss the procedure for checking and diagnosing modem problems in a communications network.

3.28   Compare and contrast each of the following:

    acoustic coupling
    inductive coupling
    direct coupling

3.29   Because modems may be characterized by their modulation techniques, their operating speed and mode, and their error performance, describe how each of these affects the performance of a communications network.

3.30   Discuss the trade-offs that occur for modem selection between noise detection and speed, reliability, and cost.

3.31   What is the role of conditioning or equalization as it applies to modems? Compare these functions when applied to the communications line and to the modem. Are they different?

3.32   In what regard does the selection of the type of phone line impact the type of modem, the speed of the modem, and the effective data throughput?

3.33   Compare the advantages and disadvantages of private leased data lines to dial-up lines.

3.34   What are some of the problems that have to be overcome as an acoustic connection (via an acoustic coupler) is made to the network?

3.35   Why is there not a one-to-one correspondence between the baud rate and the bit rate in a communications network? What is the role of timing in this discussion?

3.36   Discuss the effects of phase jitter and impulse noise on a signal. Is it possible to correct both problems simultaneously for a given modulation technique?

3.7 References

1   Abrams, M.; Blanc, R. P.; and Cotton, I. W., *Computer Networks: Text and References for a Tutorial.* New York, NY: IEEE Computer Society, 1976.

2   Abramson, N., and Kuo, F. F. (eds.), *Computer-Communication Networks.* Englewood Cliffs, NJ: Prentice-Hall, 1973.

3   AT&T Technical Reference Number 54016, 1981.

4   Bartee, T. C. (ed.), *Data Communications, Networks, and Systems.* Indianapolis, IN: Howard W. Sams & Co., Inc., 1985.

5   Bell Telephone, "Acoustic and Inductive Coupling for Data and Voice Transmission." Bell System Tech Reference No. 41803, Murray Hill, NJ, October 1972.

6   Bellamy, John, *Digital Telephony.* New York, NY: John Wiley and Sons, 1982.

7   Bell Laboratories, *Transmission Systems for Communications*, Number 500-036. Holmdel, NJ, 1982.

8   Black, U., *Physical Interfaces*. Arlington, VA: Information Engineering Educational Series, 1986.

9   Black, U., *Communications: An Introduction*. Arlington, VA: Information Engineering Educational Series, 1987.

10   Black, U., *Physical Level Interfaces and Protocols*. Washington, DC: IEEE Computer Society Press, 1988.

11   Black, U., *Data Networks: Concepts, Theory, and Practice*. Englewood Cliffs, NJ: Prentice-Hall, 1989.

12   Buckley, J. E., "Bandwidth: Information Capacity and Throughput." *Computer Design, 11*, 4, April 1973.

13   Campbell, J., *The RS-232 Solution*. Berkeley, CA: Sybex, Inc., 1984.

14   Couch, L. W., *Digital and Analog Communications Systems* (2nd edition). New York, NY: MacMillan Publishing Company, 1987.

15   Davey, T., "Modems." *Proceedings of the IEEE*, November 1972.

16   Doll, D. R., *Data Communications: Facilities, Networks, and System Design*. New York, NY: John Wiley and Sons, 1978.

17   Doweier, V. L., "Transmission Measurements: Part One." *Telecommunications, 7*, 8, August 1973.

18   Doweier, V. L., "Transmission Measurements: Part Two." *Telecommunications, 7*, 9, September 1973.

19   Electronics Industries Association (EAI), *Dial and Answer Systems*. EIA-366, 1966.

20   Ellis, R. L., *Designing Data Networks*. Englewood Cliffs, NJ: Prentice-Hall, 1986.

21   Freeman, R., *Telecommunication Transmission Handbook*. New York, NY: John Wiley and Sons, 1981.

22   GTE Lenkurt Inc., *The Lenkurt Demodulator, 20*, 10, San Carlos, CA, October 1971.

23   Halsall, F., *DataCommunications, Computer Networks, and OSI* (2nd edition). Reading, MA: Addison-Wesley, 1988.

24   Hammond, J. L., and O'Reilly, J. P., *Performance Analysis of Local Computer Networks*. Reading, MA: Addison-Wesley, 1986.

25   Jayant, N. S., and Noll, P., *Digital Coding of Waveforms: Principles and Applications to Speech and Video.* Englewood Cliffs, NJ: Prentice-Hall, 1984.

26   Jurenko, J. A., "All About Modems and Related Topics." Huntsville, AL: Universal Data Systems, 1981.

27   Kennedy, G., *Electronics Communication Systems.* New York, NY: McGraw-Hill, 1970.

28   Krechmer, K., "Integrating Medium Speed Modems into Communications Networks." *Computer Design, 17,* 2, February 1978.

29   Levine, S. T., "Focus on Modems and Multiplexers." *Electronics Design, 27,* October 25, 1979.

30   Lyon, D., "How to Evaluate a High-Speed Modem." *Telecommunications, 9,* 10, October 1975.

31   Martin, J., *Telecommunications and the Computer.* Englewood Cliffs, NJ: Prentice-Hall, 1977.

32   McNamara, J. E., *Technical Aspects of Data Communication.* Bedford, MA: Digital Press, 1982.

33   McQuillan, J. M., and Cerf, V. G., *A Practical View of Computer Communications Protocols.* Washington, DC: IEEE Computer Society Press, 1978.

34   McShane, T. J., "Acoustic Coupling for Data Transmission." *Digital Design, 10,* 6, June 1980.

35   Pooch, U. W.; Greene, W. H.; and Moss, G. G., *Telecommunications and Networking.* Boston, MA: Little, Brown and Company, 1983.

36   Rey, R. F. (ed.), *Engineering and Operations in the Bell Systems* (2nd edition). Murray Hill, NJ: AT&T Laboratories, 1983.

37   Seyer, M. D., *RS-232 Made Easy.* Englewood Cliffs, NJ: Prentice-Hall, 1984.

38   Sherman, K., *Data Communications: A User's Guide* (2nd edition). Reston, VA: Reston Publishing Company, Inc., 1985.

39   Sherman, K., *Data Communications: A User's Guide.* Reston, VA: Reston Publishing Company, Inc., 1985.

40   Sondak, N. E., "Line-Sharing System Multiplexing and Concentrating." *Telecommunications, 12,* 4, April 1978.

41   Stallings, W., *Data and Computer Communications.* New York, NY: MacMillan Publishing Company, 1985.

4

TELECOMMUNICATIONS TRANSMISSION MEDIA

4.1 Introduction*

Telecommunication transmission media are the facilities for the transmission by wire (all physical lines) or radio of all types of messages or information in analog or digital forms, including voice, telegraph data at various rates, facsimile data, videophone, television, and visual display.

There are two main categories: physical lines and radio. The former includes open wires, paired cables and coaxial cables (land and submarine), optical fibers, while the latter includes microwave, troposcatter (radio HF), and communication satellites.

Many factors affect the choice of a transmission medium. Some factors are obvious, such as economics; other factors are technical in nature; while still other factors are tied directly to the services and to the environment in which the services are to be provided. A wide range of transmission media are now available (see Figure 4.1).

Wire media are available through two basic options, leased common user services or dedicated services that are built, leased, or purchased for specific applications. Two-wire and four-wire media are available to provide a wide range of data speeds and low error rates. The predominant service in this area is the 4-kHz voice-grade line provided by the major carriers or local telephone companies. Groups of these 4-kHz channels are available to produce effectively wider bandwidths and faster speeds.

Voice circuits for data communications can be extended through the use of conditioning and equalization. Subscribers are tied to central offices by dedicated (single-party) wires or by shared (party-line) wire pairs. Each pair is a voice channel. Toll

---

* see references 4, 8, 10, 17, 23, 34, 35, 37, 41, 46, 60, 62 and 66.

offices or switches provide linkages between central offices and other switches by voice channels that are multiplexed and travel over wideband channels. Typical links are provided by coaxial cable, microwave, and satellites. It is between switches that multiplexing schemes called *T carriers* are found. The T1 carrier consists of 24 channels, the T2 carrier of 96 channels (6 Mbps), the T3 carrier of 672 channels ($\approx$45 Mbps), and the T4 carrier of 4032 channels ($\approx$274 Mbps).

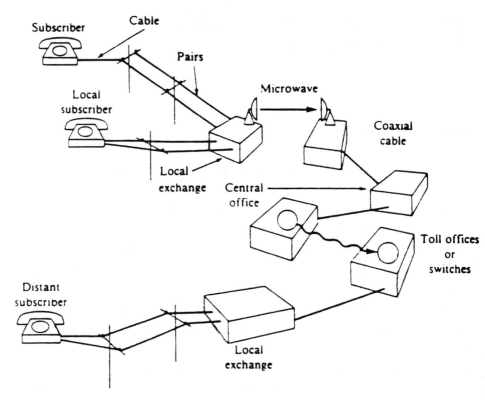

Figure 4.1. A wide range of transmission systems.

The interface between users (data) and common carriers (e.g., phone system or leased lines) is usually the modem or the data set. The standards for this interface are called RS-232-C. More formally it is known as the *interface between data terminal equipment and data communication equipment employing serial binary data interchange*. This standard is designed, among other things, to protect against voltages that can harm personnel, against incorrect signals with either too high an amplitude or too high a frequency, against line imbalances, and against improper control signals.

As the demand for more line facilities continued, the first *land coaxial cable* carrier system L1 was developed (1940). The L1 carrier system provided greater bandwidth (3 MHz), larger capacity (600 voice circuits) and better performance (less cross talk and distortion) than type J and K (12 voice circuits) carrier systems. The capacity of the coaxial system was further increased with the introduction of the L3 system (1860 voice circuits, 8 MHz-bandwidth) in 1953, the L4 system (3600 voice circuits, 18 MHz-bandwidth) in 1967, and the L5 system (10,800 voice circuits, 60 MHz-bandwidth) in 1974.

During these years, the number of coaxial tubes per cable has been increased from 2 to 20 (see Figure 4.2). The L5 carrier system is therefore capable of providing 10,800 x 9 or 97,200 voice circuits per cable (10 pairs of coaxial tubes with 1 pair as spare).

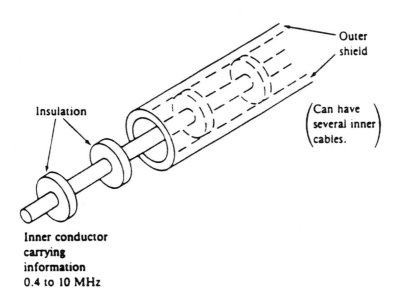

Figure 4.2. Coaxial cable construction.

Submarine coaxial cable was introduced for transmission in bodies of water, particularly across oceans, before the use of satellite communication. Its channel capacity is comparable to that of satellites. The use of high-capacity and wideband (48 voice circuits and 160-kHz bandwidth per pair of coaxial cables) submarine coaxial cable for long transmission began in 1956. This early system used two coaxial cables, one for each direction of transmission.

Subsequently, large-capacity systems were introduced: 128 voice circuits with 1100-kHz bandwidth in 1963; 720 voice circuits with 59,000-kHz bandwidth in 1970; and 4000 voice circuits with 12,000-kHz bandwidth in 1976. These larger capacity systems used one simple coaxial cable for two-way transmission. In all submarine coaxial cable systems, 3-kHz voice circuits instead of 4-kHz voice circuits were used to economize the frequency space.

Microwave has a channel capacity comparable to coaxial cables. The chief advantage of this transmission media is the low cost per channel mile, especially in high-capacity systems. Enough system gain margins are provided to take care of signal fading during poor propagation conditions.

The first microwave carrier system (TDX) was placed in operation in the 4-GHz band in late 1947 by the Bell Telephone System. This system provided 240 voice circuits and 10-MHz bandwidth per radio-frequency (RF) channel. The next system, designated TD-2, used the same RF band of 4 GHz but with 600 voice circuits and 20-MHz bandwidth per RF channel (1953). An improved version of this system, designated TD-2A (1968), could carry 1200 voice circuits with the same bandwidth of 20 MHz per RF channel. In 1961, a higher-capacity system, TH (1860 voice circuits and 30-MHz bandwidth per RF channel) operating in the 6-GHz band was introduced.

The bandwidth of microwave radio is in the order of 10 to 30 MHz per RF channel due to the limited frequency spectrum assigned to this service. Microwave radio depends on line-of-sight transmission (see Figure 4.3). Antennas must be mounted on towers high above ground. For economic reasons, towers of about 100 feet are commonly used, thus restricting the repeater spacing to about 30 miles for level terrain.

The development of *troposcatter radio* was intended to find an alternative or complementary system operating under severely restricted environmental conditions where line-of-sight microwave radio may not be feasible.

The troposcatter mode of propagation has the characteristic of large path loss and severe fading, resulting in the need for large transmitting power, large antenna, low-noise receiver, and a diversity in reception. The range of communication per link (i.e., repeater spacing) is between 100 to 300 miles (see Figure 4.4). Because of the multipath effects, the usable bandwidth in the medium is limited to a channel capacity of about 240 voice circuits (each 4 kHz) for 100-mile repeater spacing. The frequency band of 0.4 to 20 GHz is generally used.

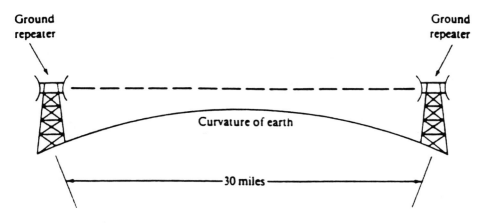

Figure 4.3. Microwave line-of-sight system.

Communication satellites provide coverage and a line-of-sight mode of transmission similar to microwave transmission. The signal has little fading if the main beam of the earth station antenna points at an elevation angle greater than 5 (see Figure 4.5). With a geostationary orbit of 22,300 miles above earth, three satellites can cover the entire globe.

The first satellite transmission service, inaugurated in 1965 (using INTELSAT I), carried one transponder with 240 voice circuits with single access by only two earth stations. Subsequently, INTELSAT II (1966) with 240 voice circuits and access by several earth stations, and INTELSAT III (1968) with 1200 voice circuits and multiple access by earth stations were put into service. Each of these satellites carried two transponders, maintaining one transponder as a spare.

INTELSAT IV (1970) carried 12 transponders, each of which provided 300 voice circuits, while INTELSAT IV-A (1975) carried 20 transponders, each providing 300 voice circuits.

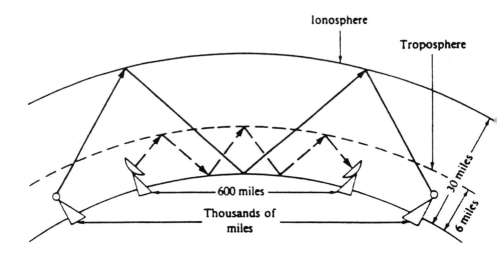

Figure 4.4. Tropospheric scatter and high-frequency (HF) transmission.

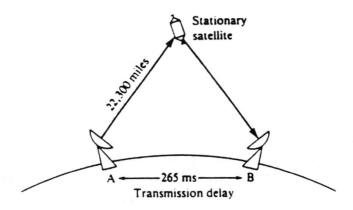

Figure 4.5. Communications satellite in geostationary orbit.

4.2 Coaxial Cable*

In communications systems it is very often necessary to interconnect points some distance apart, and as a result be concerned with the properties of the interconnecting wires. Transmission lines, a means of conveying signals from one point to another, are of two types: the twisted pair of the balanced line of Figure 4.6(b), and the coaxial, or unbalanced, line of Figure 4.6(a).

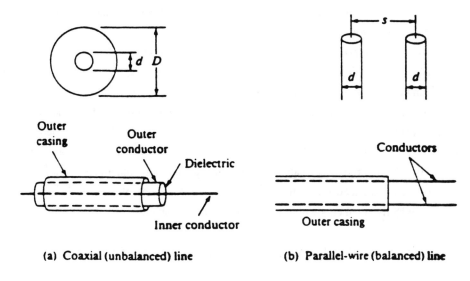

(a) Coaxial (unbalanced) line   (b) Parallel-wire (balanced) line

Figure 4.6. Transmission lines and their corresponding geometry.

Any system of conductors is likely to have cross talk if the conductor separation approaches a half-wavelength at the operating frequency. This is more likely to occur in a parallel-wire line than in a coaxial line, in which the outer conductor surrounds the inner conductor and is invariably grounded. Thus, parallel-wire lines are never used for frequencies up to at least 18 GHz.

Rigid coaxial air-dielectric lines consist of an inner and outer conductor, with spacers of low-loss dielectric separating the two conductors every few inches. There often is an

---

* see references 1, 4, 9, 12–14, 25, 37, 40, 46 and 52.

outer covering around the outer conductor to prevent corrosion, but this is not always the case. A flexible air-dielectric cable in general has corrugations in both the inner and the outer conductor, running at right angles to its length, and a spiral of dielectric material between the two.

There are three ways in which signal losses can occur in transmission lines: magnetic interference, electrostatic interference, and cross talk.

Magnetic interference is created when a conductor is located within a varying magnetic field. This may occur when a conductor carrying an electrical current is adjacent to another current-carrying conductor. Magnetic interference is reduced by twisted cable conductors so that the magnetic effect at one point is counteracted by the effect of the field on the other conductor one-half twist down.

Electrostatic interference occurs when a conductor acquires an unwanted electrical charge from an adjoining electrical field. This type of interference is reduced or eliminated by surrounding the cable with a grounded conductive shield.

Cross talk occurs when pulsating dc or ac signals are transmitted on one pair of a multipair cable, and for this signal to be superimposed on signals that are carried within the same cable or adjacent pairs. Twisting the conductor with varied distance between each twist ("staggered lay") can eliminate this problem in balanced (parallel-wire) systems. In unbalanced (coaxial) systems, cross talk can be eliminated by enclosing various conductive elements within their own conductive shield.

4.2.1 Twisted-wire pairs [1,4,9,25,40,48,49,60,63]

The twisted-wire pair has been the most common type of transmission media for analog signals. Each individual pair is wrapped with a metallized polyester material to shield the wires. This shield is terminated with a drain wire that connects the metallized layer to a ground. Shielded twisted-wire pairs are bundled together into cables consisting of as few as 2 pairs, but most often there will be 8, 12, or 24 pairs in one cable (see Figure 4.7).

4.2.2 Coaxial cable [4,12-14,37,48,52,60,63]

Coaxial and twinaxial cable (two coaxial cables in a single jacket) are used for high frequencies, digital information, and wide-bandwidth applications. Examples of services available ıor coaxial cable are given in Table 4.1.

Table 4.1 Transmission Media [4,60,66]

Designation	Year in service	Operating freq. (MHz)	Modulation	1- or 2-Carrier channel			Per system			Repeater spacing (miles)	System length (miles)
				Operating band (MHz)	Voice cap. (ccts)	Binary cap. (mbps)	Carrier channels	Voice cap. (ccts)	Binary cap. (mbps)		
Open wire (2 wire, a pair of open wire)											
A(Bell)	1918		SSB/SC	0.020	4	—	16	64	—	—	—
C(Bell)	1925	0.005–0.030	SSB/SC	0.025	3	—	16	48	—	130/180	2000
J(Bell)	1938	0.036–0.143	SSB/SC	0.107	12	—	16	192	—	30/100	1500
CCITT	—	0.003–0.300	SSH/SC	0.300	28	—	—	—	—	—	1600
Paired cable (4 wire, two cable pairs)											
K(Bell)	1938	0.012–0.060	SSB/SC	0.048	12	0.048	48	288	1.152	17	1500
CCITT	—	0.012–0.552	SSB/SC	0.480	120	0.480	—	—	—	—	1600
Land coaxial cable (4 wire, two coaxial tubes)											
L1(Bell)	1941	0.068–2.78	SSB/SC	3.000	600	3.000	2 + 2	600	3.000	6/8	4000
CCITT	—	0.060–4.09	SSB/SC	4.000	960	4.000	—	—	—	6	1600
L3(Bell)	1953	0.312–8.28	SSH/SC	8.000	1860	8.000	6 + 2	5580	24.000	3/4	4000
L3(Bell)	1962	0.312–8.28	SSB/SC	8.000	1860	8.000	10 + 2	9300	40.000	3/4	4000
L3(Bell)	1965	0.312–8.28	SSB/SC	8.000	1860	8.000	18 + 2	16740	72.000	3/4	4000
CCITT	—	0.300–12.43	SSB/SC	12.000	2700	12.000	—	—	—	3	1600
L4(Bell)	1967	0.564–17.55	SSB/SC	18.000	3600	18.000	18 + 2	32400	182.000	2	4000
L5(Bell)	1974	3.12–60.56	SSB/SC	60.000	10800	60.000	18 + 2	97200	540.000	1	4000
Submarine coaxial cable (2 wire, one coaxial tube, except "SB" which is 4 wire with 2 tubes)											
SB(TAT 1)	1956	0.024–0.168	SSB/SC	0.160	48	0.160	2	48	0.160	48	2500
SD(TAT 3)	1963	0.108–1.05	SSB/SC	1.100	128	0.550	1	128	0.550	24	4000

Table 4.1 Transmission Media [cont.]

Designation	Year in service	Operating freq. (MHz)	Modulation	1- or 2-Carrier channel			Per system			Repeater spacing (miles)	System length (miles)
				Operating band (MHz)	Voice cap. (ccts)	Binary cap. (mbps)	Carrier channels	Voice cap. (ccts)	Binary cap. (mbps)		
SF(TAT 5)	1970	0.564–5.88	SSB/SC	5.900	720	3.000	1	720	3.000	12	4000
SG(TAT 6)	1976	—	SSB/SC	30.000	4000	15.000	1	4000	15.000	6	4000
Microwave radio (4 wire, two radio-frequency carrier channels)											
TDX(Bell)	1947	3700–4200	FDM/FM	10.000	60	0.240	8 + 0	240	0.960	30	4000
TD2(Bell)	1950	3700–4200	FDM/FM	20.000	600	2.400	10 + 2	3000	12.000	30	4000
TH(Bell)	1961	5925–6425	FDM/FM	30.000	1860	7.500	12 + 2	11160	45.000	30	4000
TD3(Bell)	1967	3700–4200	FDM/FM	20.000	1200	4.800	20 + 4	12000	48.000	30	4000
Troposcatter radio (4 wire, two radio-frequency carrier channels)											
BMEW	1961	400–2000	FDM/FM	10.000	240	0.960	2	240	0.960	100	900
EMT	1965	400–2000	FDM/FM	6.000	120	0.480	2	120	0.480	200	3200
DEW EAST	1962	400–2000	FDM/FM	3.000	72	0.288	2	72	0.288	300	2400
UK SPAIN	1962	400–2000	FDM/FM	1.000	24	0.096	2	24	0.096	400	1200
Communication satellites (4 wire, two radio-frequency carrier channels)											
INTEL SAT I	1965	3700–4200 / 5925–6425	FDM/FM	25.000	240	0.960	2 + 2	240	0.960	N/A	8000
INTEL SAT II	1966	3700–4200 / 5925–6425	FDM/FM	130.000	240	0.960	2 + 2	240	0.960	N/A	8000
INTEL SAT III	1968	3700–4200 / 5925–6425	FDM/FM	225.000	1200	4.800	2 + 2	1200	4.800	N/A	8000
INTEL SAT IV	1970	3700–4200 / 5925–6425	FDM/FM	36.000	300	1.200	24	3600	14.400	N/A	8000
INTEL SAT IV A	1975	3700–4200 / 5925–6425	FDM/FM	36.000	300	1.200	40	6000	24.000	N/A	8000

Note: Circuit performance (4000 miles)
Voice Noise 38 dBa0–44 dBr nc decibels above reference noise. C-message weighted

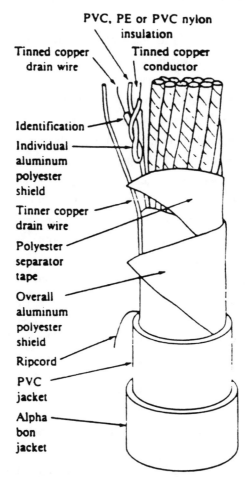

Figure 4.7. Multipair individually shielded cable [1-4,9,60].

Coaxial cables have various impedance standards, with 50, 75, and 93Ω being the most common. For data transmission, whether transmission of video information or high rates of digital information, the most frequently used impedance is 75Ω.

Coaxial cable is more susceptible to deformation than other types of wire and cable. Squeezing, hitting, or stepping on coaxial cable can result in a deformation that changes the impedance, and consequently cause a degradation of the carried signal. In addition, the connections to the cable require more skill and care than do normal electrical connections for a twisted pair. Furthermore, coaxial cables are susceptible to temperature changes.

As temperatures change, so do the attenuation characteristics of the cable. This problem is overcome in coaxial systems by the use of special repeaters, called *regulating repeaters*, at fixed intervals.

Coaxial cables are designed to compensate for radiation loss and "skin-effect" characteristics of high-frequency transmissions, providing a multichannel capability of up to 10,800 joined or separate voice channels in one cable. As microwave systems became popular, coaxial cable was regulated to areas where frequencies for microwave systems were limited; in aircraft or fixed facilities, radar systems, and in short-distance telecommunications trunking applications. Probably the most common use of coaxial cable is in the cable television (CATV) applications.

Coaxial cables, although built in many forms, typically have features illustrated in Figure 4.8. The outer shield contains the radiation within the cable and provides protection from interference and cross talk. The arrangement of the outer conductor and the inner conductors makes the cable appear as having more conductive surface, resulting in lower resistance and lower losses at higher frequencies. The proper positioning and design of the insulators provide capacitive loading that lowers the impedance, and thus the velocity, of propagation.

A typical coaxial cable system consists of the cable itself, a series of repeaters, and a multiplexing capability. The closer the repeaters are, the higher the amplification can be, resulting in increased bandwidth and increased cable capacity.

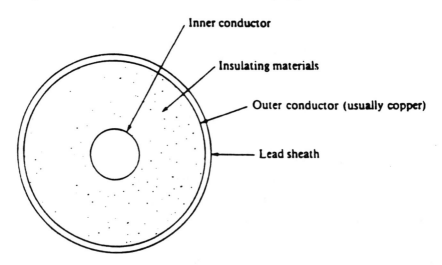

Figure 4.8. Coaxial Cable.

4.3 Microwave*

A main source of competition with coaxial systems is the microwave radio system. Microwave is a line-of-sight system; that is, the system's receivers and transmitters must be spaced in such a way that they can "see" each other along the curvature of the earth. Almost no curvature of the transmitted beam of energy is allowed, thus the terrain and the curvature of the earth dictate the spacing of receivers and transmitters that act as repeaters. The basic function of a microwave repeater is to amplify and redirect microwave signals. Passive, baseband, and heterodyne repeaters have been used almost exclusively for this purpose.

4.3.1 Microwave repeaters

Microwave repeaters are generally classified as either active or passive. The most commonly used *passive repeater* is the shield reflector, which simply redirects microwave signals by reflecting the signals from its surface. Passive repeaters are generally used on short microwave hops over inaccessible terrain, where a conventional active repeater installation would be too expensive. The principle advantages of the passive repeater are that it requires no power, provides a fixed amount of signal gain, and requires little or no maintenance. The gain of the passive repeater is proportional to its size and operating frequency. For large gains, the beam width is quite narrow, making the positioning of the reflector critical. Also, the gain of the passive repeater in the lower microwave frequency bands (see Table 4.2) is low, thus reducing its economic advantages.

The types of *active repeaters* used on microwave paths are either the demodulating-remodulating (baseband), the intermediate-frequency (IF) or radio-frequency (RF) heterodyne types. In these types of repeaters, the individual information-carrying channels are amplified and otherwise processed at frequencies usually lower than the microwave carrier frequency.

In a *baseband repeater* the incoming microwave signal is demodulated down to the baseband level, then amplified, remodulated, and transmitted to the next station. In an *IF heterodyne repeater* the incoming signal is shifted to a different frequency (usually 70

---

* see references 4, 16, 42, 44, 48, 51, 53 and 63.

MHz), which is then amplified and amplitude-modulated (heterodyned) back up to the microwave frequency for transmission to the next station. The *RF heterodyne repeater* amplifies the incoming microwave signal, then shifts the signal to a different frequency where the signal is reamplified and transmitted. In other words, the transmitting frequency is different from the carrier frequency of the input signal. Both types of heterodyne repeaters do not demodulate the signal to baseband level for amplification.

There are also RF repeaters where there is no shifting of frequencies before amplification; rather the entire incoming microwave signal is amplified and transmitted to the following repeater or terminal. There is a basic simplicity to the RF repeater in that there is only one device containing active components that operates in parallel for increased reliability. There are no frequency-generating devices, no complex automatic frequency control (AFC) circuitry, and periodic frequency checks are unnecessary. Also, the components used in the repeater are relatively insensitive to large variations in temperature and humidity, thus eliminating any requirements for temperature control, air conditioning, or special enclosures.

Table 4.2 Microwave Frequency Bands

Microwave band	Frequency range (GHz)
L	1.120-1.700
LS	1.700-2.600
S	2.600-3.950
C(G)	3.950-5.850
XN(J) (XC)	5.850-8.200
XB(H) (BL)	7.050-10.000
X	8.20-12.40
KU(P)	12.40-18.00
K	18.00-26.50
V(R) (KA)	26.5-40
Q(V)	33-50
M(W)	50-75
E(Y)	60-90
F(N)	90-140
G(A)	140-220
R	220-325

Because the input and output frequencies of an RF repeater are the same, there is the possibility of interference between the two frequencies at the repeater location. This problem is overcome by the use of special shrouded antennas. A shrouded antenna is simply a parabolic antenna that has a circular panel (shroud) that extends beyond the feedhorn (antenna). Since the shroud is made of conductive material, and in fact physically connected to the parabolic portion of the antenna, the microwave signal is maintained within the confines of the parabola, much more so than with the standard parabolic antenna, and consequently eliminates most interference from side-to-side coupling.

As with other active devices, the question of a power source is always of economic concern and trade-off. A passive repeater may be economically interesting in a location where accessibility is difficult because it doesn't require any power source, but may be restraining due to gain limitations at 2 GHz. Active repeaters, on the other hand, are very costly when installation is required at locations with difficult access (initial radio equipment costs, access roads for maintenance, utility power lines or local power generators and buildings). While the RF repeater is not limited to remote locations with difficult access, since it has various ac-dc power options, it has an important role in such areas by virtue of its unusually low power requirements (about 4 W).

4.3.2 Microwave propagation and problems

Because microwaves use short wavelengths, they are refracted or bent by the atmosphere and are obstructed or reflected by such obstacles as mountains, buildings, bodies of water, and atmosphere layers. While microwaves travel at the speed of light in a vacuum, their speed in air is reduced and varies according to the changing density and moisture content of the air.

Gradual changes in air density may cause the radio signal to refract or bend continuously so that the signal gradually curves toward the denser atmosphere. Because the atmosphere is increasingly thinner with high altitudes, radio signals do not follow a straight path but are normally refracted downward. Radio paths extend beyond the visual line-of-sight horizon, since radio signals are significantly affected by atmospheric density gradients (pressure, temperature, and humidity). The atmosphere is stratified and constantly changing, and thus these atmospheric irregularities present a varying, nonhomogeneous propagation medium to the microwave wavefront, resulting in a propagation of not only the principal body of energy, but also many refracted and reflected secondary signals that arrive at the receiver antenna at various phases and amplitudes. The amplitude of the resultant RF received signal can vary with time from 6 dB above the normal signal transmission to -40 dB below. If the fade depth is greater than the designed fade margin an outage can result. *Fading* is the fluctuation in signal strength at a receiver; it may be rapid or slow, general or frequency-selective, but in each case it is due to some sort of interference between two waves that left the same source but arrived at the destination by different paths. Fading may also occur if a single skywave is being received, because of fluctuations of height or density in the layer reflecting the wave. *Fade margin* is the amount of reserve power, in decibels, available at a receiver to overcome the effects of sudden atmospheric fades. The fade margin depends on the arrangements of the system. The closer the transmitter is to the receiver, or the more suitable the climate and terrain for microwave propagation, the smaller the fade margin necessary for required reliability.

Fortunately, most fades of this magnitude (+6 dB to -40 dB) result from atmospheric multipath and specular ground reflections and are of extremely short duration (see more details in section 4.5.1). Besides these short-term outages, long-term attenuation fades resulting from partial path obstruction or signal trapping may occur, but usually only in low-clearance paths traversing shallow standing bodies of water (e.g., swamps and lakes), especially with line-of-sight transmission. Short microwave links rarely experience a fade of such depth as to cause an outage, whereas longer paths traversing reflective terrain or water in coastal or other highly humid regions will fade far more frequently than long paths over rough terrain in dry regions.

In the receiver, the level fluctuations of the received RF signal caused by fading are removed by automatic gain control (AGC) circuits before the signal is applied to the demodulator. In most microwave receivers, AGC is provided at the intermediate frequency of about 70 MHz to which the received signal is converted by the mixer. Thus, the receiver gain varies in accordance with the received signal level, the gain being high when the received signal is fading and low when it is not. Any noise entering the receiver input, as well as noise internally generated in the input circuit, is amplified along with the desired signal, so that when the signal fades, the noise is proportionally higher and the signal-to-noise ratio is decreased.

4.3.3 Microwave transmission

Any point-to-point microwave system can carry digital or frequency-division multiplexed (FDM) channels. The information to be transmitted can be carried by the microwave signal in various forms of modulation, frequency, phase, amplitude, or any combination. FM or PM is, however, the preferred method because it facilitates AGC capabilities, and amplitude linearity is not required in the RF and IF circuits. Hence, FM techniques have been consistently used in commercial microwave radio systems for multichannel voice and data transmission.

When the information to be transmitted is in digital form, either digital data or voice, the modulation technique of the microwave carrier is still FM or PM, which keeps the envelope of the microwave signal as constant as possible. Thus the original FM microwave equipment designed to transmit such analog signals as FDM voice or video is still suitable for the transmission of digital data. The only thing required is a conversion of the digital signal into a signal similar to the normal analog modulating signal in level and frequency spectrum.

Because the bandwidth of a microwave transmission is on the order of 2 to 6 GHz, the voice channels are combined using FDM. Equipment to accomplish multiplexing is therefore associated with the radio system terminals, or with any other site where one or more voice channels are to be separated from the main signal system.

4.4 Satellites*

Satellites are a specialized form of microwave transmission. In use, the satellite replaces microwave or cable repeaters, often resulting in superior service at a low cost. Stationary satellites, referred to as geosynchronous or geostationary, hover 22,300 miles above fixed areas providing telecommunication links and pathways to widely dispersed and in some cases previously "unreached" locations. These systems provide multichannel capabilities, wide bandwidths, and high data rates. Satellites are widely used today across the total communications spectrum, including commercial and military applications (see Table 4.3).

Satellites have had a dramatic impact on telecommunications topologies, pricing, and optimizing techniques. Telecommunications systems are designed to provide a required service with minimal costs. Minimizing costs often consisted of finding optimum combinations of telecommunications services based on mileage charges and carrying capacities. Multiplexing and concentrating techniques were used to minimize the length

---

* see references 2–4, 11, 17, 21–24, 27–32, 35, 37, 45, 47, 50, 55, 57 and 59–65.

of service links. With the use of satellites, the mileage techniques have had to be changed and alternate procedures considered for optimizing topologies and charges.

Because most microwave signal degradation is caused by atmospheric conditions, and a satellite link passes essentially through refraction-free space for a significant part of its length (22,280 out of 22,300 miles), satellite circuits have fewer signal fades and distortions than long-distance microwave (terrestrial) circuits. Furthermore, since background noise on earth facilities increases with distance, satellite channels are often more quiet. For these reasons, as well as the lower cost, many traditional voiceband data transmissions have been moved to satellite channels.

Voiceband data transmission via satellite is almost indistinguishable from such transmission on earth channels (e.g., microwave circuits). In fact, the same modem may be used as long as the accepted time-out interval includes the propagation-delay time. However, in some cases users must compensate for time delays in their initial hand-shaking (line connection) procedure by proper modem selection. Aside from this time compensation all long-distance voiceband data modems (up to 9600 bps) will operate normally on satellite circuits.

Most standard satellite voice circuits are designed to satisfy the Bell C4 (frequency-response and delay-distortion) and D1 (impulse-and-hit) specifications. Typical noise performance is 2 to 3 dB better, while impulse-and-hit counts are one order of magnitude better than earth circuits.

Satellite connections do require uplinks and downlinks. Since it is relatively easy to supply high transmitter power and antenna gains at earth stations, the performance of the satellite is determined by the downlink. The limitations of satellite power and the necessity for covering the appropriate earth area limit the overall performance. Satellite power is directly translatable into weight and cost. In addition to these problems, satellites need to be placed into orbit (cost), do not stay in orbit indefinitely (need to be replaced), and require extremely complex and expensive ground terminals.

Nonetheless, with communication satellites instant and reliable, contact can be rapidly established between any points on earth, with capabilities beyond available land lines, microwave links, and other techniques. Satellites also offer flexibilities not only to fixed points on earth, but also to moving terminals, such as ships, planes, and space vehicles.

The key satellite system capabilities can be best described in terms of multiple access, direct links, multiplexing modes, demand assignments, and propagation delays.

Table 4.3 Characteristics of Communications Satellites [30]

(A) Geosynchronous Satellites in the Eastern Hemisphere

Location	Up (GHz)	Down (GHz)	Service	Name of Satellite	Operator	Transponders	EIRP	Launch	Life
E002.7	0.15, 0.4, 2.1	0.14, 0.5, 1.7	MET	METEOSAT-2	EURO MET SAT	2		81	3
E002.7	0.15, 0.4, 2.1	0.14, 0.5, 1.7	MET	METEOSAT-OPN'L	EURO MET SAT	2		87	3
E003	6, 8, 14	4, 7, 12	DOM, GOVT	TELECOM-1C	FRANCE	12	26-47	85	7
E007	6 and 30	4, 20, 40, 90	REGIONAL	ATHOS	CNES & FR. PTT	8 and 14	37.5 and 51	87	5
E007	14	11 and 12.5	REGIONAL	EUTELSAT 1-3	EUTELSAT COUNCIL	11	39.8	85	10
E010	14	11 and 12.5	REGIONAL	EUTELSAT 1-2	EUTELSAT COUNCIL	11	39.8	84	10
E013	30 and 50	20 and 40	DOM	ITALSAT	ITALY	13		88	5
E019	6	2.5 and 4	FSS & BSS	ARABSAT-1	ARAB SAT COMM	25	41 and 31	84	7

Table 4.3 Characteristics of Communications Satellites, Eastern Hemisphere (cont.)

Location	Up (GHz)	Down (GHz)	Service	Name of Satellite	Operator	Trans-ponders	EIRP	Launch	Life
E023.5	14, 30	11, 12, 20	DOM & BSS	DFS-1	GERMANY	11	48, 49	87	10
E026	6	2.5 and 4	FSS & BSS	ARABSAT-2	ARAB SAT COMM	25	41 and 31	85	7
E028.5	14, 30	11, 12, 20	DOM & BSS	DES-2	GERMANY	11	48 and 49	87	10
E056.8	6	4	INTL.	INTELSAT IVA-F2	INTELSAT	20	20 to 29	76	7
E057	6 and 14	4 and 11	INTL	INTELSAT V-F1	INTELSAT	27	21 to 42	81	7
E059.8	14	12	BSS	YURI (BS-1)	MOPT JAPAN	2	46 to 55	78	3
E060	2, 8	2, 7	GOVT	DSCS-2-FO4	DOD USA	4	28, 43	73	5
E060	2, 8	2, 7	GOVT	DSCS-3-FO4	DOD USA	7	23-44	84	10
E060	1.6, 6, and 14	1.5, 4, and 11	INT & MARIT	INTELSAT V-F7	INTELSAT	28	21 to 42	83	7
E063	1.6, 6, and 14	1.5, 4, and 11	INTL	INTELSAT V-F5	INTELSAT	28	21 to 42	82	7
E065	6, 17	4, 12	DOM, BSS	PRC-1	CHINA B/C SAT			87	5
E070	6	4	DOM	STW-2	PR CHINA	1	50	85	3
E071.9	6	0.714 and 3	BSS	EKRAN-09	USSR PT&T	1	49	82	2
E073.3	0.3, 8	0.25	GOVT	FLEETSATCOM -2	US NAVY	23	16 to 28	79	5

Table 4.3 Characteristics of Communications Satellites, Eastern Hemisphere (cont.)

			DOM/BSS/M	INSAT-1B	ISRO-INDIA	14	32 to 42	83	7
E074	0.46, 6	2.5, 4							
E075	0.3 and 8	0.25	GOVT	LEASAT-1	HUGHES COMM SVC	13	17 to 28	84	10
E080.2	6	4	DOM	PALAPA-A1	PERUMTEL (INDON)	12	32	76	7
E080.2	6	4	DOM	PALAPA-A2	PERUMTEL (INDON)	12	32	77	7
E085.4	6	0.714 and 3	BSS	EKRAN-08	USSR PT&T	1	49	82	2
E092	17	12	DOM	PRC-3	PR CHINA			88	5
E102	0.148 and 6	0.136 and 4	DOM	APPLE	INDIA	1	30.5	81	2
E102.2	14 and 2	12 and 2	BSS	YURI-2A	MOPT JAPAN	2	46 to 55	84	3
E108	6	4	REGIONAL	PALAPA-B1	INDONESIA	24	34	83	8
E110	14 and 2	12 and 2	BSS	BS-2B (SPARE)	MOPT JAPAN	2	46-55	85	3
E113	6	4	REGIONAL	PALAPA-B2			34	86	8
E120	30	20	DOM	(REPLACE-MENT)	INDONESIA	24		87	10
E120	30	20	DOM	NTT-1	NIPPON TEL & TEL			95	10
E120.8	6 and 30	4 and 20	DOM	NTT-2	NIPPON TEL & TEL		29 and 37	83	5
E125.8	6.225-0.425	4.000-4.200	DOM	CS-2B	NASDA & NTT	8	35	84	3
E132.0	6 and 30	4 and 20	DOM	STW-1	PR CHINA	2	29 and 37	83	5

Table 4.3 Characteristics of Communications Satellites, Eastern Hemisphere (cont.)

Location	Up (GHz)	Down (GHz)	Service	Name of Satellite	Operator	Trans- ponders	EIRP	Launch	Life
E140	0.4, 2.0, 2.2	0.5, 1.7, 2.3	MET	CS-2A (SAKURA)	NASDA & NTT	8	4 to 16	84	7
E156	14.0-14.5	12.25-0.75	DOM/BSS	GMS-3A (HIMIWARI)	KDD	4	36 to 48	85	7
E160	14.0-14.5	12.25-0.75	DOM/BSS	AUSSAT-1	AUSTRALIA	15	36 to 48	85	7
E160	0.4, 2.9, 2.1	0.5, 1.7, 2.3	MET	AUSSAT-2	AUSTRALIA	15	4 to 16	85	7
E164	14.0-14.5	12.25-0.75	DOM, BSS	GMS-3B (HIMIWARI)	KDD	4	36 to 48	88	7
E173.1	0.3, 8	0.25	GOVT	AUSSAT-3	AUSTRALIA	15	16.5-28	80	5
E174	6	4	INTL	FLEETSATCOM	US NAVY	23	20 to 29	78	7
E175	2, 8	2, 7	GOVT	INTELSAT IVA-F6	INTELSAT	20	23-44	84	10
E176.5	0.3 and 8	0.25	GOVT	DSCS-3-F2	DOD USA	7	17 to 28	84	10
E177.5	1.6, 6	1.5, 4	MARITIME	LEASAT-2	HUGHES COMM SVC	13	17 to 35	84	7

Table 4.3 Characteristics of Communications Satellites [30]

(B) Geosynchronous Satellites in the Western Hemisphere

Location	Up (GHz)	Down (GHz)	Service	Name of Satellite	Operator	Trans-ponders	EIRP	Launch	Life
W001	6 and 14	4 and 11	INTL	INTELSAT VA-F1	INTELSAT	28	21 to 42	84	7
W004	6	4	INTL	INTELSAT AO SPARE 5	INTELSAT			0	0
W005	6, 8, and 14	4, 7, and 12	DOM, GOVT	TELECOM-1B	FRENCH PTT	12	26-47	85	7
W008	6, 8, and 14	4, 7, and 12	DOM, GOVT	TELECOM-1A	FRENCH PTT	12	26-47	84	77
W011.33	6	4	EXP	SYMPHONIE-2	FRANCE & GERMANY	2	29	75	5
W011.5	2, 8	2, 7	GOVT	DSCS-2-F14	DOD USA	4	28, 43	79	5
W014.9	1.6 and 6	1.5 and 4	MARIT	MARITSAT-ATLANTIC-101	COMSAT GENERAL	8	29 and 19	76	8

Table 4.3 Characteristics of Communications Satellites, Western Hemisphere (cont.)

Location	Up (GHz)	Down (GHz)	Service	Name of Satellite	Operator	Trans-ponders	EIRP	Launch	Life
W016.2	2, 8	2, 7	GOVT	DSCS-3-F1	DOD USA	7	23-44	82	10
W018.5	1.6, 6, and 14	1.5, 4, and 11	INTL	INTELSAT V-F6	INTELSAT	28	21 to 42	83	7
W019	17	12	BSS	HELVESAT-1	SWISS TEL-TEC	5	64	87	7
W019	17	12	BSS	HELVESAT-2	SWISS TEL-TEC	3	64	88	7
W019	17.3-17.7	11.7-12.1	BSS	LUXSAT	RADIO TELE LUX	5	63	88	7
W019	13, 18, 30	12, 12, 20	EXP, BSS	OLYMPUS 1	ESA	9	46, 53, 63	87	5
W019	17	12	BSS	TDF-1A	TELE-DIF-FRANCE	3	63.9	85	7
W019	17	12	BSS	TDF-1B	TELE-DIF-FRANCE	5	63.9	87	7
W019	17	12	BSS	TDF-2	TELE-DIF-FRANCE	5	63.9	90	10
W019	17	12	BSS	TV-SAT-A3 F1	W. GERMANY	3	65.6	85	7

Table 4.3 Characteristics of Communications Satellites, Western Hemisphere (cont.)

W019	2.1, 17	2.3, 12	BSS	TV-SAT-A5	GERMANY	5	65.6	90	10
W019.1	2, 8	2, 7	GOVT	NATO 111C	NATO	3	31 and 36	78	7
W023	0.3 and 8	0.25	GOVT	LEASAT-4	HUGHES COMM SVC	13	17 to 28	85	10
W024.5	6 and 14	4 and 11	INT & MARIT	INTELSAT VA-F3	INTELSAT	28	21 to 42	84	7
W025	0.148 and 2.1	0.137 and 1.7	MET & EXP	SIRIO-2 REPLACEMENT	ESA			85	5
W031	14 and 18	11 and 12	BSS & FSS	UNISAT-1	UNITED SATS LTD	6	45 and 63	86	10
W031	14 and 18	11 and 12	BSS & FSS	UNISAT-2	UNITED SAT LTD	6	45 and 63	86	10
W031	14 and 18	11 and 12	BSS & FSS	UNISAT-3	UNITED SAT LTD	6	45 and 63	87	10
W037.5*	14	11	INTL	ORION-1	ORION SAT CORP	22	44-47.4	87	7
W040.2	2 and 15	2.2 and 13	TRACKING	TDRS-F1	SPACECOM	5	26 to 52	83	10
W041	2, 15	2+, 13	TRACKING	TDRS SPARE	SPACECOM		53	86	10

Table 4.3 Characteristics of Communications Satellites, Western Hemisphere (cont.)

Location	Up (GHz)	Down (GHz)	Service	Name of Satellite	Operator	Trans- ponders	EIRP	Launch	Life
W041	2 and 15	2.2 and 13	TRACKING	TDRS-F2	SPACECOM	5	26 to 52	85	10
W045.2	0.3, 8	0.25	GOVT	FLEETSATCOM -5	US NAVY	23	17-27	81	5
W047*	14	11	INTL	ORION-2	ORION SAT CORP	22	44-47.4	87	7
W050*	14	11	INTL	ORION-3	ORION SAT CORP	22	44-47.4	87	7
W057*	6	4	DOM	DIGISAT 1B	DIGITAL TELESAT	24	37	88	10
W057*	14	12	DOM	DIGISAT-1A	DIGITAL TELESAT	24	44	88	10
W057*	6.4 and 14	10.7-11.2	INTL	PANAMSAT-1	PAN AM SAT CORP	12 (6N. 6S bound)			
W065	6	4	DOM	SBTS A-2	BRAZIL	24	38	85	8

Table 4.3 Characteristics of Communications Satellites, Western Hemisphere (cont.)

W067	14	12	DOM	SATCOM K3	RCA AMERICOM	16	38-39	86	10
W067	6	4	DOM-INTL	SATCOM V1	RCA AMERICOM	24	37	87	10
W069	6 and 14	4 and 12	DOM	SPACENET-2	GTE SPACENET	18	34, 36, and 39	84	7
W070	6	4	DOM	SBTS A-1	BRAZIL	24	35	85	8
W072	6	4	DOM	SATCOM 11R	RCA AMERICOM	24	34-35	83	8
W073*	6 and 14	4 and 12	FSS	FORDSAT-3	FORD A.S.S. CORP	48	35-50	88	10
W073*	14	12	DOM	GALAXY H5	HUGHES COMM INC	16	50	86	10
W073*	14	12	DOM	M.M.-73	MART. MARIETTA	28	47-53	88	10
W074.0	6	4	DOM	GALAXY II	HUGHES COMM INC	24	34	83	9
W075*	14	12	DOM	GALAXY H6	HUGHES COMM INC	16	50	86	10

Table 4.3 Characteristics of Communications Satellites, Western Hemisphere (cont.)

Location	Up (GHz)	Down (GHz)	Service	Name of Satellite	Operator	Trans- ponders	EIRP	Launch	Life
W075*	14	12	DOM	M.M.-75	MART. MARIETTA	28	47-53	88	10
W075*	14	12	DOM	RAINBOW-3	RAINBOW SAT INC	24	44-47	87	10
W075*	6	4	DOM	SPOTNET-C2	NAT EXCHANGE	24	34	87	9
W075*	14	12	DOM	SPOTNET-K3	NAT EXCHANGE	24	57-60	87	10
W075*	14	12	DOM	SPOTNET-K4	NAT EXCHANGE	24	57-60	87	10
W075*	14	12	DOM	USAT-3	US SAT SVCS INC	20	43-46	88	8
W075.4	6	4	DOM	SATCOLIA	COLUMBIA	24	34.6	87	10
W076	6	4	DOM	TELSTAR 302	AT&T COMM.	24	32-34	84	10
W077	14	12	DOM	SATCOM K1	RCA AMERICOM	16	38-39	85	10

Table 4.3 Characteristics of Communications Satellites, Western Hemisphere (cont.)

W079	14	12	DOM	RAINBOW-2	RAINBOW SAT INC.	24	44-47	88	10
W081	6 and 14	4 and 12	DOM	ASC-2	AMER SAT CO	24	34, 36, and 42	86	8
W081*	6	4	DOM	WESTAR VII	WESTERN UNION	24	34+	88	10
W083	14	12	DOM	ABC1-1	ADV BUS COMM	16	41-53	87	10
W083	6	4	DOM	SATCOM IV	RCA AMERICOM	24	32	82	10
W085	14	12	DOM	USAT-1	US SAT SVCS INC	20	43-46	86	8
W085*	0.8, 1.6, 14	0.8, 1.5, 12	MOBILE	MOBILESAT I	MOBILE SAT CORP	2	50, 53, 45	87	7
W086	6	4	DOM	WESTAR VIII	WESTERN UNION	24	35	88	10
W087*	14	12	DOM	WESTAR C	WESTERN UNION	16	46+	89	10
W088.5	6	4	DOM	TELSTAR 303	AT&T COMM.	24	32-34	85	10

Table 4.3 Characteristics of Communications Satellites, Western Hemisphere (cont.)

Location	Up (GHz)	Down (GHz)	Service	Name of Satellite	Operator	Trans- ponders	EIRP	Launch	Life
W091	14	12	DOM	SBS-4	SAT BUS SYST	10	37-44 and 53	84	7
W093*	6, 14, and 30	4, 12, and 20	DOM	ASC-4	AMER SAT CO	46	34, 42, and 52	89	8
W093*	14	12	DOM	COMSTAR K1	COMSAT GENERAL	16	47-50	88	10
W093*	6	4	DOM	EQUASTAR-1	EQUATORIAL COMM	24	36	87	10
W093*	6 and 14	4 and 12	DOM	FORDSAT-2	FORD A.S.S. CORP	48	35-50	88	10
W093*	14	12	DOM	GALAXY H7	HUGHES COMM INC	16	50	86	10
W093*	14	12	DOM	RAINBOW-4	RAINBOW SAT INC	24	44-47	87	10
W093*	14	12	DOM	WESTAR A	WESTERN UNION	16	46+	88	10

Table 4.3 Characteristics of Communications Satellites, Western Hemisphere (cont.)

W093.5	6	4	DOM	GALAXY III	HUGHES COMM INC	24	34	85	9
W099	6	4	DOM	WESTAR IV	WESTERN UNION	24	34	82	10
W099*	14	12	DOM	SBS-6	SBS	14	47-49	87	10
W100	30	20	EXP	ACTS-1	NASA			88	3
W100	0.3 and 8	0.25	GOVT	LEASAT-3	HUGHES COMM SVC	13	17 to 28	85	10
W101*	6 and 14	4 and 12	DOM	ASC-3	AMER SAT CO	24	34, 36, and 42	87	8
W101*	17	12.2-12.7	BSS	CBS-101	CBS INC	6	61	87	7
W101*	14	12	DOM	COMSTAR K2	COMSAT GENERAL	16	47-50	88	10
W101*	17	12.2-12.7	BSS	RCA-DBS-1	RCA AMERICOM	6	58	86	7
W101*	6	4	DOM	SPOTNET-C1	NAT EXCHANGE	24	34	87	9
W101*	14	12	DOM	SPOTNET-K1	NAT EXCHANGE	24	57-60	87	10

Table 4.3 Characteristics of Communications Satellites, Western Hemisphere (cont.)

Location	Up (GHz)	Down (GHz)	Service	Name of Satellite	Operator	Trans-ponders	EIRP	Launch	Life
W101*	14	12	DOM	SPOTNET-K2	NAT EXCHANGE	24	57-60	87	10
W101	17	12.2-12.7	DBS	STC-101A	SAT TV CORP	6	57	86	7
W101	17	12.2-12.7	DBS	STC-101B	SAT TV CORP	6	57	86	7
W101*	17.3-17.8	12.2-12.7	BSS	USSB-1	HUBBARD B/C	6	57	87	7
W103	14	12	DOM	GSTAR A-1	GTE SATELLITE	16	42	84	10
W104.5	6	4	DOM	ANIK D1	TELESAT CANADA	24	36	82	9
W105	14	12	DOM	GSTAR A-2	GTE SATELLITE	16	42	85	10
W105**	14	12	DOM	ANIK C2	TELESAT CANADA	16	48	83	8
W106.5	0.868 and 14	0.823 and 12	MOBILE	M-SAT	CANADA/USA	5	37-38	87	7
W107.5	14	12	DOM	ANIK C1	TELESAT CANADA	16	48	84	8

Table 4.3 Characteristics of Communications Satellites, Western Hemisphere (cont.)

W110	6	4	DOM	ANIK D2	TELESAT CANADA	24	36	85	9
W110*	17.3-17.8	12.2-12.7	BSS	USSB-1 ALTERNATE	HUBBARD B/C	6	57	87	7
W113.5	6 and 14	4 and 12	DOM	MORELOS-1	MEXICO	22 to 24	39 and 45	85	9
W116.5	6 and 14	4 and 12	DOM	MORELOS-2	MEXICO	22 to 24	39 and 45	85	9
W117.5	14	12	DOM	ANIK C3	TELESAT CANADA	16	48	82	8
W119*	17	12.2-12.7	BSS	RCA-DBS-2	RCA AMERICOM	6	58	86	7
W119*	17	12.2-12.7	BSS	VSS-1	VIDEO SAT SYST	6	56	86	8
W120	6 and 14	4 and 12	DOM	SPACENET-1	GTE-SPACENET	18	34, 36, and 39	84	7
W122	14	12	DOM	USAT-2	US SAT SVCS INC	20	43-46	87	8
W122*	6	14	DOM	EQUASTAR-2	EQUATORIAL COMM	24	36	87	10

Table 4.3 Characteristics of Communications Satellites, Western Hemisphere (cont.)

Location	Up (GHz)	Down (GHz)	Service	Name of Satellite	Operator	Trans- ponders	EIRP	Launch	Life
W123.0	6	4	DOM	WESTAR V	WESTERN UNION	24	34	82	10
W124*	14	12	DOM	SBS-5	SBS	14	47-49	87	10
W125*	0.8, 1.6, 14	0.8, 1.5, 12	MOBILE	MOBILESAT 2	MOBILESAT CORP	2	50, 53, 45	87	7
W125*	6	4	FSS	TELESTAR 304	AT&T	24	32-34	88	10
W128	6 and 14	4 and 12	DOM	ASC-1	AMER SAT CO	24	34, 36, and 42	85	9
W130	14	12	DOM	ABC1-2	ADV BUS COMM	16	41-53	87	10
W132	14	12	DOM	RAINBOW-1	RAINBOW SAT INC	24	44-47	87	10
W134*	14	12	DOM	DIGISAT II	DIGITAL TELESAT	24	44	88	10
W134.0	6	4	DOM	GALAXY I	HUGHES COMM INC	24	37	83	10

Table 4.3 Characteristics of Communications Satellites, Western Hemisphere (cont.)

W135	2,8	2,7	GOVT	DSCS-3-F3	DOD USA	7	23-44	83	10
W137*	6	4	DOM	AURORA II	ALASCOM, INC.	24	34	89	10
W137*	6	4	DOM	GALAXY IV	HUGHES COMM INC	24	34.5	86	9
W139	6	4	DOM SPARE	SATCOM 1R	RCA AMERICOM	24	36	83	10
W141*	6	4	DOM	AURORA III	ALASCOM, INC.	24	34	91	10
W143	6	4	DOM	AURORA I	ALASCOM, INC.	24	34	82	10
W148*	17	12.2-12.7	BSS	CBS-148	CBS INC.	6	61	88	7
W148*	17	12.2-12.7	BSS	DBSC-2	DBS CORP	10		87	7
W148*	17	12.2-12.7	BSS	RCA-DBS-3	RCA AMERICOM	6	58	87	7
W148	17	12.2-12.7	DBS	STC-148A	SAT TV CORP	6	57	87	7
W148*	17.3-17.8	12.2-12.7	BSS	USSB-2	HUBBARD B/C	6	57	87	7
W148*	17	12.2-12.7	BSS	VSS-2	VIDEO SAT SYST	6	56	86	8

Table 4.3 Characteristics of Communications Satellites, Western Hemisphere (cont.)

Location	Up (GHz)	Down (GHz)	Service	Name of Satellite	Operator	Transponders	EIRP	Launch	Life
W157*	17	12.2-12.7	BSS	RCA-DBS-4	RCA AMERICOM	6	58	87	7
W171	2 and 15	2 and 14	TRACKING	TDRS-F3	SPACECOM	5	26 to 52	85	10

*Location request pending at the Federal Communications Commission

**Temporary location until Gstar A2 is operational

The second and third columns identify the up- and downlink communications frequencies in gigahertz.

The equivalent isotropically radiated power (EIRP), column eight, is expressed in terms of dBW (decibels referenced to 1 W).

The final two columns identify the launch year and the anticipated lifetime, in years. A 0 represents inadequate or unavailable information.

Satellites sharing the same fequency bands and providing overlapping coerages are now placed as close as 2^0 apart. See, for example, 72 West through 76 West. In the case of Comstar D1 and Comstar D2, these satellites are placed at the same nominal location. Because they operate on the same frequencies, the combination of the two satellites is capable of providing up to 24 transponders (not 24 each, as originally designed, because of mutual interference considerations).

List of Abbreviations for Table 4.3

AO	Atlantic Ocean	MOBILE	Mobile Satellite Service
BOL	Bolivia	MOD	Ministry of Defense
BSS	Broadcasting Satellite Service	MOPT	Ministry of Posts and Telegraph
CL	Colombia	MP	Major Path
DOD	U.S. Department of Defense	NASDA	National Aeronautics and Space Development Agency
DOM	Domestic		
EC	Ecuador	NOAA	National Oceanographic and Atmospheric Agency
ESA	European Space Agency		
EXP	Experimental	NTT	Nippon Telephone and Telegraph
FORD A.S.S.		PO	Pacific Ocean
Corp	Ford Aerospace Satellite Services Corpation	PR	Peru
FSS	Fixed Satellite Services	PR China	Peoples Republic of China
GOVT	Government	PRI	Primary
IO	Indian Ocean	PT&T	Postal Telephone and Telegraph
INDON	Indonesia	RITE	Research Institute of Telecommunications and Economics
INT or INTL	International		
ISRO	Indian Space Research Organization	RRL	Radio Research Laboratory
KDD	Kokusai Denshin Denwa Co., Ltd	SBS	Satellite Business Systems
MARIT	Maritime Mobile Satellite Service	SP COMM CO	Southern Pacific Communications Co.
MET or M	Meterological	VN	Venezuela

4.4.1 Multiple access*

To exploit the geometric properties of very large area visibility and multiple connectivity inherent in satellite communications, the various communications links using the satellite must be separated from each other. This can be accomplished by using space-division multiple access (SDMA), frequency-division multiple access (FDMA), time-division multiple access (TDMA), and code-division multiple access (CDMA).

Space-division multiple access uses different antenna beams and separate amplifiers within the satellite. Flexibility is possible only at the expense of complications within the satellite, increased weight, and occasional operational difficulties.

Frequency-division multiple access uses different carrier frequencies for each transmitting station. FDMA provides the capability for many stations to use the same transponder amplifier, whose capacity is limited only by the overall noise level. Multiple carriers produce intermodulation products that raise the apparent noise level, which then requires compensation (reduction) in the amplifier drive. The reduction in capability of a transponder can be as much as 6 dB when compared to the capability of a single-carrier frequency if all available information was multiplexed. FDMA is, however, the most popular technique, especially if one is not power-limited.

FDMA can be implemented by multiplexing many channels on each carrier transmitted through the satellite, or by using a separate carrier frequency for each baseband channel within the satellite. If many carriers are used, the intermodulation products increase but approach a limiting level that is usually acceptable. The single-channel-per-carrier approach is especially advantageous for systems where many links are to be made, each one having only a few circuits to be handled at any one time. Multiplexing is only economical if each carrier has traffic in a group of 12 or more channels. The modulation techniques used for single-channel-per-carrier systems include PCM, delta modulation, and narrowband FM.

Time-division multiple access uses a separate time slot for each earth station for its transmission, but all earth stations use the same carrier frequency within a particular transponder. This technique eliminates the intermodulation noise and improves the capacity of the transponder, but requires more complex earth station equipment. A comparison of TDMA to FDMA illustrates the efficiency of the former. For example,

---

* see references 54 and 62.

consider the capacities of an INTELSAT IV global beam transponder operating with standard INTELSAT 30-m earth stations, using TDMA and FDMA, respectively. Assuming 10 accesses, the typical capacity using FM-FDMA is about 450 one-way voice channels. With TDMA using standard PCM encoding, the capacity of the same transponder is approximately 900 channels.

The trend to digital systems, both on earth links as well as via satellite, is reinforced by the ease with which TDMA can be combined with SDMA by switching transmission bursts from one antenna beam to another, depending on their destination. This time-division switching is efficient in terms of both the satellite power and the frequency spectrum.

Code-division multiple access, or *spread-spectrum multiple access*, combines the transmission from each earth station with a pseudo-random code so as to cause the transmission to occupy the entire bandwidth of the transponder. In other words, the codes used by different stations are "orthogonal" to each other. Hence it is possible for many stations to share the same transmission channel. The destination station, using a duplicate of this pseudo-random code, extracts its transmission from the bandwidth created by the simultaneous use of many other stations. This technique is advantageous for military applications because the spread-spectrum technique is used to harden the satellite receiver against jamming, while the pseudo-random sequences can be used for cryptographic security. On the other hand, it is less efficient in exploiting the satellite's power resource and frequency spectrum than even the FDMA system.

4.4.2 Direct links

The direct connection by way of the satellite between stations on earth, whatever their geographical location, is an important advantage of satellite communications. In fact, the advantage is only shared with high-frequency (HF) radio links.

4.4.3 Random Access[*]

Earth stations that have continuous traffic over a number of channels use preassigned channels. Demand assignment is a technique used for those systems that have short-term activities. A demand assignment (DA) network provides increased space segment

---

[*] see references 54 and 56.

efficiency by pooling all channels according to instantaneous traffic loads. This is contrasted with a system using a preassignment network in which all channels are dedicated and fixed. When traffic to a particular destination is light, the channel's utilization is poor. Furthermore, for any given traffic load the blocking occurrence is high, because channels are "locked in" to a particular link. In DA systems, unused channels may be made available to other users. DA systems offer two main advantages over preassigned systems: (1) more efficient space segment utilization, and (2) more efficient utilization of earth interconnect facilities.

There are many variations that DA communications systems may have. For example, a *fully variable* DA system is one in which both ends of all channels are not dedicated and any station may use any channel. A *semivariable* DA system is one in which blocks of channels are reserved to either an originating or destination station, but still used only on demand.

An alternate way of describing DA systems is by considering their traffic characteristics. When the carriers (FDMA system) or bursts (TDMA system) are assigned on demand, the system is called *DA multiple access* (DAMA). When channels on existing carriers (FDMA system) or time slots in existing bursts (TDMA system) are assigned on demand, it is called *baseband DA* (BDA).

Various combinations of these approaches can be created, depending on the traffic characteristics and the user requirements. For example, if a network has many users but few earth stations, BDA may be most suitable. For a network with many earth stations, each with low traffic, a fully variable DAMA system would seem best. If priority control of access is essential, then a semivariable DA system would enable a certain number of channels to be reserved for this priority traffic.

4.4.4 Propagational delays[*]

One major difference between earth and satellite transmission is propagational delay. In order for the satellite to be stationary on the earth's surface, the satellite's orbit has to be synchronized with the earth's revolutions. This synchronization occurs only at an altitude of 22,300 miles above the equator, and thus there is an end-to-end propagational delay of about 250 ms, or a round-up delay of 500 ms.

---

[*] see references 6, 46 and 54.

Thus, inserting a satellite link into existing networks increases the response time, but decreases throughput, if certain error-control techniques that rely on a receiver response are used. The problem has been the stop-and-wait methods of error control embedded in most line protocols. It takes a total of about 500 ms for a block of data to travel via the satellite to a receiving station and for the signal indicating whether or not the block is in error to retraverse back to the transmitting station. Solutions to this delay problem include increasing the data block length as well as using some form of continuous automatic-request-for-repeat (ARQ) error control.

The two basic modes of data transmission are continuous and stop-and-wait. In continuous transmission, data are sent as a nonstop stream of characters or blocks, and errors are not controlled in any way.

ARQ techniques are of two types: stop-and-wait and continuous. In the *stop-and-wait ARQ mode*, the transmitting station stops sending while it waits for the receiving station to check a received block of data for errors before it allows the next block of data to be sent. This means the transmitter must wait out the round-trip propagation time plus the time duration of the forward (data) and return messages. Thus, the waiting time can be so excessive on satellite channels that more time is spent waiting and retransmitting than in delivering good data to the receiver. The decrease in throughput can be minimized in stop-and-wait ARQ used over satellite channels if the data block size is optimized to the channel bit rate and bit error rate (see Figures 4.9 and 4.10). For a given propagation delay and a given block length, the throughput efficiency (ratio of usable bits received to total transmitted bits per block) goes up as the probability of the occurrence of an erroneous bit goes down. Furthermore, for any given propagation delay and any given error rate, an optimum block length can maximize throughput efficiency. Figure 4.9 shows that for the selected block lengths, the satellite link operating at its error probability of 10^{-6} has an efficiency that matches that of the earth link operating at 10^{-4} error rate.

A protocol that is well suited to satellite transmission is the *continuous-ARQ technique*. Here the transmitting terminal does not wait for an acknowledgement after sending a block, but rather immediately sends the next block. While the blocks are being transmitted, the stream of received acknowledgements is examined by the transmitting terminal.

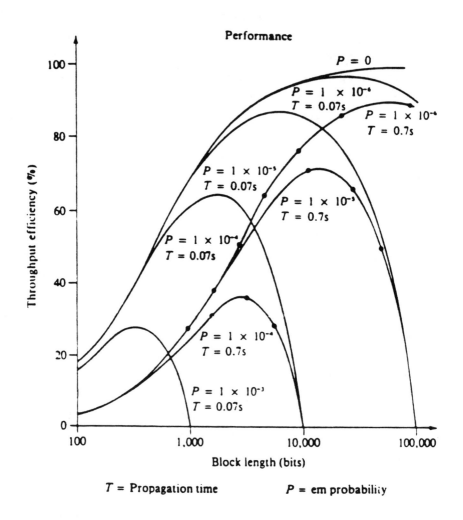

Figure 4.9.   Throughput value as a function of block length for earth circuits and satellite circuits in stop-and-wait ARQ mode [6].

When the terminal receives a negative acknowledgement or fails to receive a positive acknowledgement, it must determine which block was incorrect. The blocks are therefore numbered, and the acknowledgement contains the number of the acknowledged block.

On failing to receive a positive acknowledgement, the transmitting terminal may either back up to the block in question and recommence transmission of that block (go back N scheme) or retransmit only the block with the error without subsequent blocks (selective-repeat ARQ).

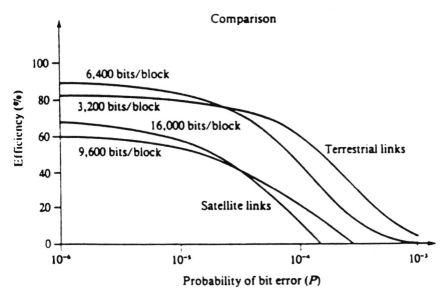

Figure 4.10.   The effects of block length and bit-error probability on throughput efficiency [6].

A comparison of throughput efficiency for the stop-and-wait ARQ and the go-back-to-7-blocks ARQ (SDLC) methods for a 9600-bps link is shown in Figure 4.11. The go-back-to-7-blocks method is clearly superior at typical error conditions for both the satellite link (10^{-6}) and the earth link (10^{-4}). The selective-repeat ARQ method is the least sensitive to a worsening error rate on the link.

4.5 Fiber Optics*

An optical communications system requires a light source, a medium over which the light signals are transmitted, and a sensor to convert the light signals back to electrical signals. The medium by which light signals are transmitted to a receiver can be one of several types of hair-thin glass fibers. An optical fiber is actually a tiny waveguide that

---

* see references 5, 7, 18, 20, 26, 33, 36, 38, 39, 43, 58, 63 and 67.

supports optical-frequency waves using the principles of total internal reflection at the boundaries of the fiber.

Transmission over optical fiber has advantages over copper wire in the form of larger bandwidths, freedom from cross talk and other types of interference, low cost, and light weight. In addition, much more information can be carried at optical frequencies than at the lower microwave frequencies. Bundles of optical fibers offer such potential advantages in future systems as bandwidth capacities of several thousand voice channels or many TV channels per single fiber.

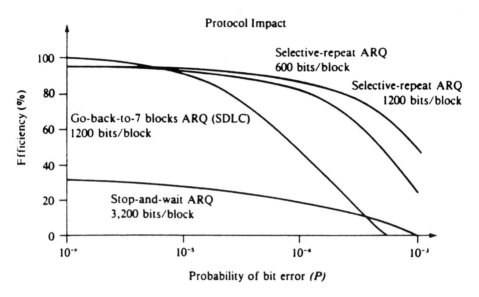

Figure 4.11. Comparison of selective-repeat ARQ, stop-and-wait ARQ, and go-back-to-7-blocks ARQ for a 9600-bps link [6].

An optical fiber data transmission link converts input electrical signals to optical signals that are then transmitted over an optical fiber waveguide to a receiver. At the receiver, the optical signal is converted back into electrical format by an optical-to-electrical converter (see Figure 4.12).

Optical-fiber transmission links accept electrical input in digital or analog form. The transmitter sends the optical signal by modulating the output of a light source (usually an LED or a laser) by varying the source drive current. At the receiver, a photodiode reconverts the light into electronic form.

The transmission distance is set by the available power margin between the transmitter and the receiver. *Power margin* is the difference in decibels between the transmitter optical output and required receiver input. Each optical data transmission system element has its associated losses expressed in decibels. The power margin has to match the accumulated losses of the associated hardware to ensure that the optical signal reaching the receiver falls within its sensitivity. To ensure this sensitivity, long links may include optical fiber splices and repeaters.

4.5.1 Optical fiber*

Light propagates along optical fibers by total internal reflection if the fiber core is surrounded by an optical cladding (or insulation) of lower refractive index. by modulating the light, data can be transmitted through the fiber.

A simple optical fiber is illustrated in Figure 4.12. It has a cylindrical glass fiber core with a uniform index of refraction. The core is surrounded by a concentric layer called the *cladding*, or optical insulating material of a lower index or graded index of refraction fibers. A ray of light entering the core of this cable at one end will internally reflect from the boundary between the two dielectric media when the ray is incident within the denser medium, and the angle of incidence is greater than a critical value defined by the refracted indices of the media. Thus the light ray will be reflected back into the original medium. This process is repeated over and over as the light passes down the core. Each time reflection occurs a slight amount of light intensity is lost. Largely due to impurities in the fiber, some additional losses are incurred as the light travels down the fiber. These two considerations are the principal causes of attenuation.

Another cable characteristic affecting light transmission is the *input light acceptance.* Figure 4.13 illustrates that light rays entering the fiber within the core shown by the dotted lines will propagate along the cable. Rays at greater angles will not. Although light energy enters the fiber end surface at an infinite number of angles, it is accepted and transmitted down the core only for those entry angles within the acceptance core, or *numerical aperture* (NA = sin θ).

---

* see references 5, 7, 15, 18, 20, 26, 33, 36, 38, 39, 43, 58 and 67.

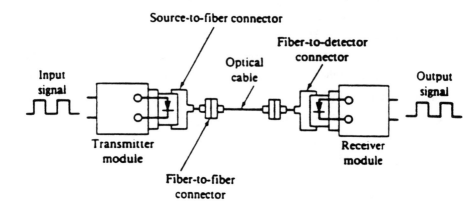

Figure 4.12. Typical optical-fiber data-transmission link [5].

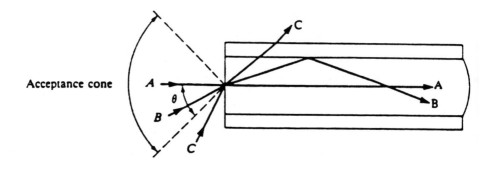

Figure 4.13. Input light acceptance [4,20].

Just as in electromagnetic waveguide propagation, only certain modes can propagate along an optical-fiber cable. For a given wavelength, the number of modes can be decreased by reducing the diameter of the core. When the diameter approaches the wavelength only a single mode will propagate. Such a *single-mode* fiber eliminates modal dispersion, which is a limiting factor on the bandwidth of fiber-optic systems.

Modal dispersion results from the fact that higher-order modes (rays reflected at higher angles) have a greater distance to travel than lower-order rays as they propagate down the fiber (e.g., Figure 4.14). Thus, the higher-order modes take more time to propagate

through the fiber with the result that a modulated light pulse broadens (or spreads). This
pulse broadening is called *dispersion*.

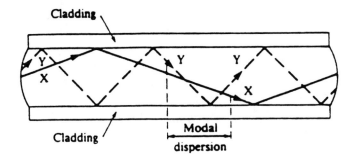

Figure 4.14. Modal dispersion [4,20].

4.5.2   Fiber-optic modes[*]

Single-mode cables eliminate modal dispersion, but the core diameter is so small that
efficient coupling between it and the light source is extremely difficult. A single-mode
fiber can function efficiently only by working in conjunction with the coherent light from
a laser, since if the fiber's core is small enough, only the fundamental mode is guided
along the fiber.

Much more efficient coupling is obtained by *multimode fibers*. There are two types
of multimode fibers: step index and graded index (Figure 4.15). The term *step index*
comes from the fact that this cable has an abrupt change of refractive index between the
cladding and the core. The difference between the refractive indexes gives a larger value to
, and the diameter of the core is much greater than in single-mode cables, thereby
increasing the light-gathering ability and the coupling efficiency. As a disadvantage, a
greater dispersion results from the larger differences in path lengths between the extreme
modes (see Figure 4.16).

---

[*] see reference 4.

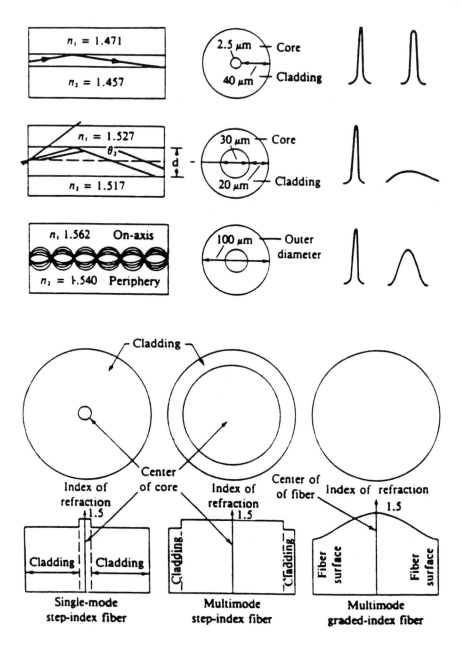

Figure 4.15. Three typical optical-fiber cables and propagation [4,20,67].

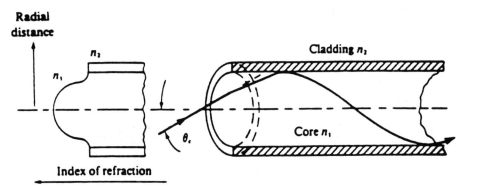

Figure 4.16. Typical step-index fiber [5].

Graded-index, multimode fiber represents a compromise that provides good coupling efficiency and reduces the effects of modal dispersion. This is accomplished by providing a graded index-of-refraction profile across the fiber cross section, instead of the uniform profile of the step-index fiber core (see Figure 4.17). The graded-core fiber's index of refraction decreases with increasing radial distance. This causes a light ray to travel more slowly as it approaches the core center, and faster with greater core radial distance. Thus, the speed of the highest-order mode approximates the speed of the lower modes. Rays in graded-index fibers are not directed by internal reflection, but rather travel in smooth paths bending toward the core axis due to the varying index of refraction.

In addition to modal dispersion, *material dispersion* results from the fact that different wavelengths of light propagate at different velocities through a given medium. Since practical light sources are not monochromatic, these sources radiate light rays with different wavelengths. A multimode fiber may be used with incoherent light sources such as LEDs (light-emitting diodes). Light rays are emitted uniformly by the LED from many points. Those rays not captured within the core of the fiber become totally absorbed by the jacket, while the others strike the interface area between the core and the cladding at angles which, by the process of total internal reflection, are forced to propagate within the boundaries of the core.

As in any communications system, the transmitted signals in an optical fiber must span the distance to the receiver and arrive there in an acceptable enough condition so that they can be detected with a certain degree of reliability. To this extent, the maximum range of the system is largely dependent on the type of light resources and light detectors, and on the purity of the optical fiber and the nature of its construction.

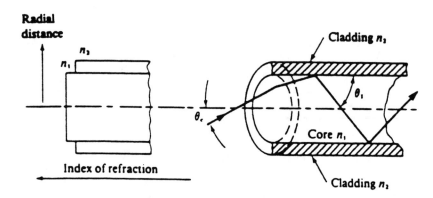

Figure 4.17. Graded-index fiber [5].

Dispersion effects, both mode and material, are the principal factors limiting bandwidth. Modal effects can be generally reduced by graded-index cable, but material dispersion effects are present in all types of cable. These can only be reduced by a truly monochromatic light source.

4.5.3 Signal degradation

Signal degradation in a fiber-optic system occurs in the form of attenuation or transmission loss (dimming of light intensity) and differential delay (the broadening of the signal in time). Attenuation in an optical fiber is measured in decibels just as in the case of wire-cable losses. The optical equivalent to wire-cable resistance is called *absorption*.

Absorption loss is caused by the presence of impurities in the fiber material. The impurities are usually found trapped in the glass from which the optical fiber is made. Impurity absorption can be reduced by carefully controlling the core material.

Another cause of absorption loss is the *scattering effect*. Scattering losses result from fundamental fluctuations in glass density and composition and from imperfections in the regions where the core interfaces with the cladding. The degradation of light by *differential delay* (*pulse broadening* or *spreading*) has more effects on transmission than scattering. The cause of pulse broadening begins with the angle at which a ray of light enters the fiber. Those rays entering a multimode step-index fiber parallel to the fiber axis travel the shortest distance to the receiver, while those entering at various angles must be reflected by the cladding and thereby travel a longer distance. The difference in time of arrival causes a spreading of individual pulses. If the difference in arrival time between the fast and slow rays exceeds the time interval allowed between pulses, a pulse overlap occurs. Because pulse spreading increases with fiber length, it is important that light rays travel as close to the core as possible. For this to occur, the difference in refractive indexes of the core and cladding must be kept small, thus also keeping the critical acceptance angle small. Pulse broadening must be especially limited in systems processing higher bit rates, since higher data speeds mean shorter time intervals between pulses, and less tolerance for errors due to pulse spreading.

Radiation losses are also present in any real fiber-optical system. *Microbends* in the fiber can cause radiation losses. These bends are sometimes incurred during cable fabrication. These can be avoided by minimizing all contact between the fibers and other bodies. Radiation losses can also result from abrasions or dirt on the outer surface of the fiber.

Any real optional-fiber system will use connectors and splices to join the fibers. Optical losses incurred in connectors and splices result from discontinuities and misalignment at the junction. The amount of loss is dependent on the fiber alignment and optical characteristics. Splice losses are lower than connector losses because splices are carefully aligned with precision fixtures and the joint is permanently bonded with a refractive index-matching agent that reduces reflection discontinuities. Connectors are detachable by definition, so their alignment is less precise (see Figures 4.18-4.19).

Splices and connectors serve four purposes: (1) to align mating fibers for efficient transmission of optical power; (2) to protect the fiber from the environment and during handling; (3) to terminate the cable strength member such that external loads will not be transmitted to the fiber termination and thereby affect alignment and coupling efficiency; (4) to couple fibers to optical sources and detectors.

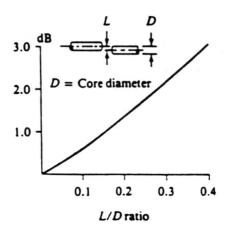

Figure 4.18. Lateral misalignment loss in decibels is a function of the misalignment/core diameter ratio. Loss is zero with zero misalignment, and infinite when L exceeds D/2 [5].

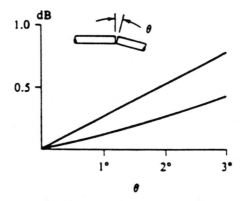

Figure 4.19. If the two optical faces (matched) are not parallel, a logarithmic angular loss occurs. With fiber loss specifications in 1 dB to 1.5 dB range, poor splitting introduces intolerable losses [5].

4.5.4 Fiber types*

Fibers are fabricated of several materials, including glass core-glass cladding and glass core-plastic cladding (PCS or plastic-clad silica). Some commonly used glasses are fused silica, quartz, and a chemical-vapor-deposited glass comprised of germanium, boron, and silicon chlorides. The cladding of PCS is either silicone or Teflon. In addition to glass-core fibers, plastic fibers made of acrylic provide considerably higher attenuation and lower temperatures.

To overcome problems such as fragility, microscopic fractures, and weakened fiber strength due to bending, flexing, or stretching, fibers are made into cables. Cables are built in various configurations, but all have, in addition to the fibers, one or more strength members, some kind of buffing material, and an overall sheath. Figure 4.20 illustrates a single-fiber cable. The optical fiber is located in the center and surrounded by the buffering material. This material has good chemical resistance and buffers against abrasion. A strength member forms the next layer, providing protection against impact, crushing, and longitudinal stretching. The outer jacket is a tubular sheath that minimizes microbending, shields from the environment, and establishes a limit of cable bending.

Fibers can also be classified in terms of the attenuation loss per kilometer into high (greater than 100 dB/km), medium (20 to 100 dB/km), and low-loss (less than 20 dB/km) fibers. For lengths less than 30 m, high-loss fiber cables are most practical. These are very efficient in coupling because of their large bundle diameter and high numerical aperture. A *bundle* is a consolidated group of single fibers used to transmit a single optical signal. Attenuation per unit length is not very important over short distances in relationship to input coupling. Thus for short spans (about 20 m) an inexpensive LED can transmit far more power over a high-loss cable than a low-loss cable. Typical fiber-cable characteristics are illustrated in Table 4.4.

4.5.5 Light sources**

A good light source for fiber must be small, bright, fast, monochromatic, and reliable. A small light source is efficient. High radiance assures that lots of light gets coupled into the fiber. Fast modulation is necessary for the transmission of high-

---

* see references 4, 20 and 67.
** see references 4, 20, 46 and 67.

bandwidth data. A narrow spectral line width helps to keep the dispersion in the fiber low. Reliability is required in terms of a lifetime of thousands of hours.

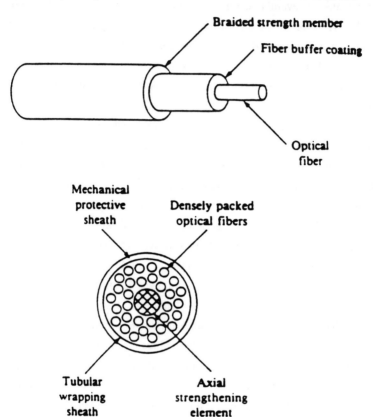

Figure 4.20. Example of single-fiber cable with axial strengthening [4,20].

The most commonly used light sources at present are Ga-As LEDs (gallium-arsenide light-emitting diodes) and injection lasers. Both are simple and inexpensive devices with sizes compatible to the fiber-core dimensions and light wavelengths in the range of 0.8 to 0.9, where fibers have low loss and dispersion.

Table 4.4 Typical fiber-cable characteristics [66,67]

Type of cable and glass	Single-mode GeO$_2$-core Silica-cladding	Multimode Borosilicate step-index	Multimode graded-index
Core index, n_1	1.471	1.527	1.562 on axis
Cladding index, n_2	1.457	1.517	1.540 on periphery
Core diameter, μm (10^{6}m)	2.5	30	100 (outer diameter)
Cladding thickness, μm	40	20	—
Numerical aperature, NA	0.20	0.17	0.26
Max launch angle, θ_1	11^0	9.8^0	15°
Max propagation angle, θ_2	7.9^0	6.5^0	9.6^0
Number of modes, M	1	200	2000
Launching efficiency, %	—	1.4	3.4
Mode dispersion, ns (10^{-9}s/km)	0	32	1
Material dispersion, ns/km for laser (2 nm)	0.18	0.266	0.280
for LED (20 nm)	1.8	2.6	2.8

LEDs are noncoherent sources capable of transmitting moderate optical power at modulation rates in the tens of megahertz. LEDs have a light power out to driving current input characteristic that is almost linear over a large driving current range. Thus, LEDs can be amplitude-modulated by varying the drive current, requiring peak driving currents of about 100 to 300 mA. With a drive current of 100 mA at 2 V, about 50 W of light power can be coupled into a multimode fiber. LEDs have a typical optical bandwidth of 40 to 50 nm, which translates to an upper limit on bit-rate capacity of about 200 Mbps (50 Mbps is a more conservative and practical number).

The laser, a semicoherent source, is a threshold device which turns on when the drive current (100 mA) reaches threshold (120 to 130 mA) and provides a large increase in output power. The light power output versus drive current input characteristic is linear over a limited region. Thus lasers are considered more appropriate for digital applications. Lasers can couple a few milliwatts of light power into a fiber and thus are about 10 to 50 times more efficient in conversion. Also, because their optical bandwidth is about 2 nm, material dispersion is not a problem and lasers can be modulated by a driving current at up to gigabit per second rates.

The most serious disadvantages relate to lifetime (reliability), driver complexity, and variations in threshold with temperature and age. Typical lifetimes are about 10,000 h. To gain wide acceptance, mean time before failure must approach 100,000 h. The laser threshold also varies with temperature and age, requiring a more complicated feedback-controlled driver to keep the laser biased near threshold.

4.5.6 Optical detectors

Optical detectors are used to transduce the light to electricity and are well developed. The choices of a photodetector device include a PIN photodiode, an avalanche photodiode (APD), a phototransistor, or a photomultiplier. Because of their efficiency and ease of use at red and near IR wavelengths, silicon PIN photodiodes and APD are most often used.

4.5.7 Design benefits

Some of the advantages of fiber-optic transmission are inherent to all fiber-optic systems because of the dielectric nature of the light conductors. Isolation, noise immunity, and safety and security are among these advantages. Repeater spacing, reliability, and cost can also be optimized. Transmitting data through totally dielectric cables permits transmission directly across very high voltage potentials without any need for isolation transformers. Similarly, fiber-optic cables eliminate the ground loops required with coaxial cables. Fiber-optic cables also do not attract lightning (because they are dielectric), pick up no inductive surges from nearby lightning flashes (they do not act as antennas) or any other electromagnetic interference (inductive fields, radio-frequency interference), nor are they susceptible to noise. Fiber-optic cables, when properly coated, do not radiate signals or pick up external electromagnetic signals. They are essentially free of cross talk regardless of data rate, cable length, or number of channels per cable. Fiber-optic systems do not spark or short circuit. They cannot cause explosions in hazardous environments or cause shocks to personnel.

Fiber-optic cables have a larger information transfer capacity than coaxial cables. Most fiber-optic systems are limited in bandwidth by the amount of energy per pulse arriving at the detector. Laser diodes and externally modulated lasers have been successfully coupled to fiber optics with information rates exceeding 1000 Mbps. Material dispersion and modal dispersion of the optical fiber limit the bandwidth for a particular source.

Low-cost fiber-optic cables can run from 5 to 10 km before repeaters are necessary, transmitting data rates in excess of 100 Mbps. Long repeater spacing results in improved system reliability, decreased initial system costs, and decreased maintenance costs. Weight savings of up to 80:1 for fiber-optic cable versus coaxial cable are possible. Weight savings have been especially significant where the electrooptics were designed into the system rather than converted by adaptive equipment, where electromagnetic noise problems are severe, and where the lengths and sizes of wire cable replaced were large.

The great multiplexing capacity of fiber-optic cables means that only a fraction of the number of coaxial cables may be required, resulting in decreased costs for both cables and interface connectors. The low losses of fiberoptic cables allow the use of fewer repeaters and attendant structures on long cables.

4.5.8 System configuration[*]

A typical fiber-optic communications system is illustrated in Figure 4.21. As shown in the figure, analog telephone signals enter the terminal and are converted to digital signals by conventional terminal equipment. The advantages of digital transmission are realized by fiber-optic systems because of the large bandwidths and negligible cross talk. However, AM is also used for low-capacity systems. At the transmitting terminal, the digital signals are used to modulate the current of a light source, such as an injection laser diode (ILD) or LED. Both of these devices are relatively inexpensive and compatible with the available optical-fiber cable. The laser could be modulated at gigabit rates, and can couple a few milliwatts of power into an optical fiber. On the other hand, a LED can only couple a few hundred microwatts of power with modulation speeds limited to a few hundred megahertz.

The light pulse output of the light source is carried over optical-fiber cable to the repeater (especially if long distances are involved). At the repeater site, the fiber terminates on an optical detector such as a photodiode, which converts the light back to digital signals for amplification and regeneration. The two most commonly used

---

[*] see references 7, 20 and 67.

detectors are the PIN photodiode and the APD. After regeneration, the digital signals modulate the current of yet another optical source for recoupling to the fiber.

At the receiving terminal, the light pulses are reconverted to digital electrical pulses by an optical detector for amplification and decoding into the original, analog telephone signal. Signals to be transmitted in the opposite direction go through exactly the reverse procedure. Except for some differences in the components and subsystems, the configuration of a fiber-optic system is similar to that of a conventional wire or coaxial cable system.

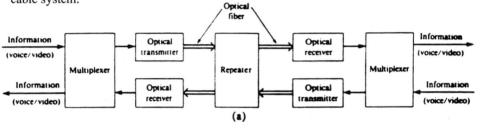

(a)

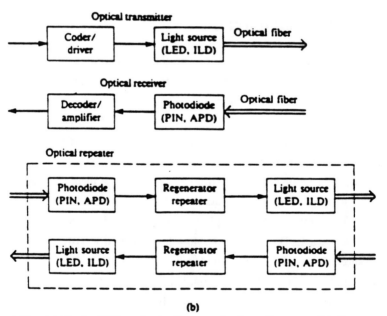

(b)

Figure 4.21. (a) Typical Fiber-Optic Communications System; (b) Components of Fiber-Optic Communications System.

4.6 Exercises

4.1   Discuss the types of transmission lines in general terms; include advantages and disadvantages of each type.

4.2   In detail, discuss reflection as regard to signal loss and signal deterioration of an electromagnetic wave.

4.3   Explain why ground-wave propagation is more effective over sea water than desert terrain.

4.4   Discuss space-wave propagation. Explain the difference between a direct and a reflected wave.

4.5   Discuss the relative merits and disadvantages of using antennas, waveguides, and transmission lines as the media used in a communications link.

4.6   Describe the basic elements of a fiber-optic communications system. Explain its possible advantages over a more standard communications system.

4.7   Describe the mode of propagation in a fiber-optic communications system.

4.8   Explain the difference between the surface wave and the ground wave for radio transmissions in the frequency range 300 kHz to 2 MHz.

4.9   What feature of microwave relay system makes it attractive for providing telephone trunk circuits? How many repeater stations would be required on a 600 km route?

4.10 Calculate the round trip or echo delay on a satellite circuit using a synchronous satellite that is located 37,000 km from station A and 40,000 km from station B.

4.11 Calculate the net loss of a trunk circuit which involves 2000 km of microwave relay circuits with an average velocity of propagation of 299×10^6 m/s. How long would this circuit have to be before an echo suppressor must be included? This question deals with the kind of repeater and S/N problem at the end of 2000 km with and without reamplification.

4.12 What is meant by the diffraction of radio waves? Under what conditions does it arise? Under what condition does it not arise?

4.13 Draw up a table showing radio-frequency ranges, the means whereby they propagate, and the maximum distances achievable under normal conditions.

4.14 Briefly discuss the reflection mechanism whereby electromagnetic waves are bent back by a layer of the ionosphere. What does the fact that the virtual height is greater than the actual height prove about the reflection mechanism?

4.15 Discuss what happens as the angle of incidence of a radio wave, using skywave propagation, is brought closer and closer to the vertical. Define skip distance and show how it is related to the maximum usable frequency.

4.16 Discuss some of the peculiarities of microwave space-wave propagation, including super-refraction.

4.17 For the three common methods of radio-wave propagation, briefly explain the mechanisms of propagation, with approximate frequency and distance ranges, and include the limitations of each of the modes of propagation.

4.18 What are the three major applications of extraterrestrial communication? Explain why they have differing requirements.

4.19 Discuss the requirements of communication with, and tracking of, satellites in close orbits and space probes.

4.20 Describe the applications, requirements, and physical aspects of communication via stationary satellites.

4.21 What would be the advantages of stationary satellites around the moon for lunar communications? Would it be possible to use scatter propagation?

4.22 Describe the communications applications of lasers. What are the outstanding advantages of lasers for communications purposes?

4.23 Discuss, in detail, at least three ways in which signal losses can occur in transmission lines and how these losses can be prevented.

4.24 What specifically in the design of coaxial cables reduces interference and cross talk?

4.25 What is the difference between a passive and an active microwave repeater? When are each used? Does one have advantages over the other?

4.26 How is the problem of frequency interference solved for microwave RF repeaters?

4.27 How are the problems of microwave fading overcome?

4.28 Why is the performance of satellite transmission determined by the downlink, and not the uplink?

4.29 Compare and contrast TDMA and FDMA as it applies to satellite access.

4.30 What problems result from propagational delays in satellite transmission? How have these problems been overcome?

4.31   Compare and contrast the effects of block lengths, protocols, and throughput on satellite versus terrestrial communications links.

4.32   Discuss in as much detail as possible the advantages that transmission over optical fiber has in relation to other transmission links.

4.33   Describe what is meant by each of the following terms:

optical cladding

light acceptance

pulse broadening

modal dispersion

material dispersion

4.34   What are the differences between step-index and graded-index multimode fibers?

4.35   Signal degradation in fiber-optics systems occurs in the form of attenuation and differential delay. Discuss each. How can these be overcome?

4.36   Discuss the problems of fragility, microscopic fractures, weakened fiber strength due to bending, flexing, or stretching. What impact does each have on fiber-optic links?

4.37   Describe several optical detectors that can be used in fiber-optic communications systems. Be sure to include advantages that each have over the other.

4.38   What bandwidth limitations apply to fiber-optic communication links?

4.7   References

1   Bates, R., and Abramson, P., "You Can Use Phone Wire for Your Token Ring LAN." *Data Communications*, November 1986.

2   Bell Laboratories, *Transmission Systems for Communications*, Number 500-036. Holmdel, NJ, 1982.

3   Binder, R., "Packet Protocols for Broadcast Satellites." In *Protocols and Techniques for Data Communication Networks* (ed. by F. Kuo). Englewood Cliffs, NJ: Prentice-Hall, 1981.

4   Black, U., *Data Networks: Concepts, Theory, and Practice*. Englewood Cliffs, NJ: Prentice-Hall, 1989.

5   Borsuk, L. M., "What You Should Know About Fiber Optics." *Digital Design*, *8*, 7, August 1978.

6   Cacciamani, E. R., and Kim, K. S., "Circumventing the Problem of Propagational Delay on Satellite Data Channels." *Data Communications*, *3*, 7/8, July/August 1975.

7   Cerny, R. A., and Hudson, M. C., "Fiberoptics for Digital Systems." *Digital Design*, *7*, 7, August 1977.

8   Chou, W. (ed.), *Computer Communications, Vol. II: Systems and Applications.* Englewood Cliffs, NJ: Prentice-Hall, 1985.

9   Clavieu, M. H., "Specifying Instrument Cables." *Instruments and Control Systems*, *51*, 11, November 1978.

10   Clement, M. A., *Transmission.* Chicago, IL: Telephony Publishing Corp., no date.

11   Crowther, W.; Rettberg, R.; Walden, D.; Orenstein, S.; and Heart, F., "A System for Broadcast Communication: Reservation ALOHA." *Proceedings, Sixth Hawaii International System Science Conference*, 1973.

12   Dineson, M. A., and Picazo, J. J., "Broadband Technology Magnifies Local Network Capability." *Data Communications*, *8*, 2, February 1980.

13   Dineson, M. A., "Broadband Coaxial Local Area Networks, Part 1: Concepts and Comparisons." *Computer Design*, *18*, 6, June 1980.

14   Dineson, M. A., "Broadband Coaxial Local Area Networks, Part 2: Hardware." *Computer Design*, *18*, 7, July 1980.

15   Duyan, P., Jr., "Fiber Optic Interconnection." *Industrial Research/Development*, *21*, 12, December 1979.

16   Freeman, R., *Telecommunication System Engineering.* New York, NY: Wiley -Interscience, 1980.

17   Freeman, R., *Telecommunication Transmission Handbook.* New York, NY: John Wiley and Sons, 1981.

18   Giallorenzi, T. G., "Optical Communications Research and Technology: Fiber Optics." *Proceedings of the IEEE*, *66*, 7, July 1978.

19   GTE Lenkurt Inc., "Incrasing PCM Span-Line Capacity." *The Lenkurt Demodulator*, *25*, 5/6, San Carlos, CA, May/June 1976.

20   GTE Lenkurt Inc., "Fiber Optics in Telecommunications." *The Lenkurt Demodulator*, *27*, 11/12, San Carlos, CA, November/December 1978.

21   GTE Lenkurt Inc., "Satellite Communications Update, Part I." *The Lenkurt Demodulator*, *28*, 1/2, San Carlos, CA, January/February 1979.

22   GTE Lenkurt Inc., "Satellite Communications Update, Part II." *The Lenkurt Demodulator*, *28*, 5/6, San Carlos, CA, May/June 1979.

23   Halsall, F., *Data Communications, Computer Networks, and OSI* (2nd edition). Reading, MA: Addison-Wesley, 1988.

24   Hartwig, G., "What the New Data Satellite Will Offer." *Data Communications*, *4*, 3/4, March/April 1976.

25   Hickey, J., "Wire and Cable--What's Happening?" *Instruments and Control Systems*, *53*, 8, August 1980.

26   International Telephone and Telegraph Corp., *Reference Data for Radio Engineers*. Indianapolis, IN: Howard W. Sams, 1975.

27   Jacobs, I.; Binder, R.; and Hoversten, E., "General Purpose Packet Satellite Networks." *Proceedings of the IEEE*, November 1978.

28   Jeruchim, M. C., "A Survey of Interference Problems and Applications to Geostationary Satellite Networks." *Proceedings of the IEEE*, *65*, 3, March 1977.

29   Kennedy, G., *Electronics Communication Systems*. New York, NY: McGraw-Hill, 1970.

30   Kullstan, P. (guest ed.), (special issue), "Satellite Communications." *IEEE Communications Magazine*, *22*, 3, March 1984.

31   Lam, S., "Packet Broadcast Networks--A Performance Analysis of the R-ALOHA Protocol." *IEEE Trans. on Computers*, July 1980.

32   Laughans, R. A., and Mitchell, T. H., "Linking the Satellite to a Data Communications Net." *Data Communications*, *8*, 2, February 1980.

33   Li, T., "Optical Fiber Communication--The State of the Art." *IEEE Trans. Comm.*, *COM-26*, 7, July 1978.

34   Martin, J., *Telecommunications and the Computer*. Englewood Cliffs, NJ: Prentice-Hall, 1977.

35   Martin, J., *Communications Satellite Systems*. Englewood Cliffs, NJ: Prentice-Hall, 1978.

36   McCaskill, R. C., "Fiber Optics: The Connection of the Future." *Data Communications*, *7*, 1, January 1979.

37   McQuillan, J. M., and Cerf, V. G., *A Practical View of Computer Communications Protocols*. Washington, DC: IEEE Computer Society Press, 1978.

38   Mier, E., "Bell Shines New Light on Digital Transmission Specification." *Data Communications*, April 1983.

39   Mokhoff, N., "Communications: Fiber Optics." *IEEE Spectrum*, January 1981.

40   Morrison, R., "Answers to Grounding and Shielding Problems." *Instruments and Control Systems, 52*, 6, June 1979.

41   Nelson, K. C., "Understanding Station Carrier." *Lee's ABC of the Telephone*, Geneva, IL, 1975.

42   Noguchi, T.; Davido, Y.; and Nossek, J. A., "Modulation Techniques for Microwave Digital Radio." *IEEE Communications Magazine, 24*, 10, October 1986.

43   Personick, S. D., "Fiber Optic Communication." *IEEE Communications Society Magazine, 16*, 3, March 1978.

44   Pickens, R., "Wideband Transmission Media I: Radio Communications." In Kuo, F. (ed.), *Computer Communications, Vol. I: Principles.* Englewood Cliffs, NJ: Prentice-Hall, 1983.

45   Pickens, R., "Wideband Transmission Media II: Satellite Communications." In Chou, W. (ed.), *Computer Communications, Vol. I: Principles.* Englewood Cliffs, NJ: Prentice-Hall, 1983.

46   Pooch, U. W.; Greene, W. H.; and Moss, G. G., *Telecommunications and Networking.* Boston, MA: Little, Brown and Company, 1983.

47   Pritchard, W., "The History and Future of Commercial Satellite Communications." *IEEE Communications Magazine*, May 1984.

48   Rey, R. F. (ed.), *Engineering and Operations in the Bell Systems* (2nd edition). Murray Hill, NJ: AT&T Laboratories, 1983.

49   Riley, E. W., and Acuma, V. E., "Transmission Systems." *Lee's ABC of the Telephone*, Geneva, IL, 1976.

50   Roberts, L., "Dynamic Allocation of Satellite Capacity Through Packet Reservation." *Proceedings, National Computer Conference*, 1973.

51   Rocher, E., "Taking a Fresh Look at Local Data Distribution." *Data Communications*, May 1979.

52   Roman, G. S., "The Design of Broadband Coaxial Cable Networks for Multimode Communications." The MITRE Corp., Report No. MTR-3527, November 1977.

53   Rush, J. R., "Microwave Links Add Flexibility to Local Networks." *Electronics*, January 13, 1982.

54   Salomon, J., "Satellite Communications Systems." *Telecommunications, 13,* 5, May 1979.

55   Scarcella, T., and Abbott, R., "Orbital Efficiency Through Satellite Digital Switching." *IEEE Communications Magazine,* May 1983.

56   Schwartz, M.; Bennet, W. R.; and Stein, S., *Communication Systems and Techniques.* New York, NY: McGraw-Hill, 1966.

57   Schwartz, M., *Computer-Communication Networks Design and Analysis.* Englewood Cliffs, NJ: Prentice-Hall, 1977.

58   Schwartz, M., "Optical Fiber Transmission--From Conception to Prominence in 20 Years." *IEEE Communications Magazine,* May 1984.

59   Spilker, J., *Digital Communications by Satellite.* Englewood Cliffs, NJ: Prentice-Hall, 1977.

60   Stallings, W., *Data and Computer Communications.* New York, NY: MacMillan Publishing Company, 1985.

61   Suda, T.; Miyahara, H.; and Hasegawa, T., "Performance Evaluation of an Integrated Access Scheme in a Satellite Communication Channel." *IEEE Journal on Selected Areas in Communications,* January 1983.

62   Tanenbaum, A. S., *Computer Networks.* Englewood Cliffs, NJ: Prentice-Hall, 1981.

63   Tanenbaum, A. S., *Computer Networks* (2nd edition). Englewood Cliffs, NJ: Prentice-Hall, 1988.

64   Tobagi, F. A., "Multiaccess Protocols in Packet Communications Systems." *IEEE Trans. on Comm.,* April 1980.

65   Withers, D. J., "Effective Utilization of the Geostationary Orbit for Satellite Communication." *Proceedings of the IEEE, 65,* 3, March 1977.

66   Yeh, L. P., "Telecommunications Transmission Media." *Telecommunications, 10,* 4, April 1976.

67   Yeh, L. P., "Fiber-Optic Communications Systems." *Telecommunications, 12,* 9, September 1978.

68   Ziemer, R. E., and Tranter, W. H., *Principles of Communications.* Boston, MA: Houghton Miffin, 1976.

5

ANALOG VERSUS DIGITAL COMMUNICATIONS

5.1 The Voice Channel*

The most familiar telecommunications system is the public telephone network. The basic building block of this system is the voice channel. A *voice channel* is usually considered to have a 4-kHz bandwidth (see Figure 5.1). In reality, the effective channel ranges from 300 Hz to 3400 Hz, with the remainder of the bandwidth used for guard or protection bands, or to accommodate special signals.

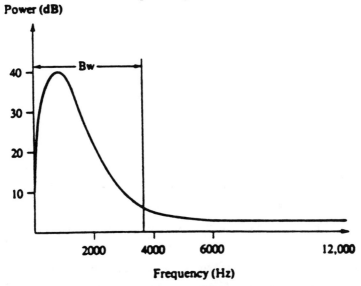

Figure 5.1. Bandwidth of a typical telephone channel.

---

* see references 4–9, 16, 19 and 21–24.

The voice channel obtains its name from the fact that it was designed to accommodate the characteristics of the human voice. Although the ear can detect frequencies from 30 Hz to 20 kHz, the voice signal can be represented quite effectively by a limited frequency range of 300 to 3400 Hz. One reason that only 3 kHz of bandwidth is required is because of the effectiveness of the receiver, the human ear. The ear, working in conjunction with the brain, reads through distortion and noise to reproduce even missing parts of words or sentences. Another contributing factor is the high redundancy of human speech. As much as 75 percent of the information content in normal speech is redundant. Furthermore, 75 percent to 85 percent of the energy content of speech is found in the 3-kHz range. Finally, the relative signal strength within the voice channel is designed to give a flat response, exceeding quickly below 300 Hz and above 3400 Hz (Figure 5.2), while the frequencies are attenuated almost equally within the center of the channel (Figure 5.3).

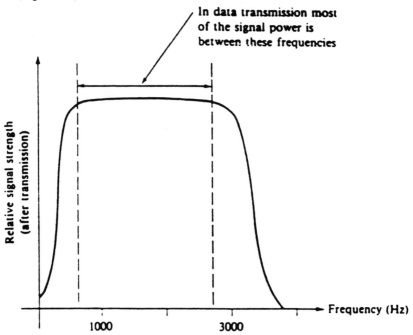

Figure 5.2. The variation of amplitude with frequency on a typical phone system.

In the earliest voice systems, speech was transmitted directly over connected telephone cables, wires, or pairs of wires. However, as the system grew and the volume increased, the necessary interconnections required some type of switching and signaling capability. At first, an operator established the connection between subscribers by a simple switchboard. The calling subscriber turned a hand crank to generate an electrical signal that lit a light on the switchboard and usually activated a bell or ringer. The operator then completed the connection with the caller. The caller then provided the name of the called party, and the operator connected the two subscribers by initiating a ringing of the called party's phone. Once a party answered, the operator got off the line and watched for the lights on the switchboard to go off or periodically checked to see if the conversation was completed. Once the call was completed, the operator disconnected the two users.

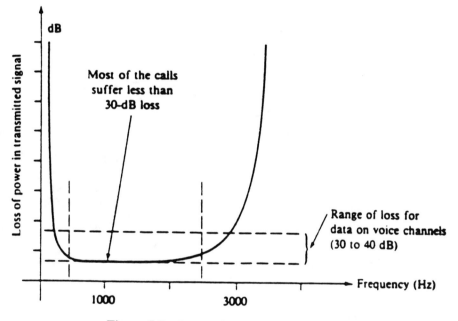

Figure 5.3. Attenuation at different frequencies.

Today most conversations take place with no operator intervention. Thus, the network provides for a user to be identified as wanting to make a call and to recognize the called number (either through a manual dialing operation or tone dialing). The system next decides if the called phone is busy or if the call can be completed. If the call cannot be completed, either from a busy line (trunks), a busy phone, or an operator intercept, then the system must direct the caller to the appropriate action (e.g., a busy ringer, to an intercept operator, or to a recording). If the call is completed, then the caller is usually advised by being hooked up to a ringer. As the system attaches the caller to a ringer, it initiates the ringer or bell at the called phone, with a recording of a ringing at the calling phone. When the connection is completed, both the called and the calling phones are placed in a recognizable busy state. After the call is complete, the system must recognize the disconnect and free up both user's phones, returning them to the available state.

Voice systems must be capable of providing not only these services but also have capabilities that include automatic billing (toll), alternate phone numbers, etc. Furthermore, in addition to these signaling capabilities, there also exist routing and switching signals between the system elements that interconnect the two users.

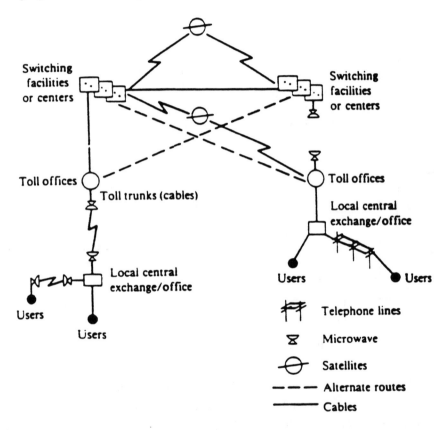

Figure 5.4. Possible routes through a network.

Figure 5.4 illustrates the myriad of possible routes that a call could take through a dialed network. Control information must travel from the caller to the called party and back at each of the stages of the call. These control signals are sometimes contained within the 3-kHz bandwidth with the voice information (in-band signaling) or outside the 3-kHz bandwidth (3400 to 4000 Hz) and separate from the voice information. In-band signaling has little or no effect on most voice users, but it can cause problems for data users. The control signals in either situation are single or repetitive appearances of a single frequency or a very small band of frequencies.

5.2 Dial-Up Versus Leased Lines*

Dial-up telephone networks consist of two simplex transmission paths between central offices and a full-duplex transmission path in each subscriber loop. From one central office to another, one simplex channel is provided for transmitting and a second channel for receiving. The outbound signal from the first office to the second office is sent on the transmit pair, while the return signal is sent on the receive pair. Amplifiers in the transmit and receive pairs prohibit two-way communications in the channel. At the central office, a balancing network combines the full-duplex subscriber loop into transmit and receive pairs (see Figure 5.5). The interchange system is called a four-wire line, while the subscriber loop is a two-wire line.

Echo suppressors can be installed in the transmit and receive paths to prevent transmission signals from coupling into the other path when no signals are present in the opposite direction. If echo suppressors are present (four-wire leased lines should always be specified without echo suppressors), the answer tone is used to disable them for full-duplex operation. Half-duplex modems must delay the transmission of data long enough to ensure that the echo suppressors are out of the circuit.

The *subscriber loop* is essentially a pair of wires without amplifiers. At the central office, the transmitted signal is sent on a unidirectional channel called the *transmit pair*. This channel is simplex, one-way only due to audio amplifiers . The far-end transmitted signal appears at the near-end of the receive pair. Transmit and receive pairs are referred to as four-wire lines. Leased circuits can be provided on either a four-wire or two-wire basis. In the latter case, the signals are combined in a two-four-wire terminating set.

Leased lines are full-term lines allocated to a single subscriber at a specified conditioning. These lines are not switched like dial-up lines.

---

* see references 7, 10, 12, 18 and 20.

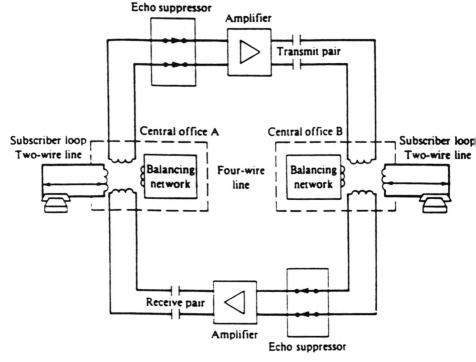

Figure 5.5. Typical long-distance telephone connection [15,17].

Leased lines, involving no switches, are generally less troubled by impulse noise and thus provide greater accuracy when compared with the dial-up network. With current terminal devices, received errors will usually not go undetected. In general, when the receiving terminal detects an error, the terminal will request that the transmitting device send the message block again. Because of the two-wire local loop, most dial-up lines operate in half-duplex mode, so that the data flow needs to be interrupted while the distant terminal sends its request for retransmission. Furthermore, numerous errors imply that the transmit terminal spends a significant part of its time retransmitting messages, thus reducing the overall data rates.

Leased lines usually operate in a full-duplex mode, reducing the time lost in requesting retransmission and increasing the effective data throughput. Another alternative is to obtain a modem with a *reverse* channel. These modems effectively operate in a full-duplex mode over the two-wire local loop, sending control signals (e.g., requests for retransmission) back to the transmitting terminal while simultaneously receiving data from it.

A leased-line *multidrop* (*multiterminal*) network is useful where the central processing unit (CPU) communicates with many modems scattered throughout a large geographical area (Figure 5.6). This approach minimizes line costs while providing each remote operator with a reasonable approximation of an on-line interactive environment. The central host site (whether CPU or concentrator) is connected in a linear fashion to many remote terminals so that the data path coming from the central site goes to the first remote location and then serially to the subsequent locations. The system operates under control from the central site, where the central site signals or polls each remote site sequentially to receive and/or transmit information. A typical response on a polled network ranges from 0.1 to 4 seconds after a request.

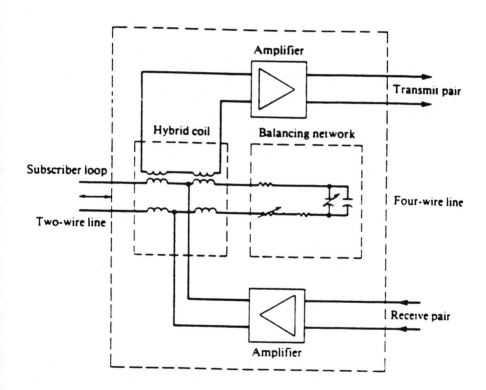

Figure 5.6. Leased-line multidrop network [15,17].

Modems, when classified according to their required transmission bandwidth, can be divided into three categories: subvoice, voice, and wideband (see Figure 5.7).

Subvoice-band modems use only a fraction of the 4-kHz voice channel for each data channel. In general these modems serve slow digital devices with speeds of up to 600 bps. Frequency-division (FDM) or time-division (TDM) multiplexing techniques are used to fill the voice channel. With FDM, a multiplexer is not needed because the modem conditions the data signal for transmission to its proper frequency position in the voice channel. On the other hand, with TDM, the multiplexer combines the digital signals in time. This new high-speed serial-bit stream then goes to a modem for digital-to-analog conversion and transmission over the voice channel.

FDM and TDM are equally suitable for voice-grade channels. However, TDM, because it is more efficient in its bandwidth utilization, and because more channels can be multiplexed on a single channel, is seldom used to multiplex low-speed signals on one single-voice channel. Conversely, FDM is best suited where signals are scattered, and where the greater reliability of individual channel modems is desired. Voice-channel modems, ranging in speed from 300 bps to 9600 bps or higher are defined not so much by speed as by the facility and the means of transmission.

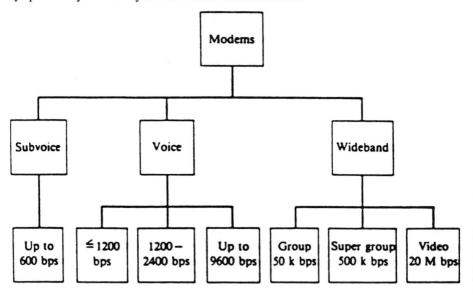

Figure 5.7.   Bandwidth and transmission speeds. The wider the bandwidth, the higher the speed [3,14].

To achieve satisfactory modem performance at 3600 bps or above requires complex equalization circuitry to precondition the signal for nonlinear or varying line parameters, such as delay distortion and attenuation. Some high-speed modems, especially those used over leased lines with relatively constant characteristics, use manually adjusted equalizers. Other high-speed modems use automatic or adaptive equalizers that continually adjust themselves to the line characteristics.

Medium-speed voice-channel modems operating in the 1200 to 2400 bps range have achieved a degree of reliability and low-error performance adequate for most data-transmission applications. Most of these medium-speed modems tolerate or precondition the signal for minor changes in line characteristics without error or interruption of transmission.

The telephone network is designed such that when the signal bandwidth exceeds one voice channel, the next transmission channel has a *group* bandwidth (12 voice channels) or a *supergroup* bandwidth (60 voice channels). Wideband modems operate at speeds from 18,750 bps to 500,000 bps. At present, the top speed is limited only by the expense of leasing wider bandwidths and the limited need to move much larger volumes of data at these rates.

Wideband modems are not true modems because they do not contain a modulator or demodulator, but rather condition a digital signal for transmission. The digital signal is sent through a scrambler, which inverts every other pulse, to eliminate sustained intervals of ones or zeros that might create an undesirable dc component in the line. The signal is then filtered to remove low-and high-frequency components. The result is an ac signal which, for 50-kbps data, has a 25-kHz bandwidth, using two bits for a cycle. There is no need to translate the wideband signal in frequency, as there is for subvoice and voice-channel modems.

This ac signal readily passes over nonloaded cable pairs with reasonable equalization and amplification. The signal can also fit a 12-channel bandwidth for analog exchange and trunk carrier systems. High-speed modems may be frequency-division multiplexed to put several in parallel on a single wideband circuit.

The great advantage of using digital transmission in wideband systems is that high data transmission rates can be obtained while keeping the data stream in serial form. In the multiplexing equipment it is not necessary to come down to the nominal voice channels (4 kHz), but the serial data streams may be modulated on a group bandwidth (48 kHz) with a data rate of 50 kbps, or a supergroup bandwidth (240 kHz) at up to 500 kbps.

5.3 Wideband Services*

The universal voice channel is between 0 and 4 kHz. Unfortunately, if all voice transmissions, whether by radio, microwave, or satellite, were sent at this frequency, no transmission would be understandable, for they would all interfere. Therefore voice channels must be moved in the frequency spectrum. This is accomplished by modulating a carrier frequency with the voice channel. The result is a voice channel that is 4 kHz wide but now exists around the carrier frequency (e.g., from 30 kHz to 34 kHz, or 270 kHz to 274 kHz). Furthermore, by limiting and separating the carrier frequencies in given regions, a significant amount of interference is eliminated.

To save on transmission and switching facility costs, many voice channels are sent over a shared transmission path. Groups of voice channels (e.g., groups, supergroups, mastergroups) are often included into the system design. In effect, wider and wider bandwidths or data paths are provided. The voice channels are placed side-by-side in the bandwidth by multiplexing. The unused portion of the voice channel's 4-kHz bandwidth provides room for the required signaling and serves as a guard band between channels to prevent cross talk (Figure 5.8).

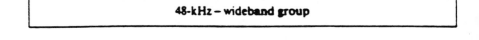

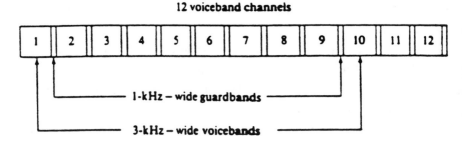

Figure 5.8. Wideband-derived voiceband channels.

---

* see references 3, 5, 8, 11, 13, 14, 22 and 23.

Taking several of these adjacent channels and treating them as one channel with a broad bandwidth makes possible some much improved capabilities for digital transmission. As a call moves through a dialed network (such as that in Figure 5.4), it is often moved around in the frequency spectrum and becomes part of a very wide bandwidth group (see Figure 5.9). The L-series transmission systems are based on a system similar to the approach illustrated in Figure 5.9.

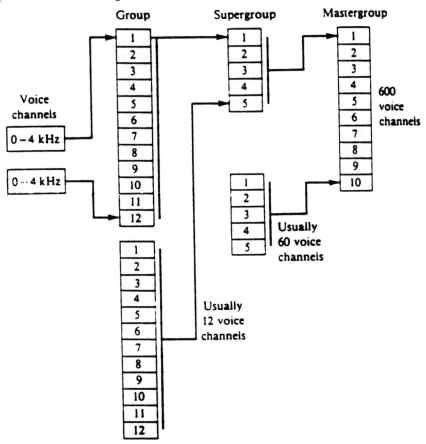

Figure 5.9. Typical grouping of channels.

The T-series transmission system does not utilize FDM but rather uses a TDM scheme based on pulse-code modulation (PCM). With this approach, voice channels are divided by sampling individual channels at defined time periods, sampling 8000 samples per second (each sample quantized into 1 of 128 levels--7-bit quantization), and superimposing 24 voice channels in a T-1 group (see Figure 5.10). These groups can then be joined to higher-speed groups, up to T-4.

In the T-1 carrier, 24 voice channels are time-division multiplexed together and transmitted in a baseband, three-level format over a twisted pair of wires (see Figure 5.10). Approximately every mile there is a digital repeater, a regenerator that detects the pulses and sends out new, noise-free, retimed pulses to the next repeater. The disadvantage of PCM is that 56 kbps (7 bits x 8000 samples per second) is required for the transmission of each voice channel. However, the quality of the used channel need not be too high because of the digital regeneration. Within the T-1 carrier system, 56 kpbs of nearly error-free data are transmitted for the cost of a single-voice telephone channel. Signaling in these systems is usually confined to a given time slot or place (bit position). Guards between channels are provided by time spacing and not frequency separation. It is these digital wideband facilities that make possible the high data rates required to support telemetry and sensory data rates.

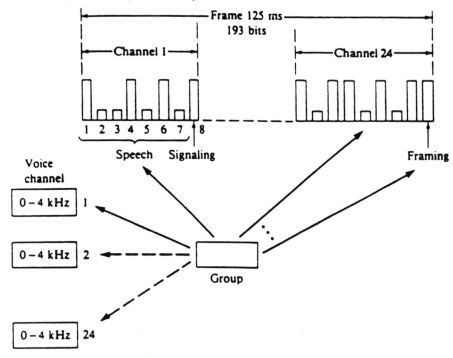

Figure 5.10. Time-division multiplexed voice channels using PCM.

5.4 Transmission Limitations*

Much of the voice-channel noise maintains a fairly constant level, and at average transmission speeds this steady noise rarely creates errors in the received data. Impulse noise, on the other hand, creates havoc with data communications. Impulse noise caused by lightning, switching equipment, or even maintenance personnel, takes the form of large narrow spikes, or impulses, that can destroy data elements completely or, possibly worse, can change the value of two or more adjacent bits, thereby complicating error-checking techniques.

When terminals communicate with each other over half-duplex links, a pause (called *turnaround time*) is generated each time the one-way channel is switched from transmitting first in one direction and then in the other. With long links over the dial-up network, this turnaround time can increase appreciably because of the presence of echo suppressors at central offices.

Echo suppressors are needed for voice conversations to prevent the caller from hearing his or her echo reflected back from the distant central office. Reflections occur whenever a four-wire trunk connects to the two-wire local loop of the called party and are only a problem on the long links, where the echo comes 45 ms or more after speech.

To eliminate the echo, suppressors are placed in both pairs of the four-wire link. When the caller speaks, the echo suppressor in the sending pair is turned off while the suppressor in the return pair is turned on, so that the voice communication proceeds to the other end while the echo is blocked. When the called party answers, the state of both suppressors is reversed, so that the 4-wire link passes the communication and blocks the echo. It takes, in general, 100 ms to reverse the suppressors, and thus data terminals must allow for this extra turnaround time when operating in the half-duplex mode.

For full-duplex operation, the terminals disable both echo suppressors, usually with a single-frequency tome of 2400 Hz. Over voice channels this tone sounds like a continuous, high-pitched whistle, recognizes as the data tone, and is used to indicate that a connection with the distant terminal is established.

Transmission errors also occur because of distortion created by the line. As the signal travels along the line, it loses strength, and this loss varies with frequency,

---

* see references 2, 7, 10, 12, 18 and 20.

increasing as the frequency gets higher. Common carriers attempt to compensate for the variable loss by a device that adds relatively large loss at low frequencies and only slight loss at high frequencies, giving the channel a fairly constant loss at all frequencies. However, there remains some variation in signal strength across the channel bandwidth, and its effect is to distort the received signals slightly, and to lower the data transmission rate that is possible for a given error performance. Equalizers may be added at each end of the line, making the signal strength more even across the bandwidth.

Another difficulty with transmission lines is that different frequencies travel at different speeds, causing the digital signal to stretch so that one bit begins to overlap with the next bit. This delay distortion can also be corrected by adding equalization at the ends of the lines.

Equalization refers to the process by which a modem corrects for distortion. *Conditioning* is the term used to indicate that the line is compensated for distortion. Delay distortion varies with the length of the line, and because of the alternate routing involved with the dial-up network, it would be impractical to condition a dialed line, and thus equalization is used via the modem.

Another problem that arises when transmitting data over voice channels results from the use of companders. *Companders* are devices that try to improve the signal-to-noise ratio of low-power signals. These devices raise the power on weak-signal components and lower the power on strong-signal components, and thereby help in solving cross-talk and noise problems. In digital systems, companders improve quantization noise by allowing quantization levels to be finer at low-speed levels. Data transmission, on the other hand, can be adversely affected if the lowering and raising of the power levels run into the quantizing margins. Companders can also cause intermodulation distortions. As a general rule, companders should be removed from voice systems that are used for data transmissions.

5.5 Noise and Distortion Advantage of Digital Systems

When properly designed, data transmission systems can offer substantial advantages relative to voice systems in overcoming distortion and noise. Using equalized, conditioned, or loaded circuits, data pulses can be accurately transmitted over short distances. If *repeaters*, which regenerate the digital signals, are added, then the chance of detecting the presence or absence of a pulse is very high. Once it is detected at a given repeater, it is regenerated as a sharp new pulse with no system degradation, no noise or distortion included in the new pulse. In short, noise and distortions are not cumulative. That is, the pulse is either detected or not, and then a new pulse or digital signal is regenerated at each repeater. When this is contrasted to an analog or voice system, distortions and noise are found to be cumulative. The noise and distortions appended to an analog signal are amplified or reduced in the same ratio as the signal travels throughout the system. The noise and distortion relative to the signal are not changed. When the signal is retransmitted by a repeater or other intermediate system component, the accumulated noise and distortion already contained in the signal are added to the new noise or distortion picked up in the next system component or transmission link (see Figure 5.11).

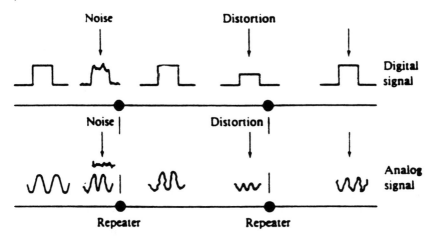

Figure 5.11. Impact of noise and distortion on digital and analog signals.

5.6 Exercises

5.1   Why are telephone lines widely used for transmission of digital data? Explain the problems involved with their use.

5.2   Explain the need for delay equalization when phone lines are used for signal transmission. If uncorrected, what would be the result of unequal delays to the different frequency components of a received signal?

5.3   Calculate the maximum number of 4-kHz channels that can be FDM into a 6-MHz television channel if 12.5 percent extra bandwidth must be allowed for each channel to prevent overlap and the system is divided into groups of 12 channels with 2 additional channel spaces unused, one at either end of the group, and supergroups of 5 groups with 1 group extra space between supergroups, and further into master groups of 10 supergroups, with no extra zone between. State the number of groups, supergroups, and mastergroups which can be used, and the number of partial groups which could be included to provide maximum usage. Compare the total to the maximum number of ideal 4-kHz channels.

5.4   Discuss, with regard to voice-grade channels, the practical versus the theoretical capabilities.

5.5   Define each of the following terms as completely as you can:
>   low-speed line
>   voice-grade line
>   high-speed line
>   switched network
>   leased line
>   fully serial
>   fully parallel
>   serial-by-bit/parallel-by-byte

5.6   Define asynchronous and synchronous data transmission. Give advantages and disadvantages for each. Describe asynchronous "start/stop" transmission. Why does this technique utilize 10 1/2 bits to send an 8-bit character?

5.7   A time-sharing system has TTY terminals, remote line printers (200 cps), remote concentrators, and one remote computer (I/O rates of 5000 cps). Draw a typical system diagram showing the communications links between all units. Indicate their capacity in terms of low-speed, voice-grade, and wideband.

5.8   How does a data set convert binary coded data for transmission over analog lines? How does the data set interface to the communications lines?

5.9   Why are echo suppressors required on two-wire loops and not on four-wire loops? Is there a difference when we use the line for voice and/or data transmission?

5.10   What is meant by in-band signaling? What effect does this have on voice and/or data transmission?

5.11   Describe the three categories of modem classifications. Include modulation techniques, transmission bandwidth, and signal conditioning.

5.12   How are voice-grade channels configured for wideband services? Also include the TDM and the PCM schemes.

5.13   How is the reverse channel used to increase the effective data throughput on leased lines?

5.14   Discuss the role that equalization and companders have in data transmission. Do they solve the same line transmission problem? Explain.

5.15   What role do repeaters have in line transmission? Are they just as effective for analog as for digital transmission? For PCM transmission? Explain.

5.16   Why is noise and distortion a problem for digital data transmission over a voice-grade line?

5.17   What is meant by intermodulation distortion?

5.18   What is the need for guard bands in wideband services? How big are these guard bands?

5.7   References

1   Abramson, N., and Kuo, F. F. (eds.), *Computer-Communication Networks*. Englewood Cliffs, NJ: Prentice-Hall, 1973.

2   AT&T Network Planning Division, *Notes on the Network*, 1980.

3   Bartee, T. C. (ed.), *Data Communications, Networks, and Systems*. Indianapolis, IN: Howard W. Sams & Co., Inc., 1985.

4   Bellamy, John, *Digital Telephony*. New York, NY: John Wiley and Sons, 1982.

5   Bell Laboratories, *Transmission Systems for Communications*, Number 500-036. Holmdel, NJ, 1982.

6   Bell Telephone Companies, selected manuals: "Communicating and the Telephone," "How the Telephone Works," "Bell's Great Invention." Available from local Bell Operating Company offices; no date.

7   Black, U., *Physical Level Interfaces and Protocols*. Washington, DC: IEEE Computer Society Press, 1988.

8   Black, U., *Data Networks: Concepts, Theory, and Practice*. Englewood Cliffs, NJ: Prentice-Hall, 1989.

9   Briley, B. E., *Introduction to Telephone Switching*. Reading, MA: Addison-Wesley, 1983.

10   Chou, W. (ed.), *Computer Communications, Vol. II: Systems and Applications*. Englewood Cliffs, NJ: Prentice-Hall, 1985.

11   Doll, D. R., *Data Communications: Facilities, Networks, and System Design*. New York, NY: John Wiley and Sons, 1978.

12   Editors, "Why Voice Channels are so Bad for Data." *The Datacomm Planner*, August 1973.

13   Freeman, R., *Telecommunication Transmission Handbook*. New York, NY: John Wiley and Sons, 1981.

14   GTE Lenkurt Inc., *The Lenkurt Demodulator*, *20*, 10, San Carlos, CA, October 1971.

15   Halsall, F., *Data Communications, Computer Networks, and OSI* (2nd edition). Reading, MA: Addison-Wesley, 1988.

16   Heath Company, *Electronic Communications*. Benton Harbor, MI, 1981.

17   Krechmer, K., "Integrating Medium Speed Modems into Communications Networks." *Computer Design*, *17*, 2, February 1978.

18   Nording, K. I., "Taking a Fresh Look at Voice-Grade Line Conditioning." *Data Communications*, *3*, 5/6, May/June 1975.

19   Pooch, U. W.; Greene, W. H.; and Moss, G. G., *Telecommunications and Networking*. Boston, MA: Little, Brown and Company, 1983.

20   Rey, R. F. (ed.), *Engineering and Operations in the Bell Systems* (2nd edition). Murray Hill, NJ: AT&T Laboratories, 1983.

21   Sherman, K., *Data Communications: A User's Guide* (2nd edition). Reston, VA: Reston Publishing Company, Inc., 1985.

22   Stallings, W., *Data and Computer Communications*. New York, NY: MacMillan Publishing Company, 1985.

23   Talley, D., *Basic Telephone Switching Systems*. Rochelle Park, NJ: Hayden Book Company, Inc., 1987.

24   Tanenbaum, A. S., *Computer Networks* (2nd edition). Englewood Cliffs, NJ: Prentice-Hall, 1988.

PART 3

Networking

6

COMPUTER NETWORKS AND THE USER

6.1 Introduction*

Computer networks are classified as either a network of computers or a set of terminals connected to one or more computers. Most computer networks consist of hosts, terminals, nodes, and transmission links. A *node* refers to a computer whose primary function is to switch data. Computers used primarily for functions separate from that of switching data are referred to as *hosts*. In some network designs, the node and host functions may be performed by the same computer. *Terminals* are devices that interface the user to the computer or computer network, and *transmission links* join this collection of subnet elements to form a network. The transmission links and nodes, along with the essential control software, make up the *communications subnet*, often referred to as the *data network*.

The underlying idea of configuring computers into a network is that of *remoteness* [7]. The early network designs were a little more than a central computer, serving both as host and a switch, with remote terminals connected to the computer by various communications media, such as dial-up access, dedicated telephone lines, or microwave. With ever-increasing subscribers, a proliferation of these simple networks resulted. Furthermore, intelligent remote terminals increasingly replaced the older nonintelligent devices. The use of intelligent terminals resulted in a concentration of information flow from users in a "local" vicinity to the computer host and improving the utilization of the communications medium. Furthermore, it was now possible to have the intelligent terminal preprocess inefficient human dialogue, thereby decreasing information flow

---

* see references 1, 4, 5, 7, 9, 10, 13, 15, 16, 20 and 21.

requirements on the communications medium [13]. It also became practical for subscribers to share communications costs by combining assets into a network of terminals and hosts.

6.2 User Perspective*

The categorization of data communications users is based directly on their computer network applications. The description of these applications will be limited to three broad categories that constitute the majority of the functions for which computer networks have been designed.

1. *Remote user access.* Whenever users are not in the same local vicinity of the computer system and need to have access to that system, they are considered to be remote users or subscribers. Remote access is made available by connecting a terminal to some communications medium, which is then interfaced to a computer. The user, based upon individual requirements, may interact with the computer for processing power or for access to data that are stored at the host facility. The interactive user expects to receive a response within seconds from having generated a stimulus. On the other hand, the response to a remote job entry is entirely dependent on the time to process the entire job and the availability of the communications medium, the latter being shared with other users.

2. *Computer-to-computer access.* Computers, when communicating directly with other computers, have created the highest demand for data communications. Given the appropriate stimulus, a computer will generate information in the form of bit strings for transfer over communications media at a much faster rate than the remote user. For example, portions of, or entire data bases can be conveniently transferred between computers without manual intervention. In fact, computer-to-computer communication is one of the general applications that requires no direct manual interface.

3. *Message traffic.* A significant portion of the communications traffic is generated by users sending messages to other users. When information is transferred to two or more terminals, it is referred to as *message traffic*. Yet another type of

---

* see references 4 and 12.

message traffic results whenever a computer generates information that is destined for some terminal. Given a predetermined sequence of events, many computers automatically transmit messages to specified remote terminals. These messages may be addressed for human use, or may be for control of hardware components (e.g., control signals to electromechanical devices used in an assembly line). Thus, computer-to-terminal communications are put into the same category as computer-to-computer communications and classified as message traffic.

It is now possible to associate user types that correspond to the three network application categories. The first user type is called the *real-time user*. A real-time computer system is defined as one that receives and processes an input and returns a result within a time frame sufficiently fast to affect the environment linked to the computer. For example, imagine a prospector in the Arctic region who has attached cans by a string to a branch adjacent to his hut. This early warning system would clearly alert the prospector of any intrusion, provided it would give him sufficient time to get out of the way. If the intrusion were an advancing glacier, then this system would provide sufficient warning time and would represent a real-time system. If, on the other hand, the intrusion were a grizzly bear, this system might not provide sufficient time for the prospector to respond to the warning. These systems are strongly dependent on the environment in which they exist and often must respond faster than normally associated with batch processing. The user of a real-time computer system is a real-time user.

The second user type is referred to as the *teleconference user*. These users communicate by sending messages to each other, each of which is a unit of information containing a complete idea or concept. These types of messages are usually context-sensitive and, therefore, have no restrictions on the order in which symbols can appear within the message. Context-sensitive messages, however, are not easily adapted for communicating with a computer because certain symbols within the message may be misinterpreted to be control symbols instead. User-to-user communications constitute the great majority of message traffic. The users of these terminals are in a teleconference mode of communications.

The third and final user type is referred to as the *data-sharing* user. The user in this context could be a computer (or the "owner" of the computer) that needs to share its data with other computers or cause data to be shared with it. The data to be shared (or communicated) can be as small as a few bits or as large as an entire data base. This has some obvious implications about the volume of information that might be communicated between computers. The data-sharing user is therefore a significant factor in the design of computer networks.

6.3 Network Design Objectives*

In the design of computer networks a delicate trade-off must be made between capabilities and cost, to achieve a proper balance to demand. The demand curve, as illustrated in Figure 6.1, will shift to the left as the design of the network includes fewer and fewer features. Obviously, a poorly balanced design would result in economic failure if the curve is allowed to shift too far to the left. This means that there exists a point on the capability curve where the demand falls very rapidly. A properly balanced computer network design must provide reliable, error-free communications within a reasonable time. These general design objectives can be restated in terms of the following design requirements:

1. Reliability (uninterrupted, error-free service).
2. Transparency (network operation invisible to the user).
3. Economy (minimum overhead with efficient use of the media).
4. Convenience (simple user access).
5. Security (as required by the user).

6.3.1 Reliability

Reliability in a computer network refers to the network's ability to provide uninterruptible, error-free service. Uninterruptible service is greatly dependent upon a design philosophy that addresses the question, "To what extent should alternate transmission paths and back-up equipment be provided?" The answer to this question generally requires a statistical analysis of cost-versus-equipment reliabilities, as well as a queueing analysis with representative load conditions. This load-condition analysis is a major factor in the design of computer networks, where the system is to redirect traffic automatically, depending on dynamic load conditions. Algorithms used for rerouting traffic are discussed in a subsequent chapter.

---

* see references 1, 4, 11, 12, 15 and 20.

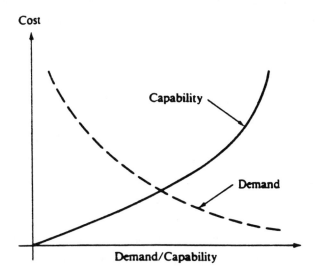

Figure 6.1. Demand/capability versus cost curve for network design.

6.3.2 Data transparency

As applied to information transfer within a network, transparency means that the network is completely impervious to the information transmitted on it. Although transparency is one of the most important design requirements, most networks do not have complete transparency. That is, there are certain values or bit configurations that cannot appear in the text of the message because they are used for control functions. For example, the automatic hardware control might mistakenly determine that the end of the text has arrived, when in fact the text only contained a bit pattern recognized as the end-of-text character. The result of such an occurrence is unpredictable and undesirable both from the network operation standpoint, as well as from the network user. Fortunately, the American National Standards Institute (ANSI) has set aside certain standard bit patterns to be used exclusively for hardware control. Examples of such bit patterns can be seen in SDLC and BI-SYNC, and are shown in Chapter 11. Since these patterns are values used exclusively for control characters, it would appear that the transparency problem has been circumvented. Unfortunately there are some categories of user information (e.g., facsimile, graphics, raw satellite weather and photographic data) that generate data with unknown value, including a high probability of designated control characters. Such occurrences would potentially degrade service or result in lost or destroyed information.

A common algorithm, called *bit stuffing*, is used in networks where SDLC, HDLC, or other bit-oriented link-control procedures are used. Assume that all messages consist of text fields (provided by the network user) and communications control information (added by the originating network processor). Text is isolated from the control information by a fixed bit pattern generally referred to as a *flag sequence* (e.g., 01111110). *Transparency* is achieved around a text field by placing a flag sequence of a zero bit followed by 6 one bits followed by another zero bit (i.e., 01111110) at the beginning and end of each text. All switching computers within the network are required to search for this sequence continuously. The occurrence of the flag sequence within the text is prevented by the following procedure for inserting zero bits. The transmitting node inserts a zero bit after each five continuous one bits anywhere between the beginning and ending flag of the next field. After receiving five continuous one bits, the receiving node inspects the sixth bit; if it is a zero, the five continuous one bits are passed as data and the zero bit is deleted. If this sixth bit is a one, the receiver inspects the seventh bit; if it is found to be a zero, a flag sequence has been received. Clearly, this would be a time-consuming test if performed by software; however, it is a simple, inexpensive test when performed by the interfacing hardware. Although other algorithms are undoubtedly possible, the zero-bit insertion method has received fairly wide acceptance as a means for obtaining a transparent communications medium.

In a byte- or character-oriented link-control procedure, text can also contain control characters. The control characters in the text are preceded by a control character called the *data-link escape* (DLC). Using the DLC character, data transparency can be achieved.

As applied to the user interface, transparency means that the user can "login" to any terminal on a network and be able to perform the same functions regardless of location. This network transparency serves to allow the network to distribute tasks for processing to nodes that are currently best able to perform the task. This type of network transparency operates in a distributed processing environment. In the packet switched network, each network communication processor decides (dynamically or statically) the best route for the message to take in order to reach its destination. There are certain priorities in packet switched networks that override the dynamic route generation, but network transparency is enabled during dynamic routing.

6.3.3 Economy

An important design consideration is the ability of a network to provide service that will accommodate the needs of the majority users without degrading service to the less frequent user. Economic considerations, though, will hamper significant wide-scale improvements in data transmission speeds over the next decade. The problem arises because existing primary communications media, land lines, were designed for voice communications at bandwidths less than those required for high-speed data transmission. In fact, considerable energy and money have been devoted to the development of sophisticated modulation schemes and hardware to maximize the use of existing communications land lines. Some success has been realized, but, in general, natural thresholds that cause high signal loss prevents any significant increase in data speeds without improving the medium. To upgrade existing land-line networks or the installation of a new medium capable of communicating high-speed data would involve costs greater than potential users are willing to pay.

A computer network must function with minimum overhead. The power of computers to which communications links are attached exceeds that necessary to saturate existing low-speed links. Thus, overhead is essentially a concern about loads on interconnecting links rather than loads within the communications processor. However, it is worth noting that less overhead results in more efficient processing and therefore can lower the investment for processing power. What is link overhead? It is those messages or that portion of messages exclusive of text that facilitate communications between computers. A certain amount of control information must be attached to each message, to be examined by the receiving computer in order to determine what should be done with the message. An efficient procedure for transmitting control information will minimize overhead without seriously affecting flexibility. This design problem is compounded by differing media and computer interface characteristics. These divergent factors make it no simple task to design a best scheme for minimizing overhead regardless of the operations environment.

6.3.4 Convenience

A critical but not so apparent factor is the ease with which the user can gain access to and make use of a network. If communicating with a specific type of computer network is troublesome, that network is placed at a competitive disadvantage to other types of networks. The reputation of a network, regardless of other advantages that it may have, can be quickly damaged because of the physical interface to the user. This means that the physical interaction required of the user must be simplified so that connectivity is established with minimum effort. Once connections are made, physical interaction should be near zero except for unusual occurrences such as failure. Disconnecting from a network by one or more users should be with minimum effort and cause no perturbations to the operation of the network.

6.3.5 Security

Data transferred through a computer network should be protected from undesired disclosure. Several state-of-the-art encryption techniques allow users to communicate using privacy keys. Network users should keep in mind, however, that there are no perfectly secure computer systems, regardless of the image a vendor may give. The network designer must therefore consider various design features that tend to enhance security rather than to seek a perfect solution to the overall problem of computer security. Some computers haves better security features than others and should be investigated for that purpose.

6.3.6 Other considerations

The operation of a geographically dispersed system that potentially interfaces with thousands of subscribers that possess equipment from different vendors, each with its own interface characteristics, poses unusual and complex problems. Aggressive management is necessary for any one institution to cope with engineering and "finger-pointing" problems that are inevitable in a multivendor environment without pricing the service out of reach. One intuitively concludes that a common technological base is necessary between users and vendors for the independent success of a computer network system. Such a base, in the form of internationally established computer interface standards, has slowly evolved through a group of academic, government, and vendor representatives called the International Standards Organization (ISO) (see Chapter 10). Although other management problems certainly exist, none approach this complexity.

There are certain social implications of linking data bases that contain information of one form or another on every U.S. citizen. The traditional security measure of using controlled access is no longer functional when contrasted to the need for rapid data transfer between computers. Regulatory bodies have already indicated a general awareness of the problem by invoking privacy bills that restrict the release of private personal information by federal agencies. Yet additional legislation will be required as more and more data bases are linked by elaborate networking. Security is given increased emphasis in both the public and private sectors. However, there exist security deficiencies which, at least for the near future, will inhibit the use of general computer networks for extremely sensitive communications.

6.4 Network Perspective*

Early computer installations in the late 1940s and early 1950s were either dedicated to particular research problems or used for finance accounting. That is to say, general-purpose systems were practically nonexistent. Since that time, the explosive growth of computer technology, both hardware and software, has placed the computer into a wide spectrum of applications. Individual installations, however, were prone to develop sophisticated software to solve a particular problem. This unique and frequently very complex software was not readily transportable to the wide diversity of machines and interfacing software. Many users were therefore required to develop duplicate software packages that could be economically adapted to their own installation.

During this time frame, military planners were becoming increasingly concerned with providing survivable, low-delay communications to support advanced weapon systems. High-speed digital computers were installed to meet the critical response times demanded by air defense operations and communications. A computerized air defense system called the Semi-Automatic Ground Environment (SAGE), installed in 1958, was the first attempt to interconnect computers on a large scale.

The immediate problem in the design of a data network in the late 1950s was to find a readily available communications medium. Designers were naturally encouraged to use existing telephone circuits along with their switching capabilities since, regardless of the many disadvantages from today's standards, these voice circuits were suitable for data transfer. Thus, SAGE was designed to use primary "dedicated" data links with the ability to switch to alternative links and routes should error or failure conditions become excessive (see Figure 6.2). The development of the SAGE switching circuits led to

---

* see references 1, 4, 7, 13 and 17.

research on other data networks that were to be used for more general-purpose communications. One such network to evolve was the Automated Digital Information Network (AUTODIN) in the early 1960s.

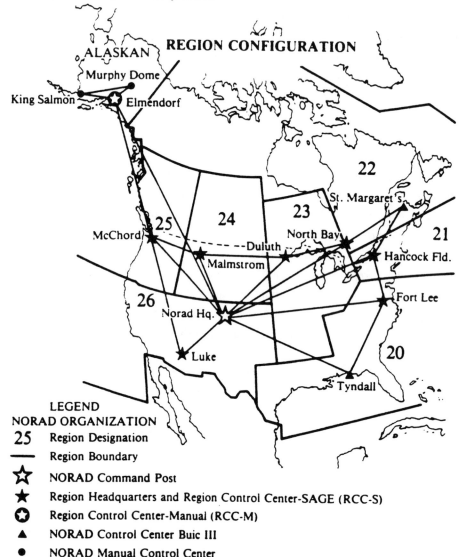

Figure 6.2. SAGE network configuration.

AUTODIN was installed to provide the Department of Defense with quasi-survivable data communications capability between major military installations in the continental United States and overseas. The major nodes of an early AUTODIN configuration are illustrated in Figure 6.3. The network was designed to transfer messages between humans, not between computers, although computers were used to format and transfer between links. A network designed for human processing is quite different from that required for direct computer processing; the latter because of its rapid processing capabilities, is very sensitive to the amount of time it takes to complete the communications process.

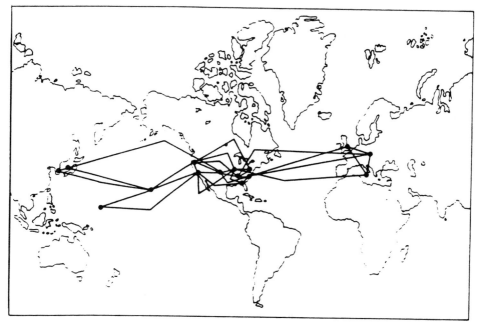

Figure 6.3. AUTODIN network configuration.

This historical perspective takes on a different flavor as the demand to gain access to data from remotely located terminals increases. Users not only wanted to gain access to data in computers thousands of miles away, but also to have information transferred between geographically separated systems. The pattern of information transferred between distant points changed drastically. The interaction of humans with computers usually occurs in short bursts, followed by longer periods of silence, with yet other short series of bursts to and from the computer. On the other hand, when computers interact with each other, they communicate for short periods in which rapid bursts of very condensed data are transferred. Dedicated circuits, using dialed connections for long distances, become very inefficient and costly when communicating in a "burst" communications environment. Actual circuit utilization under these conditions is less than 5 percent. As a result, networks designed entirely for data transmission emphasize circuit utilization as a major design factor. Switching facilities were designed, different from the traditional continuous channel switch used for telephone systems, to accommodate burst channels. Furthermore, techniques were developed to measure the communications environment to determine whether a channel should be designed for continuous or burst conditions [13]. One such technique utilizes the peak-to-average ratio as a standard for measurement. The average bit rate is determined from the total amount of information transferred between two points in the network, while the peak rate is calculated for the period of maximum desirable data flow.

Large peak rates are characteristic of such applications as graphics or video, in which peak-to-average ratios approach 200,000 to 1 or greater. On the other hand, the human-to-computer interaction has a peak-to-average ratio greater than 10 to 1. With such a wide range of peak-to-average ratios, networks should be designed using burst channels; however, such a mass medium capable of efficiently communicating burst data was not yet available.

The experience of the early network planners and supporting contractors led to the development of systems relying heavily on common carriers rather than dedicated lines. High-speed store-and-forward networks first began to appear in 1969 as a cost-effective common-carrier approach for time-shared systems. These time-shared systems allowed many users to interact simultaneously with the computer. Because the utilization of these systems was not spread uniformly throughout the day, activities needed to be scheduled. Administrative procedures for scheduling terminal usage produced a better utilization of the machine during slack periods, but did not prevent periodic peaks from saturating the systems. The basic problem was one of incompatibilities: user incompatibilities with the various types of accessible communications media and scheduling incompatibilities with the normal daily work schedule. The advancement of network technology was encouraged as a means of finding solutions to the problem of program transportability and peak machine saturation.

Better utilization of resources came about by 1967 with such improvements as load-leveling, the elimination of functional duplication, and specialization in hardware and software. *Load-leveling* was accomplished by automatically selecting a host computer within the network that had the least backlog of work, providing more immediate processing capabilities. Furthermore, load-leveling was made possible with routing mechanisms that directed communications needs around heavily saturated links of the network. The former is referred to as *distributed processing*, while the latter is referred to as *distributed communications*.

Functional duplication occurs when similar processing needs exist at two different locations, each meeting that need with functionally identical capabilities. In many cases, the requirements could have been satisfied at both locations by providing a logical connection between them; that is, a connection transparent to the user. The additional function for the use of networks is also part of distributed processing.

Finally, *specialization of hardware and software* is an extension of the concept of functional duplication. If there exists a processing need common to many locations, then it becomes feasible to provide a service that meets those needs. The likelihood that a sufficiently large requirement exists within one locale is small and, thus, remote access should be provided. If the service requires special hardware and software, it is logical to provide access to the special service via a network to which many of the potential users are attached. Such is the design of several processing services that are frequently advertised in business and data processing journals [8,18,13]. Two examples are COMPUSERVE, a general business-processing agency attached to the TYMNET Switching Network, and MicroNET, which is accessible by telephone dialing procedures.

Earlier, the Advanced Research Projects Agency (ARPA), largely as a result of research by L. G. Roberts [1-3], proposed building a distributed switchpoint system with heterogeneous hosts and lines. Such a network, according to the design of ARPA, would have specialized capabilities throughout the system to meet unique requirements of each user, regardless of the interfacing characteristics of systems needing the communications. The research efforts through ARPA have provided the impetus for the rapid growth of computer networks during the 1970s. Other networks that added insight to the distribution of both processing and communications were the local network at the UK National Physical Laboratory and the Societe International de Telecommunications Aeronautics (SITA), which now operates a worldwide message network serving more than 150 airlines [1-3,7].

6.5 Network Classification Schemes*

Classification of a network generally depends on such factors as the message routing procedures used within it, the geographical appearance or topology that is associated with it, the major functions it performs, or any combination of these.

6.5.1 Topological classifications

Network topology, as a means of categorizing data communications networks, evolved from graph theory. A formal introduction to graph theory and its relationship to computer science is provided in a fine text by Deo [8]. *Topology* refers to properties of a network that are independent of its size and shape, properties such as the connection pattern of the links and nodes within the network. Topology plays an important role in network design in regard to its reliability, message delay, and the like [6]. *Graph* is the mathematical term for network, i.e., a collection of points joined by links. Terms borrowed from graph theory include the *node*, which is analogous to the network computer switch; the *path*, which represents a logical connection between any two nodes in the network; and the *link*, which provides a physical connection between any two adjacent nodes and is analogous to the communication channel. Channel bandwidth, either in time or space, may be subdivided by many different methods depending on such considerations as the type of medium and the type of information to be communicated (refer to chapter 3). The specific discussion on the classification according to network topology is given in chapter 8.

6.5.2 Classifying networks by switching discipline

There are three basic technologies for interconnecting computers, each with its own characteristics. These technologies are distinguished by the manner in which resources are allocated in support of the communication process and therefore assume a perspective as

---

* see references 1, 2, 4, 6, 8, 14, 16, 18 and 22–24.

viewed by the network designer who must make maximum utilization of available resources. The technologies are:

1. *Circuit switching*, a process in which all physical links are established between source and destination, and remain connected during the time of communications.

2. *Message switching*, in which physical links continuously exist between two adjacent nodes in a network and logical paths are defined between users by allocating capacity on the physical links.

3. *Packet switching*, which is similar to message switching, but where logical paths are derived at each node in the communications process based upon varying load conditions within the network.

6.5.3 Classifying networks by centralized versus distributed routing

Extensive research has been done on the design and modeling of network routing algorithms by Prosser [15, 16], Boehm and Mobley [3,15,23,24], Doll [15,16,18], Gerla [2,15,16], Metcalfe [15,22], McQuillan [15,16,18,19,22,24], Kleinrock [15,16], and many others. There is considerable overlap between classifying networks according to the type of routing algorithms used and according to the configuration of their topology. Many routing procedures in use today are little more than extensions of routing mechanisms developed for voice (analog circuit) switching networks as they evolved in the 1950s. Little has been done to improve on the early research of circuit-switching algorithms for analog data communications purposes. This is primarily because of the relatively large time intervals needed by most hardware devices to establish a link between two potential users. Indeed, the communications process in circuit switching typically has involved more time making and breaking circuits than actually performing communication.

The burst nature in which computers interact with other computers and in which humans interact with computers is an obvious factor. Thus, there has been a tendency to shy away from the wide use of circuit switching as a viable alternative to the rising demand for efficient and inexpensive data communications. The future holds some interesting developments in hardware that will again make circuit switching a strong competitor to the other switching technologies.

6.6 Exercises

6.1   Categorize the various classes of computer users and contrast them with users of networks as described in this chapter.

6.2   Any information, regardless of its form, can be transformed into corresponding digital data for processing by a computer or for transmission through a computer communications network. What is the feasibility of using computer networks for video telephone conversations in the near future? Describe essential features necessary for two-way video telephone communications.

6.3   Review the related literature to determine the peak-to-average ratio for the following:

   a. Interactive calculations using a language such as BASIC.

   b. Airline reservations on a visual-display terminal.

   c. Data entry with an operator filling in a form displayed on a video screen.

   d. Inquiry/response interaction with a time-sharing system.

6.4   Find a terminal that is connected to a data communications network. Observe the operator in action; interview the operator; find out the type of information communicated by way of the terminal, how it communicates, and over what medium it communicates. Calculate the peak-to-average ratio and write a brief description of the purposes, the operation, and the characteristics of the data communications system that you have observed.

6.5   In analyzing a computer communications network, the designer must consider the following issues: terminal configurations, processor configurations, network architecture, network design. Describe how each of the above interrelate and how they affect user access, reliability, cost, and throughput.

6.6   The basic task of system network architecture is to optimize the distribution of system resources over the network in accordance with predetermined criteria. Although these criteria may be application-dependent, consider cost, availability, reliability, security, and compatibility with existing resources in discussing this optimization.

6.7   Correlate the various network user types to the three network application categories. Describe the demands and the resulting requirements that these user types impose on the network.

6.8   What specifically is meant by information transparency?   How is this implemented in networks?

6.9   Compare the departments of SAGE to AUTODIN, especially in terms of the network demands, functions, and utilization.

6.10   Describe what is meant by each of the following terms:

   load-leveling

   functional duplication

   distributed communications

6.7 References

1   Abramson, N., and Kuo, F. F. (eds.), *Computer-Communication Networks*. Englewood Cliffs, NJ: Prentice-Hall, 1973.

2   Abrams, M.; Blanc, R. P.; and Cotton, I. W., *Computer Networks: Text and References for a Tutorial.* New York, NY: IEEE Computer Society, 1976.

3   Abramson, N., "The ALOHA System--Another Alternative for Computer Communications." *Proceedings of the FICC*, 1970.

4   Black, U., *Data Networks: Concepts, Theory, and Practice.* Englewood Cliffs, NJ: Prentice-Hall, 1989.

5   Chou, W. (ed.), *Computer Communications, Vol. I: Principles.* Englewood Cliffs, NJ: Prentice-Hall, 1983.

6   Davies, D. W., and Barber, D. L. A., *Communications Networks for Computers.* London: John Wiley and Sons, 1973.

7   Davies, D. W.; Barber, D. L. A.; Price, W. L.; and Solomonides, C. M., *Computer Networks and Their Protocols.* New York, NY: John Wiley and Sons, 1979.

8   Deo, N., *Graph Theory with Applications to Engineering and Computer Science.* Englewood Cliffs, NJ: Prentice-Hall, 1974.

9   Doll, D. R., *Data Communications: Facilities, Networks, and System Design.* New York, NY: John Wiley and Sons, 1978.

10   Ellis, R. L., *Designing Data Networks.* Englewood Cliffs, NJ: Prentice-Hall, 1986.

11   Lane, M. G., *Data Communications Software Design.* Boston, MA: Boyd & Fraser Publishing Co., 1985.

12   Markley, R. W., *Data Communications and Interprobability.*   Englewood
        Cliffs, NJ: Prentice-Hall, 1990.

13   Martin, J., *Future Developments in Telecommunications.*   Englewood Cliffs,
        NJ: Prentice-Hall, 1977.

14   McQuillan, J., "Adaptive Routing Algorithms for Distributed Computer
        Networks." Report AD-781-467, *NTIS*, May 1974.

15   McQuillan, J. M., and Cerf, V. G., *A Practical View of Computer
        Communications Protocols.* Washington, DC: IEEE Computer Society Press,
        1978.

16   Pooch, U. W.; Greene, W. H.; and Moss, G. G., *Telecommunications and
        Networking.* Boston, MA: Little, Brown and Company, 1983.

17   Rustin, R. (ed.), *Computer Networks.* Englewood Cliffs, NJ: Prentice-Hall,
        1972.

18   Schwartz, M., *Computer-Communication Networks Design and Analysis.*
        Englewood Cliffs, NJ: Prentice-Hall, 1977.

19   Schwartz, M., *Telecommunication Networks, Protocols, Modeling and
        Analysis.* Reading, MA: Addison-Wesley, 1987.

20   Sherman, K., *Data Communications: A User's Guide* (2nd edition). Reston,
        VA: Reston Publishing Company, Inc., 1985.

21   Sherman, K., *Data Communications: A User's Guide.* Reston, VA: Reston
        Publishing Company, Inc., 1985.

22   Stallings, W., *Handbook of Computer Communications Standards*, Vol. 2.
        New York, NY: MacMillan Publishing Company, 1987.

23   Tanenbaum, A. S., *Computer Networks.* Englewood Cliffs, NJ: Prentice-Hall,
        1981.

24   Tanenbaum, A. S., *Computer Networks* (2nd edition). Englewood Cliffs, NJ:
        Prentice-Hall, 1988.

7

SWITCHING TECHNIQUES

7.1 Introduction*

Networks are sometimes characterized according to the type of equipment with which they interface. A network is said to be *heterogeneous* if it is made up of a variety of different equipment and nodes. This frequently implies the need for so-called front-end processing to isolate the communications subnet functions from the varying interface protocols. A network is said to be *homogeneous* if it uses only one protocol procedure, thus obligating host functions with whatever protocol translations are necessary for interfacing with the network. Networks are typically heterogeneous, while the communications subnet will commonly be configured so that it is homogeneous.

Another pair of network descriptors deals with how the communications processors in a network maintain control signals on connecting circuits. A circuit is said to be *synchronous* if the interfacing nodes are in a constant active (timed) state with each other. This means that when normal communications processes on the circuit have reached a lull, the two attached computers will retain synchronization with a continuous stream of synchronization pulses. Since the two interfacing computers are always synchronized, the communications process may begin immediately without formatting each block or packet with a synchronization preamble. This is not the case with *asynchronous* circuits. Here, synchronization is allowed to decay between each communication. A continuous stream of synchronization pulses is not placed on the circuit and it is therefore not kept active. Synchronization occurs by preceding each packet with a series of synchronization characters long enough to allow the receiving computer to synchronize its clock. This typically will range from two to four characters.

---

* see references 1–4, 8–10 and 13–16.

Trade-offs between whether a circuit should be synchronous or asynchronous depend on the importance of the circuit. Maintaining the circuit in an active state allows continuous testing for error conditions, ranging from real-time statistical analysis of the bit error rate to the immediate recognition that the circuit has failed. These error test functions are of little importance on low precedence communications.

It is generally recognized that interlinked computers require an accurate clocking mechanism for synchronization. For example, unless a receiving computer knows exactly when to start measuring a bit that represents information, it may only recognize part of the bit, a signal that is perhaps too short to correctly represent the information. The partial bit is therefore ignored. In synchronous operations, one of the two interfacing computers will be assigned the master clock responsibilities while the other computer synchronizes its operation with the master clock signal. However, both synchronous and asynchronous procedures will achieve synchronization between the clocking mechanism of the interfacing computers.

7.2 Circuit Switching*

Circuit switching, analogous to the telephone (voice) switching networks where a complete circuit is established prior to the start of communication, comes in two forms, manual or automatic, both involving the dedicated use of circuits for the duration of the communication session. Manual circuit switching is used mostly with remote terminals, generally for interactive communications. In this mode, the user dials the telephone circuits for access to the desired computer system. If the circuit is unacceptable or if access to another computer is desired, the user terminates the existing connection and redials (switches) to another circuit. Automatic circuit switching systems, on the other hand, require the use of electronic switching mechanisms that automatically connect the required circuit when pulsed with the proper signal, usually a predefined bit stream. Both modes of circuit switching experience line contention delays (this is when many users attempt to use the circuit simultaneously) when distant end-user circuits are busy.

Circuit-switching, although widely used for individual remote terminal access, has not been considered as having significant network potential, both in terms of efficiency and economy.

---

* see references 5, 7 and 12.

7.3 Message Switching*

A *message* is defined to be a logical unit of information for the purposes of communicating to one or more destinations. In telecommunications, a message is typically composed of three parts: (1) a headline, referred to as the *header*, which contains information suitable for maintaining control of the network operations involved in the delivery of the message; (2) the *body* or *text*, which contains the information to be transferred; (3) a *trailer*, which contains fields that signify the end of the message. Telegrams, programs, and data files are examples of messages.

A *message-switching subnet* is a collection of physical circuits interconnected by switches that are able to examine message control fields for determining such subsequent action as flow control or routing. This differs from circuit switching because now circuits are no longer dedicated for exclusive use. For the regular user, message switching is less expensive because circuit costs are divided among the users sharing the system. However, message switching can cause unacceptable delay for the real-time user, noting that any significant increase in switching speeds, by perhaps evolving technology, would perturbate the cost relationships between circuit and message switching.

Messages within a message-switching network are transferred between switches on a message-by-message basis. This means that a message, sometimes broken into blocks of data, must have been either transmitted and received in its entirety or canceled across a link before the next message can be transmitted. Each block of the message must be transmitted in its proper sequence so the receiving switch can rebuild the message and verify to the sending switch that it has received it (Figure 7.1; note that only the initial block has sufficient control information for further routing). If the message is not accepted, it must be retransmitted until accountability can be verified by the receiving switch. Direct access auxiliary storage is often used to prevent unreasonable restrictions on message lengths and to store messages in case of circuit failure or heavy loading. Message switching is frequently referred to as *store-and-forward* (S/F) message communication because of these characteristics. In general, real-time statistics are not maintained, and thus dynamic rerouting is impractical because heavy loading on any one circuit is not normally a sufficient criterion to take manual steps to reroute traffic.

---

* see references 5, 7 and 12.

Alternate routing in message-switching networks is reserved almost entirely for circuit or switch failure.

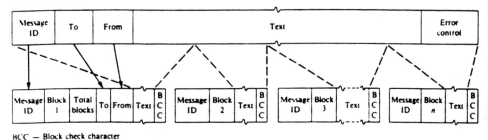

HCC — Block check character

Figure 7.1. Example format for message-switching network.

CYBERNET, a nationwide public commercial computer communications network designed and implemented by Control Data Corporation (CDC), is an example of a message-switching network where the network is heterogeneous while the communications subnet is homogeneous. The network, formed to connect CDC's existing data centers, provides the following services to the public:

1.   "Supercomputer" processing.
2.   Remote access (batch and interactive).
3.   A multicenter network.
4.   File management.
5.   Applications library and support.

By virtue of the distributed network topology and central processing power, the user has the following advantages:

1.   Better reliability; an alternate machine is available in case of local system failure.
2.   Greater throughput as a result of load-leveling across time zones and throughout the system.
3.   Greater manpower utilization by capitalizing on shared program libraries and data bases.
4.   Enhanced processor utilization by allowing users to select the computer configurations most suited for their job.

These services and advantages translate directly into dollar savings for the users.

The processing power of the CYBERNET is derived from powerful computers distributed across the country. The network operation is enhanced by the use of front-end processors and concentrators throughout the system (see Figure 7.2). CYBERNET supports single terminals, special peripheral equipment, satellite computers, and large computer complexes at its nodal interfaces.

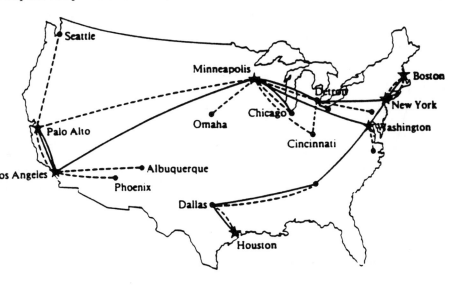

Figure 7.2.   The CYBERNET network.

The CYBERNET communications subnet is connected by switched, leased, and private lines and satellite links, with speeds ranging from 2400 bps to 40.8 kbps. Remote low-speed terminals use dial-up lines to multiplexers rather than directly to remote computers. The mix of line types and speeds has been designed to meet user needs without incurring the cost of underutilizing larger facilities. However, the high expense of communications in message switching has led to the design of more sophisticated switching techniques, including packet switching.

7.4 Packet Switching*

Another technique for data communications that has evolved over many years is called *packet switching*. Just as with message switching, each message is subdivided into blocks of data, called *packets*. However, in packet switching each packet has attached to

---

* see references 1, 5, 7, 11, 12, 14 and 17.

it sufficient control information so that the packet can be transmitted across a network independent of all other packets belonging to the same message (Figure 7.3). The following example, whose notation can be traced to Kleinrock [6], describes how a message might traverse a packet-switching network.

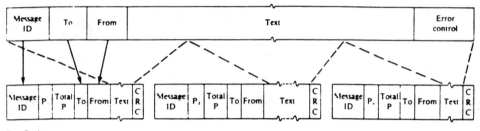

P — Packet
CRC — Cyclic redundancy check

Figure 7.3. Example format for packet-switching network.

Consider a five-packet message (Figure 7.4) which must traverse the six-switch (node) network from A to F.

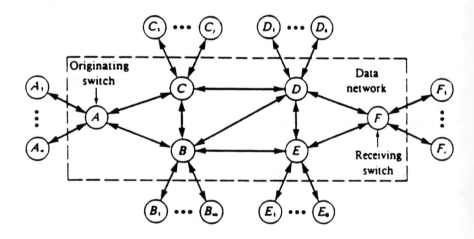

Figure 7.4. Example of packet-switching network.

The path of each packet can be represented by a set of ordered pairs to designate the circuit between two nodes, i.e., the circuit, P, from A to C is designated P(n) = (ac) and the circuit from C to D is designated P(n) = (ac, cd), where n is a unique number assigned to a particular packet traversing path P. Note that all links communicate in both directions, so that a packet going from C to A would have path P(n) = (ca). Packet-switching computers are generally programmed to alter the routing to the circuit dynamically with minimum loading, by evaluating individual circuit and switch loads. For simplicity, assume that unique numbers 1 through 5 have been assigned to packets 1 through 5, respectively. The originating switch, node A, may determine that packets should be transmitted alternately to nodes B and C such that P(1) goes to B and P(2) goes to C, etc. Now node B may determine that P(1) and P(5) should go to D and P(3) should go to E. Node C, on the other hand, has also sent P(2) and P(4) to D. Node D, now with four of the five packets, dynamically determines that it can lower its load by alternately transmitting the packets to nodes E and F. The end result is that packets arrive at F out of sequence. This presents no problem, however, since node F has been programmed to hold final delivery of the message until the entire message is received. If node F or any node between A and F received a garbled packet, the sending node will be requested to retransmit the packet. However, if F has not received all of the packets after a specified time interval, node A will be requested to retransmit the missing packets, F having assumed that the first transmission was lost in noise, equipment failure, etc. Table 7.1 provides both time-interval and path descriptors to emphasize the flexibility with which a message may traverse such a packet-switching network. Note, however, that some networks that have a "datagram" interface deliver packets independently to subscribers and do not assemble entire messages before delivery.

The ability to transmit a packet immediately without having to wait for a complete message and the ability to adjust to varying load factors dynamically minimize resource requirements at each node. Nodes that become saturated, however, are generally programmed to reject traffic until their load is normalized. The overall effect of packet transmission is a decrease in system cost resulting in a corresponding effect on user rates.

A popular and well-known packet-switching network is the Advanced Research Projects Agency (ARPA) net referred to as ARPANET. Initially started with four locations in 1969, the ARPANET now connects over 90 host computers on three continents. The heterogeneous distributed computer communication network is supported by a communication subnet of 60 minicomputer nodes connected by 50 kbps leased lines, DDS, and satellite channels [1,5,11,14,17].

The primary goal of the ARPANET was and still is to achieve effective sharing of computer resources. This goal has been accomplished successfully, as illustrated by the University of Illinois, who, because of greater computing needs, considered leasing and purchasing more hardware. The University of Illinois was able to reduce existing operating costs by 60 percent by accessing the needed services via the ARPANET. Other users have done likewise. Network use falls into three types:

1. Remote access to time-sharing systems.
2. Fast remote batch (mostly numerical) processing.
3. File transfer.

Table 7.1 Example of Packet-Switching Timing

			Time intervals			
	1	2	3	4	5	6
ab	P(1)	P(3)	P(5)			
ac	P(2)	P(4)				
bd		P(1)		P(5)		
be			P(3)			
cd		P(2)	P(4)			
de			P(1)	P(4)		
df			P(2)		P(5)	
ef				P(1)	P(3)	P(4)

Path descriptors

P(1) = (*ab,bd,de,ef*)
P(2) = (*ab,cd,df*)
P(3) = (*ab,be,ef*)
P(4) = (*ac,cd,de,ef*)
P(5) = (*ab,bd,df*)

The geographic structure of the ARPANET is shown in Figure 7.5. This distributed heterogeneous network is composed of ARPA-supported research centers and numerous government agencies. Host computers are independent of the communications subnet, which is interface message processors (IMPs) and terminal interface processors (TIPs). IMPs are used to interface with host computers or computer networks, while TIPS are provided to allow remote terminals to interface with the ARPANET, thereby having access to its vast computing power. Access to network hosts is available only if (1) prior authorization has been obtained and (2) the user is familiar with the operating procedures of the designated installation.

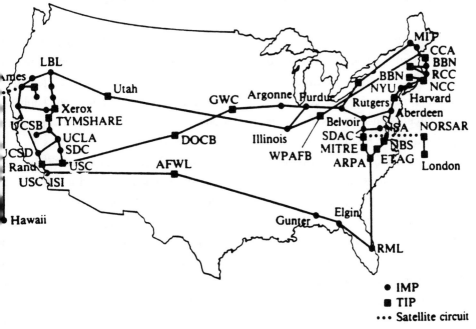

Figure 7.5.   ARPANET.

The basic communication path of the ARPANET is still the 50 kbps leased line, operating in a synchronous full-duplex mode, connecting the IMPs and TIPs of the subnet. The use of DDS and satellite circuits has reduced the transmission costs significantly while improving the error rates.

Host-IMP connectors are, for nearby hosts, accomplished by an asynchronous-bit serial interface that requires special hardware on the host side. Hosts located at greater distances from the IMPs are connected by standard communication lines. The TIP-remote-terminal connection is made by the asynchronous transmission of characters at speeds up to 19.2 kbps.

The IMP-TIP minicomputers handle all subnet end-to-end error correction and adaptive routing, gather performance statistics, maintain local routing tables, test unused lines at half-second intervals, and perform speed/code translations necessary to converse with assigned hosts.

7.5 Integrated Packet-Circuit Switching*

The evolution of computer networks took advantage of existing telephone switching design (circuit switching) and evolved to the more cost-effective designs of message and packet switching. Newer technology has now made circuit switching a viable alternative to achieve inexpensive data communications with remote locations. For heavy, nonburst users, circuit switching has already become a popular method because of its flexibility (i.e., capability to reach any location that has a telephone circuit).

Experience has shown that packet-switching technology is very cost effective for bursty, low-average-data-flow communications between computers and terminals [6]. Bursty communications are characterized by interactions that typically occur between humans and computers in a real-time interactive environment. The opposite, steady-flow communications are common when two computers are directly connected, for example, to transfer digitized voice or video information. Pure packet switching has serious shortcomings in high-data-flow environments because of overhead and excessive delay times between packet arrivals of the same message. Circuit switching, on the other hand, has significant advantages when operating under the same conditions. The probability of completing the communications process on switched circuits, however, without the ability to detect errors at occasional intervals, is very small when considering the noise experienced on most telephone circuits. Therefore, as with other switching procedures, messages must be divided into some logical entity so that appropriate error-test fields can be attached. This allows retransmission of smaller segments when an error is detected without having to resend the entire message. Whether messages are divided into blocks (as with message switching) or into packets (as with packet switching) depends on the individual needs of the user. Typically, however, packet formatting will be used in lieu of message formats, primarily to allow the additional flexibility for interfacing packet-switching networks. The hybrid circuit switching network using packet-formatting

---

* see references 5, 7, 10 and 12.

procedures will become a popular data communications technique as available switching speeds are improved.

7.6 Exercises

7.1 Describe the three major categories of data network communications. Include in this description distinguishing factors, along with advantages and disadvantages of each.

7.2 In designing message and packet formats for a packet-switching network, what considerations must be taken into account over and above format design for a message-switching network? Illustrate your answer with a block structure of the message and packet formats.

7.3 Two commonly used forms of switching network are store-and-forward and packet. Briefly discuss each, specifically mentioning switch centrality, network delay, message format, and error correction techniques.

7.4 Define:

   contention terminal system

   switched network

   dial-up network

7.5 Consider the following properties of a packet-switching network:

   random delay

   random throughput

   out-of-order packets and messages

   lost and duplicate packets and messages

   nodal storage

   speed matching between subnet and the access net

Discuss the network functions that must be provided to accommodate these properties.

What impact will these functions have on the design of these nodes.

7.6 Review other available literature to find other networks, one of each type described in this chapter. Describe their topology, characteristics, and geographical configuration using the terms defined earlier.

7.7 Numerous problems, which seem relatively small when using DDD circuit-switching procedures, become very significant when using store-and-forward switching procedures. Some of these problems are interface protocols, security, and misrouted messages. Discuss as many of the type problems that you can think of.

7.8 Networks can be classified by functional form into random- access networks (RAN), value-added networks (VAN), and mission-oriented networks (MON). Compare and contrast these different functional categories and include example networks of each.

7.9 In a circuit-switched network a physical end-to-end path, as opposed to the store-and-forward process of packet networks, is found before communication circuits and buffers are committed for the duration of the connection. Discuss the advantages and disadvantages of each type of network, including class of data traffic, user applications, interface complexity, and user transparency.

7.10 Data network-switching designs are based on circuit or store-and-forward principles. Discuss the performance between circuit and store-and-forward switching, especially how the crossover or crossbar efficiency can affect this performance.

7.11 Why is packet switching a more desirable technique as compared to message switching? Discuss the problems of routing, buffer allocations, retransmission, and load factors.

7.12 Compare the formats of packet- and message-switching networks and discuss their impact on throughput.

7.13 What impact does a saturated node have in a packet-switching network in comparison to a message-switching network?

7.14 Compare and contrast homogeneous networks to heterogeneous networks. Include in your discussion remote access, file-transfer capabilities, formats, and routing.

7.15 Discuss how network deadlocks and degradations come about as a result of reassembly store-and-forward lock-up, buffer saturation, and route loops for each of the switching techniques.

7.16 Compare the different types of network architectures, classified according to their communications structures, with reference to the following factors: switching delay, line utilization, efficiency, expandability, and reliability.

7.17 What are some of the inherent packet- and message-length limitations, especially when comparing asynchronous versus synchronous transmission?

7.18   Message switching can provide substantial improvement in circuit utilization over circuit switching if (1) resource utilization is balanced against delay; and (2) short messages are given a reasonable service. Discuss the second requirement by considering priority scheduling and message-length priorities.

7.19   Discuss the packet-switched subnetwork design considerations for ARPANET, including NCP characteristics, source-destination functions, and store-and-forward functions.

7.20   What impact do retransmissions caused by errors in entire messages, message forward fragments, and packets have on throughput for both packet- and message-switched networks?

7.7 References

1   Abramson, N., and Kuo, F. F. (eds.), *Computer-Communication Networks*. Englewood Cliffs, NJ: Prentice-Hall, 1973.

2   Abrams, M.; Blanc, R. P.; and Cotton, I. W., *Computer Networks: Text and References for a Tutorial*. New York, NY: IEEE Computer Society, 1976.

3   Bartee, T. C. (ed.), *Data Communications, Networks, and Systems*. Indianapolis, IN: Howard W. Sams & Co., Inc., 1985.

4   Black, U., *Data Networks: Concepts, Theory, and Practice*. Englewood Cliffs, NJ: Prentice-Hall, 1989.

5   Chou, W. (ed.), *Computer Communications, Vol. II: Systems and Applications*. Englewood Cliffs, NJ: Prentice-Hall, 1985.

6   Geria, M., and Mason, D., "Distributed Routing in Hybrid Packet and Circuit Data Networks." *Proceedings of the IEEE COMPCON*, Fall 1978.

7   Halsall, F., *Data Communications, Computer Networks, and OSI* (2nd edition). Reading, MA: Addison-Wesley, 1988.

8   Martin, J., *Future Developments in Telecommunications*. Englewood Cliffs, NJ: Prentice-Hall, 1977.

9   McQuillan, J. M., and Cerf, V. G., *A Practical View of Computer Communications Protocols*. Washington, DC: IEEE Computer Society Press, 1978.

10   Pooch, U. W.; Greene, W. H.; and Moss, G. G., *Telecommunications and Networking*. Boston, MA: Little, Brown and Company, 1983.

11   Rustin, R. (ed.), *Computer Networks*. Englewood Cliffs, NJ: Prentice-Hall, 1972.

12   Schwartz, M., *Computer-Communication Networks Design and Analysis*. Englewood Cliffs, NJ: Prentice-Hall, 1977.

13   Sippl, C. J., *Data Communications Dictionary*. Princeton, NJ: D. Van Nostrand Reinhold, 1976.

14   Stallings, W., *Data and Computer Communications*. New York, NY: MacMillan Publishing Company, 1985.

15   Tanenbaum, A. S., *Computer Networks*. Englewood Cliffs, NJ: Prentice-Hall, 1981.

16   Tanenbaum, A. S., *Computer Networks* (2nd edition). Englewood Cliffs, NJ: Prentice-Hall, 1988.

17   Weissler, R.; Binder, R.; Bressler, R.; Rettberg, R.; and Walden, D., "Synchronization and Multiple Access Protocols in the Initial Satellite IMP." *Proceedings, COMPCON Fall 78*, 1978.

8

NETWORK TOPOLOGIES

8.1 Introduction*

In the past, computer networks were comprised of a single host with multiple terminals used for access. The topology used to connect these terminals to the central host was relatively simple. As computers advanced to enable multiple hosts and distributed services to coexist, connections between terminals and processing hosts changed to better suit the new environment. The connections from terminal to host, host to host and from terminal to terminal (intelligent terminals) are called links. The actual physical media used for links is known as the path. Each terminal and host is known as a node. The most generic network topology classifications are centralized, decentralized and distributed, each will now be detailed (see Figure 8.1).

8.2 Centralized Networks**

The centralized network, in which control functions are centralized, is the simplest of data communications arrangements where switching has been introduced into the network [14]. This topological scheme, essentially a star topology, requires that a link be dedicated for communications between the central node and each terminal connected to the node during periods of operation. Star networks are typically used for smaller data communications systems where the node (or switch) is also used for data processing or applications programming. That portion of processing not dedicated to network functions is referred to as *host* processing.

---

* see references 1, 2 and 18–22
** see references 3, 10, 13 and 14.

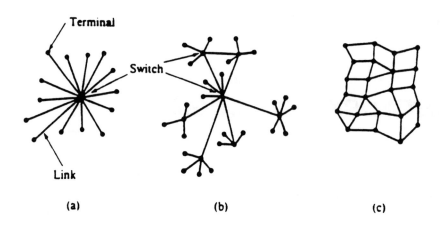

Figure 8.1. (a) Centralized network; (b) decentralized network; (c) distributed
network

An example centralized network may consist of a central time-sharing computer with
remotely connected terminals. Using the network functions of the computer, terminals
may be allowed to send messages between each other in much the same manner as
sending telegrams. The computer would also perform host functions in support of user
processing requirements. Network functions are performed by communications messages
from one terminal to one or more terminals within the same building, or one or more
terminals in other buildings within the corporation. An interface may also be provided to
larger networks for communications external to the corporation. The application of these
small-scale centralized networks using mini- and microcomputer technology has
significantly improved administrative communications throughout industry.

The reliability of the centralized network is highly dependent upon the central switch.
The failure of the switch suspends all activity in the network, whereas individual link
failures affect only the device(s) connected via that link. Any significant increase in
reliability requires duplication of the network switching function. Recovery from link
failure is a fairly simple and inexpensive provision if the terminal and associated switch
uses (or at least provides for back-up) dialing equipment to reestablish the link. This
means that dedicated links can be temporarily replaced by dial-up telephone circuits in the
event that one or more of the links fail. Reinitiating a link with dial-up telephone
circuits may be manual or automatic with the use of automatic error detection and dial-up

features that allow the switch to detect a failed link and automatically reestablish communications. The latter is in more popular demand where time is critical or where both ends of the link are terminated with some form of automated intelligence, either hardware or software. Two forms of automation typically remote from the centralized switch are the multiplexer and the concentrator.

Multiplexing refers to the ability of a single facility to handle several similar but not necessarily related operations [9]. In data communications, multiplexing is the interleaving of mutually independent low-speed signals on a high-speed path so as to reduce overall circuit costs. This is achieved only because the cost of a simple high-speed circuit is generally less than the combined costs for circuits to support each independent signal. If the combined bandwidth of the low-speed signals is less than the bandwidth of a normal telephone circuit (approximately 4 kHz), then the only additional costs would be for the associated multiplexing equipment at each end. The voice telephone circuit is the minimum bandwidth that can normally be leased for multiplexing or for some single signal use.

As previously explained, multiplexing comes in two basic forms, frequency-division multiplexing (FDM) and time-division multiplexing (TDM). As a reminder, FDM organizes independent signals so that each is separated by a frequency band and does not interfere with others on the same circuit. TDM, on the other hand, has signals organized through time so that no two signals are transmitted at the same time. Each mutually independent signal must be allocated a portion of communications time in which it is the sole user of the circuit. At the end of a predetermined period of time, the next signal is then allowed to use its share of the time bandwidth.

A special system of TDM involves the use of a *concentrator*. The *concentrator* consists of a small computer and sufficient memory to allow messages to be queued for transmission. It has no switching capabilities other than to allow two or more terminals to communicate over the same circuit.

Geographically dispersed terminals frequently lead to the use of multiplexers or concentrators to conserve communications costs. Indeed, it is unlikely that terminals in close proximity to each other would be active at the same time. A hardware switch may be justified where a subset of the terminals remotely connected to a central computer are located in the same geographical vicinity (Figure 8.2). The objective is to obtain more efficient link utilization, thereby reducing costs at the expense of an occasional (mostly transparent) delay in turnaround time. A multiplexer using FDM is most suitable when traffic tends to be steady, having a relatively constant rate. If the peak transfer rate of all users attached to it exceeds link capacity, then the system should be designed to inhibit data transfer to and from attached terminals momentarily to prevent loss of data. A concentrator should be used when it is known that the potential input capacity will exceed link capacity. The somewhat more expensive contractor temporarily stores messages under peak load conditions to compensate for occasions where instantaneous input rates exceed link capacity. As multiplexers, concentrators are used to merge several low-speed links into one high-speed link. The switching capability of network concentrators and multiplexers is totally dependent upon the status of the central node.

8.3 Decentralized Networks*

Decentralized networks are little more than expanded centralized networks; that is, a decentralized network can be viewed as a network with nodes that have the added capability for switching between circuits. With that in mind, the distinction between centralized and decentralized networks comes from the organization of the switching function. Unlike centralized switching, decentralized networks are organized with independent and geographically separated switching capabilities. Graph theorists refer to such a network as a mixture of star and "mesh" components, where a mesh is a completely enclosed region [8] [note that Figure 8.1(b) contains a mesh component]. Nodes directly connected by a mesh component have the ability to "decide" and select the optimum route for data transfer. Methods for deciding on which route or link to transmit a data segment may be simple or complex, depending on the level of sophistication required of the network. The simplest routing procedures do no more than establish primary and alternate routes, using the alternate path only when the primary path has failed. Alternate paths can be selected manually or automatically. Routing procedures from this simple algorithm increase with varying complexity. The more complex techniques are able to decide on a path depending on varying load conditions and the user's needs. Optimum routing is therefore loosely defined as routing necessary to satisfy user requirements for timeliness as constrained by implementation costs.

The added reliability of decentralized switching can only be obtained with additional computers (nodes) and associated connecting links. This added reliability is usually dependent upon some (although not elaborate) form of alternate routing, in which not

---

* see references 4, 7, 8, 12, 19 and 22.

every path is duplicated [7]. Theoretically, however, methods for improving the reliability of networks are not infinite. The number of alternate paths and links can approach infinity, but perfect reliability is achieved only if the supply is infinite. As a result, cost quickly becomes the dominating factor, requiring that reliability be statistically adjusted to a given dollar threshold. The existence of at least two disjoint paths between every pair of nodes describes a third topological category of networks, the distributed network.

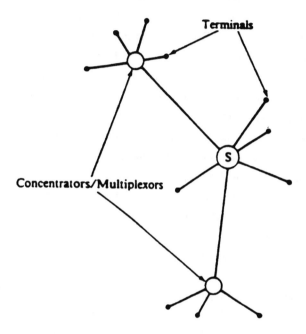

Figure 8.2. Centralized network with concentrators/multiplexers.

8.4 Distributed Networks*

The amount of material written about networks since networking of computers was first considered practical for distributed telephone systems would fill a small library. Indeed, it is literary suicide to write about computer networks without making at least a

---

* see references 1–6, 10–12 and 15–22.

casual reference to the distributed network category. The evolution of this intriguing and complex maze of computers [Figure 8.1(c)] has led to the consideration for networks with thousands and even tens of thousands of nodes [15, 16]. Therein lies much of the research by communicators and computer scientists for networks of the future.

The distributed network, a network in which the control functions are distributed to the nodes, consists of several mesh subnets where each node is connected to three or more other nodes. Each node possesses the capability to switch methodically between connected links according to some predefined routing algorithm (several of which are described in the next chapter). Routing algorithms are characteristically designed to optimize the use of network capacity. Distributed networks evolved from attempts to define military communications systems suitable for operating under hostile conditions [5]. The distributed network, using packet-switching techniques, is generally considered to have the greatest potential for networks of the future because of the inherent reliability for continuity of operation. Concepts expressed in the following paragraphs are based on work by Boorstyn and Frank, presented at the First Joint IEEE-USSR Workshop on Information Theory, Moscow, USSR [6].

Performance of distributed data networks is characterized by variables that include cost, throughput, response time, and reliability. The design of the network should consider properties of its nodes, such as throughput capabilities and reliability, along with the network's topological structure. Important considerations are listed in Table 8.1 and 8.2 [11].

For small or medium-sized networks (50 to 150 nodes), a typical network structure is fairly homogeneous with identical hardware and software at each node. Larger networks require the use of alternatives, such as topologies with embedded hierarchies, because of large processing and storage requirements in using global routing procedures. For a two-level hierarchy, the highest level can be thought of as the backbone network and the lower hierarchy as a set of subnets that accesses the backbone network through one or more high-level nodes that act as gateways. Boorstyn et al. [6] have classified four general problems which must be considered for multilevel networks:

1. Preliminary clustering of user locations.
2. Selection of nodal processor locations.
3. Backbone topological design for the upper levels.
4. Local access design.

Extensive research has developed efficient clustering algorithms for resolving problems related to items 1 and 2; it is item 3, the backbone topological design, that encompasses the greatest challenge for large-scale distributed network designers.

Table 8.1. Node characteristics

Node characteristics
Message handling and buffering methods for ensuring integrity of user-generated data and constraints on the maximum size of a message and the maximum number of messages that may be accepted by a node at any one time.
Error control--methods for ensuring that errors are detected and messages retransmitted where appropriate.
Flow control--methods to ensure orderly flow and balanced load conditions.
Routing--methods that provide optimum response for the user.
Node throughput--methods to provide the most cost-effective utilization of nodal hardware.
Node reliability--methods for maintaining user confidence at a level that sustains user participation.

Table 8.2. Topological characteristics

Topological characteristics
Link location--Is the node centrally located to provide optimum service to a maximum number of users?
Link capacity--Is link capacity statistically tuned for optimum utilization; that is, has the link been sized to requirements?
Network response time--How quickly does the network respond to a user request for information transfer? Are messages delivery times responsive to user requirements?
Network throughput--Is the network capacity suited to its operating environment and is the user satisfied with response times?
Network reliability--Can the user confidently depend upon the network to provide reliable service?

8.5 Exercises

8.1 Discuss the difference in topological structures that can be designed for communications subnet and for the user (terminal) access system.

8.2 Discuss the evolution of distributed networks, especially the evolutionary relationship to the telephone switching systems.

8.3 Consider routing algorithms for distributed networks. Discuss all the important factors to the design of an algorithm that optimizes traffic flow.

8.4 Discuss some of the multilevel "hierarchical" network design problems. Discuss any of the routing mechanisms suitable to large networks without dividing these networks into subnets.

8.5 An optimum topology for a communications subnetwork would specify the location of the packet switches, the links connecting these switches, and the individual link capacities. Discuss the problem of determining such an optimum topology, including the impact of such constraints as cost, throughput, delay, reliability and availability.

8.6 Although user requirements may suggest that a particular network have a certain terminal or processor configuration, what network topological considerations might dictate another function?

8.7 Compare and contrast centralized to decentralized network topologies from the standpoint of reliability, link failure, link reinitiation, switching functions, and routing.

8.8 Compare and contrast the functions that multiplexers and concentrators play in networks.

8.9 Why is routing more difficult in decentralized, distributed networks than in centralized networks?

8.10 Discuss the performance of distributed communications networks by considering cost, throughput, response time, and reliability. Why is it important in this discussion also to consider node properties?

8.6   References

1   Abramson, N., "The ALOHA System: Another Alternative for Computer Communications." *Proceedings of the FICC*, 1970.

2   Abrams, M.; Blanc, R. P.; and Cotton, I. W., *Computer Networks: Text and References for a Tutorial.* New York, NY: IEEE Computer Society, 1976.

3   Bartee, T. C. (ed.), *Data Communications, Networks, and Systems.* Indianapolis, IN: Howard W. Sams & Co., Inc., 1985.

4   Black, U., *Data Networks: Concepts, Theory, and Practice.* Englewood Cliffs, NJ: Prentice-Hall, 1989.

5   Boehm, B. W., and Mobley, R. L., "Adaptive Routing Techniques for Distributed Communications Systems." *IEEE Trans. on Comm. Tech., COM-17*, 3, June 1969.

6   Boorstyn, R. R., and Frank, H., "Large-Scale Network Topological Optimization." *IEEE Trans. on Comm. Tech., COM-25*, 1, January 1977.

7   Davies, D. W., and Barber, D. L. A., *Communications Networks for Computers.* London: John Wiley and Sons, 1973.

8   Deo, N., *Graph Theory with Applications to Engineering and Computer Science.* Englewood Cliffs, NJ: Prentice-Hall, 1974.

9   Doll, D. R., "Multiplexing and Concentration." *Proceedings of the IEEE, 60*, 11, November 1972.

10   Ellis, R. L., *Designing Data Networks.* Englewood Cliffs, NJ: Prentice-Hall, 1986.

11   Frank, H., and Chou, W., "Topological Optimization of Computer Networks." *Proceedings of the IEEE, 60*, 11, November 1972.

12   Halsall, F, *Data Communications, Computer Networks, and OSI* (2nd edition). Reading, MA: Addison-Wesley, 1988.

13   Hammond, J. L., and O'Reilly, J. P., *Performance Analysis of Local Computer Networks.* Reading, MA: Addison-Wesley, 1986.

14   Hasesawa; Hideo; Miyahara; Teshisawara; Tushihaa; and Yoshimi Teshigawa, "A Comparative Evaluation of Switching Methods in Computer Communications Networks." *ICC-75*, San Francisco, CA, June 16-18, 1975.

15   Hayes, J. F., "Performance Models of an Experimental Computer Communications Network, *"Bell System Technical Journal, 53*, 2, February 1974.

16   Kleinrock, L., "Advanced Teleprocessing Systems." Report AD-A034-111, *NTIS*, June 1976.

17   Martin, J., *Telecommunications and the Computer*. Englewood Cliffs, NJ: Prentice-Hall, 1977.

18   McQuillan, J. M., and Cerf, V. G, *A Practical View of Computer Communications Protocols*. Washington, DC: IEEE Computer Society Press, 1978.

19   Pooch, U. W.; Greene, W. H.; and Moss, G. G., *Telecommunications and Networking*. Boston, MA: Little, Brown and Company, 1983.

20   Stallings, W., *Data and Computer Communications*. New York, NY: MacMillan Publishing Company, 1985.

21   Stallings, W., *Handbook of Computer Communications Standards*, Vol. 3. New York, NY: MacMillan Publishing Company, 1987.

22   Tanenbaum, A. S., *Computer Networks*. Englewood Cliffs, NJ: Prentice-Hall, 1981.

9

ROUTING ALGORITHMS AND FLOW CONTROL

9.1 Introduction*

Designing and modeling network routing algorithms has been extensively investigated and formulated by Prosser [35], McQuillan [32], Kleinrock [29], and others [5, 17]. The algorithms described in this chapter are organized around the research of Fultz [15], who consolidated an excellent taxonomy for classifying network routing algorithms (Table 9.1). The transition from topological classifications to routing algorithms is easily understood, since there is a noticeable overlap between classifying networks according to the type of routing algorithms used and according to their topological structure. Also, this list should not be considered all-inclusive because of ongoing trends in network development. However, it does provide a good basis from which to proceed into a more detailed study of network theory.

Several algorithms discussed in this section are extensions of routing mechanisms developed for voice (circuit) switching networks in the 1950s [2]. Since that time, few improvements have been made to algorithms specifically designed for circuit-switching communications. This is primarily because of the low popularity of the circuit-switching techniques, resulting from their relatively slow switching speed when compared to other designs. The trend away from circuit switching is being reversed with the advent of new and more powerful electronic circuitry. As these schemes evolve, much of the research on message- and packet-switching routing algorithms will also apply to circuit switching. That is, certain algorithms developed for one switching method will also be used in

---

* see references 1, 2, 3, 5, 6, 12, 14, 15, 17, 22, 29, 32, 33, 35, 38–42 and 44.

networks that are combinations of circuit and packet or message switching. The conclusion is that the following schemes should not be associated with any particular switching philosophy. Each algorithm may have its place with a particular switching concept, but, with little adjustment or forethought, may also be applicable to two or even three switching methods.

Table 9.1 Classification of routing algorithms

Deterministic
      Flooding
            All
            Selective
      Fixed
      Split traffic
      Ideal observer

Stochastic
      Random
      Isolated
            Local delay estimate
            Shortest queue + bias
      Distributed
            Periodic update
            Asynchronous update

Flow Control
      Isarithmic
      Buffer storage allocation
      Special route assignment

9.2 Deterministic Algorithms*

The least complex procedure for routing messages across a network is to determine which path a message will take. Such a procedure is unchanging (static) and therefore "deterministic." Deterministic algorithms derive routes according to some prespecified rule that is generally designed to optimize a particular topological configuration. Each deterministic rule produces loop-free routing, so that messages never become trapped in closed paths that do not include their destination [20]. This type of routing includes at least four subschemes, some of which are divided into even more descriptive techniques.

9.2.1 Flooding techniques*

The simplest of all deterministic routine algorithms, and perhaps of all routing algorithms, is flooding [27]. According to this scheme, a message received at any node is immediately broadcast over all outgoing links except the link over which it arrived. After circulating within the network for a prespecified time, retransmission is discontinued. The communications time frame is calculated from knowing the maximum time that a message of highest precedence takes to traverse the network.

Since a node must only remember the link on which the message was received, it is not required to retain large tables for statistical routing data; it simply retransmits over other connected links. The decision mechanism for selecting a transmit link remains very simple in contrast to some of the more flexible routing algorithms to be discussed. Flooding always finds the minimum delay path for any given network state. However, if the flooding process is allowed to continue, the network quickly becomes congested after an initial stabilization period. This is because of the rapid increase of traffic within the network. It should be clear that the network traffic load would continuously increase by an average rate of n-1, where n is the average number of links per node.

Flooding has also been suggested as an initial pathfinder to route selection and path-delay statistics required in support of other techniques that may be installed [9]. However, efficiency considerations rule out flooding as a day-to-day routing procedure, even where

---

* see references 20, 21, 24 and 39–43.
* see references 9, 23 and 27.

retransmission is constrained only to links that meet certain predefined criteria. Except for determining optimum paths at initialization, flooding is used almost exclusively to communicate time-sensitive, high-priority traffic, as may be envisioned in a military situation where attack is imminent.

9.2.2 Fixed routing techniques*

Fixed routing techniques, another category of deterministic routing, assume the existence of fixed topologies and known traffic patterns. Optimal route selection is essentially reduced to a multicommodity flow problem, which has well-defined solution techniques [11]. Appropriate routing is obtained via a routing directory look-up procedure that is fixed for any given network configuration. A routing directory contains the link address for passing a message between any two nodes in the network. By searching the directory for a given destination, a cross-reference is made to the appropriate link for transmitting the packet. Fixed routing techniques do not perform well in hostile environments because of their inability to account dynamically for a changing topology. However, minor adjustments that allow the use of alternate paths in the event of a disconnect provide a reasonable degree of survivability.

9.2.3 Split-traffic techniques**

Split-traffic routing, sometimes referred to as traffic bifurcation, allows traffic to flow on more than one path between a given source and destination. If two different paths, R(1) and R(2), are available for transmitting a message, then a packet at node S would be routed over R(1) with probability P and routed over R(2) with probability 1 - P. Similarly, traffic loads can be split over more than two routes with a different probability for each, the sum of which must, of course, equal one.

This algorithm uses a directory look-up to determine the probability for each alternative, and a record of past choices to derive the current choice with greater confidence. The number of alternatives must be fewer than the total number paths at the disposal of node S.

_____

* see references 24 and 40–43.

** see references 9, 23 and 27.

Mathematical descriptions of split-traffic algorithms are not difficult to formulate; however, when placed into practice, the algorithms always turn out to perform less than optimally. This is because the assignment of link-selection probabilities is based on average traffic loads. Thus irregular traffic patterns will cause nonoptimum routes for a given network state. When compared to fixed techniques, split-traffic routing is nevertheless able to maintain a good balance of traffic throughout the network and can therefore achieve smaller average message delays than fixed routing procedures.

9.2.4 Ideal observer techniques*

A fourth deterministic algorithm is the ideal observer technique, which, as suggested by its name, requires total and continuous knowledge of the system at any given instant of time. For each new message arriving in the network, the receiving node computes a route that minimizes the travel time to the destination. This computation is based on the complete current information about the packets that previously entered the network and their selected routes. Because of inherent network delays, the ideal observer technique is of only theoretical interest. For example, when a message arrives at the destination mode, the source node is advised of its arrival with an acknowledgement message. The source node learns that a transmitted message has arrived at its destination only after an acknowledgement message sent by the destination node works its way back to the source node. Although only very short periods of time are required for this acknowledgement, an observer cannot know the exact current traffic load of the network, only what the load was recently, depending on link speeds and the rate of load variations. The use of the ideal observer technique is in providing an upper bound on network performance.

9.3 Stochastic Algorithms**

Stochastic algorithms operate as probabilistic decision rules as opposed to deterministic rules. Routes are selected that utilize network topology, perhaps combined with estimates concerning the state of the network. These estimates are statistically derived from delay information communicated from node to node between user traffic.

---

* see references 9, 23 and 27.
** see references 21, 24 and 39–43.

Each node is programmed to maintain a routing table that contains the required delay information; the table is updated any time new delay information is received. The algorithms use the delay information contained in the table in much the same manner the split-traffic and fixed-routing algorithms use table look-up (cross-reference) directories. The difference hinges on the possible alternatives; i.e., routing tables for stochastic algorithms maintain delay information for all possible paths to a destination, not just to adjacent nodes. It is a permutation of all possible combinations of links from the source to the destination. Clearly, the addition of even one node to an already fairly large network can have explosive impacts on memory requirements at each node and the number of messages for transmitting delay information.

The frequency of updating delay tables depend on such factors that include link and path delays, nodal congestion, and link speeds. Much research remains before these relationships can be well understood. It is generally recognized that, from a practical sense, each network must be tuned with various derivatives of a particular routing scheme in order to optimize the utilization of its resources. That is, traffic patterns and physical characteristics of any two networks will never be identical and, thus, fine-tuning of a routing algorithm will be necessary to ensure the most efficient use of resources. Even so, the three algorithms discussed next provide a good basis for understanding the complexity of the stochastic algorithms.

9.3.1 Random techniques*

Random routing algorithms assume that each node knows only its own identity. This means that delay tables are no longer required for determining the next path for transmission. Each message is transmitted on a link chosen at random, eventually arriving at the destination in what has been referred to as a *drunkard's walk* [9,38]. The algorithm can include a bias to guide the message roughly in the right direction. The use of a bias evolved from the need for orienting the direction of transmission; however, the algorithm should retain a substantial random routing to cope with possible link or node failures. Although algorithms using pure random routing are generally inefficient, they are surprisingly stable for networks having high probabilities of link or node failure.

---

* see references 9 and 38.

9.3.2 Isolated techniques[*]

The isolated routing technique, using local delay estimates, assumes that traffic loads are roughly equivalent in both directions between any given source and destination pair. This technique is sometimes referred to as *backward learning*, because delay estimates to destination nodes are based on combinations of transmit message times received from those nodes over the various alternative routes. A routing table is formed at each node containing the most current estimated delay to each destination. When a message is to be transmitted to a particular node, the routing table is scanned for the minimum delay path.

Needless to say, this procedure is not very appropriate for low-speed networks in which the communications circuits create the greatest delay (seldom do low-speed networks become processor-bound). The reason is, of course, that changing conditions can quickly make information contained in the delay table invalid. Also, the greater number of full-duplex circuits on the network, the more inaccurate the delay tables. Full-duplex communications remove any relationship of link delay between transmitted and received messages. Expected delay on half-duplex circuits is influenced by transmitted messages and will therefore be reflected in delay intervals of received messages. Thus, delay tables using isolated routing techniques tend to be more accurate when using half-duplex circuits. A practical use of isolated routing is only appropriate for networks with limited-load conditions.

The second of the isolated techniques, called the *shortest queue procedure*, originates from early research to develop a routing method that could automatically adjust message routing in response to link or node failures [4]. This procedure, also referred to as the *hot-potato* method, requires that intermediate nodes retransmit a packet immediately after being received. Each node in the network contains a prioritized list of connected lines leading to neighboring nodes for every destination. Packets are directed to the highest-priority line that is free for a given destination or, should all lines be in use, to the line containing the shortest queue. Although initially developed over a decade ago as an adaptive routing alternative for military voice communications networks, investigation of the hot-potato routing technique is generally acknowledged as having simulated much of the research and development on packet-switching concepts.

---

[*] see reference 4.

9.3.3 Distributed techniques[*]

The distributed class of algorithms is dependent on the exchange of observed delay information between nodes within the network. This approach introduces an inordinate amount of measurement information into the network and is therefore impractical for large networks. Modified procedures of distributed routing have been proposed, one of which uses a "minimum delay table" [16] and the other which advocates the "area approach" method [32].

The former procedure has each node exchange a delay vector with each of its nearest neighbors. Upon inserting internal delays into the vector, each neighboring node contains a copy of the delay vector and subsequently passes it to each of its nearest neighbors. The permutation of transmitting updated delay vectors between nodes eventually provides each node with a table of delays to all possible destinations via each possible path. A transmission node need only scan the delay vector table to determine which path offers the least delay to a particular destination node. Repeated updates may be prompted on either a periodic or an irregular basis as dictated by the load characteristics of the network.

The area-approach procedure partitions the network into disjoint areas in which a particular node exchanges delay information with every node within its area. Information is exchanged with adjacent areas as though each were a single node. This approach can be extended to a hierarchy of routing clusters at many levels. The objective of this approach is to reduce the total problem to a set of related subproblems that are more easily managed. The attendant impact on each node is a reduction in the amount of routing information that each node must retain, subsequently reducing demand on nodal memory. Various methods have been investigated for determining an optimum topological clustering scheme. A suitable algorithm, however, must be sufficiently general to account for the many factors (geography, user population, cost, etc.) that vary in the design from one network to another. One series of operations proposed is [10]:

1. Attach each terminal to a concentrator or node as appropriate.
2. Form clusters for concentrators.
3. Form clusters for nodes.
4. Locate concentrators and nodes.
5. Reconsider allocations of terminals.

---

[*] see references 10, 16 and 32.

6. Adjust concentrator and node locations for optimum configuration.

Clustering of concentrators (step 2) is generally a function of physical separation in which the nearest concentrators are formed into a cluster. This cluster centers around one node to which each concentrator in the cluster is attached for service. Clusters of nodes (step 3) is more complex and usually involves some heuristic clustering method that iterates on each variable having an impact on network design. The variables are bounded by more pragmatic considerations that include cost and physical size. Additional steps can be added to form clusters of clusters by iterating the above procedure for each additional level in the hierarchy. Although much research remains, the area-approach technique provides a basis for one solution to many control problems that have troubled designers of networks with large (> 200) numbers of nodes.

9.4 Flow and Congestion Control Algorithms*

Although flow control and congestion control are closely related they differ in that flow control is imposed in order to assure that messages leaving the source will be accepted by the destination with a high probability while this is not true for congestion control. Flow control is of course necessary even when there are only two nodes in the network. Congestion can occur within a network on either a global or a local basis. This congestion can be reduced by the use of a hierarchy of protocols that indicates which of several alternative actions is appropriate. This information can be contained in message- and packet-control fields. The hierarchy of protocols consist of:

1. Host-to-host (message protocols), in which the source and destination hosts decide on how to communicate a message.
2. Source node-to-destination node (packet protocols), in which respective nodes determine alternative transmit and receive actions for traffic between them.
3. Node-to-node (link protocols), in which nodes actively participate in the control and use of a link between them.

---

* see references 8, 10, 18, 19, 25, 30, 31, 34, 41 and 42.

The latter of these attempts to relieve congestion from node to node and is therefore local in nature. The other two methods, sometimes referred to as end-to-end protocols, are global in nature since they attempt to control traffic flow in the network. Three schemes that use one or more of these protocols in their communications process are the isarithmic, buffer storage allocation, and special route assignment routing algorithms.

9.4.1 Isarithmic techniques*

An isarithmic network is one in which the total number of packets is held constant [8]. This is accomplished by replacing data-carrying packets with dummy packets. A dummy packet has a special identification block, is always addressed to the nearest neighbor by a node along the path in which it is inserted, and contains a text block of all zeros or some other meaningless pattern. Each packet of user information must capture a dummy packet in order to enter the network. Holding the number of packets in a network stability under high user demand. Routing procedures are greatly simplified even though their design does not inherently consider some of the more complex problems such as packet looping (which corresponding user packet can be released for transmission). The isarithmic technique provides an inexpensive communications alternative for the noncritical host functions but could be unacceptably slow for more important user communications needs.

9.4.2 Buffer storage allocation technique**

With buffer storage allocation, the source node requests allocation of message reassemble space from the destination node prior to the release of the message for transmission. The alternative, to transmit the message without allocated reassemble space, would occasionally find the destination node's receiving buffer full, especially under heavy traffic conditions. This could turn into a disaster. Packets would not clear the last link in the path from source to destination and would therefore accumulate in the last node preceding the destination. The domino effect takes place as more messages close up paths into the destination, creating a barrier. When this occurs, nodes trapped in the barrier that have new messages to transmit will be unable to free their transmitting buffers in order to

---

* see reference 8.

** see reference 25.

process locally generated traffic. This results in a local-area deadlock that eventually seizes the entire network so that no communications can take place. Extraordinary steps are justified to prevent the occurrence of global deadlock.

The buffer storage allocation procedure was proposed as a solution to message reassemble lock-up [25]. Initially, it was intended that the destination node discard packets that cannot be accepted and then notify the source node of the action. The main problem with this approach is that it produces unnecessary duplicate packet transmissions in order to communicate a message. Advance allocation of reassembly buffers, resulting in occasional transmission delays, was concluded to be more efficient than recovering from discarded packets. Although easy to implement, neither the packet discard nor the buffer storage allocation procedure is considered adequate for the real-time or data-sharing users.

9.4.3 Special route assignment techniques*

Yet another alternative to the buffer storage allocation technique has been proposed in the form of assigning special routes. Route assignment is based on:

1. Status information received from adjacent nodes.
2. Traffic patterns encountered by the node over the past several seconds.

Thresholds are established to prevent the use of alternate routes in response to rapid changes in traffic flow. This is accomplished by combining measurements on the rate of change of traffic on each path with a predefined interval of time before alternate routing can be established. For example, refer to Figure 9.1, in which a neutral state, s, is a set of conditions that must be met before the network is altered because of changing loads. State n is defined as the "and" of two thresholds, functions A and B. Function A is a predetermined load level that must be exceeded to meet the first condition for adjustment. Function B is an interval of time over which the excess load must be sustained in order to meet the second and final condition for action. Resulting adjustments should compensate for sustained load levels above function A.

---

* see reference 25.

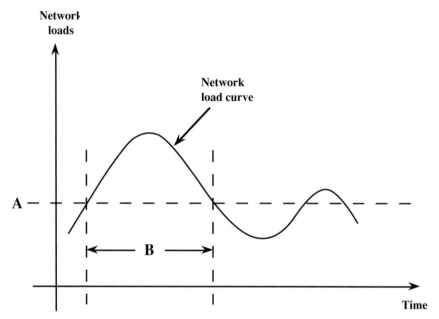

Figure 9.1. The neutral state, S, for serial route assignment.

The following procedure describes specific properties of the flow control routing algorithm.

1. The routing selection is performed independently by each node based upon information received from adjacent nodes and traffic patterns encountered.
2. The algorithm attempts to guarantee that individual routing decisions possess global continuity for the network.
3. Interval (synchronous) updating of routing tables is continuous, and dynamic (asynchronous) updating occurs where justified by wildly fluctuating network loads.
4. In selecting routes, the network is decomposed into a union of identical and overlapping subnetworks with separate routing desired within each subnetwork.
5. For an unloaded set, links are selected that result in transmitting the fewest nodes to the destination.
6. For a loaded net, traffic is diverted from fully occupied links whenever possible.
7. Changes in routing will occur only due to the sustained flow of traffic according to a new traffic pattern.

8. Additional paths will be established for a given destination that will allow individual packets to depart on separate links.

9. Traffic flow on any link in a subnetwork may occur in only one of the two directions at a time (half-duplex operation).

10. Directions of flow may change infrequently only after passing through a neutral state for a short interval of time.

11. The maximum allowed traffic through each node in a subnetwork is regulated so as to change slowly according to some prespecified time interval (reference function B, Figure 9.1). This provides routing stability and yet allows adjustments for increased traffic flow.

12. Loops in routing are more easily detected than in most other routing schemes.

9.5 An Alternate Classification Scheme*

Another view, that of Rudin [36], opposes a classification scheme in which routing techniques are combined with topological categories. This scheme, Table 9.2, divides all routing algorithms into eight classes, all but one (network routing center) of which has previously been described in one form or another.

Type A.2 of the centralized techniques uses a network routing center (NCR) that periodically accepts updated traffic load information from each node within the network. The NRC uses this information to update routing tables which then remain fixed until the next traffic-load message arrives. The primary disadvantages of this technique are:

1. The single-network switchpoint, the NRC, where the routing strategy is allowed to change between any two packets and where routing becomes fixed if the NRC fails.

2. The constrained system behavior that occurs because of single paths which develop for each source-destination node pair. As a result, Rudin [36] concludes that the use of the NRC approach caused instability in otherwise well-balanced networks.

---

* see reference 7, 17, 26, 36 and 37.

Table 9.2 Non-topological classification scheme

A.*Centralized techniques*
>   A.1. Fixed routing
>   A.2. Network routing center
>   A.3. Ideal observer routing

B.*Distributed techniques*
>   B.1. Updated routing table
>> B.1.a. Cooperative updating
>> B.1.b. Periodic updating
>> B.1.c. Asynchronous updating
>   B.2. Isolated with local delay estimates
>   B.3. Isolated with shortest queue
>   B.4. Random routing
>   B.5. Flooding

Centralized routing techniques have been extensively implemented and perform well within their natural constraints. Total system collapse due to failure of the central control facility is an example of a natural weakness of centralized control networks. Another weakness is the inflexibility for adjustments to load variations. In general, networks using routing algorithms under stable traffic flows [17]. The properties of a highly centralized network are well understood and, thus, raise few radically new problems beyond the existing technology of computer-communications systems [26].

In evaluating the relative strengths and weaknesses of centralized and distributed routing techniques, an alternative hybrid procedure referred to as *delta routing* was proposed [37]. In this scheme, topological decisions are divided into two categories. Decisions having only local network impact are implemented via the NRC. Although delta routing appears to take advantage of the more favorable attributes of the centralized and distributed classes, it still suffers from the inherent weaknesses introduced by the requirement for a central control facility.

Static (deterministic) routing strategies, exemplified by the fixed routing category of the centralized algorithms, provide optimal routing where total reliability and fixed load patterns can be assumed. In general, these assumptions make the static scheme usable only for analytical purposes. The obvious solution is an adaptive routing policy (types B.1, B.2, and B.3) in which changes in routing decisions are based on periodically updated information about the best routes to each destination. Hence, adaptive routing strategies, which take advantage of knowledge of the current state of the system, having generally been used in such networks as the ARPANET, with nonhomogeneous hosts or large aggregates of nodes and links.

Distributed routing algorithms suffer from two major shortcomings: there exists a tendency to route all messages to a given destination through a single neighboring node. Looping is characterized by a message that repeatedly traverses the same set of nodes. It may occur as a result of deficient interprocess communication or unfortunate timing. No computational solution to loopless distributed routing is known, although methods for forming loopless paths for centralized routing have been developed [7].

Traffic-flow measurements are useful tools for providing efficient routing policies. Such apparently uncomputerlike subjects as priority pricing and commodity flow are adapted from the management sciences to analyze, contrast, and improve network routing algorithms. Commodity flow is the study of the movement of such items as fruits and vegetables, or coal and other minerals, from farm or mine to the market. The parallel between movements of commodities across the country and movement of messages through a network is clear. Priority pricing affects prices on commodities in such a way as to reduce demand at the market and thus impede the movement of expensive items or, conversely, to maintain the movement of fixed proportions of various commodities at minimum cost. Simulation has also been used to derive traffic patterns under assumed distributions. Statistics resulting from simulation have been compared with results of traffic flow measurements to determine the validity of efficiency predictions for various routing algorithms [13,28].

The distributed class of routing algorithms using cooperative, periodic, or asynchronous updating (type B.1), possibly with some bias term, has substantial advantage over other networks offer one of the greatest challenges to the data communications industry.

9.6 Exercises

9.1   Extensive research has been done in the design and modeling of network routing algorithms. Briefly describe each of the following: deterministic, stochastic, and flow control.

9.2   Can you design a distributed routing algorithm which you believe will work? If so, express it in ALGOL notation. How would you go about testing the algorithm to ensure its validity?

9.3   The importance of properly considering all of the relevant factors when designing a routing algorithm cannot be overemphasized. Rank the design factors you consider important and briefly discuss why each is ranked in its relative position.

9.4   Discuss the problems of designing routing algorithms for distributed networks. What specific (unique) problems occur as the network increases in the number of nodes.

9.5   Several methods exist to validate routing algorithms. List as many such techniques as you can and discuss the advantages and disadvantages of each. Which do you prefer and why?

9.6   Consider the use of the radio-frequency media such as TDMA as a network communications path. How do the routing algorithms described in this chapter conform to a multiple-access media such as TDMA?

9.7   Looping is a very common problem in distributed networks. What procedure can you think of or prevent or to minimize looping? What mechanisms could be installed to detect looping, and if looping occurred, how could one recover from this problem?

9.8   Consider an isarithmic network. Under what circumstances is it possible to have a single node monopolize loop resources?

9.9   Discuss the following problems as they apply to distributed networks: central control, routing, flow control, and congestion.

9.10   A partially distributed (tree) or star network is generally one-connected. The best known implementation of this type is IBM's SNA network. Discuss the problem of operating such a network in a degraded mode.

9.11 Distributed routing algorithms suffer from several major shortcomings. Discuss such problems as looping, multipath routing, adaptive routing, and the inclusion of a bias term in delay vectors.

9.12 Routing design involves the joint cooperation between an appropriate network routing algorithm and a switching structure to effect the steering of a transaction between network subscribers. Discuss circuit switch routing, and compare it to store-and-forward routing.

9.13 Flow-control link design must address problems associated with mixing classes of traffic over a common transmission medium. Discuss the problem of flow control as it applies to packet speech. How could voice multiplexing be used to permit more efficient utilization of a voice link?

9.14 Major factors that impact directly on the need for flow controls are (1) synchronization of information flow on the data links, (2) detection and recovery from transmission error, (3) traffic routing from node to node, and (4) interfacing of subscriber processes to each other and the network. Discuss each of these factors.

9.15 Discuss the two extremes of flow control when applied to the transfer of data between a subscriber process and the subnet. Include switch connection, packet sequencing, bandwidth utilization, error detection, buffer allocation, and subscriber responsiveness.

9.16 Discuss congestion prevention, deadlock prevention, end-to-end flow control, and fair allocation of communication resources.

9.17 Discuss the performance impact that *progressive alternate routing* would have on distributed networks. With this method each node has a primary and an alternate path. If blocking occurs at some node during connection initiation, the alternate route is tried for route completion. If this connection fails, the transaction is either queued at the packet node or considered a system loss at the circuit node, depending of its class.

9.18 There are basically four functions which must be taken into account for any adaptive or dynamic routing strategy. Discuss the impact that each of these has on the routing strategy:
  (a) Reporting the local state to neighbors or to a centralized network routing center.
  (b) Assembling the global state based on these reports.

(c) Finding optimum routes based on the global state or information derived from the global state.

(d) Modifying the routing tables in the various nodes that are consulted by the nodal processors to determine which path to use to route a packet to or toward its destination.

9.19 Packet switching has been implemented in two rather distinct forms: ring networks and distributed packet-switching networks. Discuss the routing decisions that are required in view of the topology of each of these subnetworks.

9.20 What considerations arise when we include nonswitched point-to-point, nonswitched multipoint, and switched point-to-point techniques into communications control procedures?

9.7 References

1   Abramson, N., and Kuo, F. F. (eds.), *Computer-Communication Networks*. Englewood Cliffs, NJ: Prentice-Hall, 1973.

2   Baran, P., "On Distributed Communications: An Introduction to Distributed Communications Networks." Report RM-3420-PR, Rand Corp., Santa Monica, CA, August 1964.

3   Black, U., *Data Networks: Concepts, Theory, and Practice*. Englewood Cliffs, NJ: Prentice-Hall, 1989.

4   Boehm, S. P., and Baran, P., "On Distributed Communications II: Digital Simulation of Hot-Potato Routing in a Broadband Distributed Communications Network." Memo RM-3103-PR, Rand Corp., Santa Monica, CA, August 1964.

5   Boehm, B. W., and Mobley, R. L., "Adaptive Routing Techniques for Distributed Communications Systems." *IEEE Trans. on Comm. Tech.*, *COM-17*, 3, June 1969.

6   Chou, W. (ed.), *Computer Communications, Vol. II: Systems and Applications*. Englewood Cliffs, NJ: Prentice-Hall, 1985.

7   Chu, W. W., and Konkeim, A. G., "On The Analysis and Modeling of a Class of Computer Communications Systems." *IEEE Trans. on Comm.*, *COM-20*, 3, June 1972.

8   Davies, D. W., "The Control of Congestion in Packet Switching Networks." *Proceedings of the Second ACM/IEEE Symposium on the Optimization of Data Communication Systems*, Palo Alto, CA, October 1971.

9   Davies, D. W.,and Barber, D. L. A., *Communications Networks for Computers*. London: John Wiley and Sons, 1973.

10   Davies, D. W.; Barber, D. L. A.; Price, W. L.; and Solomonides, C. M., *Computer Networks and Their Protocols*. New York, NY: John Wiley and Sons, 1979.

11   Dantzig, G., *Linear Programming and Extensions*. Princeton, NJ: Princeton University Press, 1963.

12   Dijkstra, E., "A Note on Two Problems in Connection with Graphs." *Numerical Mathematics*, October 1959.

13   Fishman, G. S., "Statistical Analysis for Queueing Simulations." *Management Science*, *20*, 3, November 1973.

14   Ford, L., and Fulkerson, D., *Flows in Networks*. Princeton, NJ: Princeton University Press, 1962.

15   Fultz, G. L., and Kleinrock, L., "Adaptive Routing Techniques for Store-and-Forward Computer Communications Networks." *Proceedings of the IEEE International Conference on Communication*, June 1971.

16   Fultz, G. L., "Adaptive Routing Techniques for Message Switching Computer-Communications Network." Ph.D. Dissertation, University of California, Los Angeles, CA, June 1972.

17   Gerla, M., "The Design of Store-and-Forward (S/F) Networks for Computer Communications." Report AD-758-204, *NTIS*, January 1973.

18   Gerla, M., and Kleinrock, L., "Flow Control: A Comparative Survey." *IEEE Trans. on Comm.*, April 1980.

19   Gerla, M., "Routing and Flow Control." In Kuo, F. (ed.), *Protocols and Techniques for Data Communication Networks*. Englewood Cliffs, NJ: Prentice-Hall, 1981.

20   Greene, W. H., and Pooch, U. W., "A Review of Classification Schemes for Computer Communications Networks." *Computer*, *10*, 11, November 1977.

21   Halsall, F., *Data Communications, Computer Networks, and OSI* (2nd edition). Reading, MA: Addison-Wesley, 1988.

22   Halsall, F., *Data Communications, Computer Networks, and OSI* (2nd edition). Reading, MA: Addison-Wesley, 1988.

23   Heggestad, H. M., "The Testbed for Evaluation of Network Routing and Control Techniques." *MICOM 85*, October 1985.

24   Hurley, B. R.; Seidl, C. J. R.; and Sewell, W. F., "A Survey of Dynamic Routing Methods for Circuit Switched Traffic." *IEEE Communications Magazine, 25*, 9, September 1987.

25   Kahn, A. E., and Crowther, W. R., "A Study of the ARPA Computer Network Design and Performance." Report 2161; Bolt, Beranek, and Newman, Inc. Cambridge, MA: August 1971.

26   Kimbleton, S. F., and Schneider, M. G., "Computer Communication Networks: Approaches, Objectives, and Performance Considerations." *ACM Computing Surveys, 7*, 3, September 1975.

27   Kleinrock, L., *Communications Nets: Stochastic Message Flow and Delay.* New York, NY: McGraw-Hill, 1964.

28   Kleinrock, L., "Analytical and Simulation Methods in Computer Network Design." *Proceedings of the AFIPS SICC*, 1970.

29   Kleinrock, L., "Advanced Teleprocessing Systems." Report AD-A034-111, *NTIS*, June 1976.

30   Martin, J., *Systems Analysis for Data Transmission.* Englewood Cliffs, NJ: Prentice-Hall, 1972.

31   Martin, J., *Computer Networks and Distributed Processing.* Englewood Cliffs, NJ: Prentice-Hall, 1981.

32   McQuillan, J., "Adaptive Routing Algorithms for Distributed Computer Networks." Report AD-781-467, *NTIS*, May 1974.

33   McQuillan, J. M., and Cerf, V. G., *A Practical View of Computer Communications Protocols.* Washington, DC: IEEE Computer Society Press, 1978.

34   Pouzin, L., "Methods, Tools, and Observations on Flow Control in Packet-Switched Data Networks." *IEEE Trans. on Comm.*, April 1981.

35   Prosser, R. T., "Routing Procedures in Communications Networks--Part I: Random Procedures," and "Routing Procedures in Communications Networks--Part II: Directory Procedures." *IRE Transcripts on Communication Systems*, December 1962.

36   Rudin, H., "On Routing and Delta Routing: A Taxonomy of Techniques for Packet-Switched Networks." Report RZ-701, IBM Research, Zurich, Switzerland, June 1975.

37   Rudin, H., "A Performance Comparison of Routing Techniques for Packet-Switched Networks." Report RZ-702, IBM Research, Zurich, Switzerland, June 1975.

38   Schwartz, M., *Computer-Communication Networks Design and Analysis.* Englewood Cliffs, NJ: Prentice-Hall, 1977.

39   Schwartz, M., and Stern, T. E., "Routing Techniques Used in Computer Communication Networks." *IEEE Trans. on Comm.*, April 1980.

40   Schwartz, M., *Telecommunication Networks, Protocols, Modeling and Analysis.* Reading,MA: Addison-Wesley, 1987.

41   Stallings, W., *Data and Computer Communications.* New York, NY: MacMillan Publishing Company, 1985.

42   Tanenbaum, A. S., *Computer Networks.* Englewood Cliffs, NJ: Prentice-Hall, 1981.

43   Tanenbaum, A. S., "Network Protocols." *Computing Surveys*, December 1981.

44   Tanenbaum, A. S., *Computer Networks* (2nd edition). Englewood Cliffs, NJ: Prentice-Hall, 1988.

10

LAYERED NETWORK SERVICES

10.1 Introduction*

During the last decade, there has been a shift in the network marketing approach of data processing companies. In the 1970s, such a company would ensure that its customers would be able to communicate with one another within the company's network facilities. The marketing argument was to provide the customer with equipment that would permit access to a very reliable, high performance, expandable network. This led to the creation of various heterogeneous commercial networks such as IBM's SNA, DEC's DECnet, or the Advanced Research Project Agency's Network known as ARPANET. Different network design decisions generated heterogeneity among these systems and prevented them from collaborating. The end user of a given network was unable to communicate with any kind of end user in another given network.

However, a new marketing trend soon emerged: networking equipment would be more attractive if it could allow communication between entities located in different heterogeneous systems. A company whose equipment provided access to its own network as well as to that of other communication systems had a better chance to win market share.

The concept of internetworking implies dealing with partial or total heterogeneity: two networks may differ by the physical medium used, the character format, the mechanisms used to control accurate data transmission, the way of logically and physically naming different nodes on the backbone, and so on. As a consequence, protocols needed to be established in order to allow meaningful exchange of information between two or more parties located in various heterogeneous networks.

---

* see references 10, 17, 21, 27, 29, 36, 45, 49, 56, 64 and 71.

In 1978, the International Standards Organization (ISO), through its Technical Committee on Information Processing, recognized the urgency of creating an international standard for networks of heterogeneous systems. A subcommittee, called SC16, was created to deal with "Open System Interconnection" (OSI). In 1983, this subcommittee presented the OSI Reference Model, which provides a standard for network services and protocols. Hence, the interconnection of two networks, whose design conforms to the OSI Model, is made possible.

The organization of the OSI Reference Model stems from the steps required to ensure accurate data transmission between two or more end users of any type on a network. When an end user wishes to establish communication with another entity, an agreement has to be reached as to how the parameters involved in the transmission process should be set to satisfy needs at both ends. For example, the data sent by the first party has to be formatted in such a way that it can be understood by the other party, since a correct delivery of packets whose contents are not understandable is useless. The transmission parameters (half-duplex, full-duplex) and the data rate have to match the capabilities of both ends. The source and destination entities need to agree about the size and the format of the packet sent. Also involved in the communication process is the correct, error-free delivery of data packets, which implies some sort of error detection/correction mechanisms, as well as sequencing mechanisms. Routing the packets through the network compels the end user to give complete and accurate information about the other party's location. However, the need for transparency arises, in which case the user has to be aware of only the minimum information about the destination location.

It is now obvious that handling all these functions involved in network communication requires a certain level of modularity in the design of the network architecture and its protocols. The fact that service and protocol tasks are executed in a predetermined ordered fashion has led to the concept of hierarchical layered structuring. The complex network design problem is divided into smaller manageable modules. These modules are chosen so that they build on each other. Each layer or level in the structure uses the functions provided by the lower levels, through their interfaces, and provides some new or additional functions to the higher levels above it through its interface.

When a communication network is designed as a layered hierarchical structure and then distributed, the corresponding communication protocol is also layered into a number of hierarchical protocols. Each protocol supports one of the layers in the hierarchical structure. The flow of information through the layers can be categorized by way of interfaces and protocols.

The first approach of a network layered architecture is to consider that communication between two entities involves two kinds of services. First, network services must ensure an end-to-end data transfer: this means dealing with the problems of routing, flow control, error-free transfer of data packets from one node to another, among other issues. Second, once communication is established by the network services, higher-level services are needed in order to ensure that the packets sent and received are understood by both entities. End user functions or protocols are the ones in charge with this higher level of communication handling. Figure 10.1 illustrates this concept of end user vs network protocols. The end user services are provided locally at each end of the communication path, whereas network protocols involve every node along the path.

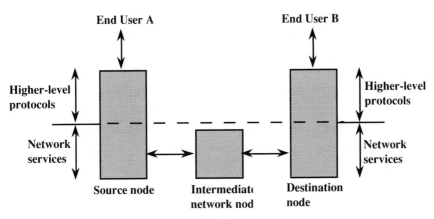

Figure 10.1. Level of protocols in a layered architecture.

The OSI Model follows this concept, with a higher granularity of detail, since end user and network protocols are further broken down into four and three layers respectively, giving rise to a global seven layer architecture, that will be described in detail later in this chapter. The network protocol layer is divided into the Physical, the Data Link, and the Network Layers. The end user protocol level is broken into the Transport, Session, Presentation and Application layers. The OSI Reference Model is summarized in Figure 10.2.

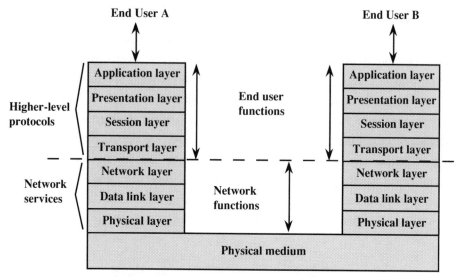

Figure 10.2. The OSI reference model.

From an organizational viewpoint, the OSI network specifications are described in a top-down approach, allowing for three levels of abstraction. The general OSI Reference Model is a framework for building communication systems that can communicate with one another. It describes generic types of architecture objects and their relationships. Many systems may match the OSI architecture. Fewer systems, however, can fit the next level of description, called OSI Service Specifications. Tighter constraints on network systems are defined, dealing with layer interfaces and services without implementation details. The OSI Protocol Specifications are the greatest level of constraints for network systems. They describe precisely the structure of the protocols and what information has to be exchanged for complete communication. Obviously, fewer systems agree with the OSI Protocol Specifications. But as soon as two computers follow the OSI specifications, they are able to communicate with each other. This is the very reason for the creation of such a standard, which does not represent a "best implementation" but rather allows systems built according to the specifications to intercommunicate [20].

10.1.1 Layered Services in the OSI Architecture

Introduced above is the concept of a layer, and the basic principle behind it. It is now clear that any information packet sent from a user A to a user B has to be first processed locally by the seven layers successively. Then the packet is sent through a physical medium, and processed by the lower layers throughout the network. Upon arrival at the node where user B resides, the packet is again successively processed by the layers from the bottom to the top, to be finally delivered to user B. An important feature of a layered architecture is that each layer is independent of the ones it interfaces with. That is, the services provided by a layer to the one above it are independent of the internal implementation of these services. By describing only the interface between layers, the OSI Model allows modifications to be performed internally for any layer.

Each layer communicates with the one directly above it, and the one directly below. Each layer uses the services provided by the layer below, and by processing the information received, provides - possibly extended - services to the layer above. From this viewpoint, no distinction can be made between any layers of the OSI Model, since the services exchanged are similar at any level of the architecture. These services are now described on a generic basis, and each service feature can be applied to any layer of the OSI Model.

Consider a generic layer, called N-layer, communicating with the (N+1)-layer above it. Similarly, call the entity residing in the N-layer an N-entity. The communication between the two layers involves the transfer of user data, as well as control information according to the established protocol. At the source node, an information packet (user and control data) sent by the (N+1)-layer to the N-layer is called a (N+1)-protocol-data-unit (N+1-PDU). Upon reception by the N-layer, this data unit becomes a N-Service-Data-Unit (N-SDU). The N-layer processes this service data unit, appending it to a header containing additional control information used by the next layer (Figure 10.3). This new N-PDU is then sent to the (N-1)-layer. Figure 10.4 summarizes the evolution of a data unit, initially composed of user data, as it goes down through the seven layers. At the receiving end, the inverse operation is performed by the layers, which successively drop the headers associated with the data unit.

The association established between two or more N-entities for communication purposes is called a N-connection. This peer-to-peer communication always follows the same protocol, independent of the layer. It is possible to distinguish three types of interactions between N-entities during the communication session: connection establishment, data transfer, and connection release. The primitives that are exchanged between the layer providing the service and the one using it are only of four types: **Request** (from a service user to ask for a service), **Indication** (from a service provider to indicate that a procedure has been invoked), **Response** (from a service user to complete an invoked procedure), and **Confirm** (from a service provider also to complete a service). For example, during the first phase (connection establishment), the N-entity receives a Connect-Request message from one of the interfacing layers and propagates a Connect-Indication message to the other layer. After a moment, it receives a message from this latter layer, which can be a Connect-Response if the connection has been accepted, or a Disconnect-Request otherwise. The N-layer will then send a Connect-Confirm or a Disconnect-Indication message to the originating layer (Figure 10.5).

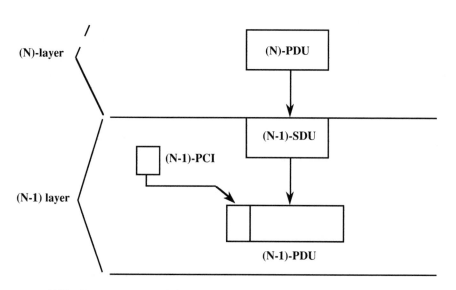

PCI = Protocol-control-information
PDU = Protocol-data-unit
SDU = Service-data-unit

Figure 10.3. Association of a header and a data unit [20].

Once the connection has been established, the data transfer phase can start, and the protocol is as follows: the N-layer receives from one of the layers a Data-Request primitive and forwards a Data-Indication primitive to the next layer (Figure 10.6). The OSI Model does not prescribe a response for each data unit sent, even though this is done at the Data Link Layer by the HDLC protocol (see Section 10.3). The disconnect phase is quite simple: a Disconnect-Request is received by the N-layer, which forwards a Disconnect-Indication primitive to the next layer. Figure 10.7 shows how a connection release can be initiated by either the service user or both service providers.

A somewhat different protocol has to be used in the case of connectionless communication [15]. This type of data transmission uses datagrams, which are data units that are independently routed through the network. Therefore, each datagram must carry full information about its destination. Datagrams which are part of a piece of information are sent in sequence, but may arrive out of order, because they do not follow the same path through the network. The main feature of communication by datagrams is that there is no connection phase required. This implies that the N-entities at each end of the network are aware of the existence and the characteristics of their party. The protocols exchanged between layers concern only the data transfer phase: a Data-Request is received by the N-layer and forwarded as a Data-Indication. Depending upon the implementation, the N-layer may sent a Data-Confirm primitive to the layer that sent the request message.

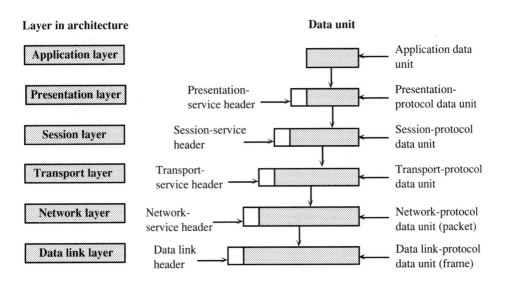

Figure 10.4. Evolution of a data unit through the layers [55].

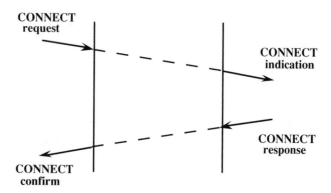

(a) **Successful Connection Establishment**

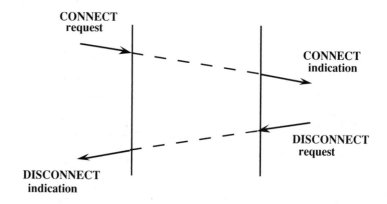

(b) **Rejection**

Figure 10.5. Connection establishment protocols.

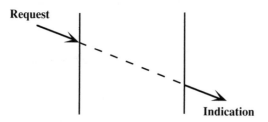

Figure 10.6. Data transfer phase.

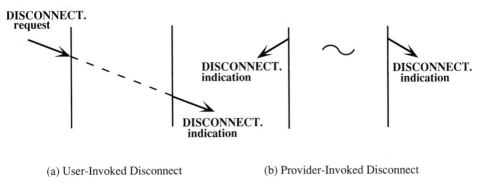

(a) User-Invoked Disconnect   (b) Provider-Invoked Disconnect

Figure 10.7.   Connection release.

10.1.2 Overview of the OSI Layers[*]

As an introduction to the OSI Model, its seven layers were listed: Physical, Data Link, Network, Transport, Session, Presentation and Application. Their basic functions are now described.

The **Physical Layer** is the most fundamental one in the OSI Model. It is the interface to the physical medium and provides standards for electrical, mechanical, and functional transmission parameters.

The **Data Link Layer** deals with procedures and services related to the node-to-node data transfer. Its main purpose is to ensure error-free delivery of data packets from a point-to-point network viewpoint. Hence, it is concerned with such problems as error detection, error correction, and retransmission. However, since the Data Link Layer is highly dependent upon the physical medium, there is not a universal protocol at this level. We can cite HDLC for point-to-point and multipoint connections, as well as IEEE 802.2 with Media Access Control (MAC) and/or Logical Link Control (LCC) for Local Area Networks (LANs). These particular protocols are described in greater detail in subsequent sections.

The **Network Layer** is charged with the task of ensuring that a packet generated at the source arrives at its destination in a reasonable amount of time. Therefore, this layer

---

[*] see references 21, 24, 25, 34–36, 46, 64 and 69.

handles routing procedures as well as flow control functions. It hides the physical implementation of the network from the upper layers, that need not know whether fiber optics, LANs, or satellite communications are used. Hence, it creates a media-independent transmission from the point of view of the upper layers.

The **Transport Layer** is the lowest among the layers that only provide services locally for an end user. It ensures that the lower three layers are providing adequate services for application communication, as far as the transmission medium and the information flow are concerned. The Transport Layer creates a logical transparent "pipe" between end users.

The **Session Layer** controls the communication between applications. It is responsible for ensuring synchronization in data exchange, so that it is performed in an orderly manner. Two-way simultaneous and two-way alternate communication are allowed by the Session Layer.

The **Presentation Layer** deals with the differences in data representation between the communicating applications. A syntax is provided by the layer so that any application can understand the content of the piece of information received.

The **Application Layer** is the only one that does not provide any service to another layer. It deals with the user applications and handles the communication at a semantics level. It is concerned by problems such as interprocess communication, file transfer, virtual terminal and manipulation services, job transfer and broadcast communication.

The next sections are devoted to a more detailed approach and description of each of these layers, particularly the lower ones. Several protocols specified by the OSI Model are also introduced.

10.2 The Physical Layer*

10.2.1 Architecture and Services

As stated earlier, the Physical Layer is the lowest layer addressed in the OSI Model. Its role is to interface with the transmission medium, and provide services to the Data

---

* see references 4, 7, 9, 10, 47, 63 and 64.

Link Layer. It is conceivable that the Physical Layer protocols should be as medium-independent as possible, for adaptability and flexibility purposes. However, no implementation of these protocols has followed this concept, mainly because of the little intelligence the physical relays (such as modems and transducers) have. But physical relays have their capabilities continuously improving, and it will be possible to have a modem check the bit stream structure with regard to the protocol used and make whatever decision is necessary for enforcing accurate data communication.

The Physical Layer provides various services to the Data Link Layer [47]:

1. physical connection between Data Link entities;

2. physical service data units: amount of physical interface data whose identity is preserved from one end of a physical connection to the other;

3. data circuit identification: communication path between physical entities, as well as the facilities necessary for the transmission of bits on this path.

Also provided for are sequencing, fault condition notification, and quality of service parameters. Each direction of transmission (bit stream from user A to user B and vice versa) in the case of a (full or half) duplex communication is specified in the Physical Layer service definition.

The ISO has worked in parallel with the CCITT on Physical Layer standards [4]. While the specifications made by each organization differ slightly, it is interesting to mention that CCITT has presented more than fifteen years ago a physical layer recommendation for the communication between a terminal and the network equipment it is directly linked to (X.21 recommendation). In the CCITT terminology, the former is called a Data Terminal Equipment (DTE), whereas the latter is know as a Data Circuit terminating Equipment (DCE). It is important to mention that X.21, which is not a standard but only a recommendation, establishes a point-to-point synchronous circuit between a DTE and a DCE. Two pairs of connectors, one for data and control information transfer from the DTE to the DCE, and the other from the DCE to the DTE, ensure balanced communication. In fact, the X.21 recommendation not only specifies a Physical Layer implementation, but also deals with features concerning the Data Link and the Network Layers.

The next sections focus on issues that concern the Physical Layer: mechanisms for network access, and protocols for contention-access. The following is not part of the strict OSI model description but is heavily related to the Physical Layer and its characteristics. Other examples of protocols concerning the Physical Layer and their various implementations will be given in Chapter 13.

10.2.2 Network Access Mechanisms: Polling*

The Physical Layer, as well as the Data Link Layer, is concerned by mechanisms created to access a network. Even though there is no particular OSI specification for these mechanisms, it is interesting to have some ideas on issues where the Physical Layer is involved. There are basically two types of access mechanisms: **polling** and **random-access**. The latter is described in the next section. Polling involves the central control of all nodes in the network. It is a form of master-slave(s) operation in which the master queries each slave to determine if it has anything to say. If the answer is affirmative, the slave is either given permission to transmit or scheduled to transmit at a later time. Although several polling schemes are known, two prominent procedures form the basis from which all others are derived. They are hub polling and roll-call polling.

10.2.2.1 Hub Polling

A network of terminals can operate with hub polling only if the network is properly configured. Each slave node is serially connected to another slave node until a path is completed back to the master node, thus creating a "hub" configuration (Figure 10.8(a)). The master node initiates a polling request to the first slave node on the hub that passes the request to the next slave node if it has nothing else to communicate. This process continues until the request has completed the hub cycle. The cycle is broken and must be restarted anytime a slave node needs to communicate with the master node. This places slave nodes on the far end of the hub at a disadvantage since each slave node on the hub preceding any other slave node lessens the probability that the request will reach that slave node. Also, any time a slave node on the hub fails, the hub is broken and must be reconfigured in order to continue operation. The additional complexity for recovering from such a failure must be shared by each slave node on the hub, thus increasing expense. These disadvantages make the hub polling procedure less popular than other schemes, even though a cost savings in communications circuitry may be realized. An alternative, referred to as roll-call, is not dependent on the hub configuration for operation.

---

* see references 10, 30, 49, 55, 64, 65 and 68.

(a) Hub polling network

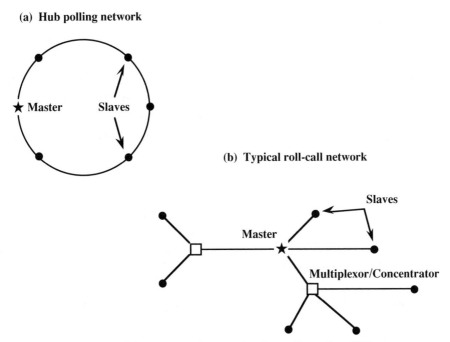

(b) Typical roll-call network

Figure 10.8. Master-slave network configuration [55].

10.2.2.2 Roll-Call Polling

The concept of roll-call polling, while on the surface is quite simple, adds a dimension of flexibility for meeting changing demands more typical of most data-processing environments. The terminal node need only be cognizant that it is a slave node of a network and be able to appropriately respond when requested by the master node. The roll-call terminal is considerably less complex when contrasted to the hub terminal that must also be able to reconfigure itself in the event that an adjacent slave node fails. Complexity for the master has the potential for great increases depending on the particular roll-call scheme used. A simple roll-call network configuration might appear as in Figure 10.8(b).

The simplest of roll-call procedures is to establish a predefined communication sequence of nodes that will ensure that each slave node has an opportunity to communicate with the master node and only then proceed to another cycle. The interval of delay between sequential transmissions is constant. Suppose, however, that some slave nodes require communications more frequently than other nodes or perhaps less frequently but with a higher priority. Both of these conditions warrant special consideration by allocating more opportunities for communications than would otherwise be typical. This, of course, decreases the opportunities that the remaining terminals have to communicate with, and so a careful balance between the needs of the users against available resources must be made. This additional alternative allows a slave node, for example node A in Figure 10.9, to receive a roll-call more frequently than the other slave nodes. Changes to the roll-call algorithm occur only in the master node.

Alternative	Roll call sequence
1	*ABCDEABCDEABC* •••
2	*ABCADEABCADEA* •••
3	*ABCADE* ••• *BCDEBEA* •••

Figure 10.9. Demonstration of alternate roll-call algorithms [55].

A third alternative, an extension of the second technique, dynamically alters the roll-call algorithm to reflect the changing demand in the network. Thus, because of changing conditions in the network, the master node must retain historical data for each slave node's communication needs. Frequent statistical analysis of the historical data allows the master node to alter the roll-call algorithm dynamically to reflect current need. Once again it is the master node that must become more intelligent. In general, roll-call procedures have been widely accepted and efficiently applied to a variety of applications involving the master-slave relationship.

10.2.3 Contention-Access Protocols[*]

Contention-access protocol procedures, popular because of their simplicity, will function adequately only if the user has a sufficient understanding of the demands made of the network. In pure contention, a user will arbitrarily transmit information hoping that no other user will interfere with the transmitted signal. More sophisticated schemes require that transmission begin only on prespecified intervals, thereby lowering the

---

[*] see references 1, 5, 40, 49, 55, 58, 64, 65 and 68.

likelihood of interference. The contention-access procedures require a mechanism to acknowledge the receipt of a signal. If this acknowledgement does not occur, the originator assumes that the transmitted data was interfered with and retransmits until such acknowledgement does occur.

Contention access is applicable to both land-line and radio media, but is more useful in radio communications where frequency allocation constraints require users to share frequencies. A contention-access network using the radio-frequency (RF) medium will typically have several users that will need to communicate data with other users on the same network. An example of a network well known for contention-access procedures is the ALOHA network that connects terminals in Hawaii with various locations in the mainland.

10.2.3.1 ALOHA Packet Radio

The ALOHA packet radio system uses a contention-access scheme that allows users to transmit information randomly on two 100 kHz channels assigned for use by the net. These channels reside at 407.35 and 413.475 MHz frequencies. Whenever two packets try to occupy the channel at the same time, there is collision and both messages are garbled. A collision between packets is assumed if no acknowledgement is received after a reasonable interval of time. The collision may have occurred on the original data or on the acknowledgement signal transmitted by the receiving terminal. The result is the same for the originator in either case: the data are retransmitted until a valid acknowledgement is received. The receiving terminal must retain a record of recently received packets to prevent processing a second identical packet in the event the original acknowledgement was not received by the originator. The receiving terminal continues to acknowledge each received packet even if it has been previously received correctly.

With the assumptions that message generation is an independent and random process, the efficiency of the ALOHA contention-access protocol can be derived. Abramson [1] uses the assumptions to derive the utilization factor and shows that a maximum channel utilization of 18.4 percent can be achieved using the ALOHA contention-access procedure. It is certainly not difficult to understand that this represents a poor utilization of a resource, the RF medium. Efforts to improve the efficiency of the ALOHA scheme resulted in the slotted ALOHA contention-access protocol.

10.2.3.2 Slotted ALOHA

In the slotted ALOHA contention scheme packets can be transmitted only at the start of a predefined clock interval. This limits the times in which collisions can occur. If a collision is going to occur, it will occur only at the beginning of the clock interval. Thus, random collisions do not occur in a transmission once communication is started.

The slotted ALOHA contention-access scheme functions properly only if all terminals in the network are synchronized. This requires a fairly accurate clocking mechanism in addition to the procedure for implementing this synchronization. In general, one terminal node is designated as the master node, and it is with this node that all other nodes synchronize themselves. Once the network is synchronized, each node can reestablish fine synchronization each time a signal is detected, whether the signal is intended for that terminal or not. Synchronization is then maintained as long as some terminal transmits within the accuracy of the time interval. Once synchronization has been achieved, the individual data clocks will maintain sufficient accuracy in the UHF range (400 to 500 MHz) for 4 to 5 hours. Thus, once the network is synchronized, or will remain synchronized without further transmission for up to 5 hours.

Restricting the start of a transmission to a predetermined time interval decreases the probability of collision by about one-half. The maximum utilization rate, using load-factor analysis, for a slotted ALOHA channel increases to 36.8 percent [40]. The probability of collision can be even further reduced by issuing a warning signal that a lengthy transmission is being initiated. And because all nodes listen to the network during intervals in which they are not transmitting, the issuance of several preamble warning signals can be used to indicate either a long transmission or a high-priority message. These preambles, which may include an indication of the time interval to be reserved, can be used to inhibit transmissions from other nodes automatically. While the probability of collision is greatly minimized, this technique does increase the probability of wasting transmission slots. Not only are opportunities for successful simultaneous transmissions excluded, but a certain amount of the bandwidth will be used by the preamble sequence. An obvious trade-off must be made by the networks using such contention access methods.

10.3 The Data Link Layer*

10.3.1 Introduction: Data Link Layer Services

The Data Link Layer was one the first layers to be identified, and protocols for this layer have been around for a long time. As stated earlier, the Data Link Layer is charged with ensuring correct and reliable delivery of data on a point-to point or multipoint basis between nodes in the network. The term data refers to user data as well as network control information. The physical media involved in the transmission can be of any type, coaxial cable, twisted pair, fiber optics, microwave or satellite channels. The interconnecting links may be of various types: public or private point-to point, multipoint, switched or non-switched.

The services provided by the Data Link Layer to the Network Layer immediately above it follow the OSI generic architecture. Four standard primitives are used for this interaction: **Request, Indication, Response** and **Confirm**. Three types of services are offered by the Data Link Layer: **connection establishment, data transfer**, and **connection release**. For any of these services, say for example communication establishment, the four primitives are involved: **Connection Request** (from the Network Layer to the Data Link Layer at the source node, i.e. the originating end of the physical link), **Connect Indication** (from the Data Link Layer to the Network Layer at the destination node, which is located at the end of the virtual link, and not necessarily where the actual end user resides), **Connect Response** (opposite from Indication), and **Connect Confirm** (opposite from Request).

10.3.2 Functionality of the Data Link Layer

Multiple functions are required from the Data Link Layer, to fulfill both user needs and communication medium needs. As identified in [19], they are:

Initialization: In order to establish a connection between entities, control frames

---

* see references 3, 8, 10, 28, 42, 46, 64 and 66.

need to be exchanged to ensure that both parties are ready for communication.

Identification: In the case of a multipoint communication, or when numerous end points exist in the network, identification of a particular sender or receiver needs to be performed, generally through a data link addressing mechanism.

Synchronization: The Data Link Layer needs to be able to recognize the "meaning" of the bit sequence delivered by the Physical Layer. This implies being able to detect the beginning and end of a frame, and may involve character synchronization, i.e. having the receiver decoding mechanism in phase with the transmitter encoding mechanism.

Segmenting and Delimiting: The information to be transmitted in generally of various length. Since it is not reasonable to transmit long bit sequences because of error occurrences, neither cost effective to send series of small sequences, long messages have to be fragmented and an optimum message size has to be used for better efficiency.

Transparency: User data have to be transparent to the Data Link Layer, that is, the Layer should never interpret user data as Data Link control information. Mechanisms, such as bit stuffing, have to be implemented to avoid such confusion.

Flow Control: The transmitter and the receiver need not have the same data rate capabilities, therefore the flow of incoming data at the receiver may submerge its processing capacity. Thus, the Data Link Layer has to provide some flow control schemes.

Error and Sequence Control: Transmission over a noisy physical link implies that errors might be present in the frames received. Mechanisms have to be implemented to detect and possibly correct these errors. With sequencing schemes, provisions can be made for frame retransmission.

Abnormal Condition Recovery: A loss of frame acknowledgement may create a situation where either end waits for the other to transmit data or control frames. Procedures, such as timeout schemes, must be implemented to recover from situation such as deadlocks or illegal bit sequences.

Termination: In a similar way as the initiation process, the Data Link Layer must be able to gracefully terminate a connection, for instance making sure that all data have been properly received.

Every Data Link protocol encompasses most of the features above. There exist many different such protocols, which are either character-oriented or bit-oriented. A character-oriented data link protocol uses special control characters, called transmission control characters, to frame user data, whereas a bit-oriented protocol uses positionally located control fields instead of a set of control characters for supervisory control [18]. A particular bit-oriented protocol, named High Level Data Link Control (HDLC) protocol, has been defined in the OSI reference by the International Standards Organization. HDLC is described in details in Section 10.3.4. The next section presents the basic principles of a character-oriented data link control protocol.

10.3.3 Character-Oriented Data Link Control Protocol*

These protocols are still very popular for two way alternate, and even two-way simultaneous communication. They are not as flexibles and adaptable as bit-oriented protocols which emerged in the late 1970s. Character-oriented protocols can be implemented on dedicated or switched lines, full- or half-duplex links, and with point-to-point or multipoint communication. Many standards have been designed, but they have generally the same features. The American National Standard Institute (ANSI) created the protocol X3.8, ISO designed a very similar protocol known as "Basic Mode," IBM uses Binary Synchronous Communication (BSC), which also resembles the two previous ones, and Digital Equipment Corporation uses Digital Data Communications Message Protocol (DDCMP). DDCMP is not a pure character-oriented protocol since it uses a combination of characters and byte-length fields for supervisory control. Therefore, DDCMP is called a byte-count protocol.

The structure of any character-oriented data link protocol must provide means of segmenting information, since a long message has a low probability of arriving error-free at the destination node. Provision must be made to identify the beginning and the end of the information being transferred. Also, it is important that an addressing mechanism be implemented to identify a particular sender or receiver, especially for multipoint communication. A protocol has to provide methods for error checking as well as error recovery mechanisms whenever an error is detected by the receiver. Finally, character

---

* see references 6 and 18.

synchronization between the sender and the receiver must also be ensured by the protocol.

Listed below in Table 10.1 is a subset of the code set of the ANSI protocol, X3.4 [18]. Note that the ISO standard "Basic Mode," as well as IBM's BSC, have the same subset of control characters. This subset concerns control characters known as communication characters. For purposes of clarity, we define a message as being an ordered sequence of characters carrying information, and a block as being a unit of data transmission. Therefore, a block may contain a messages or part of it, whereas a message is composed of one or more blocks.

Table 10.1 ANSI protocol code set.

SOH (Start of Heading): Identifies the beginning of "heading information" containing addressing and routing information.
STX (Start of Text): Indicates the beginning of the part which constitutes the text of the message. It is often used to terminate a header started with SOH.
ETX (End of Text): Indicates the end of the text portion of the message.
EOT (End of Transmission): Is used to terminate a transmission and clear the connection.
ENQ (Enquiry): Is used to request a response from another station, asking for station status or identification.
ACK (Acknowledgment): Acknowledges the error-free reception of a block of information.
DLE (Data Link Escape): Changes the meaning of several of the following control characters.
NAK (Negative Acknowledgment): Is transmitted from the receiver to the sender to indicate the reception of an erroneous block of information, which therefore must be retransmitted.
SYN (Synchronous Idle): Is used to establish and maintain (especially during idle periods) character synchronization between the sender and the receiver.
ETB (End of Transmission Block): When a message is divided into different blocks, ETB indicates the end of the total message.

It is also possible that the data being transmitted contains control characters, such as those defined above. Therefore, the protocol must provide a way of achieving transparency for user data. This is done by preceding each control character by the DLE character. For example, DLE STX initiates the transparent mode for the following data block. Also, DLE ETB ends a block of transparent data. If a DLE character is part of the user message, then DLE will be transmitted. When the receiver reads the sequence, it automatically deletes one DLE.

Error detection is made possible by appending to each block of data additional and redundant information: a block check character (BCC) is calculated from the block and appended before transmission. The receiver checks if the BCC is coherent with the rest of the block. If not, an error is detected, and a NAK is issued, requesting retransmission. Techniques used for the calculation of the block check character are explained in details in Appendix IV.

Figure 10.10 shows how a message is split into multiple blocks, each of which is transmitted with various control characters appended to it.

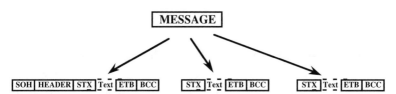

Figure 10.10.   Message transmission with a character-oriented protocol.

Character-oriented data link protocols have serious drawbacks. Their efficiency is limited by the fact data and control characters have to be distinguished, either at the hardware or at the software level. User data transparency is not achieved with simple mechanisms. Also, error checking is not performed on supervisory sequences, which may create problems when erroneous control sequences are not detected by the receiver. Finally, character-oriented protocols have a rigid structure, and provide little expandability. This is the motivation for bit-oriented data link protocols, which were designed after character-oriented ones, and have more powerful features. The ISO standard bit-oriented protocol, HDLC, is presented in the next section.

10.3.4 High Level Data Link Control (HDLC) Protocol*

There exist many protocols for communication control at the data link layer, and many of them are very similar. HDLC has become the ISO standard protocol, and its specification is very close to that of the protocol designed by the American National Standard Institute (ANSI), called Advanced Data Communications Control Procedures (ADCCP). These two protocols are so similar that the following description of HDLC is also a valid presentation of ADCCP. IBM created its own data link protocol, called Synchronous Data Link Control (SDLC), which highly influenced the design of HDLC. As a consequence, many features of SDLC, to be presented in Chapter 11, are included in HDLC.

Since a data link control protocol has to fit various types of network communications, such as point-to-point, multipoint, two way simultaneous or alternate, HDLC was designed to support three different modes of data transfer [11]. They are:

Normal Response Mode (NRM) This mode is suited for a centralized environment, where secondary stations are required to receive explicit permission from the primary station, in order to initiate transmission. This happens generally in the case of polled multipoint communication.

Asynchronous Response Mode (ARM) This mode resembles the previous one, i.e., it also concerns centralized environments. The role of a secondary station is still a passive one, however, the secondary station is allowed to initiate a transmission without permission from the primary station. This mode is better suited for communication between a single primary station and a single secondary station.

Asynchronous Balanced Mode (ABM) With this mode, two logically equal stations are able to communicate: each station has the ability to initialize the link, activate the other station, control its own flow of data and initiate an error recovery mechanism. ABM therefore provides fully balanced, independent data transfer between two stations.

---

* see references 10, 22 and 64.

10.3.4.1 HDLC Frame Format

The typical frame format for HDLC is show in Figure 10.11. A frame has six fields, respectively called flag (F), address (A), control (C), information (I), frame check sequence (FCS), and another flag (F). Each field of the frame is now described in detail.

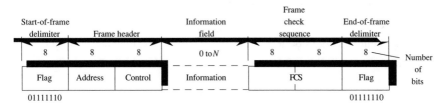

Figure 10.11. HDLC frame.

Flag Sequence The flags at the beginning and the end of the frame are the same 8-bit pattern 01111110. These flags are used to synchronize the receiver with the frame. Therefore, the receiver constantly checks for such pattern. However, if user data contains such a pattern, the receiver may be confused and consider the user data 01111110 as the terminating flag. This problem is solved by data transparency and is addressed by HDLC using a technique called bit stuffing: each time the transmitter notices five consecutive ones in the user data, it automatically inserts a zero after this series of ones. Hence, no 6-bit sequence of ones can occur, except in the terminating flag. The receiver, in turn, checks the bit following a sequence of five ones. If it is a zero the bit is dropped, since the receiver knows that this bit has been added by the transmitter. If it is a one, the receiver knows that the current sequence is the flag sequence. In the case where seven consecutive ones are received, the frame is erroneous, and an error recovery mechanism is initiated.

Address Field The address field (A) contains the identification of either the sending or receiving station. For a command frame, the field contains the address of the destination, whereas response frames have the address of the sending station. Therefore, with NRM and ARM, the address field identifies the secondary station, and with ABM, it identifies the source of the frame.

Control Field At this point, a distinction needs to be made between different types of command or response frames. HDLC defines three frame types:

information transfer (I-frame), **supervisory** (S-frame) and **unnumbered** (U-frame). S-frames and U-frames have no information field and are used only for control functions. I-frames carry user data. The control field varies depending upon the type of frame, but is always eight bits long. Figure 10.12 illustrates the different types of control fields. The first bit identifies an I-frame if it is a zero. If it is a one, then the first two bits are considered: 10 identifies an S-frame, and 11 identifies a U-frame. Bits number 2, 3, 4 in the control field of an I-frame contain a frame sequence number N(S), which uniquely identifies the frame. This is done so that the receiver can manage an ordering of the frames, even if some of them are erroneous and need to be sent again.

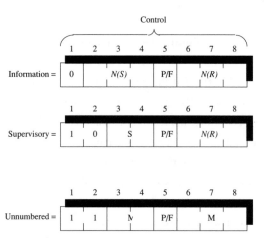

Figure 10.12. Control fields for the various types of frames.

The P/F bit (5th bit) is present in every type of control field for checkpoint purposes. It allows a response frame to be logically associated with its corresponding command frame. The P/F bit can be viewed as the P bit of the command frame and the F bit of the response frame. A response to a P = 1 must be F = 1. With NRM, this mechanism is useful for polling: P = 1 is used to poll the secondary station to which the frame is addressed. With ARM and ABM, a station having received a command frame with P = 1 will set the F bit of the next appropriate frame to 1.

I-frames and S-frames both carry a receive sequence number N(R) to perform error detection and recovery: it indicates that N(R)-1 I-frames have been correctly received, by indicating that I-frame number N(R)-1, and any preceding I-frame, has been received without error. With this field, the sender indicates that it is waiting for I-frame number N(R). HDLC supports a 3-bit sequence number field, allowing a mod 8 frame numbering. The field can be extended to seven bits thus supporting mod 128 numbering.

Bits 3 and 4 of S-frames are used also for error detection and recovery purposes. 00 means Receiver Ready (RR): it indicates that the receiver is able to accept I-frames, it can also acknowledge N(R)-1 frames. 10 means Receiver Not Ready (RNR): it is used to indicate to the sending node that the receiver cannot accept an I-frame, for example because of buffer shortage. 01 means Reject (REJ): it requests the retransmission of all the I-frames commencing with the frame indicating by N(R). REJ is commonly sent to clear a RNR condition.

Unnumbered frames (U-frames) do not carry any sequence number. They provide additional link control functions. The five M bits in the control field allow the specification of up to 32 different link control frames.

Information Field This field consists of user data, and can be of any desirable length. As stated earlier, only I-frames have an information field. Transparency for user data is provided by bit stuffing, as explained above.

Frame Check Sequence This 16-bit field is used to detect if a frame is erroneous. It contains a Cyclic Redundancy Check (CRC) performed on the content of the address, control and information fields. The transmitter calculates the FCS field from the previous ones, and the receiver checks if the received FCS matches the A, C, and I fields received. If not, the frame is declared in error, and the receiver will ask for a retransmission. CRC mechanisms are explained in Appendix IV.

Various types of U-frames are used in HDLC. Several of them are listed below:

Unnumbered Acknowledgment (UA): used by either node on the link to acknowledge the receipt of an Unnumbered command frame.

Set Asynchronous Balanced Mode (SABM): sets the send and receive sequence number to 0 and any outstanding frames are not acknowledged. For the normal response and asynchronous response modes, there exist similar U-frames, respectively SNRM and SARM.

Frame Reject Response (FRMR): used by either node to indicate an error condition where the retransmission will not help recovery. The FRMR frame has a 3 byte information field: the first byte is a copy of the control field of the frame being rejected; the second byte contains the send and receive sequence number; the third byte indicates the type of error detected, i.e., invalid control field, or invalid information field, or information field too large (buffer overflow), or invalid receive sequence number.

Disconnect (DICS): indicates to the receiving node that the sending node is terminating the communication link. The receiver will send a UA command, then enter the link-down state after a predefined time interval. This predefined time period must have its value greater than the time taken to transmit a maximum size frame (dictated by buffer sizes) and to receive two similar frames plus the propagation time of the signals through the physical link.

10.3.4.2   Example of Data Transmission

Figure 10.13 is an example of data transmission between two stations A and B. Both stations send data to each other. The communication is first established by station A which sends a SABM(B) to reset the parameters and set the Communication mode. Station B replies with an Unnumbered Acknowledgment UA(A). The stations are now ready to exchange information frames. Station A starts by sending three consecutive I-frames, numbered with N(S) = 0, N(S) = 1 and N(S) = 2, and with N(R) set to 0 since station A hasn't received any frame from station B yet.

Station B, in turn, sends two I-frames, with its own sequence numbers N(S) = 0 and N(S) = 1, requesting an acknowledgment upon reception by station A by setting the P/F bit to P = 1. In the mean time, it acknowledges the three frames received with N(R) = 3 (frame #3 is expected). When station A receives the frames, even though it has not any I-frame to send, it immediately sends the acknowledgment requested with an RR frame having the P/F bit set to F = 1. The exchange of information frames continues between stations A and B, until station B rejects two I-frames numbered 5 and 6. The error recovery mechanism functions as follows: station B sends a REJ frame indicating that it rejected all frames starting from and including frame number N(R) = 5. Therefore, station A retransmits these two frames, requesting an immediate acknowledgment by setting the P/F bit to P = 1. Upon reception, station B sends an RR frame with its P/F bit set to F = 1 to confirm correct receipt of the frames 5 and 6.

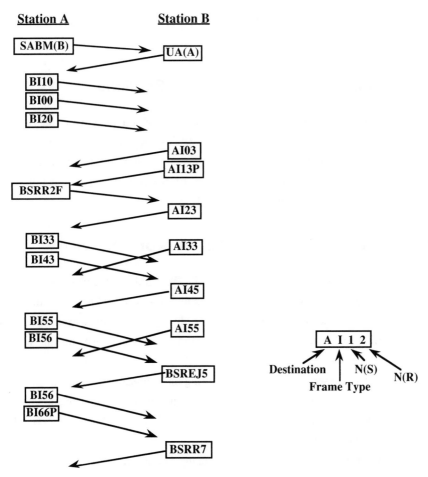

Figure 10.13. Example of communication with the HDLC protocol.

10.4 The Network Layer*

The Network Layer is the upper layer of the ones which are involved with communication at each node of the network. This layer is charged with routing and flow control in the network. At the source or destination nodes, it provides services to the

---

* see references 10, 12, 31, 43, 50, 60–64, 68 and 70.

Transport Layer. A description of the features of the Network Layer as presented in the OSI Model is given below [72].

10.4.1 Introduction: OSI Network Services*

At each end of the communication path, the Network Layer provides services to the Transport Layer. The specification of these services, and of the communication at the network layer in general, is independent of the actual transmission facilities on which the communication relies. There exists two different types of services: connection-oriented network services and connectionless network services.

10.4.1.1 Connection-Oriented Network Services

Following the generic recommendation of the OSI model, three phases occur during a Network Connection: a connection establishment phase, which sets the various communication parameters, a data-transfer phase, during which data is exchanged in either direction with provisions for flow control, and a release phase, during which the communication terminates.

There is only one service element used during the connection establishment phase, N-CONNECT. It can be used to negotiate the quality of service during the connection. With an N-CONNECT, up to 128 bytes can be transmitted by a Network Service User to specify connection parameters.

Several service elements can be used during the data-transfer phase:

N-DATA provides for the transfer of user data, also called Network Service Data Units (NSDU). There is no limit imposed on the size of the data transmitted.

N-DATA-ACKNOWLEDGE is used to acknowledge the receipt of a Data Unit. An acknowledgment for any unit is not compulsory, but the sender can request it, and thus, a N-DATA-ACKNOWLEDGE is sent back upon reception of the NSDU. The negotiations occurring during the connection establishment phase can decide whether or not a systematic acknowledgment mechanism is to be used.

---

* see references 10, 12, 51 and 64.

N-EXPEDITED-DATA provides a means for the transfer of NSDUs of limited size (up to 32 bytes) which can bypass normal N-DATA NSDUs and be accepted at the receiving end, even though normal NSDUs are refused by the receiver because of flow control on the path. This service element is useful to indicate exception conditions; it also provides an expedited service to the transport layer. This service element is also optional and is generally negotiated during the connection establishment phase.

N-RESET is used for resynchronization purposes. All outstanding NSDUs that have not been received or acknowledged yet are discarded.

The Release Phase consists of a single service element, called **N-DISCONNECT**. This element terminates the communication, and can be invoked at any time during any phase, either by the service users or the service provider. Data being transferred during the release phase may be lost.

10.4.1.2 Connectionless Network Services

The principle of connectionless communication consists of the transmission of independent data units between two entities without any connection establishment or maintenance phase. A single service element, called N-UNITDATA provides a means of transferring an NSDU without using an existing logical network connection. All N-UNITDATA NSDUs are independent of one another.

10.4.2 Internal Structure of the Network Layer*

As stated above, the Network Layer is involved at both ends of the communication path between entities, as well as at each intermediate node on this path, like the Data Link and the Physical Layers. The functions the Network Layer performs at an intermediate node system are dependent upon the subnetwork which lies between nodes. Subnetworks directly connected to a given node are not necessarily homogeneous, which means that the methods of access, the services provided and the functions performed by these subnetworks may be different. As a consequence, the functions performed by the

---

* see reference 25.

Network Layer are divided into two categories: **subnetwork-independent** and **subnetwork-dependent** functions. The former include relay and routing functions, which imply address interpretation, among other route selection criteria. Subnetwork-independent convergence (SNIC) functions are also part of the former category. They represent functions that are performed by peer Network Layer entities without the need of information about the actual subnetworks used in the communication.

Subnetwork-dependent convergence (SNDC) functions and Subnetwork access (SNAC) functions belong to the subnetwork-dependent category. SNDC functions are used to make the appropriate transformation from subnetwork service and the corresponding generic service used or provided by the SNIC function. SNAC functions deal with the interface protocol of the subnetwork. Figure 10.14 is a summary of the internal architecture of the Network Layer as defined by the OSI Model.

The OSI description of the Network Layer has been made to allow internetworking. Depending upon the level of heterogeneity of the subnetworks involved in the entire network, the influence and the role of subnetwork-dependent and independent functions will vary. Interconnection of heterogeneous facilities generally creates very complex internetworking processes, and the OSI Model is an attempt at standardizing such processes. A detailed description of the CCITT recommendation X.25, which resides at the Network Layer, is given in Chapter 13.

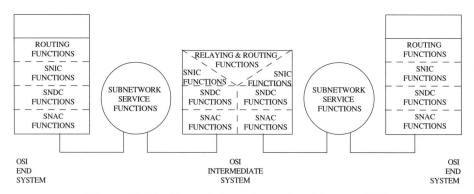

Figure 10.14. Network layer internal architecture [72].

10.5 The Transport Layer*

As discussed earlier in this chapter, the Transport Layer is the lowest of the end user layers. It is only involved at each end of the communication path between users. It uses the services provided by the Network Layer and in turn provides service to the Session Layer. The purpose of the Transport Layer is to ensure transparent and reliable end-to-end data transfer for the Session Layer and the layers above. The Transport Layer deals with the problem of offering services to a completely network-independent layer, using the highly network-dependent services of the Network Layer. The Session Layer requires a certain quality of service for parameters such as: [41] throughput, transit delay, residual error rate, communication establishment delay, resilience, cost, security, and priority. The existence of many of these parameters depend upon the actual underlying network.

Because of the variety of types of data transfer, the International Standards Organization has defined five classes of transport services, named Class 0, 1, 2, 3 and 4:

Class 0 is the simplest: a transport protocol of class 0 must be able to establish an end-to-end communication, and to segment messages during data transfer, but it is not required to perform any error recovery.

Class 1 is also a simple class, but provides for basic error recovery mechanisms.

Class 2 is the first one which has multiplexing capabilities. Class 2 protocols assume a reliable network connection.

Class 3 provides error recovery mechanisms as well as multiplexing capabilities.

Class 4 represents the most elaborate class of transport services. It provides for full error detection and recovery mechanisms. Because it ensures a higher level of reliability, it is intended for low-quality network media.

10.5.1 Transport Services

The OSI definition of the services at the Transport Layer follow the same pattern as described in Section 10.1.1. However, the OSI model specifies parameters that must be

---

* see references 14, 16, 26, 36, 37, 44, 46, 48, 52, 53, 57, 62, 64, 67 and 69.

associated with each service primitive. Table 10.2 presents these primitives with their parameters for the three phases occurring during a communication: connection establishment, data transfer, and connection release.

Table 10.2 Transport layer service primitives [41].

Primitive	Parameters
T_CONNECT.request	(Called Address, Calling Address,Expedited Data Option, Quality of Service, TS User Data)
T_CONNECT.indication	(Called Address, Calling Address,Expedited Data Option, Quality of Service, TS User Data)
T_CONNECT.response	(Quality of Service, Responding Address, Expedited Data Option, TS User Data)
T_CONNECT.confirm	(Quality of Service, Responding Address, Expedited Data Option, TS User Data)
T_DATA.request	(Transport Service User Data)
T_DATA.indication	(Transport Service User Data)
T_EXPEDITED_DATA.request	(Transport Service User Data)
T_EXPEDITED_DATA.indication	(Transport Service User Data)
T_DISCONNECT.request	(TS User Data)
T_DISCONNECT.indication	(Disconnect Reason, TS User Data)

It is important to notice that during the data transfer phase, there is no confirmation of delivery by the receiving end. This is because the Transport Layer is totally responsible for correct delivery of user data. As far as the primitive parameters are concerned, the Expedited Data option is negotiated between the two Transport Layer peers: it allows the transfer of up to 16 bytes which bypass normal data end-to-end flow control. The Quality of Service parameter carries the user requirements for throughput, transit delay, reliability and priority of the connection to be established. The Transport Service User Data (TS-User Data) parameter used in the connection establishment and release primitives allow the transfer of up to respectively 32 and 64 bytes of user data. Figure 10.15 summarizes the exchange of primitives involved in the connection establishment phase, where the Transport Layer is the service provider.

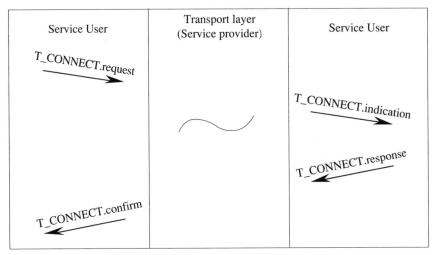

Figure 10.15. Connection establishment [41].

The state diagram given in Figure 10.16 illustrates the various states a transport endpoint may reside in, depending on the primitive sent or received. Arrows leaving a state indicate the invocation of a primitive. Any transport endpoint can be idle (state 1) if it is not connected to any other transport peer. Upon reception of a CONNECT-REQUEST or CONNECT-INDICATION, the endpoint enters the connection establishment phase (respectively states 2 and 3). State 4 corresponds to the data transfer phase.

10.5.2 Transport Protocols

The basic protocol data unit used at the Transport Layer is called Transport Protocol Data Unit (TPDU). There are two types of TPDUs: control and data. A TPDU is created from a Transport Service Data Unit (TSDU) issued by the Session Layer directly above the Transport Layer. Segmenting a TSDU or appending two TSDUs may be necessary to match protocol defined data unit sizes.

As presented in the introduction, five classes have been defined in the protocol specifications. Different classes have generally different options. Both classes and options are negotiated through the connection establishment primitives. The classes of services have been designed to fit three types of Networks Connections: type A Networks

Connections are those which have an acceptable rate of signaled failures (like Disconnect or Reset). Network Connections of type B have an acceptable residual error rate, but have an unacceptable rates of signaled failures. Finally, Network Connections with residual error rate not acceptable to the Transport Service User are defined as being of type C.

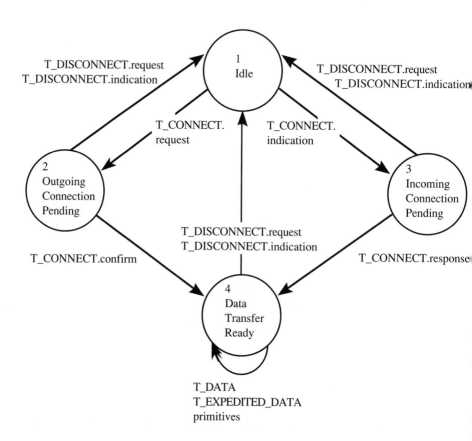

Figure 10.16. State transition diagram for a transport layer endpoint [62].

Such descriptions do not represent formal definition, since they depend on the quality of service required. For example, a Network Connection may be of type C for a certain application, and will be of type B for another one. However, Network Connections of type A are generally associated with Classes 0 and 2. Effectively, class 0 provides few functions to establish a connection, transfer data with segmentation if necessary, and report errors. Class 2 provides all functions available in class 0, plus multiplexing capabilities, as well as flow control and expedited data transfer. With Class 2 services, it is also possible to exchange user data during the connection establishment phase.

Type B connections are associated with Classes 1 and 3 (Class 1 provides the same functions as Class 2 except for multiplexing, Class 3 is an enhancement of Class 2 allowing recovery from network signaled errors), whereas type C connections are related to Class 4 services. These services could detect a lost TPDU or a duplicated TPDU.

There exist different types of TPDUs which are listed below (the amount of data that can be carried with the TPDU is indicated between parentheses).

CR: connection request (up to 32 bytes)

CC: connection confirm (up to 32 bytes)

DR: disconnect request (up to 64 bytes)

DC: disconnect confirm (none)

DT: data (the maximum length is negotiated)

AK: acknowledgment (none)

ED: expedited data (up to 16 bytes)

EA: expedited acknowledgment (none)

ER: TPDU error (none)

All TPDUs have the same basic structure: they are divided into four parts. The first one is Length Indicator Field (LI). The second part is a fixed one which contains the code of the TPDU and other control information. The third part has variable length, however, the total length of the first three parts cannot exceed 254 bytes. The variable part can contain checksum information for error detection (especially for Class 4 services) and various other information depending on the type of the TPDU and the class of service concerned. Figure 10.17 presents the format of a CR TPDU. The four bits called CDT (for credit allocation) are used for flow control, discussed next. The Source-reference field contains an identification of the entity requesting a connection. The field called Class/Option represents information concerning Class and option parameters: the first four bits describe the class (0010 for Class 2, 0100 for Class 4) and the last four bits provide flow control options.

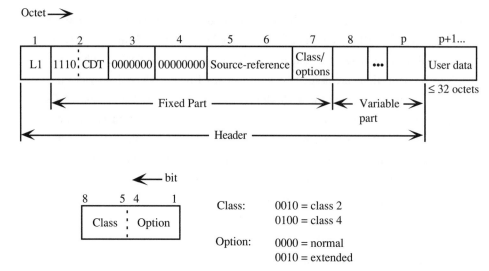

Figure 10.17. Format of a connection request (CR) TPDU [62].

10.5.3 Flow Control

Flow control is performed on an end-to-end basis at the Transport Layer. Class 4 uses a sliding window mechanism shown in Figure 10.18. At each end of the connection, the peer uses two variables: a Lower Window Edge (LWE) and an Upper Window Edge (UWE). The LWE is initially set to zero as no TPDU has been sent, and the UWE is set to the initial window credit negotiated through the CR TPDU (parameter CDT). The LWE is incremented as Data-TPDUs are sent. The UWE is incremented as acknowledgments are received for Data-TPDUs sent. Therefore, the window size (UWE-LWE) represents the number of Data-TPDUs that can be sent before an acknowledgment is necessary. The flow is stopped when as soon as the UWE reaches the credit limit value (CDT). Note that the credit limit can be modified by AK-TPDUs, which contain a CDT field.

This concludes the overview of transport protocols. A description of a non-OSI protocol, called Transmission Control Protocol (TCP), is given in Chapter 12. TCP was developed for the Department of Defense and the ARPA network. TCP has become very popular among American universities, companies and government.

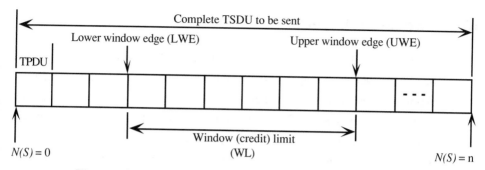

Figure 10.18. Transport layer flow control mechanism [29].

10.6 Upper Layers: Session, Presentation, Application*

The discussion about the Transport Layer was an introduction to the concept of end-to-end services used in peer to peer communication. The upper three layers of the OSI model deal in a similar way with end-to-end services. The actual implementation of the underlying network is hidden from the user, and the upper three layers focus on application processes and communication. Until recently, the definitions for these layers were still imprecise, and few systems have actually implemented OSI standards at the application, presentation or session levels. However, the last few years have seen a significant growth in the interest towards development of standardization at these layers, which are software-intensive.

Recall that the Session Layer is charged with ensuring organized and structured interaction between application processes. The Presentation Layer deals with syntax issues: it provides a unique, abstract way of representing exchanged data. The Application Layer deals with the semantics of the messages: it provides means for accessing distributed processing services. The following sections discuss in greater detail the OSI descriptions of each of these layers.

---

* see references 2, 13, 33, 38, 54, 64, 66 and 69.

10.6.1 Session Layer*

The services provided by the Session Layer to an application process through the Presentation Layer, include the capability of establishing a session connection (which is a logical communication path) with another application entity. Synchronization points during a communication must also be provided, as well as the possibility of resuming a dialogue after occurrence of an error. Dialogue interruption must also be possible, with options for resuming the dialogue later. Finally, the Session Layer has to be able to inform the Presentation Layer using its services that network exceptions may have occurred.

Various primitives are used to perform the session services [23,39]. S-CONNECT is used to establish a connection, and during this phase, the parameters of communication are negotiated. The data transfer phase is mainly based on the S-DATA primitive. Like the Transport Layer, the Session Layer may have to segment or concatenate the Session Service Data Units (SSDUs) passed by the Presentation Layer, in order to form Session Protocol Data Units (SPDUs) with adequate format. The data transfer phase involves the notion of synchronization. When an error is detected, provisions need to be made to reset the session connection to a previously known and agreed point in communication. This is done through synchronization primitives called S-SYNC-MAJOR and S-SYNC-MINOR. They allow the Session Service user to mark a precise point in the data flow, with acknowledgement of the receiver. Upon detection of an error in the data flow, the resynchronization primitive S-RESYNCHRONIZE allows both users to go back in the dialogue flow to the previous synchronization mark, and start the communication again, discarding all data that was sent after the synchronization mark. As a summary, the data transfer phase allows the Session Service user to transfer data, control the dialogue, insert synchronization marks in the data flow and resynchronize the communication due to previous synchronization marks.

The Session Layer also provides two modes of data transfer: normal and expedited. The primitives associated with these modes are S-DATA and S-EXPEDITED-DATA. Finally, the connection release phase can be invoked with the use of the S-RELEASE primitive. The Session Layer defines tokens that are exchanged between peers to control the exclusive right of performing certain functions. These tokens can be transferred from one end to the other thanks to the primitives S-TOKEN-GIVE and S-TOKEN-PLEASE.

---

* see references 2, 13, 33, 38, 54, 64, 66 and 69.

Errors can be detected by two different entities: the Session entity (the service provider) or the Presentation entities (which represent the Session service users). In the case of an error detected by the Session entity, this entity can send two primitives to the user: S-P-EXCEPTION-DATA, which will start an error recovery mechanism, or S-P-ABORT, which aborts the current session connection. In this latter case, part of the service user data might be lost. If the error is detected by one service user (Presentation entity), the same types of primitives can be sent to the other user: S-U-EXCEPTION-DATA to attempt an error recovery, or S-U-ABORT to abort the current session connection.

10.6.2 Presentation Layer

The description of the Presentation Layer is very similar to that of the Session Layer. The Presentation Layer ensures that the transfer of data can be made at a syntactically abstract level. The Presentation Layer provides a language (i.e. the protocol) that allows systems to communicate about the syntax of Application Layer information exchanges [32].

The functions exercised by the Presentation Layer include: the negotiation of an appropriate syntax for the exchange of Presentation Service user data; the translation of the message from the initial syntax to the new selected abstract syntax; the translation of the message received from the exchange syntax to the one utilized by the other Presentation Service user; as well as functions corresponding to the ones described in the Session Layer for synchronization purposes and token management.

The primitives designed for the Presentation Layer are as follows: P-CONNECT, P-DATA, P-EXPEDITED and P-RELEASE. They are used for the three communication phases, in a similar way as for the Session Layer primitives. P-SYNC-MAJOR, P-SYNC-MINOR and P-RESYNCHRONIZE are used for synchronization purposes as provisions for error recovery. P-TOKEN-GIVE and P-TOKEN-PLEASE are also part of the primitive specifications of the Presentation Layer. They reflect the Session Layer services and are used to control the right of a peer to exercise certain functions. Figure 10.19 summarizes the exchange of primitives between the Presentation Service Users and the Presentation Service Provider during a typical communication, as well as how these primitives relate to the Session Layer primitives.

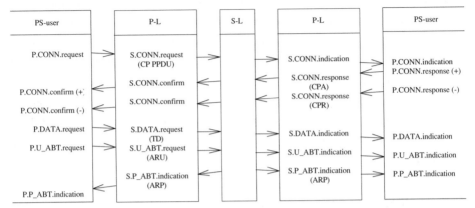

Figure 10.19. Presentation and session layer primitives [29].

A new concept, that of context, is introduced at the Presentation Layer: a presentation context is represented by the association of a user abstract syntax with a transfer syntax. For a single instance of communication between peers, there may be multiple contexts, therefore two primitives are designed to define and select a particular association of a user syntax and a transfer syntax: P-CONTEXT-DEFINE and P-CONTEXT-SELECT. The use of a current context is terminated by the primitive P-CONTEXT-SELECT, which allows an already defined context to become active in the communication.

There is currently only one standard transfer syntax. It is called the basic encoding rule for Abstract Syntax Notation 1 (ASN.1). It is used by the application recommendation X.400, discussed in Chapter 13. However, the complexity of ASN.1 makes it difficult for systems to conform to this standard.

10.6.3 Application Layer

The Application Layer is the highest one in the OSI Reference Model. It is the layer which contains the most functionality, and on which the biggest amount of work is currently being done. The Application Layer is designed to offer a "framework to design Application Layer protocols for communication among distributed application processes which are cooperating to perform information processing" [3]. The Application Layer deals with semantic issues associated with the messages (the meaning of the information exchanged) whereas the Presentation Layer deals with syntax issues.

In order to use the services provided by the lower layers, an application process interfaces with a facility called User Element (UE). The UE in turn interfaces with the Application Entity (AE), which deals directly with the Presentation Layer (Figure 10.20). Through an Application Entity, an application process can access service primitives, called Application Service Elements (ASE). Each ASE represents a set of functions supporting a certain application. Initially, the Application Layer was designed to perform two types of service, differentiated by the type of their service elements: Common Application Service Elements (CASE) and Specific Application Service Elements (SASE). The former was defined to provide general services such as setting or terminating an association between application processes. These services are independent of the nature of the application itself. The latter class of service elements was designed to provide information transfer capabilities, that is, application-dependent services. Today, however, less distinction is made between CASE and SASE, and both are often referred to as ASE.

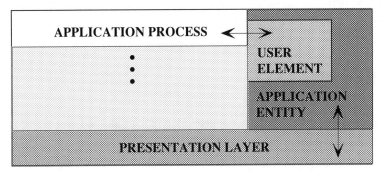

Figure 10.20. Structure of the application layer [59].

Among the protocols currently being studied for the Application Layer are the following:

File transfer, access and management (FTAM): provides for data storage and retrieval by an application process from an information storage facility, without requiring the process to know about the actual file system implementation.

Virtual Terminal Protocol (VTP): allows an application process to access and communicate with another application process in a remote system in a standard way, which does not depend upon the actual systems involved in the communication.

Message Handling System (MHS): provides a facility for exchanging electronic mail between users or application processes. Such electronic messages can be text, facsimile, graphics, voice, or any combination of these.

Job Transfer and Manipulation (JTM): provides to an application process the possibility of submitting a job for execution to a remote application process. A job is defined as an activity resulting from some specific information processing requirements. This implies the concepts of job submission, job monitoring and job manipulation.

Several protocols have started to emerge for the Application Layer. CCITT has presented recommendations for this layer, known as X.400, as part of ISDN and X.400 recommendations. This X.400 standard is discussed in Chapter 13. It is now obvious that the Application Layer is very important in the OSI Model, and the standards community is highly concerned with defining more precise structures and specifications for this layer.

10.7 Exercises

10.1   Explain the difference between network protocols and end user protocols and their respective roles in data communication.

10.2   What is the goal of the OSI Reference Model? Describe the seven OSI Layers. For each layer, explain how is involved in the data transfer process.

10.3   In the OSI terminology, what is an N-entity? an N-Service-Data-Unit? an N-Protocol-Data-Unit? Explain the notions of service user and service provider.

10.4   What are the service primitives involved in the connection establishment phase at the level of a generic OSI layer? Draw a figure for the cases of successful and unsuccessful phases. Do the same for the data transfer phase and the connection release phase.

10.5   What is a datagram? Explain the concept of connectionless data communication. What is the impact of communicating with datagrams on the exchange of service primitives between OSI layers?

10.6   For each of the seven layers of the OSI Model, describe an error that can occur.

10.7 For the following errors that occur in data transmission, point out what layer is responsible for it and explain how such an error can be possible.

    (a) Reception of a frame (data link data unit) out of sequence.

    (b) Duplicated packets are received at the same destination.

    (c) A series of various bits are set to 1 during transmission.

    (d) D packet arrives at the wrong destination.

10.8 Discuss the similarities and differences of polling and addressing; include grouping, unit selection operation in half-duplex system, action in the case of possible responses, higher-priority terminals.

10.9 Several advantages and disadvantages exist between the hub poll and roll-call procedures that warrant consideration of one or the other schemes. List and describe advantages and disadvantages for each. Describe an operating environment for each procedure and indicate the appropriateness of one over the other.

10.10 Why is contention access more appropriate to the RF medium that it is to land-lines? Contrast the advantages and disadvantages of contention-access over polling.

10.11 Consider the ALOHA contention-access procedure. Presume an average arrival rate of Lambda packets per second and that the transmit interval is fixed at t seconds. Channel utilization can then be expressed as the ratio of the time the channel is in actual use to the total time it is available for use. Make the necessary additional assumptions and derive channel utilization for ALOHA contention-access.

10.12 For the Data Link Layer, explain why synchronization is important and why packet segmenting or appending is sometimes necessary.

10.13 What is the difference between a character-oriented protocol and a bit-oriented protocol?

10.14 What is meant by "transparent" data communication? How is this done in character-oriented protocols? In bit-oriented protocols? Give example systems of each.

10.15 In the HDLC protocol specification, what is the role of the control fields $N(R)$ and $N(S)$. Explain how error recovery is made possible by the use of these fields, as well as the P/F bit.

10.16 In a similar way as Figure 10.13, describe three examples of data communication using the HDLC protocol, using NRM, ARM and ABM. Be precise as to what control field is sent. Assume that errors occur in communication, and show how error recovery is achieved by HDLC.

10.17 Explain the concept of expedited data in the context of the Network Layer. Describe a circumstance justifying the use of expedited data.

10.18 At the Transport Layer, what are the different classes of transport services, and how are they related to the various types of networks (A,B,C)? Justify the association of a class of service to a type of network.

10.19 How is flow control performed at the Transport Layer? Show by example how the window variables are incremented and how the flow of data can be stopped.

10.20 Explain how synchronization primitives used at the Session and Presentation Layers can help recover from error in dialogue. What is the purpose of the TOKEN-GIVE and TOKEN-PLEASE primitives? With a diagram, show how the exchange of primitives is performed between the Application, Presentation and Session Layers, for each the three phases in data communication (consider two end users and the upper three layers at each endpoint).

10.8   References

1   Abramson, N., "The ALOHA System: Another Alternative for Computer Communications." *Proceedings of the FICC*, 1970.

2   Bachman, C., and Canepa, M., *The Session Control Layer of an Open System Interconnection*. International Organization for Standardization OSIC/TG 6/79-10, 1979.

3   Bartoli, P. D., "The Application Layer of the Reference Model of Open System Interconnection." *Proceedings of the IEEE, 71*, 12, December 1983.

4   Bertine, H. U., "Physical Level Protocols." *IEEE Trans. on Comm., 28*, 4, April 1980.

5   Binder, R.; Abramson, N.; Kuo, F.; Okinaka, A.; and Wax, D., "ALOHA Packet Broadcasting--A Retrospect." *Proceedings, National Computer Conference*, 1975.

6   Black, U., "Data Link Controls: The Great Variety Calls for Wise and Careful Choices." *Data Communications*, June 1982.

7   Black, U., *Physical Interfaces*. Arlington, VA: Information Engineering
        Educational Series, 1986.

8   Black, U., *Computer Networks: Protocols, Standards and Interfaces*. Englewood
        Cliffs, NJ: Prentice-Hall, 1987.

9   Black, U., *Physical Level Interfaces and Protocols*. Washington, DC: IEEE
        Computer Society Press, 1988.

10   Black, U., *Data Networks: Concepts, Theory, and Practice*. Englewood Cliffs,
        NJ: Prentice-Hall, 1989.

11   Carlson, D. E., "Bit-Oriented Data Link Control Procedures." *IEEE Trans. on
        Comm.*, *COM-28*, 4, April 1980.

12   Cerf, V., and Kristein, P. T., "Issues in Packet-Network Interconnection."
        Proceedings of the IEEE, November 1978.

13   Chandy, K., and Ramamoorthy, C., "Rollback and Recovery Strategies for
        Computer Programs." *IEEE Trans. on Computers*, June 1972.

14   Chapin, A., "Connectionless Data Transmission." *Computer Communication
        Review*, April 1982.

15   Chapin, A. L., "Connections and Connectionless Data Transmission."
        Proceedings of the IEEE, *71*, 12, December 1983.

16   Chou, W. (ed.), *Computer Communications, Vol. I: Principles*. Englewood
        Cliffs, NJ: Prentice-Hall, 1983.

17   Chou, W. (ed.), *Computer Communications, Vol. II: Systems and
        Applications*. Englewood Cliffs, NJ: Prentice-Hall, 1985.

18   Conard, J. W., "Character-Oriented Data Link Control Protocols." *IEEE Trans.
        on Comm.*, *COM-28*, 4, April 1980.

19   Conard, J. W., "Services and Protocols of the Data Link Layer." *Proceedings of
        the IEEE*, *71*, 12, December 1983.

20   Davies, D. W., "The Control of Congestion in Packet Switching Networks."
        *Proceedings of the Second ACM/IEEE Symposium on the Optimization of Data
        Communication Systems*, Palo Alto, CA, October 1971.

21   Day, J. D., and Zimmerman, H., "The OSI Reference Model." *Proceedings of
        the IEEE*, *71*, 12, December 1983.

22   ECMA-61. HDLC, European Computer Manufacturers Association, August
        1979.

23   Emmons, W F., and Chandler, A. S., "OSI Session Layer: Services and

Protocols." *Proceedings of the IEEE, 71*, 12, December 1983.

24   Folts, H., "Coming of Age: A Long-Awaited Standard for Heterogeneous Nets."
        Data Communications, January 1981.

25   Folts, H., *OSI Workbook*. Vienna, VA: OMNICOM, Inc., 1983.

26   Garlick, L.; Rom, R.; and Postel, J., "Reliable Host-to-Host Protocols:
        Problems and Techniques." *Proceedings, Fifth Data Communications
        Symposium*, 1977.

27   Green, P., "An Introduction to Network Architectures and Protocols." *IEEE
        Trans. on Comm.*, April 1980.

28   Green, J. H., "Microcomputer Programs Can Be Adapted for Data Network
        Designs." *Data Communications*, April 1986.

29   Halsall, F., *Data Communications, Computer Networks, and OSI* (2nd edition).
        Reading, MA: Addison-Wesley, 1988.

30   Hammond, J. L., and O'Reilly, J. P., *Performance Analysis of Local Computer
        Networks*. Reading, MA: Addison-Wesley, 1986.

31   Heggestad, H. M., "The Testbed for Evaluation of Network Routing and Control
        Techniques." *MICOM-85*, October 1985.

32   Hollis, L. L., "OSI Presentation Layer Activities." *Proceedings of the IEEE,
        71*, 12, December 1983.

33   Honeywell Information Systems, Inc. *Distributed Systems Architecture*, CT37-
        01, 1982.

34   Institute for Electrical and Electronic Engineers. *IEEE Project 802, Local
        Network Standards*, 1983.

35   International Organization for Standardization, "Information Processing Systems-
        -Open Systems Interconnection--Basic Reference Model." DIS 7498, 1984.

36   International Organization for Standardization. *Basic Reference Model for Open
        Systems Interconnection*, DIS 7498, 1983.

37   International Organization for Standardization. *Connection Oriented Transport
        Protocol*, DP 8073, 1983.

38   ISO 8822/3. *OSI: Presentation Service/Protocol Specification*, 1985.

39   ISO 8326/7. *OSI: Session Service/Protocol Specification*, 1985.

40   Kleinrock, L., and Lam, S., "Packet Switching in a Slotted Satellite Channel."
        NCC, AFIPS Conference Proceedings, Vol. 42, 1973.

41   Knightson, K. G., "The Transport Layer Standardization." *Proceedings of the

IEEE, 71,12, December 1983.

42   Linnington, P. F., "The Virtual Filestore Concept." *Computer Networks*, February 1984.

43   Lippman, R., "New Routing and Preemption Algorithms for Circuit-Switched Mixed Media Networks." *MILCOM 85*, October 1985.

44   Markley, R. W., *Data Communications and Interoperability*. Englewood Cliffs, NJ: Prentice-Hall, 1990.

45   Martin, J., *Teleprocessing Network Organization*. Englewood Cliffs, NJ: Prentice-Hall, 1970.

46   Martin, J., and Kavanaugh, C. K., *SNA: IBM's Networking Solution*. Englewood Cliffs, NJ: Prentice-Hall, 1987.

47   McClelland, F. M., "Services and Protocols of the Physical Layer." *Proceedings of the IEEE, 71*, 12, December 1983.

48   McFarland, R., "Protocols in a Computer Internetworking Environment." *Proceedings, EASCON 79*, 1979.

49   McQuillan, J. M., and Cerf, V. G., *A Practical View of Computer Communications Protocols*. Washington, DC: IEEE Computer Society Press, 1978.

50   Narendra, K. S., and Srikantakumer, P. R., "A Learning Model for Routing in Telephone Networks." *SIAM Journal of Control and Optimization, 20*, 1, January 1982.

51   National Bureau of Standards. *Features of Internetwork Protocols*, ICST/HLNP-80-8, July 1980.

52   National Bureau of Standards. *Features of the Transport and Session Protocols*, ICST/HLNP-80-1, March 1980.

53   National Bureau of Standards. *Specification of a Transport Protocol for Computer Communications*, ICST/HLNP-83-1 to ICST/HLNP-83-5, January 1983.

54   Neumann, J., "OSI Transport and Session Layers: Services and Protocol." *Proceedings, INFOCOMM 83*, 1983.

55   Pooch, U. W.; Greene, W. H.; and Moss, G. G., *Telecommunications and Networking*. Boston, MA: Little, Brown and Company, 1983.

56   Pouzin, L., and Zimmerman, H., "A Tutorial on Protocols." *Proceedings of the IEEE*, November 1978.

57   Rauch-Hindin, W., "Upper-Level Network Protocols." *Electronic Design*, March 3, 1983.

58   Roberts, L., "ALOHA Packet System With and Without Slots and Capture." *Computer Communications Review*, April 1975.

59   Roux, E., "OSI's Final Frontier: The Application Layer." *Data Communications*, January 1988.

60   Schwartz, M., *Computer-Communication Networks Design and Analysis*. Englewood Cliffs, NJ: Prentice-Hall, 1977.

61   Schwartz, M., and Stern, T. E., "Routing Techniques Used in Computer Communication Networks." *IEEE Trans. on Comm.*, April 1980.

62   Schwartz, M., *Telecommunication Networks, Protocols, Modeling and Analysis*. Reading, MA: Addison-Wesley, 1987.

63   Sherman, K., *Data Communications: A User's Guide*. Reston, VA: Reston Publishing Company, Inc., 1985.

64   Stallings, W., *Data and Computer Communications*. New York, NY: MacMillan Publishing Company, 1985.

65   Stallings, W., *Handbook of Computer Communications Standards*, Vol. I. New York, NY: MacMillan Publishing Company, 1987.

66   Stallings, W., "Here is One Way to Get a Close Estimate of a Data Link's Efficiency." *Data Communications*, October 1986.

67   Sunshine, C., "Transport Protocols for Computer Networks." In Kuo, F., *Protocols and Techniques for Data Communications Networks*. Englewood Cliffs, NJ: Prentice-Hall, 1981.

68   Tanenbaum, A. S., *Computer Networks*. Englewood Cliffs, NJ: Prentice-Hall, 1981.

69   Tanenbaum, A. S., "Network Protocols." *Computing Surveys*, December 1981.

70   Unsoy, M., and Shanahan, T., "X.75 Internetworking of Datapac and Telenet." *Proceedings, Seventh Data Communication Symposium*, 1981.

71   Zimmerman, H., "OSI--Reference Model--The ISO Model of Architecture for Open System Interconnection." *IEEE Trans. on Comm.*, April 1980.

72   Ware, C., "The OSI Network Layer: Standards to Cope with the Real World." *Proceedings of the IEEE, 71*, 12, December 1983.

11

PROTOCOLS AND EXAMPLE NETWORKS

11.1 Introduction*

Since the OSI Model was not released before the early 1980s, many manufacturers have implemented their own network architecture which generally does not exactly match the OSI requirements. This is the case with IBM, which designed its own System Network Architecture (SNA), and Digital Equipment Corporation (DEC), which implemented Digital Network Architecture (DNA). Although created a decade before the OSI Model recommendation, these networks have many features that are very close to it. Both networks rely on a layered architecture with seven layers which have slightly different specifications. The philosophies underlying both networks are different. SNA was initially designed to meet the requirements of mainframe-oriented IBM customers, whereas DNA users were more minicomputer-oriented. It is important to keep these ideas in mind when looking at SNA and DNA architectures, since the first architectural design always influences the evolution of a network. Today, however, there is no longer such a distinction between the two networks, since they provide a much broader range of services than they did initially. Both share many networking goals; each offers a common user interface and user transparent network routing and management functions. The following sections describe both architectures, comparing their respective features with those of the OSI Model.

---

* see references 2, 13–15, 25, 32 and 33.

11.2 IBM's System Network Architecture*

IBM announced the creation of its System Network Architecture (SNA) in 1974. It was aimed at allowing communication between users of IBM products. Since IBM customers were highly mainframe-oriented, SNA was designed as a centralized network, with a mainframe as the host and many remote terminals connected to it. SNA has evolved towards greater flexibility and can now be considered as a decentralized network. The objectives of SNA include [24]:

Distributed Processing Orientation   This provides for the possibility of running distributed processing applications using distributed information storage resources.

Unification   All IBM's teleprocessing products use the same set of protocols. New products have to be compatible with these standard protocols.

Reliability   This is achieved by the use of high-performance error recovery procedures.

Ease of modification   A layered architecture such as SNA helps for modular modifications at a specific layer without forcing changes at the other layers.

Versatility   The protocols and formats used by SNA must allow for interconnection of various hardware and software products.

The next sections are devoted to a more detailed presentation of SNA, and its layered organization. The components involved in SNA are introduced, several service primitives are presented, and the functionality of IBM's Data Link Layer control protocol (SDLC) is explained.

11.2.1 SNA vs OSI Layered Organizations

SNA is built around a seven layer concept. The functionality of these layers is very close to that of the layers of the OSI Model. Figure 11.1 illustrates the comparison between SNA and OSI layers. The seven SNA Layers are called Physical Control, Data

---

* see references 17, 23, 24, 32 and 36.

Link Control, Path Control, Transmission Control, Data Flow Control, Function Management, and Application. As shown in Figure 11.1, there is not a one-to-one mapping between the SNA layers and the OSI layers. However, the same global functions are performed, even though they may be exercised at different layers, depending upon SNA or OSI.

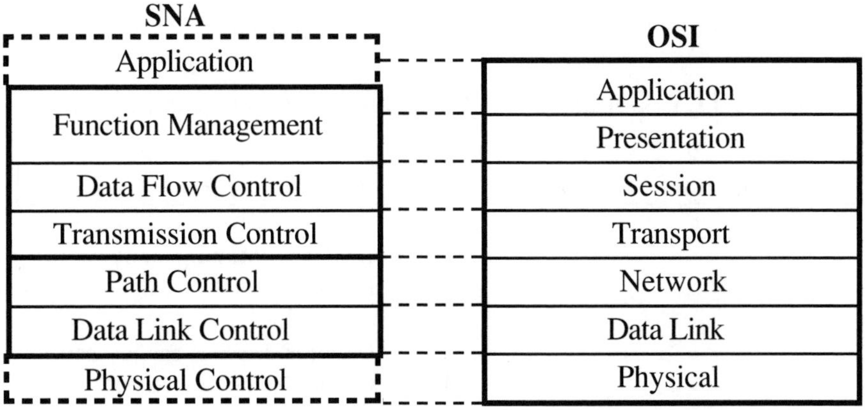

SNA	OSI
Application	
	Application
Function Management	Presentation
Data Flow Control	Session
Transmission Control	Transport
Path Control	Network
Data Link Control	Data Link
Physical Control	Physical

Figure 11.1. OSI and SNA layered organizations [24].

The Physical Layer is not exactly part of the SNA definition. It is considered as applying to international standards totally similar to that of OSI. As a reminder, the Physical Layer is responsible for the transmission of bit streams between two Data Link endpoints over a physical medium. The SNA Data Link Control Layer is responsible for the error-free transmission of data over a physical connection. SNA's HDLC counterpart is called Synchronous Data Link Control (SDLC) protocol, and it will be described in Section 11.2.4. The definition of SNA's Path Control Layer is such that it encompasses features of OSI's Data Link and Network Layers. It is responsible for routing and sequencing messages.

The upper layers in SNA resemble those of OSI. The Transmission Control Layer is analogous to the Transport Layer and is charged, among other services, with virtual route control (which is an equivalent of quality of service concepts in OSI) and global sequence numbering. The Data Flow Control Layer corresponds to the OSI Session Layer and is charged with ensuring integrity of the end-to-end data flow. The services provided include establishing and managing dialogue between end users. There is no Application Layer per se in the SNA architecture, since SNA leaves the responsibility of managing applications issues to the applications interfacing to SNA. However, the Function Management Layer includes many features of both OSI Presentation and Application Layers. Services at the Function Management Layer include presentation services (formatting of data streams, syntax issues), application-to-application services (e.g. synchronization), maintenance services, management services, and configuration services (e.g. activation and deactivation of nodes and lines, maintenance of network names and addresses). Table 11.1 is a summary of the comparison between OSI and SNA organizations.

Table 11.1 Comparison of OSI and SNA services [24,32].

SNA Function Management	OSI Application Layer
	Application Management • Initiation and termination of applications Deadlock detection and prevention • Checkpoint and recovery•
Configuration Services • Activation and deactivation of nodes and links • Program loading and dumping • Reconfiguration and restarting of the network • Maintenance of network names and addresses • Maintenance of NAU and link status	**System Management** • Activation and deactivation of network resources • Loading of programs • Reconfiguration and restart of network • Monitoring and reporting of network status
Maintenance and Management Services • Identification and analysis of failures • Collection and test results and error statistics	• Detection, diagnosis and recovery from errors • Monitoring and reporting of network statistics

Table 11.1 Comparison of OSI and SNA services (cont.)

Session Services	Application Services
• Activation and deactivation of sessions	• Determination of availability of internal partners
• Verification of LU authority	• Establishment of authority
• Conversion of network names to network addresses	• Identification of intended partners
• Determination of protocols and rules	• Identification of dialogue discipline, responsibility for error recovery and procedures for control of data integrity
• Determination of virtual route	• Determination of quality of service
• Initiation of request queuing	• Determination of adequacy of resources

Application-to-Application Services	
• Program-to-program communication	• Information transfer
• Synchronization	• Synchronization
	• Agreement on privacy mechanisms
	• Authentication of intended partners
	• Determination of cost allocation methodology
	• Identification of constraints on data syntax

	OSI Presentation Layer

Session Presentation Services	
• Formatting of data streams	Data representation syntax
• Compression and compaction of data	• Transformation between syntaxes
• Formatting of data display	Data formatting syntax

Table 11.1 Comparison of OSI and SNA services (cont.)

SNA Data Flow Control	OSI Session Layer
• Determination of send/receive mode	• Management of transmission interaction
• Grouping of messages into chains	• Providing quarantine services
• Identification of logical units of work with brackets	• Brackets (candidate for extension)
• Control of request/response processing	• Synchronization
• Interruption of data flow, on request	• Stop-and-go transmission (candidate for extension)
	• Expedited data flow
	• Expedited reporting
	• Security (candidate for extension)

SNA Transmission Control	OSI Transport Layer
• Session level pacing	• Flow control
• Sequence numbering	• Sequencing of data units
• Request/response headers	• Error detection and recovery
• Multiple sessions sharing virtual routes	• Multiplexing and splitting of transport connections into network connections
• Encryption	• Monitoring quality of service
	• Conversion of transport addresses into network addresses
	• Segmenting, blocking and concatenation of data units

Table 11.1 Comparison of OSI and SNA services (cont.)

SNA Path Control	OSI Network Layer
• Sequencing of message units	• Providing data units in sequence
	• Interruption of data flow, on request
• Sharing of explicit route by multiple virtual routes	• Multiplexing
• Segmenting and blocking of message units	• Segmenting and blocking of data units
• High-priority transfer	• Expedited data flow (optional)
	• Reset services (optional)
	• Release of network connection, on request

	OSI Data Link Layer
• Routing	• Use of multiple physical connections for data link connection
• Sequencing of message units across transmission group	• Synchronization of receipt of data units
• Virtual route pacing	• Flow control

SNA Data Link Control	
• Creation of link headers and trailers	• Delimiting data as frames
• Transmission of data over a physical circuit	• Transfer of data over a physical link
• Error detection and correction	• Error detection and correction

11.2.2 SNA network structure[*]

SNA defines an end user as being a human terminal user, an application program, a device (e.g. a printer), and so on. End users have access to the network through access points called Logical Units (LUs). A Logical Unit provides various services to an end user such as establishing a session with another LU, or multiple LUs; also, a single LU can support multiple end users. To represent the actual devices involved in the

---

[*] see references 1, 2, 6, 10, 20, 21, 24 and 32.

communication process, SNA defines Physical Units (PUs). A PU is charged with managing the resources, such as communication links, at the node of the network it resides in. Finally, System Service Control Points (SSCPs) are defined as being entities which are able to establish and control the interconnections between network users. An SSCP manages all the resources within a part of the network, called a domain. A Network Addressable Unit (NAU) is any entity of the three types defined above: Logical Units, Physical Units, and System Service Control Points are all Network Addressable Units. An NAU has a network address, which allows any user to access its resources.

SNA defines seven types of Logical Units, numbered from 0 to 7 (there is no LU of type 5), depending upon the service capabilities. LU type 6 has greatly evolved over the years, and its latest version is known as LU 6.2. A Logical Unit of type LU 6.2 has the widest range of capabilities of all the Logical Units. LU 6.2 has been implemented to support Advanced Program-to-Program Communication (APPC).

SNA also defines two types of network nodes depending on their capabilities: subarea nodes and peripheral nodes. A peripheral node can only communicate with the subarea node it is directly attached to, whereas a subarea node can access any peripheral node attached to it, as well as other subarea nodes in the network. Peripheral nodes, also called cluster controllers, are further classified into type 1 and type 2 nodes. Type 2 nodes have greater processing capabilities than type 1 nodes, and they are generally user-programmable, where type 1 nodes are not. Nodes of both types will be now considered as Physical Units and referred to as PU-T1 and PU-T2. These nodes can have many user terminals attached to them. Subarea nodes are also of two types, numbered 4 and 5. A subarea node of type 5 contains a System Service Control Point, and it is generally a large computing system such as an IBM 30XX. A PU-T5 is commonly referred to as a host. A subarea node of type 4 (PU-T4) does not contain an SSCP and is usually contained in a Communication Controller (IBM 37X5). Figure 11.2 is an example of network structure comprising a host (PU-T5), a communication controller (PU-T4) and several cluster controllers (PU-T1, and PU-T2).

Domains were introduced above with the concept of SSCP. An SNA domain comprises various types of PUs, several subareas, each controlled by one subarea node, and systematically an SSCP. The SSCP is responsible for the control of all the resources within its domain. Multiple domains are allowed in an SNA network. Figure 11.3 illustrates a general SNA network with multiple domains.

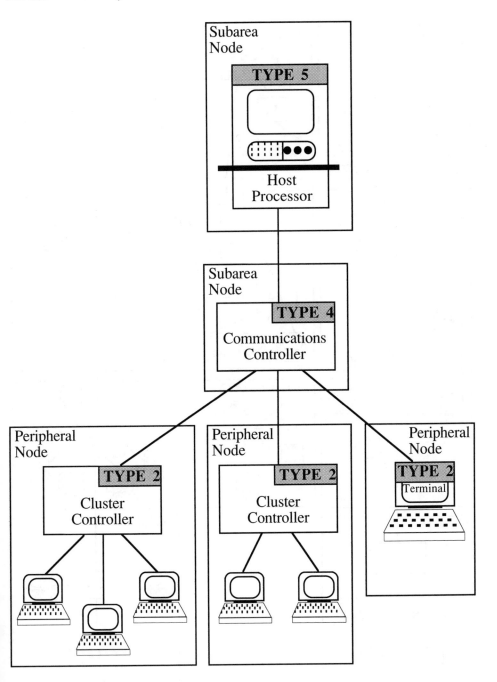

Figure 11.2.   SNA network structure [24,32].

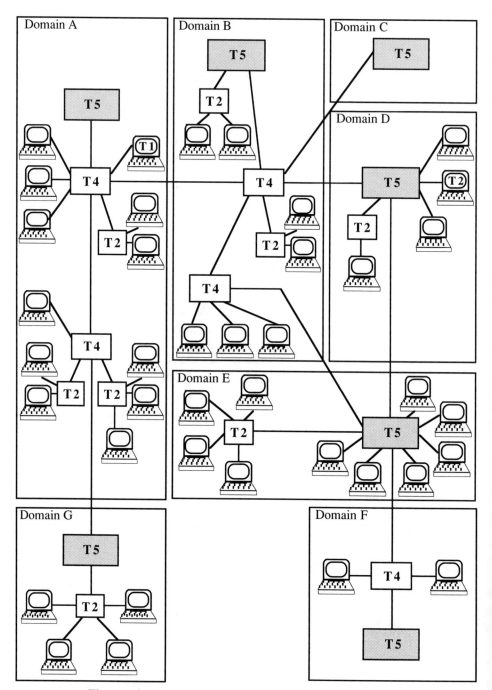

Figure 11.3. Multiple domain in SNA network [24,32].

When communication needs to be established between two users 1 and 2 in two distinct domains, say respectively A and D, first the SSCP in domain A is invoked by user 1; this SSCP has the capability of invoking the other SSCP located in domain D, set the connection parameters, and as a consequence, the connection between end users in the two different domains is established. Once this procedure is successfully achieved, end user 1 can communicate with end user 2 without invoking any further SSCP services. To be able to communicate with other SSCPs, a given SSCP uses a resource called Cross Domain Resource Manager (CDRM) which contains a table describing all the resources that are available in other domains.

11.2.3 Sessions in SNA

An important notion in SNA is that of a session. A session is a logical state that exists between two network addressable units to support a succession of transmissions between them achieving a given purpose [24]. Therefore, a session has to be established between NAUs before any data transfer can take place. A session can be either permanent (installed with the network and continuously operating) or dynamic (created when it is needed). There exist five different types of sessions:

1. **LU-to-LU sessions**   They constitute the basis of network transmissions since they allow communication between end users. Such sessions are generally dynamic.

2. **SSCP-to-SSCP sessions**   They exist only in networks that contain multiple domains. They allow exchange of control information between SSCPs. SSCP-to-SSCP sessions are usually permanent, at least as long as communication between domains is desired.

3. **SSCP-to-PU sessions**   These permanent sessions allow the exchange of control information between an SSCP and a PU.

4. **SSCP-to-LU sessions**   In order for a user to access an LU, a session between this LU and the SSCP responsible for the domain must have been established. Even though such a session is often permanent, it is not required to be so.

5. **PU-to-PU sessions**   Some tasks, like the transfer of a control program, may require that a specific session be implemented between two PUs. By nature, such

a session is dynamic.

The fact that SNA was initially designed as a centralized network greatly influenced its evolution. For example, unlike the OSI specifications which, for standard purposes, defines only peer-to-peer communication, SNA does not treat Logical Units equally. During a LU-to-LU session initiation process, SNA requires that one LU be the primary LU and the other one the secondary LU. Figure 11.4 illustrates how an LU-to-LU session is activated in three cases: initiation by a primary LU, by a secondary LU, and by a third LU which will not be further involved in the communication.

The messages exchanged between entities are called Response/Request Units (RUs). The first RU to be sent is an INIT RU (or INIT-OTHER RU, if done by a third party) and it is usually issued by the LU which desires to establish a communication. As stated before, it is compulsory sent to the SSCP, which verifies if the request is valid (i.e. if the initiating LU has the appropriate authority to initiate a session with the other specific LU).

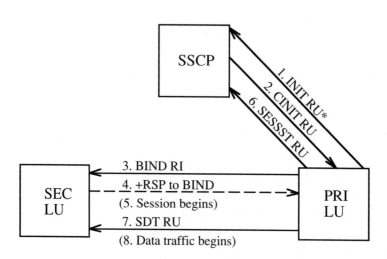

(a)

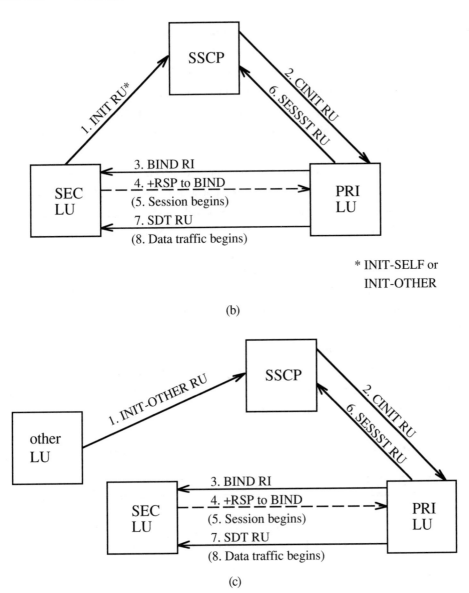

(b)

(c)

Figure 11.4. Starting an LU-to-LU session [13]: (a) primary LU initiates LU-LU session; (b) secondary LU initiates LU-LU session; (c) a third LU initiates LU-LU session.

The SSCP also resolves the name of the network destination and selects the parameters to be used while the session is active; it provides for synchronization of the initiation process as well. Upon acceptance of the session initiation, the SSCP sends a CINIT RU (Control Initiate) to the primary LU. The primary LU now has all the parameters for the session. Therefore, it sends a session activate message, called BIND RU, to the secondary LU in order to inform this LU the parameters and protocols to be used during the communication.

The secondary LU, in turn, has the opportunity of accepting or rejecting the session. In the former case, it returns a Positive Response for BIND (+RSP for BIND) with possibly additional communication parameters, which can be accepted or rejected by the primary LU. In the latter case, the secondary LU sends a Negative Response for BIND (-RSP for BIND). If the session has been accepted, the primary LU sends back to the SSCP a notification of session, through a SESSST RU (Session Started), and the data transfer between LUs can start. Otherwise, the primary LU sends a Bind Failure (BINDF) notification to the SSCP. Figure 11.5 is an example of session activation across SNA domains.

It now obvious that there exist several differences between SNA and OSI service specifications, but the primitives are very much alike. Table 11.2 illustrates the similarities between OSI Transport Layer primitives (presented in Sec. 10.5.2) and SNA LU-to-LU session establishment primitives.

Table 11.2 Comparison of OSI and SNA primitives [32,34].

OSI TPDU	SNA RU	remarks
Connection Request (CR)	BIND	
Connection Confirm (CC)	Positive Response for BIND (+RSP(BIND))	
Disconnect Request (DR)	Negative Response for BIND (-RSP(BIND))	If transport connection is pending
DR	UNBIND	If transport connection has been established
Disconnect Confirm (DC)	Positive Response for UNBIND (+RSP(UNBIND))	If DR is converted from UNBIND
DC		If DR is initiated from Gateway
TPDU Error (ER)	-RSP(BIND)	If transport connection is pending
ER	UNBIND	If transport connection has been established
Data (DT)	Data	

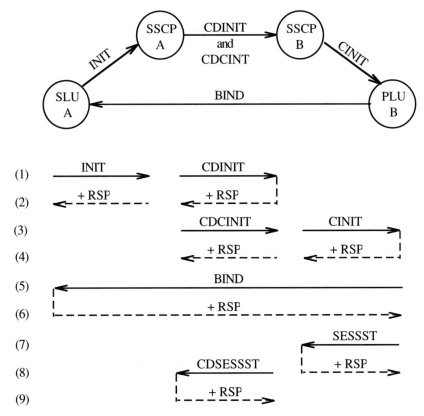

Figure 11.5. Session initiation across domains.

11.2.4   Synchronous Data Link Control (SDLC) Protocol

The protocol used by SNA at the Data Link Layer is called Synchronous Data Link Control (SDLC). It was created before HDLC and greatly influenced HDLC's specifications. As a consequence, HDLC very much resembles SDLC and therefore only a brief presentation of SDLC is given here. When an end user wants to send a message through SNA, the local services of all the layers lying under the Application Layer are requested. The message is manipulated by each layer before being sent to the physical link. Figure 11.6 shows the various steps a message, also called data unit, goes through when carried down the layers.

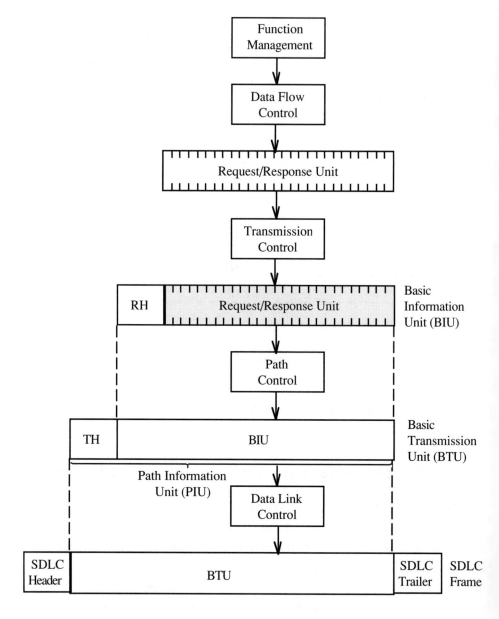

Figure 11.6. Data units in SNA [24,32].

A Data Unit given by the Data Flow Control Layer to the Transmission Control Layer is called a Request/Response Unit (RU). The Transmission Control Layer adds a Request/Response Header (RH) to the RU to form a Basic Information Unit (BIU). This BIU is then forwarded to the Path Control Layer, which in turn adds a Transmission Header (TH) to form a Path Information Unit (PIU). Multiple PIUs can be appended to form a Basic Transmission Unit (BTU), as shown in Figure 11.7. This BTU, composed of one or more PIUs, is then passed to the Data Link Control Layer, which adds a header and a trailer to form an SDLC frame.

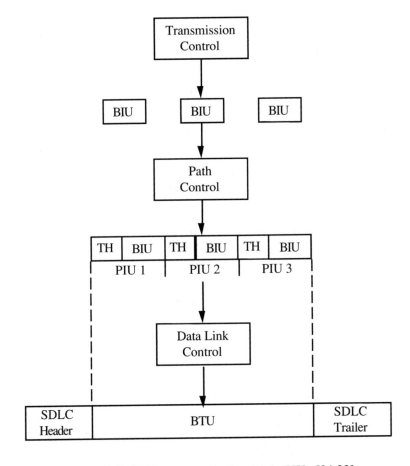

Figure 11.7. BTU composed of multiple PIUs [24,32].

The format of an SDLC frame is shown Figure 11.8. Like HDLC, is composed of two flag sequences 01111110 at the beginning and at the end of the frame, an address field, a control field, an information field (which is the BTU passed by the Path Control Layer), and a Frame Check Sequence, for error-detection purposes. When a frame goes from the primary station to the secondary one or vice-versa, the address field (one byte) contains the address of the secondary station since there is no confusion as to who the primary station is. The address field of a frame issued by the primary station can, however, contain the address of a single secondary station, or a group of secondary stations, or all secondary stations.

Figure 11.8. SDLC frame format [2,24,32].

The Control Field of an SDLC frame (Figure 11.9) is one byte in length and very similar to that of an HDLC frame. Three types of frames are distinguished: Information Frames (I-Frames), Supervisory Frames (S-Frames) and Unnumbered Frames (U-Frames). These types have the same specifications as in the HDLC protocol. The Frame Check Sequence contains a 16-bit Cyclic Redundancy Check (CRC) value used to detect if a frame is received in error (see Appendix IV). Because of the two flag sequences that must be identified at the beginning and end of a frame, bit stuffing is used to allow the transparent transfer of user data.

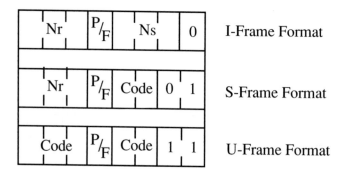

Figure 11.9. Control field of an SDLC frame [2,24,32].

Like HDLC S-Frames, SDLC S-Frames provide three types of commands: Receiver Ready (RR), Receiver Not Ready (RNR) and frame Reject (REJ). Many SDLC U-Frames have their exact counterpart in HDLC (see Section 10.3.4.1), but some of them, listed below, are more specific to SDLC.

Unnumbered Information (UI): used to transmit command or response information between stations under certain circumstances.

Request Initialization Mode (RIM): used by a secondary station to request initialization from the primary station.

Set Initialization Mode (SIM): sent by a primary station to begin initialization of a secondary station.

Request Disconnect (RD): used by a secondary station to notify the primary station that it is willing to be disconnected.

Disconnect (DISC): sent by the primary station to terminate the connection with a secondary station.

Disconnect Mode (DM): used by a secondary station to acknowledge the connection termination (DISC) by the primary station.

Exchange Station Identification (XID): allows the exchange of identification sequences between a primary station and a secondary station.

11.3 DEC's DECnet*

11.3.1 Introduction

Digital Equipment Corporation created Digital Network Architecture (DNA) as a support for DECnet. DECnet was initially designed to enable DEC users to communicate with each other. DECnet was released in 1976, and has been continuously enhanced since then. DNA also consists of seven layers, that are almost identical to the OSI layers. Figure 11.10 shows the correspondence between DNA layers and OSI layers.

---

* see references 8, 9, 19, 20, 24, 25, 27, 32, 33 and 35.

DNA Layers	OSI Model Layers
User	Application
Network Application	Presentation
Session Control	Session
End Communication	Transport
Routing	Network
Data Link	Link
Physical Link	Physical

Figure 11.10. Comparison of DNA and OSI layers.

DNA's Physical Link Layer is the equivalent of the OSI Physical Layer. It is charged with the transmission and the reception of data packets over a physical link. Its implementation depends upon the type of medium used for communication. DNA and OSI Data Link Layers have the same specifications. They are responsible for the correct delivery of data packets on a node-to-node basis. Error detection and recovery mechanisms are involved at this level. Even though it achieves the same goal, the protocol used by DNA at the Data Link Layer, called Digital Data Communications Message Protocol (DDCMP) is very different from the protocol specified by the OSI Model, HDLC. DDCMP is presented in the next section. The counterpart of OSI Network Layer in DNA is called the Routing Layer. It is responsible for the transfer of data throughout the network.

In a similar way as in the OSI Model, there are four upper layers in DNA. The End Communication Layer is the equivalent of the Transport Layer in OSI. It is the lowest layer charged with end-to-end communication. The protocol used by DNA at this layer is called the Network Services Protocol (NSP) and will be described later. The Session Control Layer and the Network Application Layer are the respective counterparts of OSI's Session and Presentation Layers. The Session Control Layer deals particularly with task-to-task communications. The Network Application Layer deals with file management operations, format operations (syntax issues) and terminal control operations. Data Access Protocol (DAP), discussed later, is used by DNA at the Network Application Layer. Finally, the User Layer is the DNA equivalent of the Application Layer in the OSI Model. It is responsible for application process communication.

The layered architecture of DNA implies that data messages are passed from the upper layers down to the lower layers at the source node, and then transferred through the network, involving the bottom three layers. Upon arrival at the destination node, the data packets are passed from the lower layers up to the User Layer. At the source node, each layer adds a header to the data packet received from the layer above, and transmits it to the layer below. Figure 11.11 illustrates the evolution of a data packet as it goes down the layers at a DNA node. As in the OSI Model, only the bottom three layers are involved at an intermediate node in the communication path (Figure 11.11). The headers added to the message at each layer follow the specifications of the protocols involved at each layer. The next sections present the three main protocols used in DNA, DDCMP, NSP and DAP.

11.3.2 DDCMP: a DNA Protocol at the Data Link Layer[*]

Digital Data Communications Message Protocol (DDCMP) allows the transmission of variable length messages over a physical link, and provides mechanisms for error detection and error recovery. DDCMP also provides for full or half-duplex, point-to-point or multipoint communications. There are three types of messages in DDCMP: data, control, and maintenance.The latter are used for specific functions such as downline loading and loop testing, and follow a special protocol called Maintenance Operation Protocol (MOP). The format of a data message is shown Figure 11.12. It starts with a synchronization character 10000001 called Start Of Header (SOH), similarly as HDLC.

---

[*] see references 2, 20, 27 and 32.

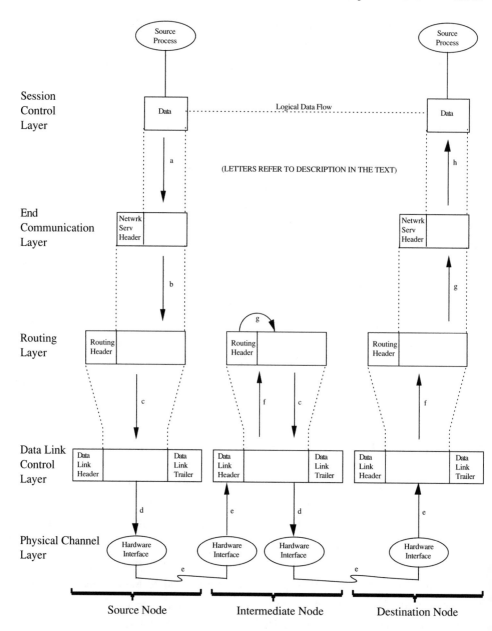

Figure 11.11. Evolution of a data packet through the DNA layers [32,39].

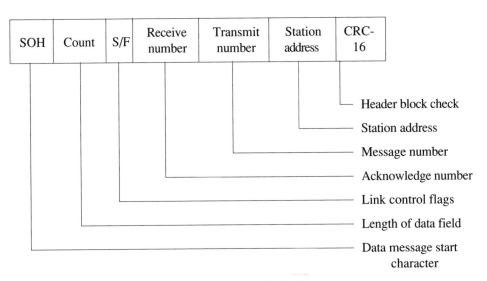

Figure 11.12. Format of a DDCMP data message.

However, there is no trailer containing the same character to signal the end of the message since the length of the message (in bytes) is specified in the message itself, in a 14-bit COUNT field. One advantage of DDCMP over HDLC or SDLC is that it does not require any bit stuffing mechanism to provide user data transparency. Indeed, since the length of the message is known, there is no control character used as a trailer, which means that user data cannot be interpreted as control data.

The next two bits following the count field are flag bits, called Select/Final bits (S/F bits), used to control link ownership and synchronization. The Final flag indicates the end of the current transmission stream, whereas the Select flag is used as a request for the receiving station to transmit a message. The next byte of the message is the response field, RESP. It is used to acknowledge messages correctly received. Each message has a number, contain in the NUM field, and the response field indicates the number of the last message received error-free. Since the message numbering is done on 8 bits, DDCMP allows 255 outstanding messages before an acknowledgement has to be sent back by the receiving station. The address field, ADDR, specifies the destination address. Because this field is one byte in length, as many as 255 stations can be addressed in multipoint communication. The header is terminated by a Cyclic Redundancy Check (CRC) field, for error detection purposes, calculated from the fields contained in the header. User data follows the header, and the only restriction on this field is that the bit count must be an integral number of bytes, since the message length in expressed in bytes. If the user data does not fulfill this format, zeros must be added to complete the field. Another CRC field, calculated from the user data field, is finally appended to the message.

Unlike HDLC, DDCMP uses two CRC fields for each data message sent. Being able to detect errors in two distinct part of the messages presents both advantages and disadvantages. The interest of such a mechanism is that if the user data is erroneous, but not the header, the receiver can use the information contained in the header (such as message acknowledgment). The drawback of this method is that it forces to transmit two additional bytes, representing redundant information, which reduces the link efficiency and will increase the probability of error during transmission.

The second type of messages exchanged in DDCMP are control messages. Figure 11.13 shows the generic format of a control message. It starts with a synchronization character 00000101, called ENQ. Next are the type of control message, and the subtype field. The latter provides additional information for some type of messages. The Select/Final flag bits are next, providing the same mechanism as explained above. The fields RESP and NUM are used to pass additional information respectively from the receiver to the sender and from the sender to the receiver. The address field ADDR follows, used similarly as for data messages. Since there is no user data transmitted in control messages and their format is fixed, there is only one CRC field and no COUNT field. DDCMP defines seven types of control messages, listed below:

Acknowledgment (ACK) Used to acknowledge messages received without errors when there is no data message to be sent that could perform the acknowledgment. An ACK control message has null subtype and NUM fields. The RESP field contains the number of the last correct message received.

Negative Acknowledgment (NAK) Used to indicate that a message (data or control) has been rejected. The RESP field carries the number of the last correct message received. The subtype field contain additional information about the reason for rejection: the CRC of the header proved that the header was in error, the CRC of the data field proved that the data field was erroneous, the buffer is temporarily unavailable, there is a receiver overrun, the message was too long, or the format of the header was incorrect.

Reply to Message Number (REP) Sent from the transmitter to the receiver if the former has not heard anything from the former for a certain period of time (timeout expiration). The receiver answers by sending a control message (either ACK or NAK) with the number of the last message correctly received.

Reset Message Number (RES) Used by the transmitter to force the receiver to reset its receiving message counter to the content of the NUM field of the RES message.

Reset Acknowledge (RESAK) Allows the receiver to acknowledge the reception of a RES message.

Start (STRT) Sent by a station willing to start sending messages to another one. The NUM field contains the number of the first message to be sent.

Start Acknowledgment (STACK) Used by the receiver of a STRT message to acknowledge reception of this message.

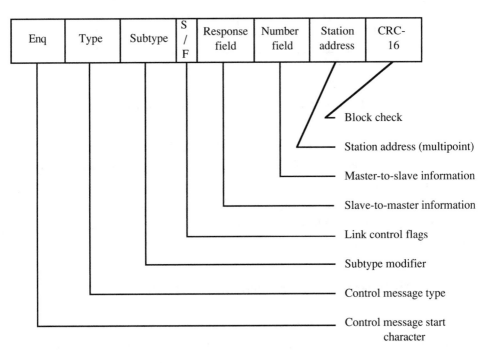

Figure 11.13. Format of a DDCMP control message.

11.3.3 Protocols at the Routing Layer

Both information and control messages are sent at the Routing Layer (corresponding to the Network Layer in the OSI Model). The following is a brief description of a typical header used at this layer. The format of such a header, sometimes called Packet Route header, is shown Figure 11.14. The first of the six characters contained in the header is a flag field indicating if the message is an alarm message, or some other type of message, and what to do with it if the delivery turns out to be impossible. DST indicates, with two bytes, the address of the destination node and SRC indicates, also with two bytes, the address of the source node. FWD is a counter of the number of nodes the message has passed through. It is incremented by each node it passes through on the communication path.

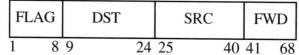

FLAG	DST	SRC	FWD
1 8	9 24	25 40	41 68

Figure 11.14. Typical DNA routing header.

Control messages are exchanged at the Routing Layer to perform routing and congestion control functions. Three types are prevalent [4]: **Routing Message**, containing the minimum cost and number of hops to all destination nodes from the node sending the message, **Test Message**, useful to test the integrity of a channel or of a node, and **Initialization Message**, used to set various communication parameters between neighboring nodes.

11.3.4   Network Service Protocol (NSP)*

NSP resides at the End Communication Layer (corresponding to the Transport Layer in the OSI Model). It is responsible for establishing, maintaining, and terminating a logical link between two processes. A logical link is defined as a "full duplex byte oriented sequential message channel" [39]. On a logical link, two processes can simultaneously exchange messages. NSP must ensure that the messages delivered to the upper layers are correctly sequenced. This imply acknowledging messages correctly

---

* see reference 39.

received and recovering from lost messages by initiating retransmissions.

In a similar way as done in the OSI Model, various primitives are used by NSP to achieve end communication functions. The connection establishment phase uses a CONNECT-INITIATE primitive, containing the address of the initiator, of the desired destination and other communication parameters. If the logical link is accepted, a CONNECT-CONFIRM message is sent back to the initiator and the logical link is created. An acknowledgment of the confirm message, DATA-ACKNOWLEDGE, is in turn sent by the initiator; therefore,for synchronization purposes, a three-way handshake is used to establish a logical link. The data transfer can start as soon as the logical link is established. Figure 11.15 is an example of a message header appended to user data at the End Communication Layer. It starts with a one byte-flag indicating the type of the message, then the fields of logical destination address and logical source address follow, with a length of two bytes each. The next field is optional. It can contain two bytes indicating the number of the last message received. Finally, the header has a message number field, and messages are numbered modulo 4096. This provides for message resequencing and error recovery at the destination node.

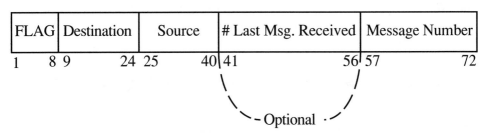

Figure 11.15. Format of an NSP data message.

NSP also has the ability of segmenting one long message into multiple short ones, and reassembling these messages at the destination node. During an exchange of data, NSP provides the possibility of transfer interruption to send high priority alarm signal messages. The primitives for the three-way handshake also used for interruption are similar to that used for the connection phase: INTERRUPT, INTERRUPT-REQUEST and SUBCHANNEL-ACKNOWLEDGMENT. The termination of a logical link can be caused by either a user request, or the failure of a user process, or the failure of a communication link. When a process wants to terminate a logical link, it sends the primitive DISCONNECT-INITIATE, and the other process sends back a DISCONNECT-

CONFIRM to acknowledge the termination of the link.

11.3.5 Data Access Protocol*

DAP resides at the Network Application Layer, which is the equivalent of the Presentation Layer of the OSI Model. It is designed to manage file operations, I/O device operations, terminal control operations, as well as to resolve the data format issues.

There exist two types of DAP messages. The first type consists of messages establishing the connection path and performing handshaking mechanisms. Messages of the second type are device-oriented and are used to control certain features of particular I/O devices. DAP has also been designed to manage file transfer, remote file access, and user identification.

This concludes the overview of Digital Network Architecture. Even though IBM's SNA and DEC's DNA are two very different approaches to networking, two such networks are able to communicate with each other. This comes from the fact that in many companies, both DEC equipment (such as VAX) and IBM equipment (very often a mainframe) coexist, and interconnection between them is necessary to help the company be efficient in data processing. As an example of adaptability, DNA specifications can be compatible with the X.25 standard recommendations (described in Chapter 13).

11.4 DoD Internet Architecture and ARPANET**

11.4.1 Introduction: a layered architecture***

ARPANET was developed by the Defense Advanced Research Projects Agency, which is part of the U.S. Department of Defense (DoD), in the late 1960s [4]. The DoD Internet Architecture Model, later called Internet Model, is the support for ARPANET. Due to military requirements, it has been designed to allow multiple heterogeneous networks to communicate with each other. ARPANET is only one such network. The

---

* see reference 26.

** see references 2–5, 7, 11, 12, 22, 29, 30, 32, 37 and 38.

*** see reference 4.

DoD Internet Model is built around seven layers, as in OSI, but there is not a one-to-one mapping between the two models, since some DoD Internet Layers have different specifications than their counterparts in the OSI Model. Figure 11.16 shows the differences of two architectural designs.

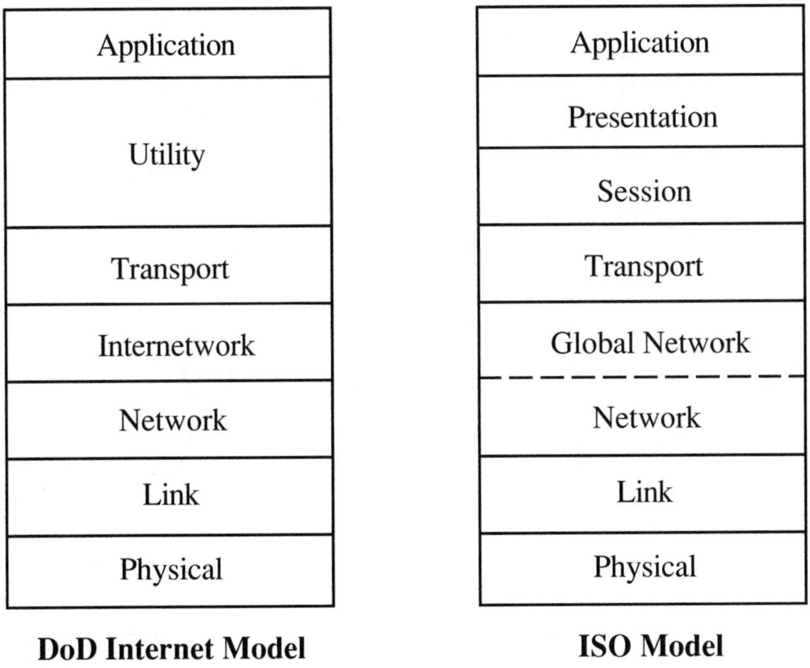

Application
Utility
Transport
Internetwork
Network
Link
Physical

DoD Internet Model

Application
Presentation
Session
Transport
Global Network
Network
Link
Physical

ISO Model

Figure 11.16. Comparison of DoD Internet and OSI models [4,18,32].

The Physical, Data Link, Transport and Application Layers reside at the same level in both models, but the layer that corresponds to the OSI Network Layer is split up into two distinct layers, Network and Internetwork, in the DoD Internet Model. Also, the OSI Session and Presentation Layers are merged together in the DoD Internet Utility Layer. The specifications for these layers are described below. The major feature of the DoD Internet architecture is that it has been designed to allow communication between networks having very different internal characteristics. As a consequence, standard gateways are used to route internet packets from one network to another (Figure 11.17). Also all the networks use a standard set of protocols for the upper layers (above the Internetwork Layer). For example, an actual implementation of a DoD internet subnetwork can be an ARPANET as well as an Ethernet. Table 11.3 is a summary of the various features of the DoD Internet Model.

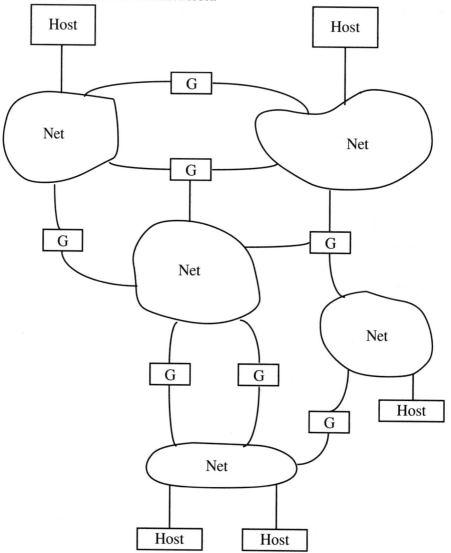

Figure 11.17. DoD Internet System Architecture [4,32].

Table 11.3 Assumptions and requirements of the DoD Internet model
[4,32]

1.	Heterogenous Packet Networks (i.e. Physical, Link, Network Layers differ).
2.	Datagram (connectionless) Service at Internet Layer.
3.	Architectural Provision for Interoperable Tactical and Strategic Communication.
4.	High Reliability and Survivability Under Hostile Conditions.
5.	Combined Voice and Data Services.
6.	Interactive, Real-Time, Transaction, and Bulk Data Transport Services.
7.	Precedence and Security at Several Layers.
8.	Broadcast/Multicast Services.
9.	Host-Host File Transfers and File Access.
10.	Widely Varying Terminal Types Using Remote Service Hosts.
11.	Electronic Message Switching Services Utilizing Different Transport Protocols.
12.	Multimedia (Text, Fax, Graphics, Voice) Electronic Messaging.
13.	Distributed, Redundant Name-to-Address Translation Services.

11.4.2 Protocols used by the DoD Internet Layers[*]

At the Physical Layer, several standards are used to allow compatibility with various types of equipment. Modem connections between hosts and packet switches use such standards as CCITT V.24, V.35, EIA RS-449 or EIA RS-232C [4]. The hardware interface can also be of various types, for instance following the Ethernet standards or the IEEE 802 Local Area Network standards (discussed in Chapter 12).

The protocols involved at the Data Link Layer can be the ISO designed HDLC supporting the CCITT X.25 recommendation, or the Advanced Data Communication

---

[*] see references 4 and 32.

Control Procedure (ADCCP) created by the American National Standard Institute (ANSI), or even IBM's Binary Synchronous Link Procedure (BSC).

The Network Layer supports point-to-point, broadcast and multicast services, and is responsible for the exchange of packets between hosts and the various packet networks. The Network Layer protocols still depend upon the type of network they manage. Packet Satellite and Packet Radio protocols are used at this layer. The Internet Layer provides for global internet addressing, internet routing and error recovery. The services are unified among all the various networks, and the nodes see only a internet datagram service. Internet Protocol (IP) and Internet Control Message Protocol (ICMP), to be described in Chapter 12, are widely used at this layer. Datagrams are fragmented at the gateways by the Internet Layer, which then routes the packets independently.

Implementations of the Transport Layer use three different protocols, called Transmission Control Protocol (TCP), which will be described in Chapter 12, User Datagram Protocol (UDP) and Stream Protocol (ST). The main characteristic of TCP is its high reliability on an end-to-end, sequenced communication. UDP is used when a lower level of requirements for control and sequencing can be accepted. ST is a protocol which provides services for applications (such as voice-oriented applications) which have heavy real-time requirements, but do not necessarily require correct delivery of data packets.

The protocols used at the Utility Layer depend upon the type of application involved. File operations use the File Transfer Protocol (FTP), which allows transparent identification, access and transfer of files between nodes. Trivial File Transport Protocol (TFTP) also allows the transfer of files between hosts. However, TFTP's simplicity implies very low performances, and TFTP is mainly used to transfer files between a host and a personal computer or a small computing system. Electronic mail is handled by the Simple Mail Transfer Protocol (SMTP), which provides the possibility of using various transport protocols for mail transmission. The mandatory knowledge of the specific characteristics of remote terminals involved in the communication process can be eliminated through the use of the TELNET protocol, which enables the hosts in the networks to consider all terminals as standard Network Virtual Terminals. A Name Server Protocol (NSP), also at the Utility Layer, provides for the translation of local names into generic internet addresses. Finally, the Network Voice Protocol version 2 (NVP-2) provides functions for the transfer of voice packets with features such as multiple-destination addressing and dynamic connection and disconnection of users on a dialogue.

NVP-2 uses services provided by ST at the Transport Layer. All the protocols existing at the Application Layer of the DoD Internet Model correspond to those presented for the Utility Layer [4,32].

11.5 Burroughs' BDLC*

Burroughs created its own data link control protocol, called BDLC, in the mid-1970s. BDLC is essentially the same as IBM's SDLC. The network architecture, message format, and protocol are almost identical. BDLC is also compatible with the ISO standard data link protocol, HDLC.

The frame format for BDLC is basically the same as that of SDLC. There are two framing flags, an address field, a control field, an optional information field and a frame check sequence. The major difference appears to be in the definition and use of the control field. SDLC has an 8-bit control field, and BDLC has an 8-bit control field that is expandable to 16 bits. SDLC is limited to 7 acknowledged messages at any one time, but with the expanded control field BDLC can handle up to 127 acknowledged messages (as can HDLC).

11.6 Exercises

11.1 Compare and contrast the network architecture, the protocol format, the line-control procedure, the message formats, and the link controls for IBM's SNA and DEC's DNA.

11.2 Explain the differences between the OSI Model Layer specifications and that of SNA.

11.3 Explain the differences between the OSI Model Layer specifications and that of DNA.

11.4 Why is SNA considered as a decentralized network and not a distributed network? Contrast with the distributed OSI approach.

11.5 What is a Physical Unit, a Logical Unit, a Network Addressable Unit in SNA terminology? For each of them give a practical example. Why are there several

---

* see reference 27.

types of Logical Units and of Physical Units in SNA?

11.6 What is the function of a System Service Control Point (SSCP) in SNA? Explain the notion of domain in SNA. What is the difference in capabilities between a PU of type 5 and a PU of type 4?

11.7 Draw a diagram of an SNA network with multiple domains. Presume that a communication needs to be established between terminals across domains. From the diagram, list what entities are involved in this process.

11.8 With the diagram drawn in exercise 7, show the exchange of messages occurring during the session establishment, data transfer, and session termination phases, for a communication between end users across domains.

11.9 What is the difference between the evolution of an OSI data unit and an SNA data unit as they are processed down the seven layers at the transmitting node?

11.10 Compare the U-Frames specified by HDLC and those specified by SDLC.

11.11 In what extent does the particular architecture of SNA influence the specifications of the data link control protocol SDLC?

11.12 Describe the ARPANET system functionally and how it structurally differs from SNA.

11.13 Discuss how SNA improves response time, decreases communications line costs, decreases main processor loads and improves system availability.

11.14 Describe the evolution of a DNA data packet as it processed down the layers at the transmitting node. Explain particularly the function of the headers that are successively added to the data unit.

11.15 Why is bit-stuffing useless in DEC's data link control protocol, DDCMP?

11.16 What are the differences between DDCMP and HDLC? In particular, compare the control messages used in DDCMP and the control frames specified in HDLC.

11.17 Presume that a communication needs to be established between two DEC users. Draw a diagram showing the exchange of messages occurring at the Data Link Layer during the connection establishment and the data transfer phases.

11.18 Explain the functionality of DEC's End Communication Protocol, NSP. Compare with the protocols used at the Transport Layer in the OSI Model.

11.19 Contrast the layered architectures of the OSI Model and the DoD Internet Model, support of ARPANET. Why is the OSI Network Layer split up into two layers (Network and Internetwork) in the DoD Internet Model specification.

11.20 Explain how interconnection of various heterogeneous networks is made possible by the DoD Internet architecture. What is the main conceptual difference between the DoD Internet Model and the OSI Model respective views of internetworking?

11.7 References

1   Atkins, J., "Path Control: The Transport Network of SNA." *IEEE Trans. on Comm.*, April 1980.

2   Black, U., *Data Networks: Concepts, Theory, and Practice*. Englewood Cliffs, NJ: Prentice-Hall, 1989.

3   Cerf, V., and Kristein, P. T., "Issues in Packet-Network Interconnection." *Proceedings of the IEEE*, November 1978.

4   Cerf, V. C., and Cain, E., "The DoD Internet Architecture Model." *Computer Networks*, No. 7, 1983.

5   Chapin, A. L., "Connections and Connectionless Data Transmission." *Proceedings of the IEEE, 71*, 12, December 1983.

6   Chou, W. (ed.), *Computer Communications, Vol. I: Principles*. Englewood Cliffs, NJ: Prentice-Hall, 1983.

7   Corrigan, M., "Defense Data Network Protocols." *Proceedings, EASCON 82*, 1982.

8   *DECnet Digital Network Architecture*, Document Number AA-X435A-TK. Maynard, MA: Digital Equipment Corporation, May 1982.

9   DECnet Publication Number AA-N149A-TC. Maynard, MA: Digital Equipment Corporation, May 1982.

10   Donnan, R., and Kersey, J., "Synchronous Data Link Control: A Perspective." *IBM Systems Journal*, May 1974.

11   Ennis, G.; Kaufman, D.; and Biba, K., *DoD Protocol Reference Model*, Sytek, TR-82026, September 1982.

12   Ennis, G., "Development of the DoD Protocol Reference Model." *Proceedings, SIGCOMM '83 Symposium*, 1983.

13   Falk, G., "The Structure and Function of Network Protocols." In Chou (ed.), *Computer Communications, Vol. I: Principles*. Englewood Cliffs, NJ: Prentice-Hall, 1983.

14   Green, P., "An Introduction to Network Architectures and Protocols." *IEEE*

Trans. on Comm., April 1980.

15 Halsall, F., *Data Communications, Computer Networks, and OSI* (2nd edition). Reading, MA: Addison-Wesley, 1988.

16 Hammond, J. L., and O'Reilly, J. P., *Performance Analysis of Local Computer Networks*. Reading, MA: Addison-Wesley, 1986.

17 IBM Corp., *System Network Architecture: Concepts and Products*. GC30-3072, 1981.

18 International Organization for Standardization. *Basic Reference Model for Open Systems Interconnection*, DIS 7498, 1983.

19 Johnson, S., "Architectural Evolution: Digital Unveils Its DECnet Phase III." *Data Communications*, March 1980.

20 Lane, M. G., *Data Communications Software Design*. Boston, MA: Boyd & Fraser Publishing Co., 1985.

21 Linnell, D., *SNA Concepts Design and Implementation*. McLean, VA: Gate Technology, 1987.

22 Markley, R. W., *Data Communications and Interoperability*. Englewood Cliffs, NJ: Prentice-Hall, 1970.

23 Martin, J., *Computer Networks and Distributed Processing*. Englewood Cliffs, NJ: Prentice-Hall, 1981.

24 Martin, J., and Kavanaugh, C. K., *SNA: IBM's Networking Solution*. Englewood Cliffs, NJ: Prentice-Hall, 1987.

25 McQuillan, J. M., and Cerf, V. G., *A Practical View of Computer Communications Protocols*. Washington, DC: IEEE Computer Society Press, 1978.

26 Padlipsky, M., "A Perspective on the ARPANET Reference Model." *Proceedings, INFOCOM 83*, 1983.

27 Pooch, U. W.; Greene, W. H.; and Moss, G. G., *Telecommunications and Networking*. Boston, MA: Little, Brown and Company, 1983.

28 Pouzin, L., and Zimmerman, H., "A Tutorial on Protocols." *Proceedings of the IEEE*, November 1978.

29 Roberts, L., and Wessler, B., "Computer Network Development to Achieve Resource Sharing." *Proceedings, Spring Joint Computer Conference*, 1970.

30 Selvaggi, P., "The Department of Defense Data Protocol Standardization Program." *Proceedings, EASCON 82*, 1982.

31   Systems Network Architecture, Technical Overview, GC30-3073-0. IBM, 1982.

32   Stallings, W., *Data and Computer Communications*. New York, NY: MacMillan Publishing Company, 1985.

33   Stallings, W., *Handbook of Computer Communications Standards*, Vol. 1. New York, NY: MacMillan Publishing Company, 1987.

34   Sy, K. K.; Shiobara, M. O.; Yamaguchi, M.; Kobayashi, Y.; Shukuya, S.; and Tomatsu, T., "OSI-SNA Interconnections." *IBM Systems Journal*, *26*, 2, 1987.

35   Tanenbaum, A. S., *Computer Networks*. Englewood Cliffs, NJ: Prentice-Hall, 1981.

36   Tanenbaum, A. S., "Network Protocols." *Computing Surveys*, December 1981.

37   Tanenbaum, A. S., *Computer Networks* (2nd edition). Englewood Cliffs, NJ: Prentice-Hall, 1988.

38   Walker, S., "Department of Defense Data Network." *Signal*, October 1982.

39   Wecker, S., "DNA: The Digital Network Architecture." *IEEE Trans. on Comm.*, *COM-28*, 4, April 1980.

12

LOCAL AREA NETWORK STANDARDS

12.1 Introduction*

Local Area Networks (LANs) represent a class of networks that are limited in physical size. LANs are generally confined to the size of a campus or a building. They consist largely of computers linked by some physical high speed media for the purpose of sharing resources. As distributed processing has become increasingly popular so have LANs due to their distributed nature.

LANs differ from traditional multiuser systems and their communication networks. Devices on a LAN are intelligent devices. Each device is capable of connecting to the LAN and exchange data with other devices. Some LANs only allow communication with file servers or resource servers and such servers are not prevalent within the network. But, most LANs allow all devices to communicate with all other devices via peer-to-peer communication via some predefined session or transport layer protocol. This peer-to-peer communication is only possible with respect to each device connected on the LAN being an intelligent device.

A unique feature of LANs is that they are prevalently privately owned. This is unlike other networks. Most other network types, including multiuser systems, are networked together through public data lines.

An interesting aspect of LANs is that, for the most part, the actual physical media are experiencing relatively little further development. Several of the physical communication standards have remained as they were when they were originally developed. But, as a contrast, upper layer protocols are continually under development and revision.

---

* see references 3, 6, 9, 10, 11, 14, 18, 37, 42, 48, 55–64, 71 and 73.

The end result of using LANs is that distributed processing is realized. Distributed processing extends itself to solving computing problems in a manner that befits many computing needs.

There are many different topologies and standards that provide communication on LANs. LANs themselves allow heterogeneous devices to communicate, and the equipment that provides access to a LAN come in several arrangements. Disjoint hardware can unite through the use of LANs.

LAN topologies are divided into 3 main types, bus, star and ring. In the case of bus and ring the difference is sometimes only visible when the data link layer is analyzed. The bus or Collision Sense Multiple Access LANs and ring topologies have been further standardized by the IEEE 802 committee. The star topology has seen little, true, standardization. There are also other non-IEEE 802 standards, each will be detailed in the following sections. There are also a few standard, or near standard (in implementation) middle to lower layer protocols (layers in terms of the OSI model). They include MAP, TOP, and TCP/IP. Each of these protocols, due there widespread use will be included in the last few sections of this chapter.

12.2 Carrier Sense/Multiple Access Networks*

The network media access scheme Carrier Sense/Multiple Access (CSMA) is utilized by both the IEEE 802.3 and Ethernet standards. Ethernet, developed jointly by Xerox, Digital Equipment and Intel Corporations, is not the same as the IEEE 802.3 standard. Ethernet is based on the experimental network designed (based on Aloha Net) in the early 1970's at Xerox's Palo Alto Research Center (PARC)[33]. The CSMA mechanism is further recognized by the use of Collision Detection (CSMA/CD), Collision Avoidance (CSMA/CA) and Collision Elimination (CSMA/CE)[34,37].

12.2.1 Ethernet**

Ethernet was created in 1973 at Xerox PARC during the concurrent development of a personal computer called the Alto[41]. Ethernet was derived from the University of

---

* see references 6, 16, 18, 31, 33, 34, 37 and 45.
** see references 21, 22, 37 and 41.

Hawaii's Aloha Packet Radio Network. Alohanet broadcast packets with randomized retransmissions. Ethernet was originally called Alto Aloha Network. Ethernet was publicly acknowledged in 1976 with the publication of the paper "Ethernet: Distributed Packet Switching for Local Computer Networks" by Robert Metcalfe and David Boggs[37].

In 1980 Digital Equipment, Intel, and Xerox Corporations jointly-developed a standard Ethernet. The result was a 10 mbs Ethernet called DIX (first initial of each participating company) Ethernet.

Ethernet allows all stations to share the network communication cable. Notice that this standard only indicates how the communication takes place, not the media used. For Ethernet can operate on several cable media, including:

1. Thin Coaxial Cable (RG58), 50 ohm
2. Thick Coaxial Cable (RG11), 50 ohm
3. Twisted Wire Pair Cable, (22/24 gauge) 150 ohm
4. Fiber Optic (100/120/140 micron fiber)

This Ethernet specification is Version 2.0, published in November 1982. With Ethernet each station has a controller and transceiver which attaches it to the network, the ether. The controller is used to build packets and disseminate packets. The transceiver which may or may not be part of the controller taps into the network to send and receive packets for the controller.

12.2.2   IEEE 802.3*

The IEEE 802.3 standard, just like Ethernet, use CSMA/CD (Collision Detection) as the media access control procedure. The IEEE 802.3 standard differs from Ethernet in the manner which messages (frames) are formed. The IEEE 802.3 standard has been adopted by the American National Standards Institute (ANSI), the United States Federal Government (FIPS 107) and the International Organization for Standards (ISO 8802/3).

The IEEE 802.3 standard was first published in 1985[24] and incorporates 10Base5 (10 mbs baseband media where the maximum segment is 500 meters, using thick, RG11 cable) physical layer and the CSMA/CD access control procedure, based upon Ethernet.

---

* see references 18, 24 and 64.

There have been several adaptations of this initial standard, first is Cheapernet, 10Base2 (using thin, RG58 cable) and the most revolutionary being the 10BaseT (T for Telephone Pair) (10BaseT is pending final IEEE approval). For a comparison of 10Base5 and 10Base2 standards see Figure 12.1.

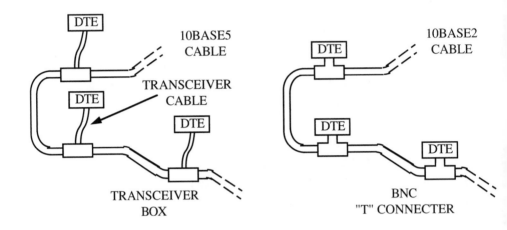

Figure 12.1. Comparison of 10Base5 and 10Base2 [64].

The IEEE 802.3 standard also has specifications that allow it to use 10Broad36 (10mbs broadband media with a maximum segment length of 3600m, using standard 75 ohm CATV coaxial cable). The 10mbs rating is maintained to stay compatible with 10Base5's Attachment Unit Interface (AUI).

The last specified broadcast medium for the 802.3 is 1Base5. This specification was designed to provide for low cost LANs. The media used is unshielded twisted pair.

The 10BaseT standard provides for 10mbs over twisted pair telephone wire. Instead of a bus where each station taps into the bus, each station wires to a concentrator. The concentrator works as a hub to provide fault isolation and network diagnostics as well as propagate network traffic. Objectives for 10BaseT Ethernet include coexistence with ISDN and AT&T's StarLan and AT&T's ISN and 100 meter minimum distance from station to concentrator, also known as a wiring closet.

The IEEE 802.3 standard also divides the functions at the data-link layer, whereas Ethernet does not differentiate. The IEEE 802.3 standard splits the data-link layer (of the OSI model) into the IEEE 802.2 Logical Link Control (LLC) layer and IEEE 802.3

Medium Access Control (MAC) layer, see Figure 12.2. The IEEE 802.2 LLC layer is concerned with maintaining maintaining and terminating logical links with other devices on the network [23]. The IEEE 802.3 MAC layer is concerned with the actual media access, the CSMA/CD algorithm is at work in the IEEE 802.3 MAC layer.

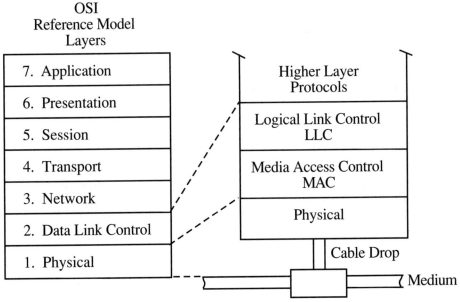

Figure 12.2. LAN protocol layers [6,44].

12.2.3   CSMA/CD

The CSMA/CD protocol was originally developed by Robert Metcalfe and David Boggs of the Xerox Palo Alto Research Center (Xerox PARC) in 1976[37]. With Collision Detection each station first listens to the bus, sending its message if the line is quiet. Quiet indicates that no messages are currently on the network bus. If not quiet, the station waits for a random amount of time before listening again. During and after the message has been transmitted, the device listens to the line to determine whether its message packet has collided with another. If a collision is detected, both sending stations wait a random yet different amount of time before re-sending their message packets, see Figure 12.3.

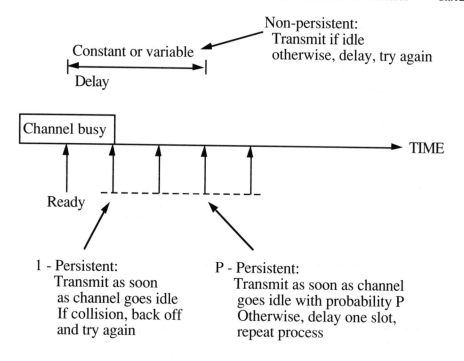

Figure 12.3. CSMA persistence and back-off [44].

12.2.4   CSMA/CA*

CSMA/CA, Carrier Sense/Multiple Access with Collision Avoidance is very similar to CSMA/CD. CSMA/CA is similar to CD in that a particular station listens for a quiet cable before sending. However, a sending station does not continue to monitor the network once a transmission has begun. The CSMA/CA scheme never has knowledge of collisions. Error recovery may be compensated for in the data-link or network layer, but there is no strict requirement. Recovering from lost data due to collision at the application layer (the unusual method, using time-outs) is rather time consuming and as a result, CSMA/CA is rarely implemented.

---

* see references 34 and 62.

12.2.5   CSMA/CE*

Collision Elimination is a distributed contention-based access method that guarantees no data collisions. The CSMA/CE algorithm is proprietary, pending adoption by the IEEE. With CSMA/CE and sending station listens for a quiescent state on the network. Once this state has been detected, an additional wait period is inserted. This additional wait is in the microsecond range. This wait period is termed the Deference Slot Time (DST). The DST is determined by a signal-processing algorithm that is executed locally at the station's controller.

The DST is key to the elimination of collisions. If several stations are waiting when the network becomes quiet, each station does not try to send its message at that moment. Instead each station waits an additional period of time (DST) before attempting transmission. If the network becomes non-quiescent while counting down the DST, then the station will wait until the next quiescent state and start again. The DST is calculated each time a packet is transmitted. The DST calculation is in silicon however and is computed in nanoseconds, which does not preempt communication[34].

12.2.6   Comparison of Ethernet and 802.3 Packet Frames

The major difference between the Ethernet and IEEE 802.3 standards is the manner which the packet frames are built, see Figure 12.4. The Ethernet frame format is seen in Table 12.1. The IEEE 802.3 frame format is shown in Table 12.2. The frame fields are explained in Table 12.3.

Table 12.1 Ethernet frame format

Field	Length in Bytes*
Preamble	6
Destination	6
Source	6
Type	2
Data	46-1500
CRC	4

*72 bytes is the minimum packet size for an Ethernet packet.

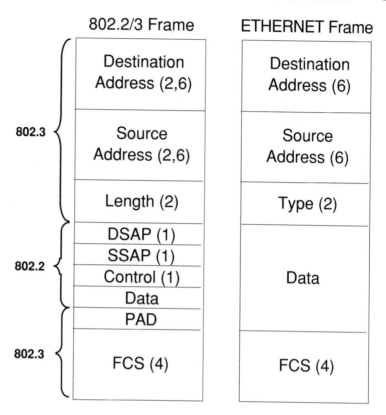

Figure 12.4 Comparison of 802.3 and Ethernet frames [44,64].

Table 12.2 IEEE 802.3 frame format

Field	Length in Bytes
Preamble	7
SFD	1
Destination	2 or 6
Source	2 or 6
Length	2
Data	4
Pad	varies. See table 12.3
CRC	4

Table 12.3 Frame fields, Ethernet vs. IEEE 802.3

Field	Ethernet	IEEE 802.3
Preamble	8 bytes (octets) in length,provides for synchronization and framing, compromised of the bit pattern 10101010 (repeated 7 times) and the eighth pattern of 10101011	7 bytes in length,provides synchronization,each byte is comprised of the bit pattern 10101010
Start Frame Delimiter (SFD)	n/a (represented by the 8th byte of the Ethernet Preamble)	1 byte in length,provides framing, represents the start framebit pattern is 10101011
Destination Address (see Figure 12.5)	6 bytes in length, represents the address of the receiving station. The most significant bit (MSB) is defined:0 indicates the field contains a unique address of the one receiving station,. NOTE: all unique addresses are being assigned by the Xerox Corporation, specifically, the first 3 bytes are assigned by Xerox and the remaining 3 bytes are specified locally. 1 indicates the field contains a logical group of recipients. NOTE: if the field contains all 1's, this indicates this packet (message) is meant for all stations, a broadcast	2 or 6 bytes (depending on implementation, 10Base5 specifies 6 byte addresses) Represents the address of the receiving station. The MSB is defined: 0 indicates an individual address, the IEEE assigns all global addresses while local addresses may be defined privately. 1 indicates a group address, may be a multicast group of logically related stations or a full broadcast if all bytes are 1's

Table 12.3 Frame fields, Ethernet vs. IEEE 802.3 (cont.)

Source Address	6 bytes in length, always set to the address of the sending station, MSB is 0	2 or 6 bytes in length,always set to the address of the sending station, MSB is 0, if 2 bytes long, the Destination Address must be 2 bytes too, same is true if this field is 6 bytes long
Type	1 byte in length. Specifies the higher layer protocol used to disseminate the message data, types are administered by Xerox Corporation	n/a
Length	n/a	2 bytes in length. Specifies the length of the data field.
Data	46-1500 bytes in length. Represents the content of the message, the data.	46-1500 bytes in length. Represents the content of the message, the data.
Pad	n/a	the minimum frame size minus the Data size plus 2 times the address size plus 6 in length, if the result is non-positive, the Pad value is 0. Used to Pad the message to ensure its size meets the minimum size requirement, this is necessary when 2 byte destination and source fields are used

Table 12.3 Frame fields, Ethernet vs. IEEE 802.3 (cont.)

Cyclic Redundancy check (CRC)	4 bytes in length, computed by the CRC-32 polynomial, note: Data field must be at least 46 bytes in length. Also note that the Ethernet frame must be between 72 and 1526 bytes in length	4 bytes in length, computed by the CRC-32 polynomial, NOTE: must be between 72 and 1526 bytes in length. A difference between Ethernet and IEEE 802.3 is that with Ethernet it is the duty of the upper layer protocols to assemble a proper length packet where such responsibility rests with the IEEE 802.3 MAC layer under IEEE 802.3

12.3   Token-Passing Networks*

The token-passing networks circulate a token. The token controls the right of access to the network's physical medium. The node that possesses the token has control of the medium. The token is passed from node to node, and as this is done, a logical ring is created. The ring is fault tolerant providing maintenance for ring initialization at each node, lost token recovery, and new station addition and deletion from the logical ring (reconfiguration).

Token-passing networks have been in wide use since 1977 when DataPoint Corporation introduced ARCnet (Attached Resource Computer Network). ARCnet is a token-ring, token-passing network. The IEEE 802.1 committee also has its version of the token-ring network, described under IEEE 802.5[26]. The IEEE committee has also defined a token-passing bus network in the IEEE 802.4 standard[25].

---

* see references 6, 7, 25, 26, 30, 62, 68 and 69.

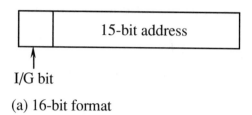

I/G bit

(a) 16-bit format

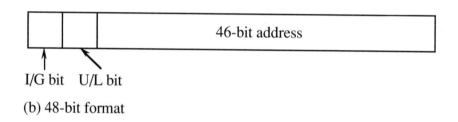

I/G bit   U/L bit

(b) 48-bit format

I/G = 0 means Individual Address
I/G = 1 means Group Address
U/L = 0 means Globally Administered Address
U/L = 1 means Globally Administered Address

Figure 12.5. IEEE 802.3 address field formats [44,64].

Token-passing networks use a single token to control all network traffic. This eliminates message packet collisions, such as those with CSMA networks. Token-passing is a deterministic access scheme. There are specific rules that each node is governed by when using the token. Discussion of token-passing rules is furthered in Sections 12.3.1, 12.3.2 and 12.3.3.

12.3.1 ARCnet[*]

ARCnet, originated by DataPoint Corporation (John Murphy was the original developer). ARCnet predates the IEEE 802 committee and its token-passing standards.

---

[*] see reference 54.

ARCnet originally utilized RG62 coaxial cable as its physical medium. ARCnet now, in addition to coaxial cable, allows the use of twisted pair, fiber optic and infrared medias. Currently ARCnet uses a 2.5 Mbps and 20 Mbs communication speed.

ARCnet is a distributed star, or an unrooted tree topology. ARCnet is an efficient token-passing network. When an ARCnet node sends a message, all of the other nodes receive the message at about the same time (only limited by the speed of light in the physical medium). All nodes except the destination node ignore the message (all taken care of by the MAC level hardware on the ARCnet controller, the COM 9026 in most cases). ARCnet passes the token based upon node address.

The ARCnet protocol also uses positive acknowledgments of message receipt. Also, the ARCnet packet length is set at 512 bytes. The first two bytes are for the source address (maximum of 255 addresses) and the next two bytes indicate the destination address. The remaining 508 bytes contain the message. The ARCnet protocol specifies a limit of one-packet-per-transmission. Each node is sequentially offered the token; when a node gets the token, it can transmit its message. Once that transmission is complete (a positive acknowledgment has been received), or if the node does not need the token, the token is passed to the next node. The next node is determined by the node's address. If more than one message needs to be transmitted, the sending node must wait until the token goes around the network again.

If an extra token is generated, (which has an almost zero chance of occurring), it cannot survive very long because of the way the ARCnet protocol works. Basically, communications from two different nodes would interfere with each other, with the end result being that both tokens would get lost. If the token is lost, the whole network will reach an idle state. Each node is continually monitoring activity on the network. If no activity is detected for 78.2 μs (microseconds)[54], then a reconfigure timer is started (see Figure 12.6). The programmed time is based on each node's address. If node addresses are unique, only one node will time-out first. This node is then responsible for initiating a new token. The network reconfigures itself and communication resumes. As compared to the IEEE's 802.4 and 802.5 standards, ARCnet's real elegance is its simplicity.

The ARCnet line protocol can be described as isochronous because each byte is preceded by a start interval and ended with a stop interval. Unlike asynchronous protocols, there is a constant amount of time separating each data byte. Each byte takes up exactly eleven clock intervals with a single clock interval being 400 ns. As a result, one byte is transmitted every 4.4 ms; the line idles in a spacing (logic 0) condition. A logic 0 is defined as no line activity and a logic 1 is defined as a pulse of 200 ns. All transmissions start with an ALERT BURST consisting of six unit intervals of mark, or logic 1. Eight bit data characters are then sent with each character preceded by 2 unit intervals of mark and one unit of space. There are five types of transmissions, each is detailed below[54]:

1. **Invitations to Transmit**

    An ALERT BURST followed by an EOT (End Of Transmission -- ASCII code 04) and two (redundant) DID (Destination IDentification) characters. This message is used to pass the token from one node to another.

2. **Free Buffer Enquiries**

    An ALERT BURST followed by three characters (six bytes): an ENQ (binary 00000101) and two (repeated) Destination Identification (DID) character, each being 2 bytes long. This transmission type is used to ask another node if it is able to accept a packet of data.

3. **Data Packets (see Figure 12.7)**

    An ALERT BURST followed by the following characters (each 2 bytes)

    -    Start of Header (SOH) binary 00000001
    -    Source Identifier (SID), source node address
    -    Destination Identifier, repeated (4 bytes), destination address
    -    a single COUNT character which is the two's complement of the number of data bytes to follow if a "short packet" is being sent or two bytes of 0's followed by a COUNT character, which is the two's complement of the number of data bytes to follow if a "long packet" is being sent.
    -    N data bytes where COUNT = 256 - N (512-N for a "long packet")
    -    two CRC characters, four bytes, using CRC 16 polynomial

4. **Acknowledgments**

    An ALERT BURST followed by one character, two bytes, the Acknowledgment character (ACK), binary 00000110. This transmission type is used to acknowledge reception of a packet or as an affirmative response to a FREE BUFFER ENQUIRY.

5. **Negative Acknowledgments**

    An ALERT BURST followed by one character, the Negative Acknowledgment character (NAK), binary 00010101. This transmission type is used as a negative response to a FREE BUFFER ENQUIRY.

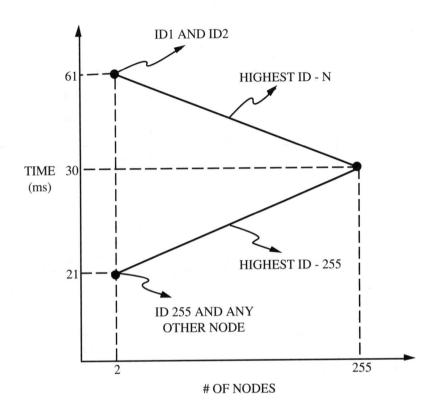

Figure 12.6. Network reconfiguration time [54].

12.3.2   IEEE 802.4 Token-Passing Bus*

In 1985, the IEEE 802.4 standard was solidified. IEEE 802.4, or token-passing bus is also recognized by ISO DIS 8802/4, which is a standard supported by the ISO, International Organization for Standardization[25]. Currently the IEEE 802.4 standard is being revised.

---

* see references 6, 18, 25, 45, 54, 58, 62 and 63.

The 802.4 standard defines for 1 mbs, 5 mbs and 10 mbs (baseband and broadband) coaxial cable attachment of the node to the medium.

Address (Byte #)	Format of Short Packet (256 or 512 bytes)	Format of Long Packet (512 Bytes)
0	SID	SID
1	DID	DID
2	Count (equal to 256 - N)	0
3		Count (equal to 512 - N)
	Not Used	Not Used
•••		
Count	Data Byte 1	Data Byte 1
	Data Byte 2	Data Byte 2
255	Data Byte N	Data Byte N-256
256		Data Byte N-255
•••		•••
•••	Not Used	•••
511		Data Byte N

N = Packet Data Length, SID = Source ID, DID = Destination ID, or 0 for Broadcasts

Figure 12.7. RAM buffer packet configuration [54].

The token-bus uses a token to control access to the network. The network formed by the token-bus is a logical ring. Each node may transmit its messages or data frames when it has the token. Although the node may transmit all the data frames that it has, generally there is a time limit in effect that prevents any one node from monopolizing the network. Further, a slot time is defined to refer to the maximum time any node need wait for an immediate response from another node. The slot time is also noted by twice the end-to-end propagation delay of the medium. And, each node assists in the error recovery and network management.

All data, token, and general information frames are passed between stations using the frame format shown in figure 12.8. Following is a discussion of each element of the frame:

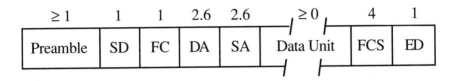

SD = Start Delimiter
FC = Frame Control
DA = Destination Address
SA = Source Address
FCS = Frame Check Sequence
ED = End Delimiter

Figure 12.8. General IEEE 802.4 frame format [54].

Preamble The preamble precedes every transmitted frame. The preamble has an appropriate length to match the physical medium used. The preamble pattern is chosen for the receiving nodes' to be able to acquire the signal level and phase lock. The preamble also guarantees a minimum ED to SD time period so that all nodes have enough time to process the previously received frame.

Start Delimiter (SD) The start delimiter indicates the beginning of the data frame. The SD is 1 byte in length. There can be up to 8,191 bytes between the SD and ED.

Frame Control (FC) The frame control indicates the class of the frame being sent. FC classes include: claim token, solicit successor, who follows, resolve contention, token and set successor.

Destination Address (DA) The destination address indicates the destination of the token. The DA may be 2 or 6 bytes in length. Which ever length is chosen, it is used in all token frames. The first bit of the first address byte indicates whether the address is an individual (0 bit) or a group (1 bit) address.

Source Address (SA) The source address indicates the source of the token. Its length is the same as chosen for the destination address. The first bit of the first address byte is always 0, indicating a local address.

Data The data field, depending on the frame's class (from the frame control byte) may have a length of 0 or a length up to 8182 bytes (with 2 byte DA and SA).

Frame Check Sequence (FCS) The Frame Check Sequence is used to check the correctness of the data frame being received. The FCS is generated with the standard generator polynomial of degree 32. And the FCS is actually the one's complement of 2 additional computations. See the reference (802.4 manual) for further details.

End Delimiter (ED) The End Delimiter ends the frame and determines the position of the FCS. The ED is a byte in length. The seventh bit in the ED indicates if there are more frames to transmit (1) or if this is the end of the transmission (0). And the eighth bit is used to indicate if there is an error with the frame (1) and if there is no error with the frame (0). The ED is defined by the transmitting node. The ED is not protected by the FCS that checks the consistency of the rest of the frame.

An aborted frame, abort sequence or frame abort is defined by a frame that has its SD immediately followed by an ED. A frame that is not an integral number of bytes is also rejected.

The token-passing bus IEEE 802.4 standard has several different faults that can occur. Tokens can be lost, failed to be passed, duplicated, also nodes can fail, and nodes can have duplicate addresses (administrative error). The IEEE 802.4 standard defines methods to trap and respond to each of these problem conditions[25].

The monitoring for token loss or duplication does not need a special monitoring node. Each node on the network (peer network, no masters) is responsible for handling token loss or duplication.

Once the sending node is done with the token, it sends (passes) the token to the next node, or successor, note: the IEEE 802.4 standard offers an optional priority mechanism for token access, see [25] for a detailed discussion therein. After the token is passed, the node passing the token listens for evidence that the successor is active (see Figure 12.9). If a valid frame is heard following the passed token frame, the original sending token presumes that the successor has the token and is operating properly. If the sending node fails to hear a valid token frame it will try to assess the state of the network.

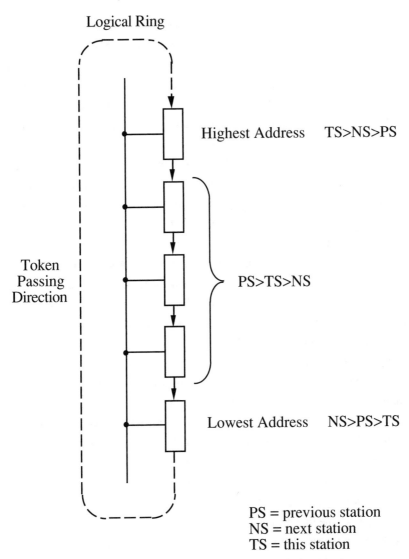

Figure 12.9. Numerical relationship in IEEE 802.4 logical ring [54].

If the sending node does not see a valid token frame, it will listen to see what type of tokens are currently active. If noise or invalid tokens are heard the sending node will presume that the noise (or invalid token) is its own token (used when passing the token) and will retransmit. Once again the sender will listen for a valid frame. If none is heard again the sending node presumes that the successor node has failed (or, perhaps is deaf, the receiving modem of that node's network controller has failed). The sender will now send a who follows frame in an attempt to pick a new successor. All nodes will compare the successor address (the failed successor) to the previous owner address. Each node remembers the previous owner address from the last time the token was passed to that node. The node that matches the successor with the previous owner sends a set successor frame. And that node is now the token holder, this bridges the failed node from the network. If a predefined number of attempts to solicit a successor fail, the sending node will stop soliciting. The network will now either enter an idle state (recourse defined below) or the sender will attempt to claim the token the next time it has a transmission.

If the sending node presumes the successor node has failed when the node has not, duplicate tokens will result. It is also possible for the sending node to hear a delayed version of its own transmission, and thus believes that the successor has taken control of the token. In this case the token will be lost. In the case of duplicate tokens, the tokens will cause chaos and eventually collide, producing noise. And the network will either continue on when one of the sending nodes hears a successor or the network reaches an idle state. The idle state is noted when all nodes are in a listen state for a predefined multiple of slot times. A lost token is noted by the entire network reaching an idle state.

The token initialization algorithm presumes that more than one node may try to initialize at the same instant. Each node attempting to claim the token issues a claim token class frame padded by 0, 2, 4, or 6 slot times based on the first two bits of the node's address. After transmitting the node listens, if anything is heard, it stops trying to claim the token. Otherwise, using the next two bits of its address, the node sends out another claim token frame. This process is repeated until all the address bits are used, the highest numbered node 'wins'. That is, the node that hears silence after its last claim token frame assumes control of the token. Response windows are used to add new nodes to the network (see Figure 12.10). Each active node issues a solicit successor frame each time the node passes the token. The solicit successor frame is solicited for any node with an address between the sending node and the next node in the logical ring. One slot time is waited, during this slot time there may be none, one or multiple responses. In the case of no response to the solicit successor frame, the token is passed to the successor previously established. If one node responds, a set successor frame is heard and the new node enters the network. If multiple nodes respond, noise will be heard. The sending node will now issue a resolve contention frame and wait for four response windows. Based on the first two bits of its address, each node attempting to begin participating in the ring issues a set successor frame. The first node(s) issue the set successor frame in the first response window, an so on. If a contending node hears any frame or noise before

its response window is present it will not transmit. If the original token sender, the one
soliciting a successor, receives a valid set successor frame it will set that node as the next
node and pass the token to it. If no valid set successor frames are heard during the four
response windows the sending node stops trying to determine a successor and passes the
token to the previously established successor.

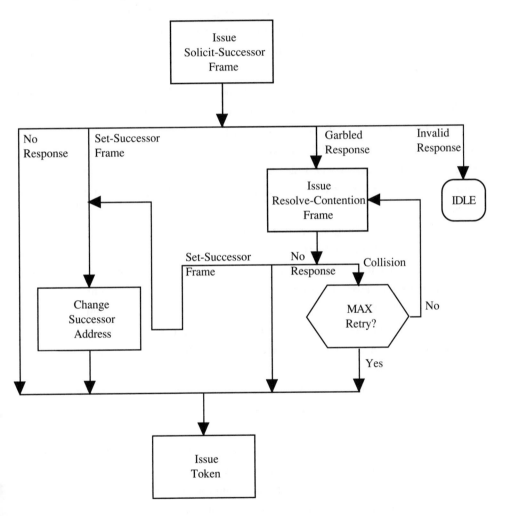

Figure 12.10. Addition of a node [54].

Nodes are removed or deleted from the network by simply not responding when the
token is passed to them. Once the node stops responding when the token is passed to it,

the fault recovery mechanisms previously discussed will remove it from the network.

12.3.3   IEEE 802.5 Token-Passing Ring*

The IEEE 802.5 standard is an outgrowth of IBM's research and development. The IEEE 802.5, or token-passing ring is also recognized by ISO DIS 8802/5, which is a standard supported by the ISO, International Organization for Standardization[26]. It should be noted that IBM was and still is a major influence in the shaping of the IEEE 802.5 standard.

The 802.5 standard defines for both 1 mbs and 4 mbs shielded twisted-pair attachment of the node to the medium, including the definition of the medium interface connector. And, in 1988, IBM has defined a 16 mbs shielded twisted-pair token-ring network in adherence with the IEEE's 802.5 standard. IBM has also defined (for the new 16 Mbs token-ring) for an Early Token Release option to the IEEE 802.5 standard. This option allows token-passing to occur very much as it does in the FDDI standard to be discussed in Section 12.3.4.

The token-ring technique uses free and busy tokens to control access to the network. The token is passed around the ring, when a node needs to transmit it first captures a free token and changes it to a busy token. Once done with the token the node will return a free token to the network. With low network utilization this technique is quite cumbersome. A node wanting to transmit must wait for the token to come back around the network. Under moderate and high network use the token performs in a round-robin manner, providing predictable performance. A new token is released to the network once:

* the owning node has finished its transmission.
* the leading edge of its transmitted frame has returned (after completing one trip around the ring) to the owning node.

If the bit length of the ring is less than the frame length, the first condition implies the second. If not, a node could release a free token after it has finished transmitting but before it receives its own busy token; the second token is not strictly necessary. If the first but not the second condition is true, multiple frames may result, requiring fault recovery. In any case, use of the token guarantees that one and only one node may transmit during any one time period.

---

* see references 1, 6, 16, 18–20, 26, 29, 32, 43, 47, 54, 62, 64, 67 and 72.

The next node downstream with data to send will be able to seize the token and transmit once the current node releases a free token (see Figure 12.11).

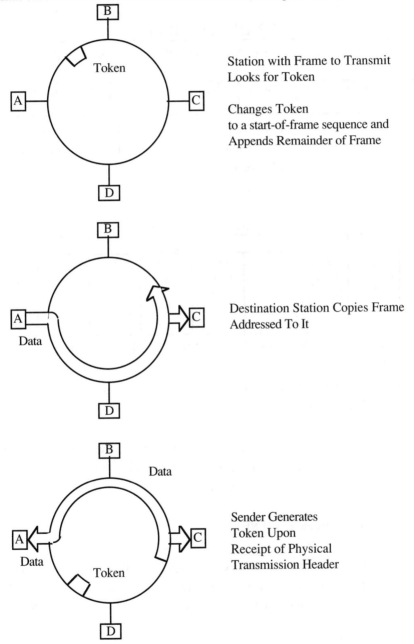

Figure 12.11. IEEE 802.5 token ring [54,64].

The format of the token and frame generated by the IEEE 802.5 protocol is shown in Figure 12.12 below, and then explained.

TOKEN FORMAT

START DELIMETER	ACCESS CONTROL	END DELIMETER
J K 0 J K 0 0 0	P P P │T│M│R R R	J K 1 J K 1 │ I │ E

J=Nondata J   PPP=Priority   I = Intermediate frame bit

K=Nondata K   T=Token bit   E=Error detected

0=Binary 0   M=Monitor bit

                   RRR=Reservation bits

FRAME FORMAT

<— SFS —>		<— FCS Coverage —>					<— EFS —>	
Start De-limiter	Access Control	Frame Check [note 1]	Desti-nation Address (48 bits)	Source Address (48 bits)	Infor-mation	Frame Check Se-quence	End De-limiter	Frame Status [note 2]

Note 1. Format of the Frame Check is FFZZZZZZ, where FF = Frame type, and ZZZZZZ = Control bits.

Note 2. Format of Frame Status us ACRRACRR, where A = Address Recognized, C = Frame Copied, and R is reserved.

Figure 12.12. Token format and frame format [19]. The frame format is used for sending MAC and LLC messages to the destination station(s). The information field is optional.

Start Frame Sequence (SFS):

Start Delimiter (SD)

Indicates the start of the token or frame. The SD is made up of signaling patterns which are always distinguishable from data. It is coded as follows: JK0JK000, where J and K are nondata symbols, 0 is a binary 0. SD is one byte long.

Access Control (AC)

Contains the priority and reservation bits, which are used for the priority mechanism and the monitor bit which is used for ring maintenance. Also, indication of this being a token or a frame is noted, if a token then the ED is the only other field. AC is one byte long.

Frame Check Sequence (FCS):

Frame Control (FC)

Indicates whether this frame contains LLC data or a MAC control frame. If MAC, the control bits indicate the type of MAC frame.

Destination Address (DA)

This field indicates the node(s) that are the intended recipient(s) of this frame. The address may indicate a single node, a group of nodes or may be global (all addresses/nodes). The address used may be 2 or 6 bytes in length and is an implementation decision. Also, the address size (2 or 6 bytes) must be the same size used in the SA and for all nodes on that particular network.

Source Address (SA)

Indicates the sending node's address. Uses the same address size as the DA.

Information (INFO)

Contains LLC data or control information for the MAC protocol. May be 0 bytes or more. There is no maximum length, though the size is implicitly limited by the amount of time a node may possess the token.

Frame Check Sequence (FCS)

A CRC 32 polynomial based on the FC, DA, SA and INFO fields.

End-of-Frame Sequence (EFS):

Ending Delimiter

Contains nondata symbols to indicate the end of the frame. It also includes indicators to indicate if there are more frames or if an error has been detected in the frame. ED is one byte long.

Frame Status (FS)

Frame Status is provided for a redundant check to detect errors. Indicators include the Address recognized and Frame copied, also known as the A and C bits (actually each is 2 bits). Errors include an FCS that appears incorrect and a frame with an incorrect priority.

See Table 12.4 for further details regarding the format of the frame.

In an aborted frame, abort sequence or frame abort is defined by a frame that has its SD immediately followed by an ED. Also, a frame that is not an integral number of bytes is rejected.

Address fields in 802.5 come with recommended structures to provide for a LAN (network) that is divided into multiple rings. The hierarchical address format provides a convenient method for a bridge to recognize frames that are destined for another ring. For 16 bit and 48 bit address fields, the hierarchical address structure is as follows:

16 bit address:

|-I/G-|-7 bit ring address-|-8 bit node address-|

(I/G stands for whether the frame is for an Individual address or a group/global address, all 1's indicates global, otherwise group. I/G is 1 bit long.)

48 bit address:

|-I/G-|-1-|-14 bit ring address-|-32 bit node address-|

(1 is an actual binary 1)

For one node to talk to another, the first node must send the message to its nearest neighbor. The neighbor then repeats the message to its neighbor, and so on. Each node introduces approximately a one bit time delay (250 ns at 4 mbs), this delay is incurred for the time it takes to examine, copy or change a bit of the message as necessary. Even the destination node repeats the message. But, once the destination node receives the token it sets the frame status byte to indicate that it has copied the frame. When the message is passed back to the originating node, it removes the message from the ring. The sending node can determine from the frame status whether the destination was nonexistent/inactive, if the destination exists but did not copy the frame or if the frame was copied (received).

There is a multiple-priority scheme that determines priority of token ownership, see Figure 12.13. There are three values designated, Pm, the priority of the message to be transmitted; Pr, the received priority; and Rr, the received reservation. The scheme works as follows:

1. A node that needs to transmit must wait for a free token where Pr <= Pm.

2. While waiting, a node may reserve a future token at its priority level (Pm). If a busy token goes by, it may set the reservation field to its priority (Rr <- Pm) if the reservation field is less than its priority (Rr < Pm). If a free token goes by, it may set the reservation field to its priority (Rr <- Pm) if Rr < Pm and Pm < Pr. This has the effect of preempting any lower-priority reservations.

3. When a node seizes a token, it sets the token bit to 1, the reservation bit field to 0 and leaves the priority field unchanged.

4. Following transmission, a node issues a new token with the priority set to the maximum of Pr, Rr and Pm, and a reservation set to the maximum of Rr and Pm.

Table 12.4 Token ring frame format fields

Bit	Description
Access Control	
Priority (PPP)	Priority of the token
Token (T)	0 in a token, 1 in a frame
Monitor (M)	Used to prevent persistent data frame or persistent high-priority token
Reservation (R)	Used to request that the next token be issued at the requested priority
Frame control	
Frame type (FF)	MAC or LLC frame
Ending delimiter	
Intermediate frame (I)	0 indicates last or only frame of the transmission; 1 indicates more frames to follow
Error detected (E)	Set by any station that detects an error (e.g. FCS error or nondata symbols)
Frame status	
Address recognized (A)	Station recognizes its address
Frame copied (C)	Station has copied frame

The effect of this scheme is that competing claims for the token are sorted with the highest priority given the token as soon as possible. This scheme has a ratchet effect on priority, driving it to the highest used level and keeping it there. To avoid this, a node that raises the priority has the responsibility of later lowering the priority to its previous level. Two stacks are maintained, one for reservations and one for priorities. In essence, each node is responsible for assuring that no token circulates indefinitely due to its priority being too high. By remembering the priority of an earlier transmission a node can detect this condition and downgrade the priority to a previous, lower priority or reservation.

A node having a higher priority than the current busy token can reserve the next free token for its priority level as the token passes. When the current transmitting node is done, it will issue a free token at that higher priority. Nodes of lower priority cannot seize the token, so it is received by a node of equal or higher priority with data to send.

Token ring maintenance specifies four conditions which can cause the failure of the network. These conditions include the loss of the token, failure to transmit a free token by the node that last had control of the token, a physical medium interruption and failure of the monitor node.

One node is designated as the active token monitor. The monitor node will periodically issue an active monitor present control frame so that other nodes will be aware that there is an active monitor present on the ring. The monitor detects the loss of the token. To reestablish the token the monitor purges the ring of any residual data and issues a free token. The monitor can detect a looping token by inspecting the monitor bit (in the Access Control byte) which it turns on every time it sees a busy token. If a busy token with its monitor bit already set is encountered, the monitor will change the token to a free token. The looping token is caused by the originating node not issuing a free token.

All other nodes participate as passive or standby monitors. If the loss of the active monitor is detected, one of the passive monitors will assume the active monitor duties. If there is a contention, the node with the highest address will become the active monitor via a contention resolution algorithm.

All nodes upon entering the network transmit a duplicate address test frame. If the frame returns with the address recognized bits set to 1 (in the Frame Status byte) then a duplicate address is detected and the entering node removes itself from the ring and issue an error to the higher level protocols.

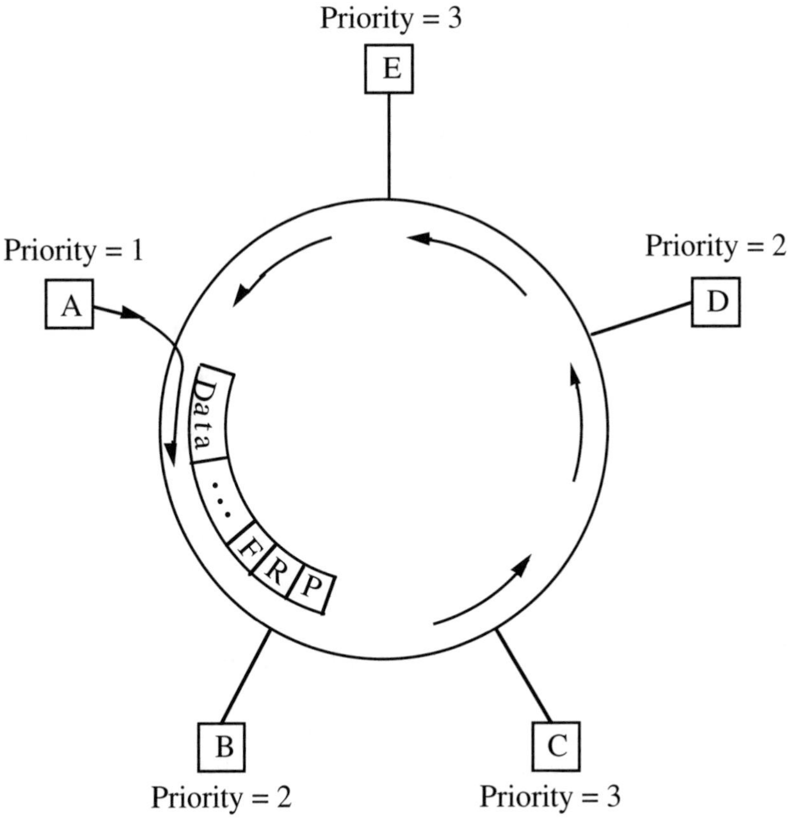

P: Priority Field of Station Using Token
R: Reservation Field
F: Flag to Indicate Ring is Busy or Free

Figure 12.13.   Token ring (priority) [64].

A beacon frame is used to isolate a ring failure, such as a break in the ring or ring medium. When a node is attempting to claim the token it will time out if it does not achieve a resolution. Once timed out, the node issues a beacon to indicate the fault. The monitor will purge the beacon frame, clear the ring and issue a free token. Beacon frames are discussed further under the FDDI section.

12.3.4   Star Networks[*]

Star networks, where every node is connected directly to a master node, require no access methods, see Figure 12.14. Nodes simply sends a request to the master node, if the master node does not respond to the sending node, the sending node will resend its message. Star networks are contentionless. And the effective bandwidth of the Star network increases every time a new node is added. There are no set standards such as IEEE, FIPS or ISO for Star connected networks.

Star networks are very susceptible to major catastrophe if the master node is lost since there is not normally a backup node. Effectively, a backup master node would have a set of connections physically separate from the original master node or somehow share the same connections, perhaps through dual communication controllers at each non-master node. See Figure 12.15 for an alternative Star layout.

Star networks commonly employ a polling technique (much like SNA). The poll is used to determine which nodes are still active and to maintain the network.

12.3.5   Fiber Distributed Data Interface[**]

The Fiber Distributed Data Interface (FDDI) standard is in the process of becoming an ANSI standard, developed by the X3T9.5 ANSI committee[64], see Figure 12.16. The FDDI standard provides for a 100 mbs optical fiber ring LAN. This standard is designed to support high speed network requirements.

The FDDI standard is designed for a 100 mbs fiber optic medium. The wavelength specified is 1300 nm. The FDDI standard also provides for fault tolerance of the network path by employing dual, counterrotating fiber optic rings to interconnect nodes in such a way as if a ring were to malfunction, the second ring can provide for network traffic, see Figure 12.17. As many as 1000 nodes may be placed on one FDDI fiber optic ring. Nodes can be up to two kilometers apart and the ring's circumference may be up to 200 km. These maximum distances are defined to minimize latency of data traveling from node to node.

---

[*] see references 8, 15, 40, 47, 49 and 62.

[**] see references 6, 18, 36, 39, 44, 45, 56, 60 and 64.

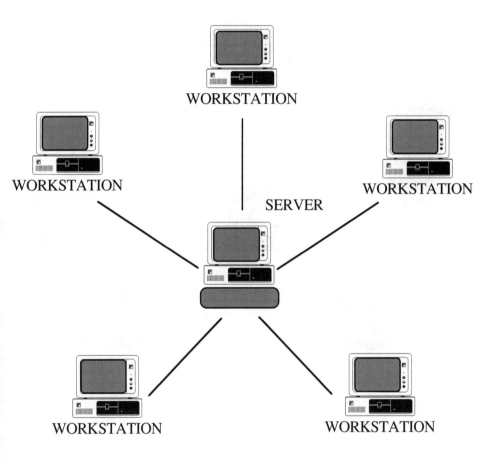

Figure 12.14.   Star topology [40].

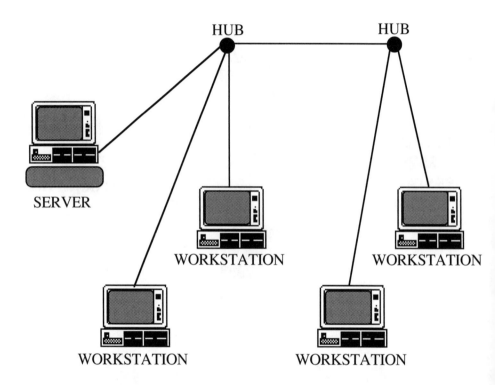

Figure 12.15. Distributed star topology [40].

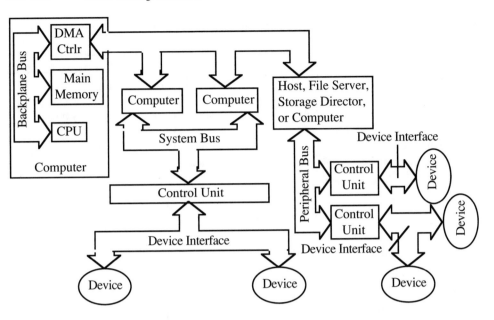

Figure 12.16. Scope of work for ASC committee X3T9.5 [64].

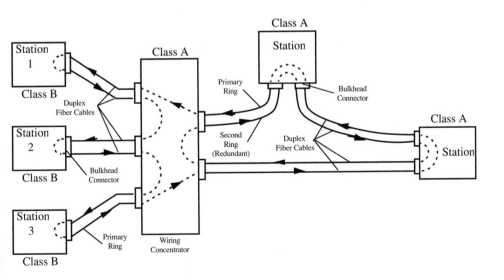

Figure 12.17. FDDI dual-ring operation [64].

The FDDI frame format is shown below in Figure 12.18. A description follows.

<— SFS —>		<— FCS Coverage —>					<— EFS —>	
PA	SD	FC	DA	SA	INFO	FCS	ED	FS

SFS = Start of Frame Sequence   INFO = Information (0 or more symbol pairs)

PA=Preamble (16 or more symbols, see text)   FCS=Frame Check Sequence (8 symbols)

SD=Starting Delimeter (2 symbols)   EFS=End of Frame Sequence

FC=Frame Control (2 symbols)   ED=Ending Delimiter (1 symbol)

DA=Destination address (4 or 12 symbols)   FS=Frame Status (3 or more symbols)

SA=Source Address (4 or 12 symbols)

Figure 12.18. FDDI frame format [64].

Start Frame Sequence (SFS):

Preamble

Synchronizes the frame to each nodes internal clock. The sender uses a field of 16 idle symbols, each symbol is one nibble long making the field 64 bits long. Each repeating node may alter the length of the field to be consistent with clocking needs. The idle symbol is a nondata pattern.

Start Delimiter (SD)

Indicates the start of the token or frame. The SD is made up of signaling patterns which are always distinguishable from data. It is coded as follows: JK, where J and K are nondata symbols. SD is one byte long. Note, symbols here are composed of 4 bits.

Frame Check Sequence (FCS):

Frame Control (FC)

Has a bit format of CLFFZZZ where C indicates this frame is synchronous or asynchronous. L is used to indicate 16 or 48 bit addresses. FF indicates whether this frame contains LLC data or a MAC control frame. If MAC, the control bits (Z) indicate the type of MAC frame.

Destination Address (DA)

This field indicates the node(s) that are the intended recipients of this frame. The address may indicate a single node, a group of nodes or may be global (all addresses/nodes). The address used may be 2 or 6 bytes in length and is an implementation decision. Also, the address size (2 or 6 bytes) may be different on different frames.

Source Address (SA)

> Indicates the sending node's address. Uses the same address size as the DA
> for that frame.

Information (INFO)

> Contains LLC data or control information for the MAC protocol. May be 0
> bytes or more. There is no maximum length, though the size is implicitly
> limited by the amount of time a node may possess the token.

Frame Check Sequence (FCS)

> A CRC 32 polynomial based on the FC, DA, SA and INFO fields.

End-of-Frame Sequence (EFS):

Ending Delimiter

> Contains nondata symbol(s) to indicate the end of the frame. It is composed
> of two symbols, if both symbols are nondata (T symbols) then the frame is
> a token. If the frame is not the token, it has only one T symbol. The
> variation is used to ensure the frame is an integral number of bytes in
> length.

Frame Status (FS)

> Frame Status is provided for a redundant check to detect errors. Indicators
> include the Address recognized and Frame copied, also known as the A and C
> bits (actually each is 2 bits). Errors include an FCS that appears incorrect
> and a frame with an incorrect priority. The field ends with a T symbol if
> need to ensure an integral number of bytes.

Address fields in FDDI come with recommended structures to provide for a LAN
(network) that is divided into multiple rings. The hierarchical address format provides a
convenient method for a bridge to recognize frames that are destined for another ring. For
16 bit and 48 bit address fields, the hierarchical address structure is the same as described
in the 802.5 standard discussion.

FDDI, just like the other token passing networks discussed, uses a token to control
access to the network. But, unlike the others, FDDI uses a multiple token-passing
protocol. The token circles the ring behind the last transmitted packet from a node, see
Figure 12.19. Any node needing to transmit data seizes the token, removes the token,
places its packet(s) on the ring and then issues the new token directly behind its data
stream. This token-passing scheme is predicated on the need for real-time applications on
the network. The timing is designed so that any node is assured of getting the token

within a specified time slot. Also unlike the other token passing topologies, with FDDI each node, as the packet passes, seizes the packet, retimes and regenerates it.

The token is recognized upon inspection of the FC field. If the inspection reveals that the FF and ZZZZ bits are set to all 0's, the frame is the token. The node captures the token by removing or absorbing it from the network. The node may now begin to transmit any frames that it has, frames are limited to a maximum of 4500 bytes. Further, each node has an elastic buffer of at least 10 bits. Data is clocked into the buffer at the clock rate recovered from the incoming data stream, but the data is clocked out of the buffer at the node's autonomous clock rate. FDDI is designed this way, distributed clocking, in an attempt to minimize jitter and make the system more robust.

The jitter phase describes timing jitter that is a deviation of clock recovery that can occur when a receiving node attempts to determine clocking as well as data from the received signal. Each node has an elastic buffer that expands or contracts to accommodate for when data on the ring runs ahead or behind the master clock. It is the size of the elastic buffer that limits frames to a maximum of 4500 bytes.

Each node inspects each token or frame that it sees, absorbing what it needs and repeating everything else. Each node introduces a one bit delay (10 ns at 100 mbs) as the time to inspect, copy or alter a bit is necessary. Each node checks for the data stream for errors and can turn on the E indicator (in the Frame Status field) if an error is discovered. If the frame inspected is destined for the node inspecting it, the node will set the A indicator and it may also set the C indicator if the node copies the frame. The sending node can, upon receipt of the frame after circulating around the ring, determine if the destination node does not exist or is inactive, if the destination node sensed the frame but did not copy it or if the destination node copied the frame.

The sending node is responsible for absorbing and thus removing its frame from the ring. If an error is detected in the received frame, the frame will not be retransmitted. This choice of whether to retransmit or not is determined by higher level protocols (non-MAC layer).

The priority algorithm utilized by the IEEE 802.5 standard is not practical for use by FDDI, this is largely due to the possibility of a sending node issuing a token before its own data frame returns. The FDDI capacity, rather than priority of 802.5, allocation scheme proposes to allow for:

* support of a mixture of bursty and data stream traffic
* support of multiframe dialogs

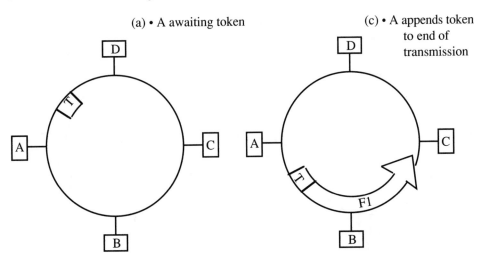

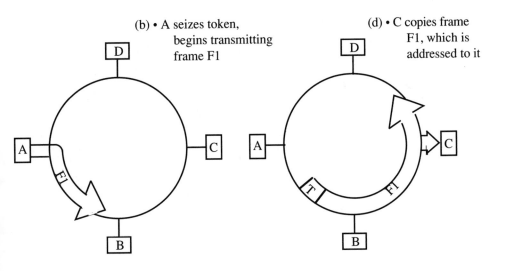

Figure 12.19a. FDDI token operation, part 1 [64].

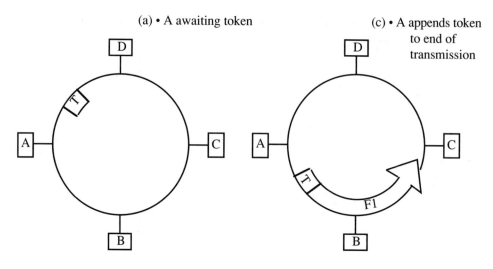

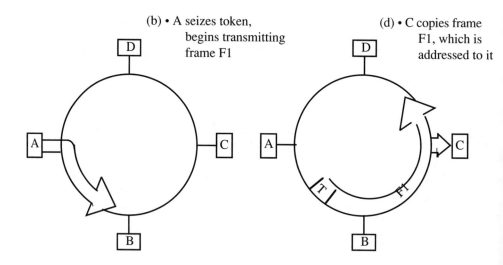

Figure 12.19b. FDDI token operation, part 2 [64].

To support bursty and data stream traffic, FDDI accommodates two types of traffic, asynchronous and synchronous. A target token rotation time (TTRT) is defined. Each node on the network remembers the same TTRT. Some, possibly all, nodes can have a synchronous allocation (SAi) that may not be the same value at each node. Allocation must be:

$$\{SIGMA\}SAi + D\_Max + F\_Max + Token\_Time <= TTRT, \text{ where}$$

SAi   -   allocation for station i

D_Max   -   propagation time for one complete circuit of the ring

F_Max   -   time required to transmit a full length frame of 4500 bytes

Token_Time   -   time required to transmit a token

The assignment of SAi is by means of a station management protocol (SMT) that uses the exchange of SMT Protocol Data Units (SMT PDUs). The protocol ensures that the allocation algorithm is satisfied. Every node has a zero allocation as it enters the network, once part of the network the node requests a change in the allocation. Synchronous allocation is optional and a node that will not support (sending or receiving) of synchronous traffic must support asynchronous traffic.

Every time a node receives the token it measures the time since it last received the token. This value is determined by the token rotation timer (TRT). This value is saved in the token-holding timer (THT). Then the TRT is set to zero and begins counting again. Now a node may transmit based on these two rules:

1. Synchronous frames may be transmitted for a time of SAi
2. After transmitting synchronous frames (if any) the THT is enabled and begins to run from its set value; now the node may transmit asynchronous data as long as THT < TTRT.

These two rules are designed to assure subsequent receipts of the token are on the order of TTRT or less. A given amount of time is always available for synchronous traffic and any excess capacity may be used for asynchronous traffic. Due to traffic loads, TRT may exceed the TTRT at any particular node. But, if there is a backlog, the opportunity to transmit rotates among the nodes thus the network becomes saturated, but still operates.

For asynchronous transmissions there are eight levels of priority. The scheme used is essentially the one used in the 802.5 standard.

FDDI also provides for dedicated multiframe traffic. When a node enters an extended dialogue it gains control of all the unallocated (asynchronous) capacity on the ring through the use of a restricted token. The node first absorbs a non-restricted token and then transmits its first data frame. Next, the restricted token is issued. Only the node that was sent the data frame may use the restricted token. The two nodes may exchange data frames and restricted tokens for as long as they wish. During this time, no other nodes may transmit asynchronous traffic. Note that synchronous frames may be transmitted by any node upon capture of either type of token (restricted or non-restricted).

Each node is responsible for maintaining and monitoring the ring. Error conditions that nodes detect include: extended period of inactivity or incorrect activity such as a persistent or looping data frame. Each node maintains how long it has been since a valid token was last detected. If this time is significantly larger than the TTRT an error condition is detected.

Nodes have three options to correct an error condition, they are:

1. **Claim token process**

   When a node detects the need for initialization of the ring it begins the initiation by issuing claim frames. These frames facilitate the assignment of TTRT and to resolve any contentions there may be among nodes attempting to initialize the ring. Each node inspects the claim frames and either abstains, repeats any received claim frames, or sends its own claim frames, absorbing any incoming frames. The following is used as a basis for the node's decision:
   - the frame with the lowest TTRT has precedence
   - given equal values of TTRT, the frame with the largest SA has precedence
   - given equal values of TTRT and address lengths, the frame with the highest address has   precedence

   The claim token process is finished when the node receives its claim token frame after it has circulated around the ring. When the node receives its own claim token back, this indicates that each node on the ring has acquiesced to this node. All nodes now have their TTRT initialized, and the TTRT will be used to allocate capacity of the ring.

2. **Initialization process**

   The node that was responsible for initializing the TTRT is also responsible for initializing the ring. This node now issues a non-restricted token. Generally, on the first circulation of the token each node uses the token to reset its TRT and change from an initial state to an operating state.

3. **Beacon Process**

The beacon process, as in 802.5, is used to isolate serious ring failures. A serious failure includes a break in the ring and/or a malfunctioning node modem. Once a node enters the beacon process (possibly due to it timing out while attempting to claim the token) it continuously transmits beacon frames. Any node upstream will yield to the beacon frames. The beacon frames will continue until the node originating the beacon frames receives its own beacon frames. At this point, the node will presume the ring has been restored and issue a claim token.

Table 12.5 summarizes the LAN standards discussed.

12.4 LAN Protocol Implementations*

12.4.1   Manufacturing Automation Protocol/Technical Office Protocol

General Motors Corporation (GM), in 1982 embraced the IEEE 802.4 token-passing bus standard through the use of Manufacturing Automation Protocol or MAP[27], see Figure 12.20. Note that MAP can, in addition to IEEE 802.4, alternately use IEEE 802.3 or IEEE 802.5. MAP has its specifications based on the OSI model. MAP is one of the first significant LAN standards developed by a user that encompasses one interface requirement that is used particularly to support the multi-vendor environment GM incorporates. MAP uses the IEEE 802.2 LLC and the ISO 8473 network layer protocol for connectionless-mode network service. Connectionless-mode service was discussed in Chapter 10.

---

* see references 2, 5, 6, 23, 27, 46, 65 and 70.

Table 12.5 LAN standards summary [44]

Standard	Media	Data Rate	Address bits	Access Control
IEEE 802.3 CSMA/CD	Baseband: 50 ohm coax Broadband: 75 ohm coax	Baseband: 10 Mbps Broadband: 5 or 10 Mbps per channel	16 or 48	Exponentially increasing retransmission delays. Max number of retransmissions.
ARCNET	Baseband: 93 ohm coax Broadband: 75 ohm coax	Baseband : 2.5 Mbps Broadband: 2.5 Mbps	2	Each station is sequentially offered the token, peer-to-peer
IEEE 802.4 Token Bus	Baseband: 75 ohm coax Broadband: 75 ohm coax (single, dual)	Baseband: 1, 5, 10 or 20 Mbps Broadband: 1, 5, 10 or 20 Mbps per channel	16 or 48	Station maintains address of preceding and following station. Logically addressed token. Multi-level priority based on allocation by higher level process.
IEEE 802.5 Token Ring	150 ohm twisted pair (TP) 75 ohm coax	1 or 16 Mbps	16 or 48	Highest priority station gets token next
ANSI X3T9.5 FDDI (Token Ring)	Primary and secondary fiber rings with cable types of 100/400, 62.5/125, or 85/125 micron diameter	100 Mbps per ring	16 or 48	Timed token. Token sent immediately after packet. Multilevel priority based on free token cycle time.

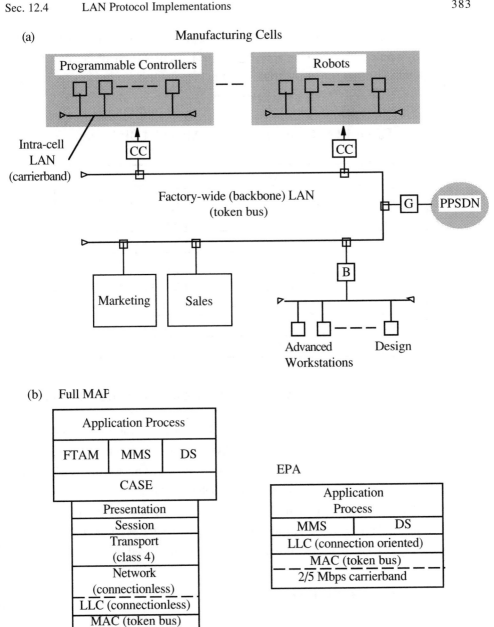

Figure 12.20. MAP network: (a) schematic; (b) protocols [17].

Boeing Computer Services has developed a protocol, the Technical and Office Products System (TOP) (see Figure 12.21). TOP is similar to MAP but uses CSMA/CD (IEEE 802.3) instead of 802.4. TOP specifies communications services for technical and office environments. Table 12.6 compares the layers used in MAP and TOP[2,5]:

Table 12.6 Comparison of MAP and TOP layers

OSI REF	MAP	TOP
Application	ISO 8571 FTAM	ISO 8571 FTAM
Presentation	ISO 8823 IPS	ISO 8822 DIS
Session	ISO 8327 IPS	ISO 8326/ISO 8327 IPS
Transport	ISO 8073 IPS	ISO 8072/ISO 8073
Network	ISO 8473 IPS	ISO 8348/ISO 8473/ISO 8648
Data Link	IEEE 802.2	IEEE 802.2
Physical	IEEE 802.3,.4,.5	IEEE 802.4

12.4.2   Transmission Control Protocol/Internet Protocol

Transmission Control Protocol/Internet Protocol (TCP/IP) was originated by Vinton Cerf in the early 1970's at Stanford University. TCP/IP represents an entire suite of protocols developed in the 1970s as research projects sponsored by the Advanced Research Projects Agency (ARPA) and the Department of Defense (DoD).

TCP/IP represents two different levels of communications. IP relates to the physical layers while TCP relates to the session layers, or specifies the services IP provides, see Figure 12.22. For a more relative discussion, IP will be discussed first and TCP second.

12.4.2.1   Internet Protocol

Internet Protocol, IP, was developed to provide the ability to interconnect heterogeneous networks thus allowing nodes on different networks to communicate. IP is also recognized by DoD IP, MIL-STD-1777 nomenclature. IP resides between the Transport and the Network layers of the OSI model. In this position, IP remains hardware independent.

(a)

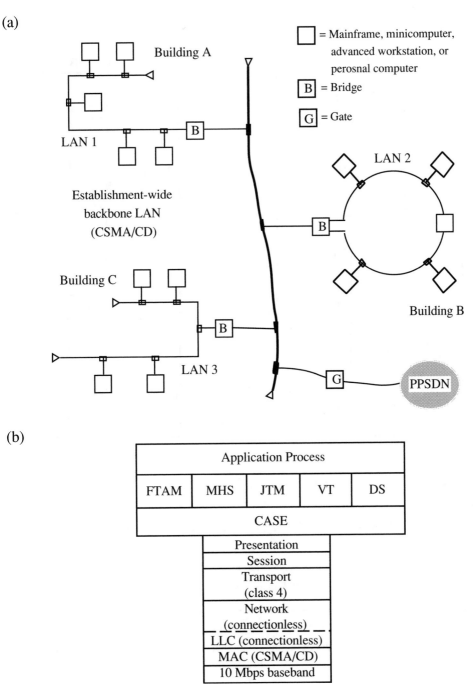

(b)

Figure 12.21. TOP network: (a)schematic; (b) protocols [17].

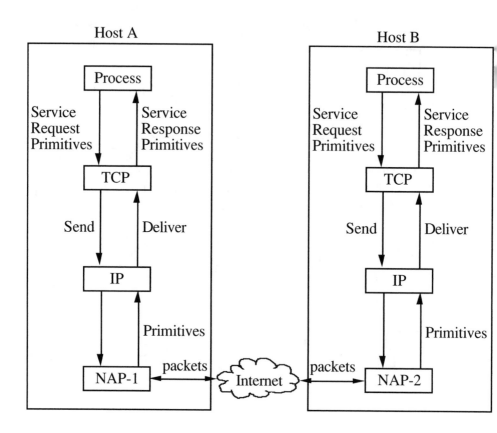

NAP = Network Access Protocol

Figure 12.22. Use of TCP and IP service primitives [65].

IP provides for connectionless service between nodes or hosts. IP's service involves datagrams, by using datagrams IP does not develop a logical connection between nodes or guarantee that the data (datagrams) will be delivered. Also, as is the nature of datagrams, the order of the data packets are received is not necessarily in the same order as transmitted. But, by providing connectionless service IP does offer a number of benefits:

Robustness

Each datagram (data packet) is routed independently through the network or internetwork by using virtual paths. This allows the datagrams to be individually routed the best way possible including around nodes that are out of service. For these reasons datagrams can arrive at their destination in any order.

Adaptable

IP can be operated across disjoint network services. Services of networks such as those that offer connection-oriented service and those that do not.

Modular

For applications requiring routing, flow control and connection oriented protocols, TCP can be used in coordination with IP to provide these services. IP defines for datagram life, datagram fragmentation and defragmentation, addressing, routing, error and flow control.

Datagram life

Every datagram is given an upper bound on its lifetime. This bound is used to determine when to remove the datagram from the internet. Datagrams that are transported normally between source and destination will usually not be affected by its upper bound. But, there exists the possibility that datagrams can loop indefinitely in the network consuming resources and preventing the timely delivery of data, or delivery at all. The aspect of timely delivery relates to the use of TCP with IP. This aspect will be discussed under the TCP heading.

Datagram Fragmentation

Due to IP's versatile nature, specifically its ability to utilize heterogeneous networks, datagrams may be fragmented or divided according to the physical restraints of intervening networks. IP does not define a standard packet (datagram) size. Since datagrams can be continually downsized or fragmented during their journey all defragmentation occurs at the destination node. Defragmentation is not performed at intervening gateways, if it was, large buffers would be required to absorb all the pieces of a datagram and this would prevent the use of dynamic routing since all packets would be assembled at some intermediary point.

The format of an IP datagram format is shown in Figure 12.23 Field definitions follow.

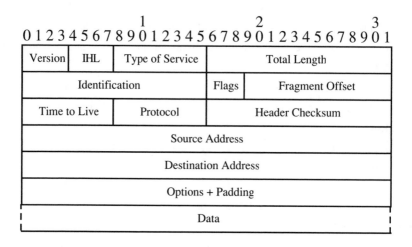

Figure 12.23.   Internet protocol format [65].

Version (V)

Version number, included to allow the evolution of the protocol. Four bits long (nibble).

Internet Header Length (IHL)

Indicates the length of the header in 32 bit words with a minimum value of five, consequently, a header is always a minimum of 20 bytes long.

Type of Service (ToS)

Used to specify reliability, precedence, delay and throughput parameters. One byte long.

Total Length (TL)

Represents the length of the entire datagram including the header in bytes. The field itself is two bytes long.

Identification (ID)

Used with the SA, DA and user protocol in an attempt to uniquely identify the datagram. Two bytes long.

Flags (Flg)

The first bit is the more flag, the next is for the don't fragment flag, the third bit is unused. The field is 3 bits long.

Fragment Offset (FO)

Used to point where this datagram fits. The offset is indicated in 8 byte units. All fragments save the last must contain a data field in some multiple of 8 bytes.

Time To Live (TTL)

Indicates in one second increments how long the datagram is to live on the internet. One byte long.

Protocol (P)

Used to indicate the next protocol that is to receive the data portion of the datagram once it arrives at its destination. One byte long.

Header Checksum (HC)

A simple one's complement checksum (see appendix QR) is applied against the entire datagram save the header checksum field. This calculation is performed at each gateway and at the receiving node. If there is a discrepancy the datagram is forsaken. The checksum is 2 bytes long.

Source Address (SA)

Used to indicate the sending network and node. The SA is four bytes long.

Destination Address (DA)

Used to indicate the destination network and node. Also four bytes long.

Options (O)

Indicates options from the sender. This field has a variable length.

Padding (P)

Used to ensure the internet header, which it is the last field of, ends on a 4 byte boundary. Also of variable length.

Data (D)

The field must be an integral number of bytes long. The maximum length is determined by 65,535 minus the size of the header in bytes [64,65].

The Options field is used to indicate the options desired concerning the current datagram. There are three options, copy flag, option class and option number. The copy flag is used to indicate where this option is to be copied into all fragments or just the first one. Options that are to be copied include security, strict source routing and stream identifier. Note that loose source routing, route recording and timestamping appear only in the first fragment.

The option class and option number identify the specific options desired.

Each datagram and fragmented datagrams have a header that indicates an ID, data length, offset and a more flag. The ID is used to uniquely identify the originating node. Further on the ID, IP's ID includes the source and destination addresses of the datagram and a sequence number. The data length is the size of the data field in bytes. The offset is the position of the fragment in the original datagram, indicated in multiples of 64 bits. The more flag is a boolean indicator for the indication of more fragments to succeed this fragment.

For instance, the original datagram would have a data length equal to the length of the datagram's entire data field and would have an offset of zero and the more flag set to false.

Unfortunately, IP does not guarantee delivery and it is quite possible that a datagram or a fragment of a datagram will not arrive at the destination. IP defines that the datagram lifetime be indicated in the header of each datagram/fragment. As each fragment is received a timer, based on the datagram's lifetime, starts to count down. As each new fragment is received (part of the original fragment, all leading to the assembly of the original datagram) the timer is incremented again by the lifetime of the datagram fragment. If the timer ever expires before all fragments are received, the entire datagram is forsaken.

Addressing

IP uses the hardware addressing scheme of the underlying network. The IP does not concern itself with the correct destination address, it does complete the source address. The destination address is handed down from higher level protocols such as TCP.

Routing

Each IP node and gateway maintains a routing table that is used to indicate the best node or the gateway to send the datagram to in order for the datagram to be routed on its way. These routing tables are static or dynamic. Static tables generally include alternate routes for when the primary route is unavailable. Dynamic routing tables are involved more with maintaining current information about the network. If a gateway became unavailable, nodes or gateways that were using it will send out messages to other nodes and gateways indicating that the gateway is down. The interested reader may desire to consult [12,46] which specifies a variety of internet control messages used in routing.

IP also allows for source routing. Source routing indicates that the transmitting node defines a list of gateways in the datagram. This list is used to indicate the route the datagram is to take. This is generally done to provide security or priority to the datagram. IP also can use route recording, where each node the datagram visits on its journey has its address appended to the end of the datagram. This allows for network analysis and debugging.

Error Control

Although the IP does not guarantee delivery, when a datagram is refused due to the timer running out, the receiving node, if the underlying network configuration allows it, will attempt to return information concerning the discarded datagram to the originating node. Datagrams may also be discarded if there is an error detected in the datagram. But, due to the bit error, the datagram may not have a recognizable ID. It is the ID field of the datagram that is used to identify the datagram and its source.

Flow Control

IP does not specify flow control. But the Internet Control Message Protocol (ICMP), which is a user of IP, does (see Figure 12.24).

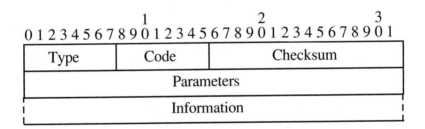

Figure 12.24. ICMP format [64].

The ICMP resides in the same layers that IP does, but ICMP is a user of IP. ICMP provides information concerning the network. ICMP messages have the following fields:

1. Type, 1 byte, indicates the type of ICMP message.
2. Code, 1 byte, indicates parameters of the message.
3. Checksum, 2 bytes, provides checksum of the entire ICMP message.
4. Parameters, 4 bytes, specifies any necessary parameters.
5. Information, n bytes, indicates additional message information.

Currently, nine ICMP message types are defined:

1. Destination unreachable
2. Echo
3. Echo reply
4. Parameter problem
5. Redirect
6. Source quench
7. Time exceeded
8. Timestamp
9. Timestamp reply

The destination unreachable message indicates one of several conditions. These conditions include: when the datagram includes a route that is unavailable, a node determines that the user protocol or another high level protocol is unavailable. Also, when a gateway determines that the destination is unreachable or if the gateway does not know how to route the datagram to its destination. Finally, the destination unreachable can be caused if a datagram has its don't fragment indicator on and an intervening gateway needs to fragment the datagram. The first 8 bytes of the IP header are returned in this message.

The echo and echo reply messages are used to test the communication between two nodes. The originating node sends an echo message and the destination node replies with an echo reply message. The first 8 bytes of the IP header are returned in this message.

The parameter problem message is used to indicate a semantic or syntactic error in the header of a datagram. The parameter field has a pointer to the point in the header, the first 8 bytes of the header are returned, where the error is suspected.

The redirect message is sent by a gateway to indicate to the sending node that a quicker route can be obtained by sending its data via another gateway. The gateway will forward the original datagram to its destination. The address of the other gateway to use is contained in the parameter field and the first 8 bytes of the original datagram header, are both returned in the redirect message.

The source quench message provides for primitive flow control. A gateway or a node may send this message to the sending node. The source quench message is a request to decrease the rate at which datagrams are being sent. The first 8 bytes of the offending datagram are sent to the originating node.

The time exceeded message is sent by a node to indicate that the lifetime of the datagram, whose first 8 bytes are returned, has expired before its delivery was complete.

The timestamp and timestamp reply messages are used to sample delay characteristics of the intervening network between two nodes. The originating timestamp is included in the information field. The receiving node appends its timestamp and returns the message as a timestamp reply.

Example transmission:

To reflect on what IP does, the following depicts the initiation and transmission of an IP datagram:

1. The sending node constructs the IP datagram based on the SEND PRIMITIVES received.
2. The checksum is calculated and inserted into the IP datagram.
3. The route is determined, either the destination can be directly sent to or an intervening gateway must be chosen.
4. The IP datagram is passed to the data-link and physical layers for delivery.

At each gateway:

1. Each gateway the datagram crosses performs the checksum calculation; if the checksum in the datagram and the calculated one do not match, the datagram is purged from the network.
2. The time to live counter is decremented; if the time has expired the datagram is purged   from the network.
3. The gateway makes the decision on where to route the datagram next. The datagram is fragmented if necessary.
4. The IP header is reconstructed to reflect the new time to live, fragmentation and new checksums.
5. The IP datagram is passed to the data-link and physical layers for delivery.

At the destination mode:

1. The checksum is calculated. If the checksum calculated does not match the datagram's, the packet is purged.
2. If the datagram received is a fragment, it is buffered in anticipation of the receipt

of the remaining fragments. Once all fragments have been received or the time
to live counter   has expired the datagram is assembled or purged.

3. If the datagram arrives successfully, the data and parameters are passed up to the
higher layers (TCP).

12.4.2.2   Transmission Control Protocol

Transmission Control Protocol (TCP) developed originally for use in ARPAnet [53],
is now used as the transport protocol standard for the U.S. Department of Defense (DoD).
TCP also has been combined with IP (TCP/IP) to provide a defacto protocol standard for
heterogeneous node communications. Acceptance of TCP/IP following DoD acceptance
is found in Table 12.7.

Table 12.7 TCP/IP momentum since 1983

1983 - Berkeley, Excelan and Sun Microsystems
1984 --Wollongong and CMC
1985 - Bridge Communications, NRC and Siemens
1986 - Novell, DEC, Ungerman-Bass and Interlan
1987 - IBM and Sytek
1988 - Microsoft, Apple and NCR

TCP resides in the Transport layer of the OSI model. It receives data to be delivered
from upper layer protocols. And proceeds to provide reliable transportation of the data, in
segments, to its destination. TCP is a connection-oriented protocol. TCP provides the
following services:

Connection
> Establishment
> Management
> Termination

Data Transport
> Full duplex
> Timely (user specified)
> Ordered

Labeled

Flow Control

Error Checked

Multiplexing

Multiple pairs of processes

Sockets

Connections

Flow   Control

Determined by receiving TCP

Sliding windows

Send/Receive message spaces

Special   Capabilities

Data Stream Push (expedited delivery)

Urgent Data Signalling (expedited receipt)

Error Reporting

TCP's services are provided by a set of primitives and parameters. Tables 12.8, 12.9 and 12.10 provide details of TCP's Request and Response Primitives and TCP's Service Parameters.

Transmission Control Protocol, a Transport layer protocol operates as an intermediary between applications and the internetwork. TCP frees the need for the higher application layers to become involved in the complex business of maintaining and communicating with other nodes. TCP is but an abstraction of the physical communication process. The services of the Internet Protocol are used by TCP to provide for the actual exchange of data. Since IP is not reliable, TCP assumes that:

1.   Segments may be lost or arrive somewhere with errors.

2.   Segments may not be received in transmitted order.

3.   Segments may be delayed at a variable rate which slows communications.

Segments produced by TCP are transmitted by IP in the form of datagrams, which were previously discussed. Segments transmitted by TCP may arrive out of order; note that one segment corresponds to one datagram. In order to manage the receipt of segments, TCP sequentially numbers each segment. The segments can be properly assembled at their destination according to their sequence number. Segments, like datagrams, can be lost. TCP sends an acknowledgment (ACK) segment for each segment it receives. If the sending TCP does not receive an ACK within a reasonable amount of time, it presumes the loss of the segment and re-sends. The repeated segment is generally re-sent with the same sequence number. TCP is only able to re-send the missing segment due to the use of a segment buffer that holds each segment transmitted until an ACK is received.

Table 12.8 TCP service request primitives [65]

Primitive	Parameters[*]	Description
Unspecified Passive Open	source port, [timeout], [timeout-action], [precedence], [security range]	Listen for connection attempt at specified security and precedence from any remote destination
Fully Specified Passive Open	source port, destination port, destination address, [timeout], [timeout-action], [precedence], [security-range]	Listen for connection attempt at specified security and precedence from specified destination
Active Open	source port, destination port, destination address, [timeout], [timeout-action], [precedence], [security]	Request connection at a particular security and precedence to a specified destination
Active Open With Data	source port, destination port, destination address, [timeout], [timeout-action], [precedence], [security], data, data length, PUSH flag, URGENT flag	Request connection at a particular security and precedence to a specified destination and transmit data with the request
Send	local connection name, data, data length, PUSH flag, URGENT flag, [timeout], [timeout-action]	Transfer data across named connection
Allocate	local connection name, data length	Issue incremental allocation for receive data to TCP
Close	local connection name	Close connection gracefully
Abort	local connection name	Close connection abruptly
Status	local connection name	Query connection status

[*] square brackets indicate optional parameter

Table 12.9 TCP service response primitives [65]

Primitive	Parameters	Description
Open ID	local connection name, source port, destination port[*], destination address[*]	Informs user of connection name assigned to pending connection requested in an Open primitive
Open Failure	local connection name	Report failure of an Active Open request
Open Success	local connection name	Reports completion of a pending Open request
Deliver	local connection name, data, data length, URGENT flag	Report arrival of data
Closing	local connection name	Reports that remote TCP user has issued a Close and that all data sent by remote user has been delivered
Terminate	local connection name, description	Reports that the connection has been terminated and no longer exists; a description of the reason for termination is provided
Status Response	local connection name, source port, source address, destination port, destination address, connection state, receive window, send window, amount awaiting ACK, amount awaiting receipt, urgent state, precedence, security timeout	Reports current state of connection
Error	local connection name, description	Reports service request or internal error

[*]Not used for Unspecified Passive Open

Table 12.10 TCP service parameters

Parameter	Description
Source Port	Identifier of the local TCP user
Timeout	The longest delay allowed for data delivery before automatic connection termination or error report. User specified.
Timeout-action	In the event of a timeout, determines if the connection is terminated or an error is reported to the user.
Precedence	Actual or requested precedence level for a connection. Takes on values zero (lowest) through seven (highest). Same parameter as defined in IP.
Security-range	Security structure that specifies the allowed ranges in compartment, handling restrictions, transmission control codes and security levels.
Destination Port	Identifier of the remote TCP user.
Destination Address	Internet address of the remote host.
Security	Security information (including security level, compartment, handling restrictions, and transmission control code) for a connection. Same parameter as defined in IP.
Data	Block of data sent by a TCP user or delivered to a TCP user.
Data Length	Length of block of data sent or delivered.
PUSH Flag	If set, this indicates that the associated data are to be provided with the data stream push service.
URGENT Flag	If set, this indicates that the associated data are to be provided with the urgent data signaling service.
Local Connection Name	The shorthand identifier of a connection defined by a local socket/remote socket pair. Provided by TCP.
Description	Supplementary information in a Terminate or Error primitive,
Source Address	Internet address of the local host.
Connection State	State of referenced connection (i.e. CLOSED, ACTIVE OPEN, PASSIVE OPEN, ESTABLISHED, or CLOSING).
Receive Window	Amount of data in octets the local TCP entity is willing to receive.
Send Window	Amount of data in octets permitted to be sent to remote TCP entry.
Amount Awaiting ACK	Amount of data in octets buffered at local TCP and pending receipt by local TCP user.
Amount Awaiting Receipt	Amount of data in octets buffered at local TCP and pending receipt by local TCP user.
Urgent State	Indicated to the receiving TCP user whether there is urgent data available or whether all urgent data, if any, has been delivered to the user.

Then TCP establishes a connection (session) between two sockets (nodes). The connection established serves two purposes:

1. To define all connection characteristics including security.
2. To allow for each TCP socket to maintain state information about the connection; state information such as the last sequence number used, last sequence number received and last sequence number acknowledged.

TCP has been designed to service multiple processes' requests within a single node. For instance, a node that is a Unix host is likely to have several processes running concurrently that will use services of TCP. Each process using a TCP service is identified by a port. A port and an internet address are combined to form a socket. The formed socket is unique throughout the entire internet. In TCP the socket is the basic communication mechanism and is a communication endpoint in each TCP. TCP proceeds to provide reliable communication between pairs of sockets. Interestingly, two processes within the same node could actually use TCP to communicate with each other because of their unique sockets.

The   fields of the TCP segment frame are described in Figure 12.25. A description follows.

Source port (2 bytes)
   Indicates source port.
Destination port (2 bytes)
   Indicates destination port.
Sequence number (4 bytes)
   Indicates the sequence number of the first data byte in this segment, except when SYN is present. When SYN (see below) is present, it is the initial sequence number (ISN) and the first data byte is ISN + 1.
Acknowledgment number (4 bytes)
   Indicates the sequence number of the next byte that the TCP entity expects to receive; used for piggyback acknowledgments (see Acknowledgment Policy at the end of the chapter).
Data offset (1 nibble)
   Indicates the number of 32-bit words in the header.

```
              1                   2                   3
0 1 2 3 4 5 6 7 8 9 0 1 2 3 4 5 6 7 8 9 0 1 2 3 4 5 6 7 8 9 0 1
```

SOURCE PORT	DESTINATION PORT
SEQUENCE NUMBER	
ACKNOWLEDGEMENT NUMBER	

DATA OFFSET	RESERVED	U R G	A C K	P S H	P S T	S Y N	F I N	WINDOW

CHECKSUM	URGENT POINTER
OPTIONS & PADDING	
DATA	

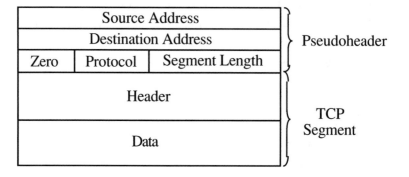

Figure 12.25. TCP Header Format [65].

Reserved (6 bits)

Not currently used.

Flags (6 bits)

URG: Urgent pointer field significant   ACK: Acknowledgment   field
significant   PHS: Push Function RST: Reset connection   SYN:
Synchronize the sequence numbers

FIN: End of data from sender

Window (2 bytes)

Flow control credit allocation in bytes, contains the number of data bytes beginning with the one indicated in the acknowledgment field that the sender is willing to accept.

Checksum (2 bytes)

One's complement of the sum mod $2^{16} - 1$ of all the 2 byte words in the segment plus a 96 bit pseudo-header that contains the source internet address, destination internet address, protocol and TCP segment length.

Urgent Pointer (2 bytes)

Indicates the byte following the urgent data; allows the receiver to know how much urgent data are coming.

Options (variable)

Currently specifies the maximum segment size to be accepted.

The TCP standard supplies a specific protocol for communication between TCP entities. TCP also supplies several implementation options. Five of these options or policies will now be discussed:

1. Send
2. Deliver
3. Accept
4. Retransmit
5. Acknowledge

Send Policy

When the Data Stream Push isn't exercised the sending TCP can transmit data whenever it is appropriate. User data is buffered by TCP, who will send each set of user data as its own segment or accumulate some prespecified amount of user data before assembling a segment. The exact implementation chosen can affect performance by increasing or decreasing network load.

Deliver Policy

Without the use of the Data Stream Push a recipient TCP node is free to deliver data to its client at its convenience. Data may be delivered in sequence order as received or TCP may buffer several data segments and deliver a lump of segments. The policy chosen affects performance from the receiving TCP's viewpoint.

Accept   Policy

The receiving TCP can choose to accept only segments that arrive in sequence order or to accept segments within the same receive window.   If the TCP determines that it will only accept segments arriving in sequence order this can create extra communication in order to reject and re-send segments.   If TCP accepts any segment arriving in the current receive window, then TCP is responsible to ensure that all segments arrive and to place them in proper order before delivery to the client (user).

Retransmit   Policy

A sending TCP maintains a queue of segments that have been transmitted but not acknowledged.   The TCP protocol specifies that the sending TCP will retransmit to any segment it fails to receive, within a specified time period, an acknowledgment.   The sending TCP has three options in regards to the retransmission of unacknowledged segments:

First-only

One timer is maintained for the entire queue. When an acknowledgment is received that segment is removed and the timer is reset. If the timer expires the segment at the beginning of the queue is retransmitted.

Batch

One timer is maintained for the entire queue. When an acknowledgment is received the segment is removed and the timer is reset (so far, just like First-only option). But, if the timer expires, the entire queue of unacknowledged segments are retransmitted and the timer is reset.

Individual

A timer is maintained for each segment in the queue. When an acknowledgment is received, the corresponding segment is removed and its timer is cancelled. When a timer expires, that segment is retransmitted and its timer is reset.

The first-only policy is useful because only unacknowledged segments are re-sent (note that an acknowledgment may be lost on its way back to the sending TCP and therefore its segment remains unacknowledged at the sending TCP). But, with the first-only policy there may be considerable delays in segment communication.

The batch policy reduces the chance of delays but at the price of possibly excessive retransmissions. But, the batch policy can be useful for receiving nodes that must receive segments in sequence.

The individual policy, generically, is the most useful policy. But, at the cost of extra overhead at the sending TCP which may be proportional to the communication needs of the network.

Acknowledge Policy

The receiving TCP has two options when acknowledging received segments. Segment acknowledgments may be sent upon the arrival of each segment. As each segment is received, note its arrival internally, waiting for an outbound segment in which an acknowledgment may be piggybacked. In the case of no outbound segments a timer is used to force the sending of the acknowledgment upon the expiration of the timer. The immediate acknowledgment is straightforward and keeps acknowledgments current at both ends of the connection. There may be extra segment transmissions to achieve this result.

The time acknowledgment policy demands additional overhead at the receiving TCP and may result in extraneous retransmissions from the sending TCP.

12.5 Exercises

12.1   Describe and discuss the main differences of LANs from other network models.

12.2   Discuss each type of network topology and the protocols that are used to provide access to each.

12.3   Discuss the different physical cabling schemes for IEEE 802.3/Ethernet and what you would use for the basis of which one to utilize.

12.4   Differentiate between the CSMA/CD, CSMA/CA and CSMA/CE access protocols.

12.5   Detail how a token is used as a means for data and control information transfer on ARCnet, IEEE 802.4, IEEE 802.5 and FDDI.

12.6   How does the FDDI token-passing implementation differ from the other token-passing standards, explain why it is better or worse.

12.7   Which of the token-passing protocols discussed in this chapter reflect the most overhead (for control purposes, i.e. non-data transfer) and why? Is this excess beneficial or necessary, in your mind?

12.8   What would you do to decrease the need for control information transfer in token-passing networks, would you use another protocol, if so why?

12.9   Describe how the priority algorithm works in IEEE 802.5, give an example. Do the same for the FDDI priority algorithm.

12.10   Discuss the differences between TCP and IP of TCP/IP.

12.11   Describe how ICMP fits into the TCP/IP protocol and what benefits it offers.

12.12   Explain the different implementation options of TCP, do you feel they are adequate? What would you add to make the TCP protocol even more viable.

12.6   References

1   Andrews, D. W., and Schultz, G. D., "A Token-Ring Architecture for Local Area Networks: An Update." Proceedings, COMPCON Fall 82, IEEE, 1982.

2   Alcatel Corporation, "Leading LAN Standards." Communications Week, no date.

3   Bartee, T. C. (ed.), Data Communications, Networks, and Systems. Indianapolis, IN: Howard W. Sams & Co., Inc., 1985.

4   Bhusri, G., "Considerations for ISDN Planning and Implementation." IEEE Communications Magazine, January 1984.

5   Black, U., Computer Networks. Englewood Cliffs, NJ: Prentice-Hall, 1987.

6   Black, U., Data Networks: Concepts, Theory, and Practice. Englewood Cliffs, NJ: Prentice-Hall, 1989.

7   Bux, W., "Local-Area Subnetworks: A Performance Comparison." IEEE Trans. on Comm., October 1981.

8   Bux, W.; Closs, F.; Janson, P. A.; Kummerle, K.; Miller, H. R.; and Rothauser, H., "A Local-Area Communication Network Based on a Reliable Token Ring System." Proceedings, International Symposium on Local Computer Networks, 1982.

9   Chou, W. (ed.), Computer Communications, Vol. II: Systems and Applications. Englewood Cliffs, NJ: Prentice-Hall, 1985.

10   Clark, D. D.; Pogran, K. T.; and Reed, D. P., "An Introduction to Local Area Networks." Proceedings of the IEEE, November 1978.

11   Cotton, I. W., "Techniques for Local Area Computer Networks." Proceedings, Local Area Communications Network Symposium, 1979.

12   Defense Communications Agency, DDN Protocol Handbook. Menlo Park, CA:
        DDN Network Information Center, SRI International, December 1985.

13   Deasington, R. J., X.25 Explained. Chicester, England: Halsted Press, 1985.

14   Derfler, F., and Stallings, W., A Manager's Guide to Local Networks.
        Englewood Cliffs, NJ: Prentice-Hall/Spectrum, 1983.

15   Dixon, R. C., "Ring Network Topology for Local Data Communications."
        Proceedings, COMPCON Fall 82, IEEE, 1982.

16   Franta, W., and Chlamtec, I., Local Networks. Lexington, MA: Lexington
        Books, 1981.

17   Halsall, F., Data Communications, Computer Networks, and OSI (2nd edition).
        Reading, MA: Addison-Wesley, 1988.

18   Hammond, J. L., and O'Reilly, J. P., Performance Analysis of Local Computer
        Networks. Reading, MA: Addison-Wesley, 1986.

19   Haugdahl, J. S., "The Token-Ring Solution." PC Tech Journal, 5, 1, January
        1981.

20   Hickey, J., "Wire and Cable--What's Happening?" Instruments and Control
        Systems, 53, 8, August 1980.

21   Hopkins, G. T., "Multimode Communications on the MITRENET."
        Proceedings, Local Area Communications Network Symposium, 1979.

22   Hopkins, G. T., and Wagner, P. E., Multiple Access Digital Communications
        Systems. US Patent 4, 210, 780, July 1, 1980.

23   The Institute of Electrical and Electronics Engineering, "Logical Link Control."
        ANSI/IEEE std. 802.2, 1985.

24   The Institute of Electrical and Electronics Engineering, "Carrier Sense Multiple
        Access with Collision Detection (CSMA/CD) Access Method and Physical
        Layer Specification." ANSI/IEEE std. 802.3, 1985.

25   The Institute of Electrical and Electronics Engineering, "Token-Passing Bus
        Access Method and Physical Layer Specification." ANSI/IEEE std. 802.4,
        1985.

26   The Institute of Electrical and Electronics Engineering, "Token Ring Access
        Method and Physical Layer Specification." ANSI/IEEE std. 802.5, 1985.

27   Kaminisky, M., "Protocols for Communicating in the Factory." IEEE
        Spectrum, April 1986.

28   Kuo, F. (ed.), Protocols and Techniques for Data Communication Networks.
        Englewood Cliffs, NJ: Prentice-Hall, 1981.

29 Liu, M. T., "Distributed Loop Computer Networks." In Advances in Computers, Vol. 17 (ed. M. C. Yovits). New York, NY: Academic Press, 1978.

30 Liu, M. T.; Hilal, W.; and Groomes, B. H., "Performance Evaluation of Channel Access Protocols for Local Computer Networks." Proceedings, COMPCON Fall 82, 1982.

31 Luczak, E. C., "Global Bus Computer Communication Techniques." Proceedings, Computer Network Symposium, 1978.

32 Markov, J. D., and Strole, N. C., "Token-Ring Local Area Networks: A Perspective." Proceedings, COMPCON Fall 82, IEEE, 1982.

33 Martin, J., Computer Networks and Distributed Processing. Englewood Cliffs, NJ: Prentice-Hall, 1981.

34 McHale, J., "Answering One of Connectivity's Interesting Challenges." LAN Times, March 1988.

35 McQuillan, J. M., and Cerf, V. G., A Practical View of Computer Communications Protocols. Washington, DC: IEEE Computer Society Press, 1978.

36 Myers, W., "Toward a Local Network Standard." IEEE Micro, August 1982.

37 Metcalfe, R. M., and Boggs, D. R., "Ethernet: Distributed Packet Switching for Local Computer Networks." Proceedings of the ACM, 1976.

38 Miller, C. K., and Thompson, D. M., "Making a Case for Token Passing in Local Networks." Data Communications, March 1982.

39 Nelson, J., "802: A Progress Report." Datamation, September 1983.

40 Novell, Inc., LAN Evaluation Report. Provo, UT: Novell, Inc., 1986.

41 Pake, G. E., "Research at Xerox PARC: A Founder's Assessment." IEEE Spectrum, October 1985.

42 Parker, R., and Shapiro, S., "Untangling Local Area Networks." Computer Design, March 1983.

43 Penny, B. K., and Baghdadi, A. A., "A Survey of Computer Communications Loop Networks." Computer Communications, August and October 1979.

44 Pickholtz, R. L. (ed.), Local Area and Multiple Access Networks. Rockville, MD: Computer Science Press, 1986.

45 Pooch, U. W.; Greene, W. H.; and Moss, G. G., Telecommunications and Networking. Boston, MA: Little, Brown and Company, 1983.

46 Postel, J. B.; Sunshine, C. A.; and Cihen, D., "The ARPA Internet Protocol."

Computer Networks, 1981.

47   Rauch-Hindin, W., "Upper-Level Network Protocols." Electronic Design, March 3, 1983.

48   Rosenthal, R. (ed.), The Selection of Local Area Computer Networks. National Bureau of Standards Special Publication 500-96, November 1982.

49   Saltzer, J. H., and Pogran, K. T., "A Star-Shaped Ring Network with High Maintainability." Proceedings, Local Area Communications Network Symposium, 1979.

50   Sastry, A. R. K., "Performance Objectives for ISDN's." IEEE Communications Magazine, 22, 1, January 1984.

51   Shotwell, R. E. (ed.), The Ethernet Sourcebook. Amsterdam, The Netherlands: Elsevier Science Publishing, 1985.

52   Schutt, T. E., et. al., "Message-Handling Systems Based on the CCITT X.400 Recommendations." IBM Systems Journal, 26, 3, 1987.

53   Schwartz, M., Computer-Communication Networks Design and Analysis. Englewood Cliffs, NJ: Prentice-Hall, 1977.

54   SMC Corporation, "Programming the COM 9026." Hauppauge, NY: SMC Corporation, 1983.

55   Stallings, W., Tutorial: Local Network Technology. Silver Spring, MD: IEEE Computer Society Press, 1983.

56   Stallings, W., "Local Network Overview." Signal Magazine, January 1983.

57   Stallings, W., "The Integrated Services Digital Network." Datamation, December 1984.

58   Stallings, W., Local Networks: An Introduction. New York, NY: MacMillan Publishing Company, 1984.

59   Stallings, W., "Local Networks." Scientific American, 1984.

60   Stallings, W., "IEEE Project 802: Setting Standards for Local-Area Networks." Computerworld, February 13, 1984.

61   Stallings, W., "Local Networks." Computing Surveys, March 1984.

62   Stallings, W., Data and Computer Communications. New York, NY: MacMillan Publishing Company, 1985.

63   Stallings, W., Tutorial: Computer Communications Architectures, Protocols, and Standards. Silver Spring, MD: IEEE Computer Society Press, 1985.

64   Stallings, W., Handbook of Computer Communications Standards, Vol. II. New York, NY: MacMillan Publishing Company, 1987.

65   Stallings, W., Handbook of Computer Communications Standards, Vol. III. New York, NY: MacMillan Publishing Company, 1987.

66   Stewart, A., "A User's Guide to ISDN Standards." Telecommunications, May 1988.

67   Stieglitz, M., "Local Network Access Tradeoffs." Computer Design, October 1981.

68   Stuck, B., "Which Local Net Bus Access Is Most Sensitive to Congestion?" Data Communications, January 1983.

69   Stuck, B., "Calculating the Maximum Mean Data Rate in Local Area Networks." Computer, May 1983.

70   Tanenbaum, A. S., Computer Networks (2nd edition). Englewood Cliffs, NJ: Prentice-Hall, 1988.

71   Tropper, C., Local Computer Network Technologies. New York, NY: Academic Press, 1981.

72   Wilkes, M. V., and Wheeler, D. J., "The Cambridge Digital Communication Ring." Proceedings, Local Area Communications Network Symposium, 1979.

73   Wood, D. C., "Local Networks." In Chou, W. (ed.), Computer Communications, Vol. I: Principles. Englewood Cliffs, NJ: Prentice-Hall, 1984.

13

WIDE AREA NETWORK STANDARDS

13.1   Introduction*

Wide Area Networks (WANs) represent a class of networks that are not bounded by physical size. WANs generally involve relatively long transmit times (incurred by distance) with relatively high error rates. WANs are also infrequently wholly owned; commonly third party carriers or common carriers are used to provide WAN services.

Wide Area Networks are used to provide a communication interface between widely separated nodes or networks. Most WANs consist of packet switching networks with multiple intervening nodes and communication links between two communicating nodes. WANs provide for timely communication of messages between distant sites. Also, they are becoming more frequently used to provide to the interchange of electronic mail.

This chapter will focus on the CCITT X.25 packet switching recommendation (it is not a standard) and the Integrated Services Digital Network (ISDN). Also the CCITT X.400 message-handling service recommendation will be detailed.

13.2   CCITT X.25 Recommendation**

The International Telephone and Telegraph Consultative Committee (CCITT) has formulated the Recommendation X.25. This recommendation specifies the protocol to be followed by the user devices (nodes) in accessing public packet switching networks.

---

* see references 6, 15, 16, 19, 20 and 23–25.

** see references 1, 2, 5–12, 19, 20, 22 and 23.

Internationally agreed upon, the X.25 protocol specifies the details of the interactions between each user packet-mode device and the network nodes (see Figure 13.1).

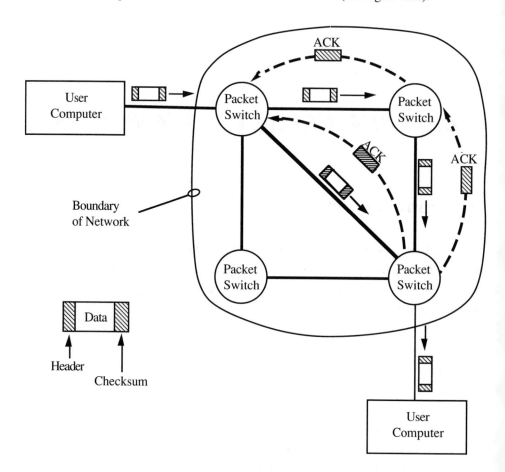

Figure 13.1. A simple model of packet switching [12].

Each user packet-mode device and the network node are called Data Terminal Equipment (DTE) and Data Circuit-Terminating Equipment (DCE) respectively. The actual equipment used and the design of the packet switched network is not a concern when implementing the X.25 protocol. In the case where the communication network utilized does not use packet switching, each DTE is connected to a Packet Assembler/Disassembler or PAD and the DTE is referred to as a character-mode device (instead of a packet-mode device), see Figure 13.2.

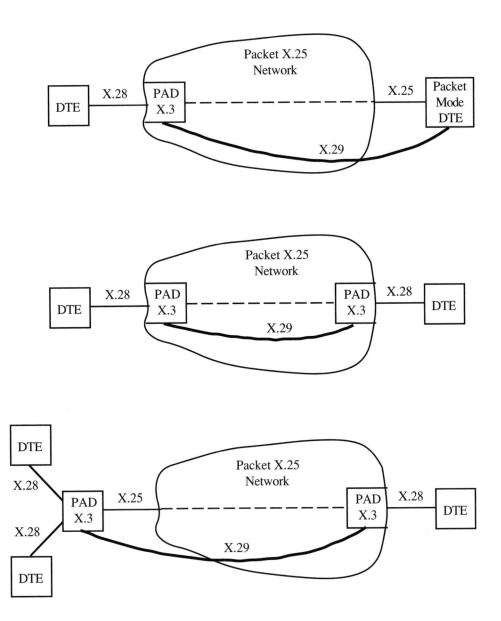

Figure 13.2. PADs and X.25 [12].

The actual implementation of the X.25 protocol is primarily through the use of software in a intelligent terminal, host or network processing node. The CCITT X.25

recommendation specifies three layers of communications, the physical, data-link and network.

13.2.1 Physical Layer

The physical layer, in reference to the OSI model, defines the interface between the network and the node that allows the exchange of data. Currently, the bulk of data communications uses telecommunications circuits although these circuits were designed for voice communications. There are, however two types of telecommunications circuits available, dial-up and leased line. The signals that traverse these circuits as connected by a modem are defined by some CCITT definition such as V.24. Generally, though not necessary, packet-switched systems use leased lines. If the communications circuit is fully digital, the interface to communicate is defined by the CCITT recommendation X.21. The definition of X.25 also specifies the subset of facilities of X.21 that it uses. X.21 is used by X.25 to provide communication. Some of the facilities X.21 offers aren't needed by a simple, fixed point-to-point X.25 network but will be discussed nevertheless. Simply stated, the X.21 interface provides for end-to-end digital transmission between DTEs and DCEs.

The following signals are provided by the X.21 interface:

Circuit ID	Name	DCE	DTE	Path Direction
G	Signal Ground		none	
Ga	DTE Common	Return		<--------------
T	Transmit			<--------------
R	Receive			-------------->
C	Control			<--------------
I	Indication			-------------->
S	Signal Element Timing			-------------->
B	Byte Timing (optional)			-------------->

Signal Ground (G)

This part of the circuit provides a reference with which the other logic states may be judged.

DTE Common Return (Ga)

This part of the circuit provides a reference for receivers in the DCE interface using an unbalanced-type configuration such as X.26.

Transmit (T)

This part of the circuit carries the digital signals between DTE and DCE devices. Either data or control information may be transmitted.

Receive (R)

This part of the circuit carries the digital signals between DCE and DTE devices. Can be used to transmit data or control information.

Control (C)

During data transfer this part of the circuit is ON. During control information exchange may be ON or OFF as the protocol specifies. This circuit is controlled by the DTE device and indicates the meaning of the data on the Transmit circuit to the DCE.

Indication (I)

During data transfer this part of the circuit is ON. During control information exchange may be ON or OFF as the protocol describes. This circuit is controlled by the DCE device and indicates the meaning of the data on the Receive circuit to the DTE.

Signal Element Timing (S)

This part of the circuit gives the timing of the bits flowing from the DCE to the DTE.

Byte Timing (B)

The optional signals on this part of the circuit provide the DTE with a byte element timing. This circuit is ON and changes to OFF to signify when the Signal Element Timing circuit signifies the last bit of a byte. This circuit may be used to indicate the end of each byte transmitted and received.

With an X.21 circuit-switched network the DTE or user sends an address to the network of the node it wants to communicate with. This is the call request. Once committed, the DTE will wait until it gets a proceed to select indication from the DCE. The DTE then transmits the address to the DCE. The DCE will send a call progress signal (see Table 13.1) to the DTE within 20 seconds after the DTE has completed communicating the desired address to the DCE.

Table 13.1 Call progress signals (from the CCITT recommendation X.96)

Code	Meaning	Category
00	Reserved	
01	Terminal called	
02	Redirected call	
03	Connect when free	Successful
20	No connection	
21	Number busy	
22	Selection Signal procedure error	Cleared due to short-term conditions
23	Selection Signal transmission	Error
41	Access barred	
42	Changed number	
43	Not obtainable	
44	Out of order	
45	Controlled not ready	
46	Uncontrolled not ready	
47	DCE power off	
48	Invalid facility request	
49	Network fault in local connection	
51	Call information service	Cleared due to long-term conditions
52	Incompatible user class of service	
61	Network congestion	Cleared due to short-term conditions
71	Long-term network congestion	Cleared due to long-term conditions
72	RPOA out of order	
81	Registration/cancellation	Confirmed
82	Redirection activated	Cleared by DTE procedure
83	Redirection deactivated	

Each established "call" through a packet-switched network, versus a leased line, creates a virtual circuit. Each DTE node can have up to 15 virtual channels or logical channel groups, each with up to 255 logical channels. Once both DTEs, the calling and the receiving, have entered the Ready for Data state, they are ready to transmit. The call can be ended by the DCE or a DTE signalling a Clear.

The X.21 recommendation does not have to be used to provide communication for

X.25. Instead, X.21 BIS may be used. This was designed for conventional analog connections using the CCITT V.24 or EIA RS-232C modem connections. The ability to connect V.24 DTEs and X.21 DTEs is defined by X.21 BIS.

The following is a cross reference between X.21 and V.24:

X.21 ID	V.24 ID	V.24 Description
G	101	Protective Ground
Ga	102	Reference Ground
T	103	Transmitted Data
R	104	Received Data
C	109	Carrier Detect
I	105	Request to Send
S	114	Signal Element Timing
B	---	-------------------

Notes: The Call Progress signals are not supported in X.21 BIS connections. There are procedures for manual answering of calls with call request time-outs of 2 (normal) to 60 seconds.

13.2.2. Data-Link

The X.25 Recommendation specifies data-link procedures that provide for the exchange of data via frames. Frames can be sent, and received. Errors in the physical layer can be detected by the data-link layer. The data-link layer used by X.25 is defined by the High-Level Data Link Control (HDLC), Link Access Procedure (LAP) and Link Access Procedure Balanced (LAPB) protocols.

13.2.3. Network Layer*

13.2.3.1   X.25

The network layer, also known as the packet layer, is where the real substance of the X.25 protocol recommendation is found. The network layer is where X.25 provides the

---

* see references 6, 12–14 and 22.

virtual circuit interface to packet switched service.

Each X.25 packet indicates a logical channel (there are 15 available) which identifies the packet as being used on a switched or a permanent virtual circuit for both directions of communications. The actual range of valid logical channel numbers is defined between the DTE and the network service being used. The logical channel numbers are only significant between the communicating DTE and DCE interface pair (see Figure 13.3).

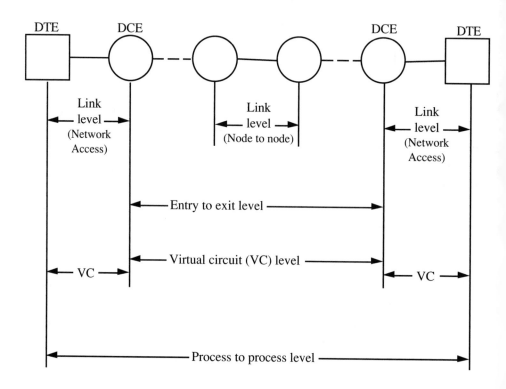

DTE: Data terminating equipment (e.g., host, terminal)
DCE: Data communication equipment (e.g., switching processor)

Figure 13.3. Network Protocol Levels [12].

Any one DTE may communicate to many other DTEs each using a switched and/or permanent virtual circuit. The X.25 recommendation has the following packet types:

Call Request

Call Connected

Clear Request

Clear Confirm

Data

Interrupt

Interrupt Confirm

Receive Ready (RR)

Receive Not Ready (RNR)

Reject (REJ)

Reset Request

Reset Confirm

Restart Request

Restart Confirm

Permanent Virtual Circuits (PVC)

Just like dial-up lines, X.25 offers the user a virtual circuit or call. And, like leased lines, X.25 offers permanent virtual circuits. The biggest difference is that there is no call setup, or disconnect operations when the permanent virtual circuits are used.

When a user DTE connects to another via a virtual circuit, a free logical channel number is selected. If the connection is a permanent virtual circuit, the logical channel number is permanently assigned. Once again, there are as many as 255 logical channels per group and each node (DTE) may have up to 15 groups.

Initiating a call

Once the calling DTE selects a free logical channel, it sends a Call Request message to its DCE. This message usually has the address of the destination node and may contain the address of the sending node. Both addresses are variable in length. The addresses may be followed by a facilities field which is also variable in length. The facilities field is present when the sending node wants a call with some optional characteristic which must be requested. A maximum data length may be specified to accommodate limited buffer capacity at either node. Also, for flow control, a maximum window size may be specified.

When the DCE receives the Call Request from the DTE, the DCE sends the information to the network in an attempt to initiate the communication. Meanwhile, the DTE changes from the Ready state to the DTE Waiting state.

The receiving DTE receives an Incoming Call message from its DCE. The receiving DTE will then determine if it is able to establish communication. If it can, a Call Accepted message is sent back to the originating DTE/DCE. The DCE receives the message and sends a Call Connected message to its DTE.

One fault that may occur is that the waiting DCE (of the originating node) may receive a Call Request from another node not currently being communicated with. If this incoming Call Request is for the same logical channel in the same group as the call currently being established, a Call Collision state is entered. The DCE will reject the incoming Call Request and proceed normally with the Call Accepted message that is pending or due.

When the call attempt (Call Request) fails, the originating DCE will receive a Clear Indication which indicates the reason why the Call Request was rejected.

The format for the Call Request and Incoming Call packets is shown in Figure 13.4 and then defined below.

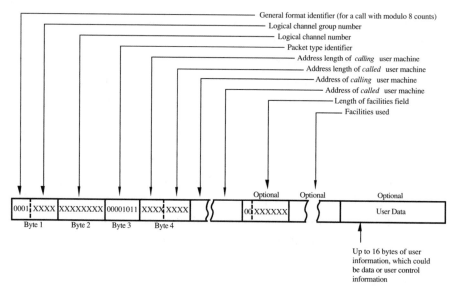

Figure 13.4. The Format of the CALL REQUEST and INCOMING CALL packets used when setting up a call [14].

General Format Identifier (GFI)

Consists of four bits, nibble, where each bit indicates:

bit 1 - may be 0 or 1, referred to as the qualifier bit, its use is not predetermined

bit 2 - not used, set to 0

bit 3 - set to 1 if modulo 128 counts are used

bit 4 - set to 1 if modulo 8 counts are used

Logical Channel Group Number (LCGN)

Consists of four bits, indicating the logical group used.

Logical Channel Number (LCN)

Consists of eight bits, indicating the logical channel used.

Packet Type Identifier (PTI) (see Figure 13.5)

Consists of one byte, the last bit (# 8) is used to indicate a data packet if 0, or a control/data-interrupt packet if set to 1.

Source (Calling) Address Length (SAL)

Consists of four bits to indicate the length of the calling address.

Destination (Called) Address Length (DAL)

Consists of four bits to indicate the length of the called address.

Source (Calling) Address (SA)

Consists of n bits that indicate the calling address.

Destination (Called) Address (DA)

Consists of n bits that indicate the called address.

Length of Facilities Field (LFF) - Optional

Consists of eight bits, bits 1 and 2 are always 0, used to indicate the length of the facilities field, notice only 6 bits available, thus only a maximum length of 64 bits is possible.

Facilities Field (FF) - Optional

Consists of n bits used to indicate that the calling DTE is requesting specific services or perhaps an agreement with the called DTE, such as reversed charges (for billing), priorities to use, alter window size; the default window sizes for the window and packet size are 2 and 128 bytes respectively; for a line speed of 2400 bits/per second (bps) a window size of 2 is commonly used, for 4800 bps the window size of 4 is used and for bps speeds of 9600 and above the full window of 7 is used; optionally, the window may be up to 128 positions, the 3 bit of the GFI field indicates if 128, or 7 bit sequence window size will be used.

Data - Optional

May consist of up to 16 bytes of information which can be used as real data or as control information.

Packet Type		Service	
From DCE to DTE	From DTE to DCE	V C	PVC
Call Set-up and Clearing			
Incoming call	Call request	X	
Call connected	Call accepted	X	
Clear indication	Clear request	X	
DCE clear confirmation	DTE clear confirmation	X	
Data and Interrupt			
DCE data	DTE data	X	X
DCE interrupt	DTE interrupt	X	X
DCE interrupt confirmation	DTE interrupt confirmation	X	X
Flow Control and Reset			
DCE RR	DTE RR	X	X
DCE RNR	DTE RNR	X	X
	DTE REJ	X	X
Reset indication	Reset request	X	X
DCE reset confirmation	DTE reset confirmation	X	X
Restart			
Restart indication	Restart request	X	X
DCE restart confirmation	DTE restart confirmation	X	X
Diagnostic			
Diagnostic		X	X
Registration			
Registration confirmation	Registration request	X	X

VC = Virtual Call   PVC = Permanent Virtual Circuit

Figure 13.5. Packet types [12].

The X.25 Recommendation optionally allows up to two levels of priority for virtual calls. A calling DTE can request that a call have a high priority. The high priority would be indicated in the facility field of the Call Request and Call Indication packets.

Once communication is established, the logical channel enters the Data Transfer state. The format of the data packet used for data exchange is shown in Figure 13.6. The following fields (defined earlier in Section 12.2.3.1) are used: GFI, LGCN, LCN, RSN, M, SSN, PT and Data.

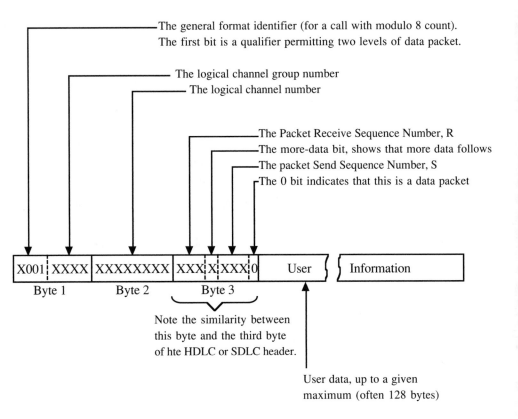

Figure 13.6. The format of the X.25 DATA packet (with 3-Bit Counts) [14].

The GFI, LCGN, and LCN fields are the same as specified earlier. The GFI field is defined as being x001. The Receive Sequence Number (RSN) functions as the one in the HDLC frame does. The More (M) bit is used to indicate if there are more frames to follow, 1 for yes, 0 for no. The Send Sequence Number (SSN) is used as the one in the HDLC frame is, the eighth bit is used to indicate if the frame is data (0) or control information (1).

The GFI field, specified to be x001, does not define the first bit. The first bit's use can be determined by the installation.

The data field is variable in length, since the frame is controlled by the HDLC protocol in the data-link layer. The HDLC Flag (01111110) is used to indicate the end of the data instead of a length being specifically given.

The More bit that follows the RSN field is used to indicate the presence of additional frames (packets). Only a packet of maximum length, which is dependent on the intervening network or may be have been previously agreed upon, can have the More bit specified. If the More bit is set and the packet is not of the maximum length, the packet will be discarded due to a procedure error.

The X.25 Recommendation specifies, or recommends a maximum data field length of 128 bytes. But, any size may be used; often with high speed communication links the data size of 1024 is used. But, once again, any integral number of bytes may be used.

The SSN field is a sequential message number that is defined at the time packets are sent. The SSN works with the window size being used to indicate that message's position in the window. The RSN field is defined by the receiver when it is able to accept a new message. The RSN field contains the sequence number of the next packet the receiving DTE expects. The RSN is communicated to the sending DTE after one of these data exchanges: Data, Receiver Ready (RR), Receiver Not Ready (RNR) or Reject (REJ). As with the data-link HDLC protocol, the RR packet is used to indicate that the receiving DTE has adequate buffer space available to begin receiving messages. The RNR packet is used to indicate that the DTE sending it is unable to accept any messages and new packets should only commence once this DTE sends an RR packet. The REJ packet type would be used if a packet was received that had to be discarded; remember that the REJ packet indicates the RSN which is the next sequence number expected. Receiving a REJ may require the need to resend one or more messages.

The format of the packet used to acknowledge a Data packet is shown in Figure 13.7.

Receive Ready:
>The following fields are used: GFI, LCGN, LCN, RSN and PTI.
>The GFI field is defined to be 0001; could be 0010 if 128 modulo counts are being used. The LCGN, LCN and RSN fields operate as defined earlier. The Packet Type Identifier (PTI) is set to 00001.

Receive Not Ready:

The following fields are used: GFI, LCGN, LCN, RSN and PTI

The GFI field is defined to be 0001; could be 0010 if 128 modulo counts are being used. The LCGN, LCN and RSN fields operate as defined earlier. The Packet Type Identifier (PTI) is set to 00101.

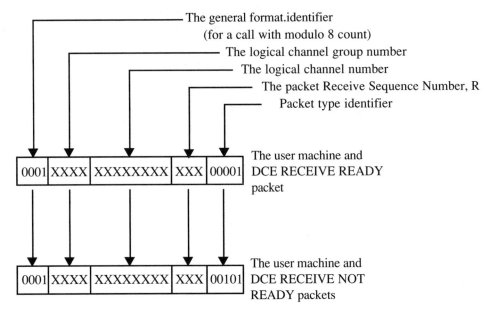

Figure 13.7. Packets used to acknowledge a DATA packet (with 3-Bit counts) [14].

To satisfy the requirement of the need to temporarily stop interactive communication, the X.25 Recommendation specifies the use of Interrupt packets. The Interrupt packet bypasses the normal flow of information, jumping ahead of Data packets in the normal queues. Normally the Interrupt packet contains only one byte of information, it can have more but usually does not. However, any one DTE cannot have more than one outstanding Interrupt packet on any virtual call in each direction. This allows for the dedication of a single one byte buffer space for each logical channel in use to capture any incoming Interrupt packet. Further, the Interrupt packet does not use a sequence number. A receiving DTE will send an Interrupt Confirmation packet to recognize the receipt of an Interrupt packet. Once the original sending DTE receives the Interrupt Confirmation packet it may once again use an Interrupt packet on that logical channel within that logical channel group.

The following is the format of the Interrupt and Interrupt Confirmation packets is shown in Figure 13.8.

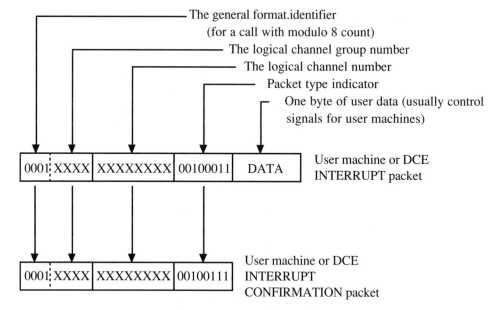

Figure 13.8. The formats of the INTERRUPT and INTERRUPT CONFIRMATION packets [14].

Interrupt:

The following fields are used: GFI, LCGN, LCN, PTI and Data.

The GFI, LCGN, LCN, and PTI fields are used as defined earlier. The GFI field is set to 0001 (for modulo 8). The PTI field is set to 00100011. The Data field is usually one byte long containing control signals for the receiving DTE. The 1984 version of X.25 allows up to 32 bytes in the Data field.

Interrupt Confirmation:

The following fields are used: GFI, LCGN, LCN and PTI.

The GFI, LCGN, LCN, and PTI fields are used as defined earlier. The GFI field is set to 0001 (for modulo 8). The PTI field is set to 00100111.

The network is capable of detecting protocol errors between DTEs, or if a DTE needs to discard a message whether it be in transit or buffered at one end of the link. When the network detects an error condition or unknown state, it issues a Reset. When the network generates the Reset Request condition, both DTEs on the link receive the packet. The network will be reset once both DTEs have replied with a Reset Confirmation packet. One of the DTEs may generate the Reset Request though. The network will intercept the Reset Request and the receiving DTE will get a Reset Indication packet. That DTE will then send a Reset Confirmation packet. The Reset, once complete will have set both the SSN and RSN counters to 0. Also, any Data or Interrupt packets that were in transit will be discarded.

The layout of the Reset Request, Indication and Confirmation packets is shown in Figure 13.9.

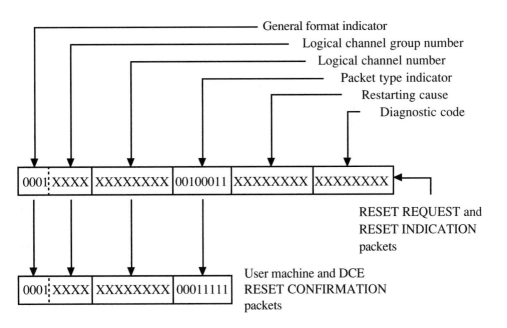

Figure 13.9. The format of packets used for resetting [14].

Reset Request and Indication:

The following fields are used: GFI, LCGN, LCN, PTI, RC and DC.

The GFI, LCGN, LCN and PTI fields operate as they do elsewhere. The GFI field is set to 0001 (modulo 8), the PTI field is set to 00011011. The Reset Cause (RC) field is one byte long and indicates the reason for the reset. The following are Reset Cause codes (bits from 1 to 8):

          00000000 - DTE initiated Reset.

          10000000 - Out of order (used only on

                        Permanent Virtual Circuits-PVC).

          11000000 - Remote procedure error.

          10100000 - Local procedure error.

          11100000 - Network congestion.

          10010000 - Remote DTE operational (used only on PVCs) .

          11110000 - Network operational (used only on PVCs).

The Diagnostic Code (DC) may be used to provide network specific information in addition to the RC given.

Reset Confirmation:

The following fields are used: GFI, LCGN, LCN and PTI.

The GFI, LCGN, LCN and PTI fields operate as they do elsewhere. The GFI field is set to 0001 (modulo 8), the PTI field is set to 00011111.

Once communication is complete, a DTE may disconnect. To disconnect, the DTE sends a Clear Request packet to its DCE. The DCE responds with a Clear Confirmation packet when it is ready to clear the channel. Then the DCE proceeds to send the Clear Request to the other DCE. The receiving DCE will send a Clear Indication to the DTE in question. When that DTE sends a Clear Confirmation back to its DCE the channel will be cleared and will once again be in the Ready state.

The Clear Request, Indication and Confirmation have their own packet structure shown in Figure 13.10.

Clear Request and Indication:

The following fields are used: GFI, LCGN, LCN, PTI and Cause.

The GFI, LCGN, LCN and PTI fields are the same as defined earlier. The GFI field is 0001 and the PTI field is 00010011. The Cause field is one byte long and indicates the cause of the Clear Request or Indication.

Clear Confirmation:

The following fields are used: GFI, LCGN, LCN and PTI.

The GFI, LCGN, LCN and PTI fields are the same as defined earlier. The GFI field is 0001 and the PTI field is 00010111.

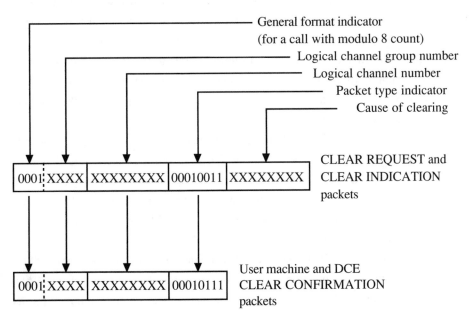

Figure 13.10. Packet formats used when disconnecting a virtual call [14].

13.2.3.2   PADs

The Packet Assembly/Disassembly or PAD is a device which provides dumb character terminal emulation while using a complex packet-switched network. Or, in other words, the PAD, defined by 3 CCITT Recommendations, is used to connect character mode terminals to packet-switched networks utilizing the Recommendation X.25. The PAD specifically employs the use of the X.3, X.28 and X.29 protocols. The X.3 protocol defines the service provided to the terminal by the PAD. The Recommendation X.28 defines how start-stop terminals are connected to the PAD via a telephone or other link and how they can control the PAD's functions. Also, X.28 defines the user interface to the X.3 services. The X.29 protocol defines the interaction between the PAD and the host machine, which is using the X.25 protocol and how the host can control the PAD.

Packet-switched networks are most efficient when exchanging relatively large blocks of data. On the other hand, a character mode terminal typically is set up to send and receive one byte or character at a time. The PAD is software (or firmware) and hardware which provides a buffering service between the character mode terminal and the block mode packet-switched network. Typically a end of message or terminating character is selected, when this character is received from the terminal, the PAD, which has been buffering the input up to this point, sends the message to its destination. Here the PAD assembles the message, then once the appropriate character is received from the terminal, sends the message out onto the network to its recipient.

Now, the decision about what determines a terminating or end of message character is different for different systems. The use of the X.3, X.28 and X.29 Recommendations is an attempt to provide a general solution. Unfortunately these 3 recommendations are from the CCITT and do not conform well with the ISO model. But, the X.25 and PAD Recommendations are widely accepted and used on a global basis, so usability has won over conformity with the ISO model.

There are a variety of PADs used to fit different terminal arrangements. PADs generally support more than one terminal, options range from 1 to 32 terminals per PAD. Each terminal using the PAD is assigned a unique logical channel number for its communication.

13.2.3.3   X.3

Each terminal connected to the PAD has 18 separate parameters which control the response of the PAD as it receives data from the terminal. The result of the parameters is that the session between the terminal and PAD can be customized to suit the needs of the terminal. The host, PAD or terminal user may alter the PAD's parameters. The following details each of the twenty two parameters[4].

Parameter 1:   Escape to PAD Command State on Receipt of DLE
> The default of this parameter is 1. The 1 indicates that escape to the PAD command state is possible. Typically this would be used if a user wanted to end a call from the PAD rather than the host. After the DLE command was sent to the PAD, the PAD would then prompt for a command. A command such as Clear or Reset might be used.
>
> If this parameter is set to 0 then escape is not possible (sounds ominous doesn't

it?). This would be useful if there is the possibility that the escape sequence, DLE, might be issued during some other processing, such as with graphics.

Parameter 2: Character Echo

The parameter defaults to 1, which indicates that echoing will be performed. This parameter determines if the PAD will echo each character back to the terminal as it is typed. Normally, the terminal would be connected to the PAD in full duplex so that each character is not displayed on the terminal until the PAD as echoed it. This parameter would be set to 0 if no echoing is desired, such as when a password or other security code is being typed in at the terminal.

Parameter 3: Data Forwarding Characters

The data forwarding characters are referring to the same terminating or end of message characters discussed earlier. Since the PAD deals with a variety of terminals, this parameter provides the means to indicate to the PAD which character codes indicate the end of a message.

If, while entering information, the PAD runs out of buffer space and the terminal flow control (parameter 5) is not enabled, the additional or overflow characters will be discarded and the PAD will issue a BEL (hex code 07) character to the terminal to be echoed.

Data, once forward to the host system by the PAD can no longer be edited by the terminal.

Data forwarding may also take place if parameter 4, Data forwarding on time out, is used. The count down timer for parameter 4 is reset each time a character is received from the terminal. Parameter 4 is especially useful when no forwarding character can be defined.

The following encoding is used to select the data forwarding character(s):

    0 -   receipt of the 129th character or time-out only

    1 -   A-Z, a-z, and 0-9

    2 -   CR

    4 -   ESC, BEL, ENQ, ACK

    8 -   DEL, CAN, DC2

    16-   ETX, EOT

    32-   HT, LF, VT, FF

    64-   All other characters less than hex 20 in value and DEL (hex 08)

To customize the data forwarding characters, the above values may be summed to indicated the desired characters. For instance, if parameter 3 is 6, then CR, ESC,

BEL, ENQ and ACK can all be used to indicate that the data buffered by the PAD needs to be forwarded.

Parameter 4: Data Forwarding on Time-out

If parameter 3 is set to 0 the value of the this parameter will be used as the method of sending the accumulated message from the PAD to the host. This parameter may be set from 0 to 255, 0 indicates that no time-out will ever be signalled. While if set to some value 1 through 255, 0.05 seconds x the parameter will be waited before sending the accumulated message to the host. The maximum delay is 12.75 seconds, that is, parameter 4 is set to 255. The use of parameter 3 set to 0 can attribute to a high load, traffic wise, on the network due to the continuous manner in which messages are exchanged.

Parameter 5: Flow Control of the Terminal by the PAD

When the PAD is connected to some type of smart terminal, there exists the possibility that the PAD may be more easily overrun with data to send to the host. This is due to the smart terminal's ability to send data at a higher rate than say, a human typist. If this parameter (5) is set to 0 then the PAD will discard all data that it cannot buffer. The PAD will also echo the BEL character back to the terminal to indicate that the most recently data has been discarded. If this parameter is set to 1 then the PAD will issue an X-OFF (DC3) character when its buffer becomes full. Once the PAD is able to once again buffer data, the X-ON (DC1) character will be issued.

Parameter 6: Suppression of Service Signals from the PAD

The PAD issues service signals in response to external events, such as the network being Cleared or Reset. If this parameter is set to 0 then these service messages will not be echoed on the terminal; if set to 1 then the terminal will be sent the messages as they are detected.

Parameter 7: Action of Receipt of a Break from the Terminal

The break, or break signal is some predefined sequence that is used to signal the host that a terminal, connected via a PAD, is in need of attention. On some PADs, the break signal is indicated when the connection between the terminal and PAD is held in the space condition for more than 100 ms. The following indicate the action the PAD will take when the break signal is detected:

0 -   No action.

1 -   Transmit an X.25 Interrupt packet to the host.

> 2 -   Transmit an X.25 Reset packet to the host.
>
> 5 -   Transmit an X.25 Interrupt packet and an Indication of Break.
>
> 8 -   The PAD enters the command state awaiting a command from the user, thus leaving the Data Transfer state.
>
> 21-   Same as 5, but parameter 8 (discussed below) is set to 1.

Option 21 is useful for slower terminals since parameter 8 will be set to 1, thus discarding any messages that are buffered for display to the terminal. Once the PAD receives an acknowledgment of the Indication of Break, it will set parameter 8 to 0, thus restoring the terminal's ability to receive messages.

Parameter 8: Data Delivery to the Terminal

> When this parameter is set to 0, data will be sent to the terminal as fast as it can receive it. When set to 1, all data destined for the terminal is discarded. Receipt of a Reset indication or confirmation sets this parameter to 0.

Parameter 9: Padding after Carriage Return

> This parameter controls the number of pad characters inserted after a Carriage Return (CR). The CR may have originated with the terminal or from the host. In any case, the pad characters are used to allow TTY or simple mechanical terminals to have sufficient time to return their print head back to the margin so that they can begin to print a new line. If this parameter is set to 0 then no pad characters are generated. But, if the PAD, under control of parameter 10 generated the CR then 2 or 4 pad characters are generated. The number of pad characters generated depends on the terminal's speed, either 110 bps or faster. If parameter 9 is set between 1 and 7 then 1 - 7 pad characters will be issued regardless of the origin of the CR.

Parameter 10: Line Folding

> To prevent the loss of data at the terminal due to the terminal having a narrower print line than the host is using, parameter 10 is used. The PAD keeps track of how many non-format-effectors it has sent to the terminal. If this count reaches the value of the line folding parameter then the PAD automatically generates a CR. If parameter 9 is nonzero, additional pad characters will also be generated. If parameter 10 is 0 then the PAD will not insert any format effectors. Otherwise, if this parameter is set between 1 and 255 then the PAD will issue a CR after this many non-format-effectors are displayed on the terminal.

Parameter 11:   Terminal Speed

> The CCITT sets the values for possible terminal speeds, though in an illogical

manner:

0 - 110 bps	10 - 50 bps
1 - 134.5 bps	11 - 75/1200 bps
2 - 300 bps	12 - 2400 bps
3 - 1200 bps	13 - 4800 bps
4 - 600 bps	14 - 9600 bps
5 - 75 bps	15 - 19.2 kbps
6 - 150 bps	16 - 4800 bps
7 - 1800 bps	17 - 56 kbps
8 - 200 bps	18 - 64 kbps
9 - 100 bps	

This parameter is read-only, the host may view it, but not change. The value is also sent as an option during the Call Request packet which is sent when the virtual circuit is being initialized.

Parameter 12:   Flow Control of the PAD by the Terminal

When the terminal has intelligence and some manner of recording its messages, the terminal may indicate to the PAD when to temporarily stop sending data. The terminal accomplishes this by sending an X-OFF signal to the PAD. The PAD resumes data transmission once it receives an X-ON signal from the terminal. Parameter 11 is only in effect when it is set to 1. If set to 0, parameter has no effect. If the PAD enters the command state, it will be cleared as if an X-ON had been issued.

Parameter 13:   Line Feed Insertion after Carriage Return

To accommodate the variety of terminals and hosts the PAD connects, the following options are allowed for in respect to line feed insertion:

    0 -   None.

    1 -   Inserted after every CR transmitted.

    2 -   Inserted after every CR received from host.

    4 -   Line Feed inserted after every CR locally echoed to the terminal.

    5 -   values 1 + 4.

    6 -   values 2 + 4.

    7 -   values 1 + 2 + 4 (data transfer only).

Parameter 14:   Padding Characters Inserted after Line Feed

This parameter has the same effect as with Parameter 9. Except pad characters are sent after a Line Feed to the terminal. If this parameter is set to 0, no padding occurs, if set 1 to 7, that many pads will be inserted. Optional, 8-255 pads may be used.

Parameter 15:   Editing

This parameter, if set to 1 allows edited of characters in the send buffer, but where such characters have not yet been transmitted to the host. If set to 0, editing is not allowed. Also, if set to 1, parameters 16, 17, and 18 have significance.

Parameter 16:   Character Delete Character

When this parameter is set to 0 then deletion of characters in the PAD's buffer is disallowed. When nonzero, the value used indicates the character code that performs the act of backspacing and deleting. Often the value of 08 is used.

Parameter 17:   Buffer Delete Character

As with parameter 16, when set to 0, this parameter has no effect. Otherwise, when nonzero, that value indicates the character code that will erase the entire buffer pending transmission. Typically the value used (in hex) is 18, which happens to be the Cancel character in the ASCII code table.

Parameter 18:   Buffer Display Character

This parameter, as with parameter 16, must be set to a nonzero value to have an effect. When nonzero, the value indicate is the character code that will cause the contents of the PAD's buffer to be displayed on the terminal. Usually DC2, code 12 (hex) is used to display the current buffer contents.

Parameter 19:   Editing PAD Service Signals

This parameter controls the format of the editing PAD service signals.

       0 -   no editing

       1 -   editing for printing terminals

       2 -   editing for display terminals

       8 -   editing using characters from the character code range 20-7E (hex)

Parameter 20:   Echo Mask

This parameter is used to control which characters will and will not be display upon the terminal when Parameter 2 is enabled.

       0 -   all characters echoed

       1 -   no echo of CR

       2 -   no echo of LF

       4 -   no echo of VT, HT, or FF

       8 -   no echo of BEL, or BS

16 -   no echo of ESC, or ENQ

32 -   no echo of ACK, NAK, STX, SOH, EOT, ETB, or ETX

64 -   no echo of editing characters

Parameter 21:   Parity Treatment

This parameter dictates how the checking and generation of parity on characters to/from the terminal will be performed.

0 -   no parity detection or generation

1 -   parity checking

2 -   parity generation

3 -   values 1 + 2

Parameter 22:   Page Wait

This parameter is used to indicate the number of lines to be displayed before waiting for a continuation prompt from the terminal.

0 -   no page wait

23 -   number of line feed characters before waiting, optionally may be other values.

13.2.3.4   X.28

The X.28 protocol defines how the control of the data flow between the non-packet mode user terminal and the PAD is performed. The terminal issues commands to the PAD; the commands that can be issued were just discussed. These commands summarize the procedures for the establishment of the link, initialization of the service, orderly exchange of data and control data. The X.28 recommendation requires the PAD to return a response when a terminal sends a command. The link established may be transparent, this is where the services of the PAD are transparent to both the terminal and the host (or other terminal) or the link may be simple, this is where the terminal has access to the X.3 commands.

13.2.3.5   X.29

The X.29 Recommendation defines how the PAD and a remote node will exchange control information during an X.25 call. The remote node is either another PAD or an X.25 DTE. As introduced earlier, the Qualifier bit of the General Format Identifier field doesn't have a specific definition. With the use of X.29, the Qualifier bit is set to 0 to indicate that the packet has user data or is set to 1 to indicate that the packet contains PAD control information.

The X.29 Recommendation has 7 control messages, they are called PAD messages and they are:

0: **Parameters Indication:** Returned by the PAD in response to the Read and Set messages.

1: **Invitation to Clear:** Allows X.25 call clear by a remote DTE; PAD clears to local   connection.

2: **Set Parameters:** Changes an X.3 value.

3: **Indication of Break:** PAD indicates that the terminal has transmitted a break.

4: **Read Parameters:** Reads an X.3 value.

5: **Error:** Response to an invalid PAD message.

6: **Set and Read:** Changes an X.3 value and requires the PAD to confirm the change.

13.3   Integrated Services Digital Network*

The Integrated Services Digital Network or ISDN as it is commonly referred to, is an emerging standard orchestrated by the CCITT. ISDN gives the user the capability to simultaneously transmit data, facsimile, video and voice over a single communications link (see Figure 13.11). ISDN is an evolutionary technology.

As networks become more complex, ISDN seeks to make the network more ubiquitous by joining LANs, WANs and other topologies. The most significant limitation of ISDN is that transmission speeds are limited to 64kbps. In a Wide Area Network (WAN) this does not present as cumbersome a problem as it does under a Local Area Network (LAN). This is because LANs, as discussed earlier, have transmission speeds referenced in megabits per second and WANs are typically in kilobits per second.

---

* see references 4, 11, 17, 21 and 27.

| SERVICE | BANDWIDTH | |
	Digital Voice (64 Kbps)	Wideband (>64Kbps)
Telephone	Telephone Leased Circuit Information retrieval (by voice analysis and synthesis)	Music
Data	Packet switched data Circuit switched data Leased circuits Telemetry Funds transfer Information retrieval Mailbox Electronic mail Alarms	High-speed computer communications
Text	Telex Teletex Leased circuits Videotext Information retrieval Mailbox Electronic mail	Teletex
Image	Videotex Facsimile Information retrieval Surveillance	Teletex TV conferencing Videophone Cable TV distribution

Figure 13.11. Candidate services for integration [21].

One experimental technique now under investigation is the grouping of 64 kbps channels to create the illusion of a single, high speed link. There is also a broadband ISDN under investigation; it would allow for transmission speeds of 1.4 mbps.

In any case, ISDN offers a single interface for users connecting to a LAN, WAN or PBX (telephone system, Private Branch eXchange). Currently such users must employ a separate technology for each of these communication links. ISDN is not entirely theoretical, the first complete installation in the United States was in November 1986 at the Arizona Department of Transportation, installed by Northern Telecom.

Companies that do not have their own PBX system, which is a key component to ISDN technology, will be able to utilize Centrex switches such as those operated by the Bell Operating Companies (BOC). Each Centrex switch operates individually as a PBX for each customer as if that customer were the only one. The first Centrex switch with ISDN functions was installed by Illinois Bell for McDonald's Corporation in December 1986.

It should be noted that these ISDN's just discussed do not conform with the emerging CCITT standards as they are still under development [3,17,21].

13.3.1   ISDN Goals

ISDN has five primary goals[4],

1.   To provide for a worldwide homogeneous digital network that supports numerous services and uses the same standards of access at any point in the network;

2.   To provide for a uniform set of standards of digital transmission across all ISDN networks;

3.   To supply a standard user interface regardless of network access methods or changes;

4.   As with the 3rd goal, to provide an application independent user definition. This goal is in accordance with the objectives of the OSI committee in its defining of an Application Layer interface and is thus not limited to ISDN only;

5.   Building on goals 3 and 4, to supply for the portability of user DTEs and applications.

Further, ISDN focuses on three specific themes[4],

1.   Standardization of services to the user with the intent of a global standard;

2.   Standardization of user to network interfaces with the intent of defining an independent standards for terminal and network devices;

3.   Standardization of network capabilities for user-to-network and network-to-network communications.

The CCITT describes ISDN with the following attributes[21]:

1.   The ISDN is to evolve from the existing telephone networks, which themselves are evolving into integrated digital networks.

2.   New services introduced into ISDN should be compatible with the basic 64

kbps switched digital connections.

3.   ISDN will require from 10 to 20 years (from the early 1980's) for full transition.

4.   During the transition, ISDN will rely on internetworking among the national ISDNs and other non-ISDN networks.

5.   ISDN will contain intelligence for the provision of service features, maintenance and system control, and network management.

6.   ISDN will use a layered functional set of integrated protocols for the various access arrangements.

The CCITT is still developing the standards for signaling, network interfaces and protocols. The CCITT has adopted, in 1984, what is called the first family of ISDN standards. The main focus of the standards adopted deal with the customer interface. The second family of standards, in 1988, will focus on refinements to the first family and more details on the functions internal to the network.

13.3.1.1 ISDN Channels

The typical ISDN interface supports a bit rate of 144 kbps. This rate is divided into two 64 kbps channels, called B (Bearer) channels, the remaining 16 kbps channel is called the D (Delta) channel. Actually, ISDN provides framing control and other overhead bits which accumulates into an additional 48 kbps, making the total ISDN interface 192 kbps[4]. The 144 kbps interface provides its service via a synchronous, full-duplex connection, see Figure 13.12. This 144 kbps interface utilizes time division multiplexing (TDM) for the 3 channels, the two B and one D channel. The B channels can be further multiplexed into subchannels. There is no strict definition on the use of the B channels supplied, the user may use the full band of each channel or subdivide it.

The B and D channels allow for different data transfer needs. The B channels are generally intended for user data. Whether that data be voice at 64 kbps; data transfer at 64 kbps or less; broadband voice at 64 kbps or less; video at 64 kbps. The D channel is primarily intended for control and signalling information. But, the D channel can also be used for user data transfer. Note that the B channel is not intended to carry signalling information.

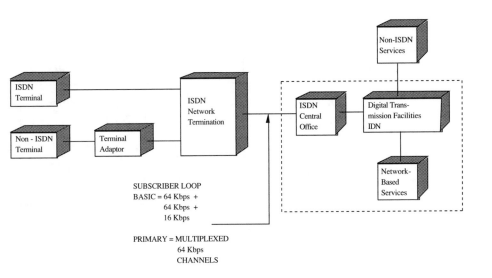

Figure 13.12. Block diagram of ISDN functions [21].

The transmissions that ISDN does via the D channel are divided into three types: the s-type or signalling information; the p-type or packet data; and the t-type, telemetry information. Further, the D channel can carry all three types of information concurrently by the use of statistical multiplexing.

The second family of standards proposes to include definitions for E and H channels. The E channel will carry signalling information for circuit switching at 64kbps. The H channel will be designed for user data and split into the H0 channel, operating at 384 kbps, the H11 channel operating at 1536 kbps and the H12 channel operating at 1920 kbps.

13.3.1.2   ISDN Interfaces

ISDN, in accordance with the ISO seven layer model, has definitions for the basic service layers (1-3) (see Figures 13.13, 13.14.).

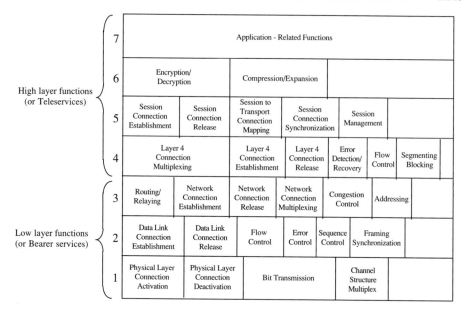

Figure 13.13. ISDN layers [4].

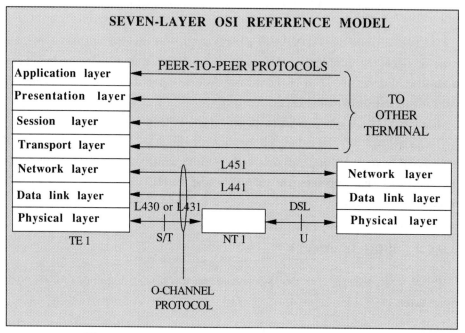

Figure 13.14. Seven-layer OSI reference model [27].

The **physical layer** is defined by the I430 recommendation. It details the interface to be used and methods to be used for bit and byte channel synchronization, D channel access control and power feeding. The **data link layer** is defined by the I440/1 recommendations. This recommendation details the virtual interface for D channels. These 2 service definitions (I440 and I441) are based on the previously discussed LAPD protocol of HDLC. These services do utilize the Unnumbered Information (UI) frame that is part of LAPD. The **network layer** is defined by the I450/1 recommendations. This layer is responsible for setting up virtual connections (via circuit or packet switched calls). Also, the control of the data transferred is found in this layer. These 2 service definitions (I450 and I451) provide for connectionless (unacknowledged datagram) or virtual circuit (acknowledged) services.

ISDN offers different interfaces to accommodate different data rates and requirements. ISDN defines:

> **Functional groupings** - are a set of capabilities required in an ISDN user interface. The specific functions in each functional grouping may be performed by multiple pieces of equipment and software.
>
> **Reference points** - are the points dividing functional groups. Typically a reference point corresponds to a physical interface between communication equipment, see Figure 13.15.

Terminal Adapters (TA) is a protocol convertor that convertors signals from the interface used (like X.21, V.24, RS232, etc) to the standard ISDN interface.

Terminal Equipment 1 (TE1) is the first of the two different types of TEs that ISDN specifies. It is simply a TE that plugs into the ISDN network using ISDN interface.

Terminal Equipment 2 (TE2) is the second type of TE ISDN specifies. This type of TE works with conventional interfaces such as X.21, V.24, RS232, etc. The ISDN interface allows for a TA to be combined into a TE2. The functions of the TE's are:

> upper level protocol handling
> maintenance
> interface functions
> connection services

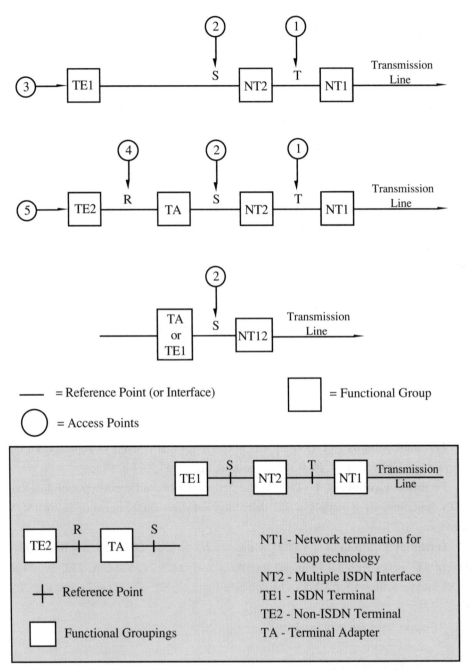

Figure 13.15. Basic ISDN configurations [4,27]. In this figure the following functional groups are found: TA, TE1, TE2, NT1, NT12 and NT2 functional groups.

Network Termination 1 (NT1) supplies functions that are like those of the physical layer of the OSI model. The NT1 gives the user transparency in their dealings with the ISDN network thus abstracting the user from the physical concerns of the ISDN. The NT1 provides for:

      termination of the circuit

      physical layer maintenance and performance monitoring

      transmission signalling and timing

      power feeding for the channel

      multiplexing at the physical layer (if needed)

      interface termination

Network Termination 12 (NT12) contains the functions found in the NT1 and NT2. The NT12 is provided in anticipation of the fourth generation of PBXs being developed.

Network Termination 2 (NT2) contains functions found in the physical layer and upper layers of the OSI model. The NT2 can also be referenced as a PBX, LAN, Terminal or Cluster Controllers. The NT2 is an end-user equipment interface. The NT2 is responsible for switching, multiplexing, and protocol handling. The NT2's functions are:

      protocol handling for the data link and network layers

      multiplexing of the data link and network layers

      switching and concentration functions

      link maintenance

      termination of the physical layer functions

Figure 13.16 illustrates a summary of configurations for the ISDN user network interface. Reference points S and T (as shown in Figure 13.15) use the I412 Recommendation for channel interface structure. The reference point R is defined by some CCITT or EIA Recommendation (such as X.21, V.24, V.32, RS232C, etc.)

The B channel interface at Reference points S and T are required by ISDN to comply with one the of the following interface structures:

      The 2B + D option. This is the basic interface composed of 2 B channels and a D channel.

      The 23B + D option (30B + D European). This interface has 23 B channels (1.544 Mbps) and one D channel at 64 kbps. In Europe, there are 30 B channels (2.048 Mbps) and one 64 kbps D channel. This is also known as the primary rate B channel.

This is the same as the above interface, but is used when an NT2 device connects to the network by more than one B channel. There are still 23 B channels, and one D channel. And in Europe there are 30 B channels and one D channel.

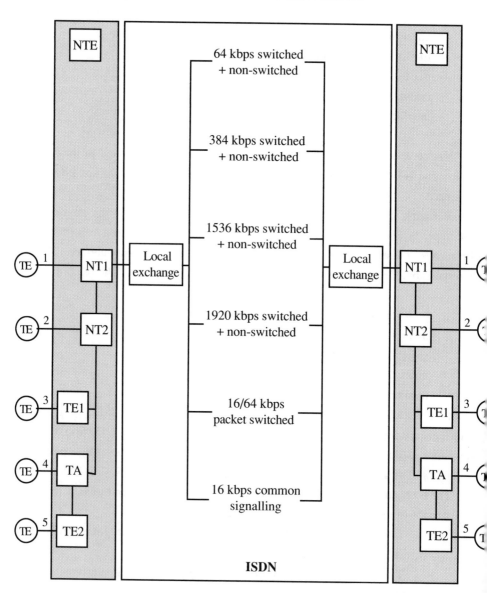

Figure 13.16. User networks interface summary [11].

13.4   CCITT X.400*

13.4.1 CCITT X.400 Recommendation

The CCITT has proposed a series of recommendations for message-handling systems. X.400 is the nomenclature used to refer to these set of recommendations. The X.400 standard, as it has become to be known, was approved in 1984 by the CCITT, and since then has had widespread acceptance and implementations are continuing.

The X.400 standard specifies rules for two different computers to exchange messages. This set of recommendations, there are eight, has X.400 positioned in the Presentation and Application Layers of the OSI model, and is designed to interface to the Session Layer.

The X.400 standard has two key functional modes, referred to as the CEPT and CEN/CENELEC profiles. The CEPT functional standard provides for message exchange between private companies via a public network. The CEN/CENELEC functional standard provides for the description of interfaces used by message-handling systems within private companies.

Mentioned previously, the X.400 standard is a collection of eight recommendations, these recommendations are:

  X.400 System model-service elements

  X.401 Basic service elements and optional user facilities

  X.408 Encoded-information-type conversion rules

  X.409 Presentation transfer syntax and notation

  X.410 Remote operations and reliable transfer server

  X.411 Message transfer layer

  X.420 Interpersonal messaging user agent layer

  X.430 Access protocol for Teletex terminals

The X.400 recommendation describes the basic Message Handling System (MHS) in accordance with the OSI model. Further, X.400's recommendations are limited to the Application Layer. X.400 describes how the user or originator, interacts with the User

---

* see references 6, 18 and 22.

Agent (UA) in order to prepare, edit, send and receive messages. Note that when a message is received, the receiver is called the recipient. Also, X.400 describes the interface between the UA and the Message Transfer Agent (MTA), which is responsible for the delivery and receipt of messages from the network. Both the UA and MTA describe naming and addressing conventions.

The X.401 recommendation details services and facilities provided for both the MTA and X.420.

The X.408 recommendation specifies recommendations for code and format conversion, for instance, ASCII to Teletex.

The X.409 recommendation defines presentation transfer conventions. X.409 specifies encoding rules for messages and control information to be used by the subcomponents of the Application Layer. The Application Layer is logically divided into two sublayers, the lower one consisting of two components, X.410, X.411 and X.420 describe services provided by these sublayers.

The X.410 recommendation provides for remote operations and an entity labeled the reliable transfer server (RTS) which is a separable subcomponent of the MTA. The RTS is the newest defined subcomponent of the Application Layer and makes use of the Basic Activity Subset (BAS) of the ISO Session Layer. The RTS provides for reliable and recoverable transfer of individual messages between communicating MTAs (see Figure 13.17).

The X.411 recommendation describes the Message Transfer Layer (MTL) service. The MTL services is involved with describing how the UA transfers messages and provides delivery of message within a specific period. Also, MTL provides for type conversion of the message contents. The transfer services include the specification of the P1 and P3 protocols, see Figure 13.18. The P1 protocol specifies rules for message transfer between MTAs. And the P3 protocol identifies the protocol used by an MTA and Submission and Delivery Entity (SDE). The SDE sends and receives messages from an MTA. Further, the SDE is used when the two communicating MTA's are not in the same system, the SDE is used as a remote delivery agent. Since the P3 protocol was largely developed on minicomputers and mainframes, a new, P7 protocol is being developed for microcomputers. The main difference between P3 and P7 is that P7 allows for the MTA to be located in a central MHS server, where microcomputers can occasionally check for or send messages.

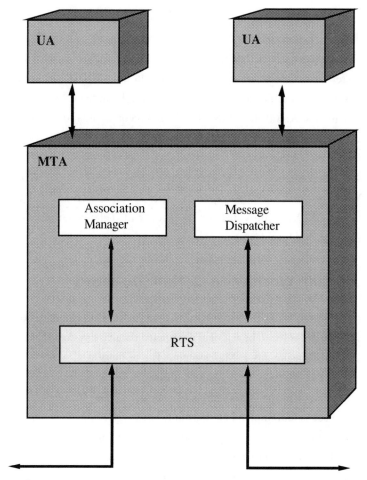

Figure 3.17. Association with adjacent Message Transfer Agents (MTAs) [18].

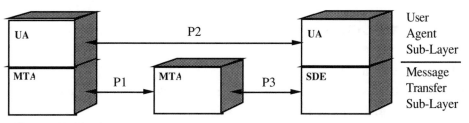

Figure 13.18. Sublayers and protocols of an interpersonal messaging system [18].

The X.420 recommendation provides a description of the Interpersonal Message Service (IPM). The semantics and syntax involved in the sending and receiving of interpersonal messages are described by X.420. Also, X.420 recommends the operation for the transfer of the electronic-mail protocol data units (PDU) through the network. X.420 is a user agent definition; other user agents can be defined to suit the needs of the community using the X.400 standards. The X.420 recommendation also specifies the P2 protocol for peer-to-peer communication between UAs and the format of the messages exchanged between UAs according to the encoding rules specified in X.409.

The X.430 recommendation describes the interface between the MHS and Teletex devices. X.430 just like X.420 also defines a user agent, known as a Teletex access unit (TTXAU). The TTXAU provides for the access of Teletex terminals to the X.400 standard; this is meant for migration purposes.

13.4.2   X.500 Worldwide E-Mail Directory

In early 1988 the CCITT and ISO drafted the X.500 Recommendation. The X.500 Recommendation proposes to be a global distributed database system that contains E-Mail addresses of persons using any E-Mail system. The primary goal of the X.500 standard is to provide a viable method to exchange messages with persons on disjoint E-Mail systems and supplement the X.400 series of standards. The X.500 Recommendation is not expected to see actual implementations until the early 1990s.

The X.500 Directory is made up of directory system agents (DSAs). The DSAs are individual portions of the Directory that exist in X.500 hosts. The DSAs are accessed by users through the directory user agents (DUAs). The user of the X.500 Directory system may be human or communication entities.

13.5   Exercises

13.1   Describe the differences between LANs and WANs.

13.2   Explain the roles of the DCE and the DTE in WAN communications such as those used by the X.25 Recommendation.

13.3   Describe the difference between a virtual call and a virtual circuit.

13.4   Detail why a PAD is useful to a protocol such as X.25 (packet switched network).

13.5   Describe the benefits of using ISDN. Is there any significant difference between ISDN and X.25, what differences? What would you use each for?

13.6   Why would you use ISDN if you could use X.25 and X.400?

13.7   What does ISDN mean to Wide Area Networking? Site examples of ISDN's implementation and design.

13.8   What benefits can be derived from accepting and using the CCITT's X.400 Recommendation(s)?

13.9   Detail what you view as the average voyage of a message through an X.400 message handling system.

13.6 References

1   Aho, A. V.; Hopcroft, J. E.; and Ullman, J. D., The Design and Analysis of Computer Algorithms. Reading, MA: Addison-Wesley, 1974.

2   Bellamy, John, Digital Telephony. New York, NY: John Wiley and Sons, 1982.

3   Bhusri, G., "Considerations for ISDN Planning and Implementation." IEEE Communications Magazine, January 1984.

4   Black, U., Computer Networks. Englewood Cliffs, NJ: Prentice-Hall, 1987.

5   Black, U., Computer Networks: Protocols, Standards and Interfaces. Englewood Cliffs, NJ: Prentice-Hall, 1987.

6   Black, U., Data Networks: Concepts, Theory, and Practice. Englewood Cliffs, NJ: Prentice-Hall, 1989.

7   Callon, R., "Internetwork Protocols." Proceedings of the IEEE, December 1983.

8   Defense Communications Agency, DDN Protocol Handbook. Menlo Park, CA: DDN Network Information Center, SRI International, December 1985.

9   Deasington, R. J., X.25 Explained. Chicester, England: Halsted Press, 1985.

10   Dijkstra, E., "A Note on Two Problems in Connection with Graphs." Numerical Mathematics, October 1959.

11   Halsall, F., Data Communications, Computer Networks, and OSI (2nd edition). Reading, MA: Addison-Wesley, 1988.

12   Kuo, F. (ed.), Protocols and Techniques for Data Communication Networks. Englewood Cliffs, NJ: Prentice-Hall, 1981.

13   Markov, J. D., and Strole, N. C., "Token-Ring Local Area Networks: A Perspective." Proceedings, COMPCON Fall 82, IEEE, 1982.

14   Martin, J., Computer Networks and Distributed Processing. Englewood Cliffs, NJ: Prentice-Hall, 1981.

15   McQuillan, J. M., and Cerf, V. G., A Practical View of Computer Communications Protocols. Washington, DC: IEEE Computer Society Press, 1978.

16   Pooch, U. W.; Greene, W. H.; and Moss, G. G., Telecommunications and Networking. Boston, MA: Little, Brown and Company, 1983.

17   Sastry, A. R. K., "Performance Objectives for ISDN's." IEEE Communications Magazine, 22, 1, January 1984.

18   Schutt, T. E., et. al., "Message-Handling Systems Based on the CCITT X.400 Recommendations." IBM Systems Journal, 26, 3, 1987.

19   Schwartz, M., Computer-Communication Networks Design and Analysis. Englewood Cliffs, NJ: Prentice-Hall, 1977.

20   Schwartz, M., and Stern, T. E., "Routing Techniques Used in Computer Communications Networks." IEEE Trans. on Comm., April 1980.

21   Stallings, W., "The Integrated Services Digital Network." Datamation, December 1984.

22   Stallings, W., Data and Computer Communications. New York, NY: MacMillan Publishing Company, 1985.

23   Stallings, W., Handbook of Computer Communications Standards, Vol. 2. New York, NY: MacMillan Publishing Company, 1987.

24   Stallings, W., Handbook of Computer Communications Standards, Vol. I. New York, NY: MacMillan Publishing Company, 1987.

25   Stallings, W., Handbook of Computer Communications Standards, Vol. II. New York, NY: MacMillan Publishing Company, 1987.

26   Stallings, W., Handbook of Computer Communications Standards, Vol. III. New York, NY: MacMillan Publishing Company, 1987.

27   Stewart, A., "A User's Guide to ISDN Standards." Telecommunications, May 1988.

Appendix I

Fourier Coefficients of Representative Periodic Functions

	Periodic function, $f(t) = f(t + T)$		Fourier coefficients (for phasing as shown in diagram)
1	Rectangular pulses		$a_n = 2A\dfrac{T_o}{T}\ s\left(\dfrac{nT_o}{T}\right)$ $b_n = 0$
2	Symmetrical triangular pulses		$a_n = A\dfrac{T_o}{T}s^2\left(\dfrac{nT_o}{2T}\right)$ $b_n = 0$
3	Symmetrical trapezoidal pulses		$a_n = 2A\dfrac{T_o + T_1}{T}\ s\left(\dfrac{nT_1}{T}\right)\ s\left[\dfrac{n(T_o + T_1)}{T}\right]$ $b_n = 0$
4	Half-sine pulses*†		$a_n = A\dfrac{T_o}{T}\left\{s\left[\dfrac{1}{2}\left(\dfrac{2T_o}{T} - 1\right)\right] + s\left[\dfrac{1}{2}\left(\dfrac{2T_o}{T} + 1\right)\right]\right\}$ $b_n = 0$

5	Clipped sinusoid $A = A_o\left(1 - \cos\frac{\pi T_o}{T}\right)$		$a_n = \frac{A_o T_o}{T}\left\{ s\left[(n-1)\frac{T_o}{T}\right] + s\left[(n+1)\frac{T_o}{T}\right] - 2\cos\frac{\pi T_o}{T} s\left(\frac{nT_o}{T}\right)\right\}$
6	Triangular waveform		$a_n = 0$ $b_n = -\frac{A}{n\pi}\Bigg\}\, n = 1, 2, \ldots$

*For $T_o = \dfrac{T}{2} = \dfrac{\pi}{\omega}$ $f(t) = \dfrac{2}{\pi} A\left(\dfrac{1}{2} + \dfrac{\pi}{4}\cos\omega t + \dfrac{1}{3}\cos 2\omega t - \dfrac{1}{15}\cos 4\omega t + \dfrac{1}{35}\cos$

$\omega t \pm \cdots\Bigg)$ (Half-wave rectified sinusoid).

†For $T_o = T = \dfrac{2\pi}{\omega}$ $f(t) = \dfrac{4}{\pi} A\left(\dfrac{1}{2} + \dfrac{1}{3}\cos 2\omega t - \dfrac{1}{15}\cos 4\omega t + \dfrac{1}{35}\cos 6\omega t \pm \cdots\right)$

(Full-wave rectified sinusoid).

$$S(x) \equiv \frac{\sin \pi x}{\pi x}$$

References

1   Bracewell, R., *The Fourier Transform and Its Applications*. New York, NY: McGraw-Hill, 1965.

2   Churchill, R. V., *Fourier Series and Boundary Value Problems*. New York, NY: McGraw-Hill, 1963.

Appendix II

Fourier Integral

Given a function of the real variable t, the integral

$$F(\omega) = \int_{-\infty}^{\infty} f(t)e^{-i\omega t}\, dt \qquad (1)$$

can be formed. If this integral exists for every ereal value of the parameter ω, it defines a function $F(\omega)$ known as the Fourier integral or fourier transform of $f(t)$. $F(\omega)$ can be rewritten as

$$F(\omega) = A(\omega)e^{i\phi(\omega)} \qquad (2)$$

where $A(\omega)$ is called the Fourier spectrum of $f(t)$, $A^2(\omega)$ the energy spectrum, and $\phi(\omega)$ the phase angle.

To represent $f(t)$ in terms of its Fourier transform $F(\omega)$, we make use of the inversion formula

$$f(t) = \frac{1}{2\pi} \int_{-\infty}^{\infty} F(\omega)e^{i\omega t}\, d\omega \qquad (3)$$

If the function $f(t)$ is shifted by a constant, its Fourier spectrum remains the same, but a linera term $-t_0\omega$ is added to its phase angle.

$$f(t - t_0) \leftrightarrow F(\omega)e^{-i\omega t_0} \qquad (4)$$

Rectangular Pulses

As a result of equation 4,

$$P_{T_0/2}(t - t_0) \leftrightarrow \frac{2 \, \text{Sin} \, (\omega T_0/2)}{\omega} \, e^{-i\omega t_0}$$

The phase angle is linear for $\omega \neq 2n\pi/T_0$, with jumps equal to π for $\omega = 2n\pi/T_0$, because of the change in the sign of $sin(\omega\tau_0/2)$ at these points. See figure II.1

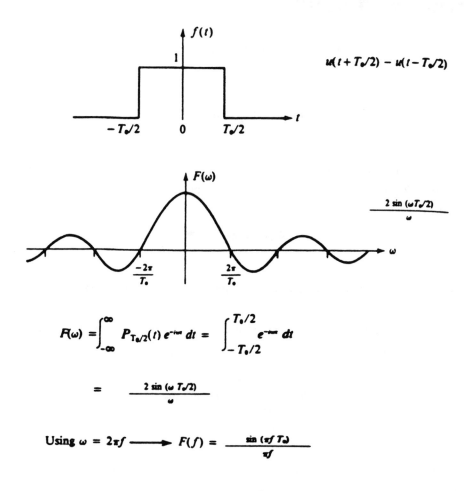

$$F(\omega) = \int_{-\infty}^{\infty} P_{T_0/2}(t) \, e^{-i\omega t} \, dt = \int_{-T_0/2}^{T_0/2} e^{-i\omega t} \, dt$$

$$= \frac{2 \, \text{sin} \, (\omega \, T_0/2)}{\omega}$$

Using $\omega = 2\pi f \longrightarrow F(f) = \frac{\text{sin} \, (\pi f \, T_0)}{\pi f}$

Figure II.1

Exponential Pulses

For

$$f(t) = u(t)\, e^{-t/T_c} \qquad 1/T_c > 0$$

using equation 1, we have

$$F(\omega) = \int_{-\infty}^{\infty} u(t) e^{-t/T_c} e^{-i\omega t}\, dt$$

$$= \int_{0}^{\infty} e^{-t/T_c} e^{-i\omega t}\, dt = \frac{1}{(1/T_c) + i\omega}$$

$$= \frac{(1/T_c)}{(1/T_c)^2 + \omega^2} - i\frac{\omega}{(1/T_c)^2 + \omega^2}$$

$$= \frac{1}{\sqrt{(1/T_c)^2 + \omega^2}}\, e^{-i\tan^{-1}(\omega T_c)}$$

Thus,

$$e^{-t/T_c}\, u(t) \leftrightarrow \frac{1}{\sqrt{(1/T_c)^2 + \omega^2}}\, e^{-i\tan^{-1}(\omega T_c)}$$

$$e^{-t/T_c}\, u(t) \leftrightarrow \frac{T_c}{\sqrt{1 + (2\pi f T_c)^2}}\, e^{-i\tan^{-1}(\omega T_c)}$$

The pair is then illustrated as in figure II.2.

For more detailed examples consult A. Papoulis, *The Fourier Integral and Its Applications*, New York: McGraw-Hill, 1962.

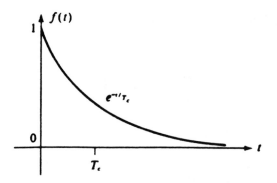

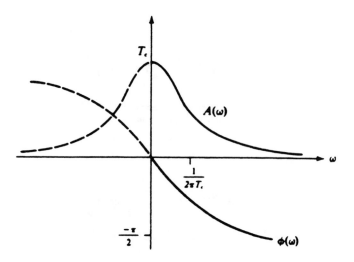

Figure II.2

Appendix III

Data Communication Codes

A conversion must always occur prior to transmission of data. This is a fundamental notion in all communications, regardless of type, simplicity, or complexity of the system being used. For example, an idea must be converted to written letters or spoken words before it can be conveyed to another individual. In electrical systems the data are converted to electrical pulses called bits. In all cases, the information or data are converted to symbols or code to which the originator and the receiver have assigned some meaning.

In data communications systems, data are best represented as on/off or true/false conditions. The code that is normally used is the binary number system, with the two symbols 1 and 0. Each number in the entire number system is represented by a unique series of 1s and 0s. If alphabetic letters are arbitrarily assigned to a specific series or sequence of 1s and 0s, the alphabet can be uniquely represented. Thus a code can be established with which numeric, alphabetic, or alphanumeric information can be transmitted. Special characters such as commas, periods, and other symbols may be represented in a similar manner. The three advantages derived from converting data are speed, efficiency, and economy.

It will suffice to discuss only some of the many possible codes that can be constructed.

Baudot Code. This type of code utilizes 5 bits in representing each character, thereby allowing only 32 combinations. This is not sufficient to represent the alphabet and the numbers 0 through 9. To compensate for this inadequacy, the Baudot code assigns a "figures" or "letters" character to many of the 5-bit combinations. The letters character is used for lowercase, and the figures character is used with uppercase. This expands the code representation to 57 characters and functions.

Data Interchange Code and ASCII. The American Standard Code for Information Interchange is an 8-bit code that uses the eighth bit for even parity checking. The alphabet, number system, and all special characters can thus be represented by the 128 character combinations. This includes 94 graphic characters and 34 control characters.

Hollerith Code. This code is normally used in card equipment and utilizes the 12, 11, or 0 zone punch for alphabetic and special character representations. The numbers 0 through 9 are represented by punching the respective zone. Upper- and lowercase characters, special characters, and alphanumerics are represented using this code.

Binary Coded Decimal (BCD). A 64-character set consisting of alphabetics, numerics, and several special characters can be developed from this 6-bit code. This coding structure is often extended to an 8-bit code which is referred to as the Extended Binary Coded Decimal Interchange Code (EBCDIC). This expansion allows for the character representation of 256 characters.

Each of the various codes is characterized by its individual limitations, advantages, and capabilities, and must therefore be evaluated according to the requirements of the individual users. Some of the factors that should be considered when selecting a coding structure must include throughput requirements, costs, information that the code contains, the number of characters and functions, and the grade of the transmission channel.

Communication Codes

Col. No.	1	2	3	4	5
Code	Baudot (Telegraphic)	CCITT·2 (International)	ASCII (With even parity)	EBCDIC (Extended BCD Interchange Code)	Field Data (6-bit)
No. Bits	5	5	7	8	6
Parity	None	None	Even	None	None
Media	Tape Channels	Tape Channels	Tape Channels	Tape Channels	Tape Channels
A	1-2	1-2	1-7	1-7-8	2-3
B	1-4-5	1-4-5	2-7	2-7-8	1-2-3
C	2-3-4	2-3-4	1-2-7-8	1-2-7-8	4
D	1-4	1-4	3-7	3-7-8	1-4
E	1	1	1-3-7-8	1-3-7-8	2-4
F	1-3-4	1-3-4	2-3-7-8	2-3-7-8	1-2-4
G	2-4-5	2-4-5	1-2-3-7	1-2-3-7-8	3-4
H	3-5	3-5	4-7	4-7-8	1-3-4
I	2-3	2-3	1-4-7-8	1-4-7-8	2-3-4
J	1-2-4	1-2-4	2-4-7-8	1-5-7-8	1-2-3-4
K	1-2-3-4	1-2-3-4	1-2-4-7	2-5-7-8	5
L	2-5	2-5	3-4-7-8	1-2-5-7-8	1-5
M	3-4-5	3-4-5	1-3-4-7	3-5-7-8	2-5
N	3-4	3-4	2-3-4-7	1-3-5-7-8	1-2-5
O	4-5	4-5	1-2-3-4-7-8	2-3-5-7-8	3-5
P	2-3-5	2-3-5	5-7	1-2-3-5-7-8	1-3-5
Q	1-2-3-5	1-2-3-5	1-5-7-8	4-5-7-8	2-3-5
R	2-4	2-4	2-5-7-8	1-4-5-7-8	1-2-3-5
S	1-3	1-3	1-2-5-7	2-6-7-8	4-5
T	5	5	3-5-7-8	1-2-6-7-8	1-4-5
U	1-2-3	1-2-3	1-3-5-7	3-6-7-8	2-4-5
V	2-3-4-5	2-3-4-5	2-3-5-7	1-3-6-7-8	1-2-4-5
W	1-2-5	1-2-5	1-2-3-5-7-8	2-3-6-7-8	3-4-5
X	1-3-4-5	1-3-4-5	4-5-7-8	1-2-3-6-7-8	1-3-4-5
Y	1-3-5	1-3-5	1-4-5-7	4-6-7-8	2-3-4-5
Z	1-5	1-5	2-4-5-7	1-4-6-7-8	1-2-3-4-5
0	•P	•P	5-6	5-6-7-8	5-6
1	•Q	•Q	1-5-6-8	1-5-6-7-8	1-5-6
2	•W	•W	2-5-6-8	2-5-6-7-8	2-5-6
3	•E	•E	1-2-5-6	1-2-5-6-7-8	1-2-5-6
4	•R	•R	3-5-6-8	3-5-6-7-8	3-5-6
5	•T	•T	1-3-5-6	1-3-5-6-7-8	1-3-5-6
6	•Y	•Y	2-3-5-6	2-3-5-6-7-8	2-3-5-6
7	•U	•U	1-2-3-5-6-8	1-2-3-5-6-7-8	1-2-3-5-6
8	•I	•I	4-5-6-8	4-5-6-7-8	4-5-6
9	•O	•O	1-4-5-6	1-4-5-6-7-8	1-4-5-6

Communication Codes (cont)

Col. No.	1	2	3	4	5
Code	Baudot (Telegraphic)	CCITT·2 (International)	ASCII (With even parity)	EBCDIC (Extended BCD Interchange Code)	Field Data (6-bit)
No. Bits	5	5	7	8	6
Parity	None	None	Even	None	None
Media	Tape Channels	Tape Channels	Tape Channels	Tape Channels	Tape Channels
U CASE	1-2-4-5	1-2-4-5		2-3-5-6	1
L CASE	1-2-3-4-5	1-2-3-4-5		2-3	2
SPACE	3	3	6-8	7	1-3
CAR RET	4	4	1-3-4-8		3
L FEED	2	2	2-4	1-3-6	1-2
BELL	•S	•J	1-2-3-8		
•	•H		1-2-6-8		
$	•D		3-6	1-2-4-5-6-7	
%			1-3-6-8	1-2-4-5-7	1-2-3-6
&	•G		2-3-6-8	3-4-6-7	
•	•J		1-2-3-6	1-3-4-5-6-7	
(	•K	•L	4-6	1-3-4-7	1-4-6
)	•L	•L	1-4-6-8	1-3-4-5-7	6
•			2-4-6-8	3-4-5-7	4-6
+		•Z	1-2-4-6	2-3-4-7	2-6
,	•N	•N	3-4-6-8	1-2-4-6-7	2-3-4-6
-	•A	•A	1-3-4-6	6-7	1-6
.	•M	•M	2-3-4-6	1-2-4-7	1-3-4-5-6
/	•X	•X	1-2-3-4-6-8	1-6-7	3-4-5-6
:	•C		2-4-5-8	2-4-5-6-7	1-2-4-6
;	•V		1-2-4-5	2-3-4-5-7	1-2-4-5-6
<			3-4-5-8	5-7-8	1-2-6
=		•V	1-3-4-5	2-3-4-5-6-7	3-6
>			2-3-4-5	7-8	1-3-6
?	•B	•B	1-2-3-4-5-8	2-4-7	3-4-6
@			7-8	3-4-5-6-7	
□					
!	•F		1-6	2-4-5-7	1-3-4-6
•	•Z		2-6	1-4-5-6-7	2-4-6
¢				1-2-3-4-5-7	
[			1-2-4-5-7-8		
\			3-4-5-7		
]			1-3-4-5-7-8		
←			1-2-3-4-5-7	3-4-7	
↑			2-3-4-5-7-8		
TAB				1-3	
PCH ON				3-5-6	

Communication Codes (cont)

Col. No.	1	2	3	4	5
Code	Baudot (Telegraphic)	CCITT·2 (International)	ASCII (With even parity)	EBCDIC (Extended BCD Interchange Code)	Field Data (6-bit)
No. Bits	5	5	7	8	6
Parity	None	None	Even	None	None
Media	Tape Channels	Tape Channels	Tape Channels	Tape Channels	Tape Channels
PCH OFF					
DELETE				3	
NULL				1-2-3	
SOM					
EOA					
EOM					
EOT				1-2-3-5-6	
WRU		*D			
RU					
ALT MODE					
STOP				1-3-5-6	1-2-3-4-6
SPECIAL					2-3-4-5-6
IDLE				1-2-3-5	1-2-3-4-5-6

*Upper case

Communication Codes (cont)

Col. No.	7	8	9	10	11
Code	Mach—10 (Chan 5 is for odd parity)	Flexowriter Model SFD	IBM Perforated Tape and Transmission Code	IBM Card Code (Hollerith)	UNIVAC Card Code (90—Col.)
No. Bits	6	6	7		
Parity	5th level odd	5th level odd	5th level odd		
Media	Tape Channels	Tape Channels	Tape Channels	Card Row	Card Row
A	1-6-7	1-6-7	1-6-7	12-1	1-5-9
B	2-6-7	2-6-7	2-6-7	12-2	1-5
C	1-2-5-6-7	1-2-5-6-7	1-2-5-6-7	12-3	0-7
D	3-6-7	3-6-7	3-6-7	12-4	0-3-5
E	1-3-5-6-7	1-3-5-6-7	1-3-5-6-7	12-5	0-3
F	2-3-5-6-7	2-3-5-6-7	2-3-5-6-7	12-6	1-7-9
G	1-2-3-6-7	1-2-3-6-7	1-2-3-6-7	12-7	5-7
H	5-6-7	4-6-7	4-6-7	12-8	3-7
I	1-4-5-6-7	1-4-5-6-7	1-4-5-6-7	12-9	3-5
J	1-5-7	1-5-7	1-5-7	11-1	1-3-5
K	2-5-7	2-5-7	2-5-7	11-2	3-5-9
L	1-2-7	1-2-7	1-2-7	11-3	0-9
M	3-5-7	3-5-7	3-5-7	11-4	0-5
N	1-3-7	1-3-7	1-3-7	11-5	0-5-9
O	2-3-7	2-3-7	2-3-7	11-6	1-3
P	1-2-3-5-7	1-2-3-5-7	1-2-3-5-7	11-7	1-3-7
Q	4-5-7	4-5-7	4-5-7	11-8	3-5-7
R	1-4-"	1-4-7	1-4-7	11-9	1-7
S	2-5-6	2-5-6	2-5-6	0-2	1-5-7
T	1-2-6	1-2-6	1-2-6	0-3	3-7-9
U	3-5-6	3-5-6	3-5-6	0-4	0-5-7
V	1-3-6	1-3-6	1-3-6	0-5	0-3-9
W	2-3-6	2-3-6	2-3-6	0-6	0-3-7
X	1-2-3-5-6	1-2-3-5-6	1-2-3-5-6	0-7	0-7-9
Y	4-5-6	4-5-6	4-5-6	0-8	1-3-9
Z	1-4-6	1-4-6	1-4-6	0-9	5-7-9
0	6	6	2-4-5	0	0
1	1	1	1	1	1
2	2	2	2	2	1-9
3	1-2-5	1-2-5	1-2-5	3	3
4	3	3	3	4	3-9
5	1-3-5	1-3-5	1-3-5	5	5
6	2-3-5	2-3-5	2-3-5	6	5-9
7	1-2-3	1-2-3	1-2-3	7	7

Communication Codes (cont)

Col. No.	7	8	9	10	11
Code	Mach—10 (Chan 5 is for odd parity)	Flexowriter Model SFD	IBM Perforated Tape and Transmission Code	IBM Card Code (Hollerith)	UNIVAC Card Code (90—Col.)
No. Bits	6	6	7		
Parity	5th level odd	5th level odd	5th level odd		
Media	Tape Channels	Tape Channels	Tape Channels	Card Row	Card Row
8	4	4	4	8	7-9
9	1-4-5	1-4-5	1-4-5	9	9
U CASE	3-4-5-6-7	3-4-5-6-7	2-3-4	9-6	
L CASE	2-4-5-6-7	2-4-5-6-7	2-3-4-6-7	12-9-6	
SPACE	5	5	5	Blank	Blank
CAR RET	8	8	1-3-4-5-7	11-9-5 (cr-lf)	
L FEED			1-3-4-5-6	0-9-5	
BELL					
•	1-2-3-4-5	•3	1-2-4	3-8	0-1-5-7
$	1-2-4-5-7	•4	1-2-4-5-7	11-3-8	0-1-3-5-9
%	•V	•5	•5	•5	0-1-5
&	5-6-7	•7	5-6-7	12	0-1-3-5-7
'	•X	•6	•6	•6	0-1-5-7-9
(	•D	•9	•9	•9	0-1-9
)	•M	•0 (Zero)	•0 (Zero)	•0 (Zero)	0-13-5
•	1-3-4-5-6	•8		•8	0-1
+			•&	•&	1-5-7-9
,	1-2-4-5-6	1-2-4-5-6	1-2-4-5-6	0-3-8	0-3-5-9
-	7	7	7	11	0-3-5-7
.	1-2-4-6-7	1-2-4-6-7	1-2-4-6-7	12-3-8	1-3-5-9
/	1-5-6	1-5-6	1-5-6	0-1	3-5-7-9
:	•4	•;	•4	•4	1-3-7-9
;	•P	5-6-7.	•3	•3	1-3-5-7-9
<	•G				0-1-5-9
=	•U		•1	•1	0-1-3-5-7-9
>	•7				0-3-5-7-9
?		•/	•/	•/	0-1-3
←	•5	•2	6	4-8	0-1-3-7
□	•E		•2	•2	0-1-3-9
!			•5		0-3-7-9
•	•W	•	•7		
¢	••		•@	•@	
[					0-5-7-9
\					0-1-3-7-9

Communication Codes (cont)

Col. No.	7	8	9	10	11
Code	Mach—10 (Chan 5 is for odd parity)	Flexowriter Model SFD	IBM Perforated Tape and Transmission Code	IBM Card Code (Hollerith)	UNIVAC Card Code (90—Col.)
No. Bits	6	6	7		
Parity	5th level odd	5th level odd	5th level odd		
Media	Tape Channels	Tape Channels	Tape Channels	Card Row	Card Row
]					1-3-5-7
←					
↑					
TAB	2-3-4-5-6	2-3-4-5-6	1-3-4-6-7	12-5-9	
PCH ON	3-4-7	3-4-7	3-4-5	4-9	
PCH OFF	1-2-3-4-6	1-2-3-4-6	3-4-5-6-7	12-4-9	
DELETE			1-2-3-4-5-6-7	12-7-9	
NULL					
SOM					
EOA					
EOM					
EOT			1-2-3-4-5	7-9	
WRU					
RU					
ALT MODE					
STOP	1-2-4	1-2-4			
SPECIAL					
IDLE			1-2-3-4-7	11-7-9	
BYPASS			3-4-6	0-4-9	
RESTORE			3-4-7	11-4-9	
±			1-2-4	**	
‡			2-4-6	0-2-8	
♦				*‡	
γ̅				*−0 (Minus 0)	
				*+0	
RDR STOP			1-3-4	5-9	
EOB			2-3-4-5-6	0-6-9	
BACKSP			2-3-4-5-7	11-6-9	
+0			2-4-5-6-7	12-0	
−0			2-4-7	11-0	
PREFIX			1-2-3-4-6		
CANCEL			5-7		

*Upper case

Communication Codes (cont)

Col. No.	12			13			14			15		16
Code	SEVEN—BIT Alphameric (Mod. BCD)			SIX—BIT Numeric			XS—3 (Excess 3)			BI-QUINARY		2—OUT—OF—5
No. Bits				6			6			7		5
Parity				None			None			Self-cont. even		Self-cont. even
Media	C	BA	8421	C	F	8421	B	A	8421	05	01234	0 1 2 3 6
A	1	11	0001				0	1	0100			
B	1	11	0010				0	1	0101			
C	0	11	0011				0	1	0110			
D	1	11	0100				0	1	0111			
E	0	11	0101				0	1	1000			
F	0	11	0110				0	1	1001			
G	1	11	0111				0	1	1010			
H	1	11	1000				0	1	1011			
I	0	11	1001				0	1	1100			
J	0	10	0001				1	0	0100			
K	0	10	0010				1	0	0101			
L	0	10	0011				1	0	0110			
M	0	10	0100				1	0	0111			
N	1	10	0101				1	0	1000			
O	1	10	0110				1	0	1001			
P	0	10	0111				1	0	1010			
Q	0	10	1000				1	0	1011			
R	1	10	1001				1	0	1100			
S	0	01	0010				1	1	0101			
T	1	01	0011				1	1	0110			
U	0	01	0100				1	1	0111			
V	1	01	0101				1	1	1000			
W	1	01	0110				1	1	1001			
X	0	01	0111				1	1	1010			
Y	0	01	1000				1	1	1011			
Z	1	01	1001				1	1	1100			
0	0	00	1010	1	0	0000	0	0	0011	10	10000	0 1 1 0 0
1	1	00	0001	0	0	0001	0	0	0100	10	01000	1 1 0 0 0
2	1	00	0010	0	0	0010	0	0	0101	10	00100	1 0 1 0 0
3	0	00	0011	1	0	0011	0	0	0110	10	00010	1 0 0 1 0
4	1	00	0100	0	0	0100	0	0	0111	10	00001	0 1 0 1 0
5	0	00	0101	1	0	0101	0	0	1000	01	10000	0 0 1 1 0
6	0	00	0110	1	0	0110	0	0	1001	01	01000	1 0 0 0 1
7	1	00	0111	0	0	0111	0	0	1010	01	00100	0 1 0 0 1
8	1	00	1000	0	0	1000	0	0	1011	01	00010	0 0 1 0 1
9	0	00	1001	1	0	1001	0	0	1100	01	00001	0 0 0 1 1

Communication Codes (cont)

Col. No.	12			13			14			15		16
Code	SEVEN—BIT Alphameric (Mod. BCD)			SIX—BIT Numeric			XS—3 (Excess 3)			BI-QUINARY		2—OUT—OF—5
No. Bits				6			6			7		5
Parity				None			None			Self-cont. even		Self-cont. even
Media	C	BA	8421	C	F	8421	B	A	8421	05	01234	0 1 2 3 6
U CASE												
L CASE												
SPACE	1	01	0000				0	0	0000			
CAR RET												
L FEED												
BELL												
•	1	00	1011				0	1	1101			
$	0	10	1011				1	0	0010			
%	1	01	1100				1	1	0001			
&	0	11	0000				0	1	0000			
'							1	0	0000			
(							1	0	1101			
)							1	1	1111			
•	1	10	1100				1	0	0001			
+							1	1	0011			
,	0	01	1011				1	1	0010			
-	1	10	0000				0	0	0010			
.	1	11	1011				0	1	0010			
/	0	01	0001				1	1	0100			
:							0	1	0001			
;							0	0	1110			
<							0	1	1110			
=							0	1	1111			
>							1	1	1110			
?							0	1	0011			
@	0	00	1100				1	0	1110			
□	0	11	1100				1	1	1101			
!							1	0	0011			
•												
¢												
[												
\												
]												
←												
↑												

Communication Codes (cont)

Col. No.	12			13			14			15		16	
Code	SEVEN—BIT Alphameric (Mod. BCD)			SIX—BIT Numeric			XS—3 (Excess 3)			BI-QUINARY		2—OUT—OF—5	
No. Bits				6			6			7		5	
Parity				None			None			Self-cont. even		Self-cont. even	
Media	C	BA	8421	C	F	8421	B	A	8421	05	01234	0 1 2 3 6	
TAB													
PCH ON													
PCH OFF													
DELETE													
NULL													
SOM													
EOA													
EOM													
EOT													
WRU													
RU													
ALT MODE													
STOP													
SPECIAL													
IDLE													
GROUP MK.	0	11	1111										
TAPE MK.	0	00	1111										
DRUM MK.	0	00	0000										
+0	0	11	1010										
−0	1	10	1010										

*Upper case

Appendix IV

Error Detection and Correction Codes

IV.1 Introduction

The effect of transmission errors will vary according to the type of data being transmitted (e.g., errors in text information are usually not too bad, while such errors would be serious for numerical data, and disastrous for control information). Thus, where necessary, the code scheme used to transmit the data may need to be modified in order to detect when a received character is in error or, further, to correct for such errors.

Any sort of error detection and correction scheme must involve the insertion of *redundancy* into the transmitted data. That is, the sending of codes that contain no additional information. Thus all error detection and correction schemes are called *redundant codes*. There are billions of such codes, only representative examples are described here.

IV.2 Classical Error Detection

IV.2.1 Even and odd parity

The even (or odd) parity check is a simple test first applied to error check pre-WW II teletype circuits. The concept is to set aside one bit of data in a field for parity. The field, typically of character length plus one parity bit, is 6 (baudot), 8 (ASCII), or 9 (extended ASCII, EBCDIC) bits in length. The parity bit was used to ensure that the transmitted field contained an even or odd number of 1 bits, depending on the implemented scheme [1]. Let us assume that a block of n binary digit needs to be transmitted. To this bit stream add an $(n + 1)$ digit to ensure the even (odd) integrity. The final test comes at the receiving end where the number of 1 bits in the field is counted. If the proper number of 1 bits does not exist in the field, the block of data containing the error is rejected. This usually results in a request for block transmission.

If the block is chosen to be small relative to the probability P that an error will occur (allowing us to ignore 1 - P) and if each error can be assumed to be an independent event, then the probability that an error will occur in $N + 1$ bits can be written as $(n + 1)P$. The probability that two errors occur is derived as $[n(n + 1)/2]p^2$. Designers should strive to achieve a better reliability than this probability value to minimize the probability of undetected errors. It follows that the optimal length of a block is a function of the desired reliability and the probability of a single error occurring, because the occurrence of an even number of errors within the same field has a good chance of remaining undetected. This is because changing two bits to their opposite state will retain the integrity of the even (odd) count. Additional schemes could be added to the simple even/odd parity test if reliability necessitates such accuracy. Figure IV.1 is a state diagram that describes the even/odd error detection algorithm (IV.2)

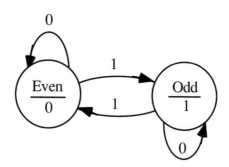

Figure IV.1 Parity check state diagram

IV.2.2   Horizontal and Vertical Tests

A two-dimensional extension of the even/odd parity detection scheme is the horizontal and vertical parity testing scheme, sometimes also referred to as the longitudinal and vertical redundancy checks, LRC and VRC, respectively. This technique is particularly appropriate to communications interfaces such as tape or disk controllers and other external media, both local and remote.

$$
\begin{array}{l}
1\ 0\ 1\ 0\ 1\ |\ 1 \\
0\ 1\ 1\ 1\ 0\ |\ 1 \\
1\ 0\ 1\ 0\ 1\ |\ 1 \quad \text{Horizontal parity} \\
0\ 1\ 1\ 1\ 0\ |\ 1 \\
1\ 0\ 1\ 0\ 1\ |\ 1 \\
0\ 1\ 0\ 1\ 0\ |\ 0 \\
\end{array}
$$

$$1\ 1\ 1\ 1\ 1\quad 1 \qquad \text{Vertical parity field}$$

Figure IV.2 Even parity horizontal/vertical error detection

To understand the vertical and horizontal error test, it is necessary to visualize transmitted data as a matrix of bits, where rows are fields (characters) such as described above and the combination of columns are blocks of fields (Figure IV.2). As before, an even (odd) parity bit is added to each field to make up the horizontal parity. The last row of bits of every block consists of a parity field sometimes called the *block check character* (BCC), which ensures an even (odd) one bit count in each column of the block. This represents the vertical parity test. Blocks must either be of fixed length or the BCC must be preceded by an ETX.

Bit streams arriving serially must be reorganized into the horizontal/vertical matrix structure for testing purposes. A quick test of the last bit received to see if it satisfies the even (odd) configuration of both the row and column parity fields must be performed before proceeding to test the remaining rows and columns. There is little need to test the user data for error if the parity fields are found to be in error themselves.

Oddly enough, the horizontal/vertical error-detection scheme also contains some error-correction power. It should be obvious by now that a parity failure in a particular row and column must mean that the intersecting bit is in error. To correct the error, it is only necessary to change the state of that bit. It is still possible, though, to pass errors undetected by the algorithm. This would occur if a double error changed the states of bits in a row and in a column. To go undetected, errors must have occurred in an even number within columns and in the same number of rows. The probability of four errors, two per field, in a two-field block, can be derived, and is $[(n**2)(N+1)**2/4]$ $p**4$. If the probability P that a single error will occur is 0.1, then the probability that offsetting errors will occur within the two-field block is 0.0225. However, in an m-field block, there are m - 1 opportunities that the same two columns can be in error. Thus the probability of an error going undetected escalates to 0.0224(m-1). What this means is that the longer the data block, the greater the probability of having an undetected error. Thus, if the medium is prone to high error rates, short blocks are warranted. Improved media justify longer blocks. If a proper balance between block length and error conditions of the medium cannot be reached, more powerful error-detection mechanisms must be employed.

IV.2.3   Check sum burst error detection

Errors result from two general categories of noise, Gaussian "white" noise, and impulse noise caused by lightning, static, power fluctuations, and the like. Certain error-detection algorithms are more prone to detect errors caused by one or the other type of noise categories. One particular scheme more appropriately used for burst error conditions is a check sum modulo 2 addition of the fields in a block. Simply stated, each field is added, without carry, to the next field. This continues for the entire block. The resulting value is included as the last field in the block (Figure IV.3). The receiving element proceeds to add modulo 2 each field for the entire block (including the check sum field). This should produce a field of binary 0s or the block was received in error. No error-correction power exists in this algorithm, consequently the block must be retransmitted. White noise error conditions increase the probability that both the user data as sell as the check sum will be altered in such a fashion that errors can pass undetected.

Transmitter   Receiver

1 0 1 0 1 0 1 1   1 0 1 0 1 0 1 1
0 1 1 1 0 1 0 1   0 1 1 1 0 1 0 1
0 0 1 1 0 0 1 1   0 0 1 1 0 0 1 1
1 1 0 0 1 1 0 0   1 1 0 0 1 1 0 0
1 0 0 1 0 1 0 0   1 0 0 1 0 1 0 0

1 0 1 1 0 1 0 1   Check sum field   0 0 0 0 0 0 0 0   Test result

Figure IV.3 Example check sum bursts error detection

IV.2.4   Constant ratio codes [4]

Constant-ratio-code algorithms are so called because their purpose is to maintain and test for a constant ratio between the number of 0s and 1s in a field. For example, a 4-of-8 code means that there should always be four 1 bits and four 0 bits for every eight bits transmitted. The receiver knows that an error has occurred whenever a field is received with the bits off-balance. The constant ratio codes were never very popular because of the obvious overhead implications and the inefficient use of costly bandwidth.

IV.2.5   Cyclic polynomial codes

One of the more powerful error-detection algorithms involves the use of cyclic redundancy codes, whose product can be represented as a polynomial. The process involves the use of a generator polynomial that is selected to detect certain types of errors that most frequently occur on the medium in use. Use of powerful cyclic polynomial codes are now flexible because of the recent advances in microtechnology hardware, which produce the required code as the data are being transmitted [5].

The following explanation is based on Davies et al. [6]. The transmitted data are treated as one long k-binary number in which the binary digits represent coefficients to a $(k - 1)$th degree polynomial. Let the message polynomial be represented by $M(x)$ and the generator polynomial by $G(x)$. Then, for the data message 1 1 0 0 1 0 0 0 1, the $M(x)$ is $1 + x + x^4 + x^8$ (the high-order exponent is transmitted first). Given $G(x)$ of degree n, the method requires that $(x^n) M(x)$ be divided by $g(x)$ and the remainder polynomial, $R(x)$, be added to $(x^n)M(x)$ to produce

$$(x^n)M(x) = Q(x)G(x) + R(x)$$

where $Q(x)$ is the quotient. Modulo 2 addition and subtraction are identical, thus the code polynomial, $C(x)$, is formed by

$$C(x) = Q(x)G(x) = (x^n)M(x) + R(x)$$

if we assume a fifth-degree generator polynomial of $1 + x^3 + x^5$, $R(x)$ becomes

$$
\begin{aligned}
R(x) &= \text{mod} \, [(x^n)M(x)/G(x)] \\
&= \text{mod} \, [x^5(1 + x + x^4 + x^8)/1 + x^3 + x^5] \\
&= 1 + x^3 + x^4
\end{aligned}
$$

The code polynomial, $C(x)$, is then derived as

$$
\begin{aligned}
C(x) &= R(x) + (x^n)M(x) \\
&= (1 + x^3 + x^4) + (x^5 + x^6 + x^9 + x^{13})
\end{aligned}
$$

This results in a coefficient bit stream of

$$1\,0\,0\,1\,1 \qquad 1\,1\,0\,0\,1\,0\,0\,0\,1$$

where the first five bits are the check digits to be forwarded with the message. Note that the remaining nine bits are identical to the original user bit stream. This must be so since multiplying $M(x)$ by (x^n) only changes the exponents and not the coefficients.

The process of deriving $R(x)$ in hardware is really quite simple. For the receiver, there exists an $n + 1$ bit register, R, which contains all n coefficients (both 1s and 0s) of the generator polynomial, $G(x)$. Another $n + 1$ register, R_m, is designated to receive the incoming data as they arrive. These data arrive through a third $n + 1$ register, R^q, which will ultimately contain the unneeded quotient. The algorithm proceeds as follows after shifting the first $n + 1$ bits through R^q into R^m.

1. Test for ETX;

2. $R_m \leftarrow R_m - R_q$;

3. If ETX then

      if $R_m = R_q$ then
          do;
          send ACK;
          stop;
          end;
      else
          do;
          send NAK;
          stop;
          end;

4. Else

      do;
      if $R_m < 0$ then $R_m = R_m + R^q$;
      accept next bit by shifting $R_m R_q$ left one bit;
      go to step 1;
      end;

Clearly, the above algorithm could be programmed in PL/1, compiled, and "burned in" to function at hardware speed. Since the data stream is altered by the process, both the transmit and the receive sides must ensure that the algorithm is deriving $R(x)$ from a copy of the data stream as it appears on the output/input ports, respectively.

Using the algorithm is easy; determining the proper $G(x)$ is far more difficult and really depends to a great extent on the characteristics of the communications media. The CCITT has recommended a generator polynomial of the form $1 + x^5 + x^{12} + x^{16}$ as suitable for most communications lines [6].

One other point is worthy of note. Cyclic polynomial codes are well known for their power to detect errors; however, little credit is given to their power to also correct errors. The reason is that the error-correcting capabilities of this subset of cyclic codes are complex and difficult to implement efficiently. This will become apparent in the following section, which reviews the error-correcting power of cyclic algorithms along with some of the better understood error-correcting procedures.

IV.3 Techniques for Forward Error Correction

Error-correcting codes can be categorized as rectangular, triangular, cubic, or n-dimensional [2]. The horizontal/vertical parity test algorithm, discussed earlier, is a rectangular code. In general, increasing the power of a correcting algorithm increases the overhead and usually increases the difficulty in implementation. For example, the horizontal/vertical algorithm, while relatively weak for correcting errors, produces a nominal amount of overhead when compared to other error-correcting algorithms. To demonstrate, assume a data field size of j bits to which is added one parity bit. Also assume a block size of i fields (Figure IV.4). Overhead isquickly calculated to be i + j + 1 bits or approximately 20 percent of the transmitted field. As we shall see, overhead for the more powerful correction codes will in some cases be larger than the actual user data that are being transmitted. It is therefore necessary to evaluate carefully the advantages and disadvantages of error correction versus simply retransmitting the data if received in error. Because of this high overhead, error-correction codes are generally used where retransmission is not possible. Communications involving time-sensitive or volatile information or using one-way media may justify the additional overhead.

IV.3.1 Triangular codes

Triangular codes are an attempt to lower the overhead while retaining the correction power in the horizontal/vertical algorithm. This is only true if the number of bits in a triangle is sufficiently large, and even then this scheme has an increased risk in not detecting errors.

$$j + 1$$

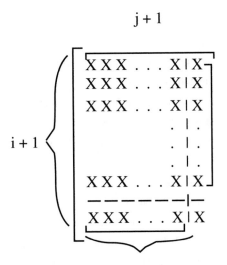

Figure IV.4 Overhead for rectangular error correcting

Assume a triangle of user data with n rows and n columns. One parity bit is added to each row such that it serves as parity bit for both the row and column in which it resides. The triangle now consists of three sides of n + 1 bits; the overhead is calculated as

$$(n + 1)\sum_{i=1}^{n-1} i$$

as shown in Figure IV.5.

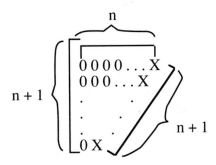

Figure IV.5 Formation of triangular coding

Plotting overhead versus n [Figure IV.6(a)] indicates that, while percent of overhead continues to decline, very little change is realized after n = 8. Thus beyond n = 8, the ratio of the risk of an undetected error to the percent of overhead is becoming worse. No direct conclusion can be made from the graph about a proper selection of n, except that if the media is average, n = 8 is a good starting point. If the media are better than average, then a larger n can be selected. However for n > 12, each additional n will improve on overhead by less than 1 percent.

The possibility of having an undetected error requires the error pattern to be similar to the pattern of the horizontal/vertical algorithm. From previous calculations, we know that the probability of two errors in a field of n bits is $[n(n + 1)/2]P^2$, where P is the probability of an error. The probability of an undetected error can thus be calculated as $\{[n(n - m)(n - m + 1)(n + 1)(n - 1)]/4\}P^4$, m < n - 1, where m is the mth row of the field containing n bits of user data. The factor n - 1 represents the opportunities that an additional field will have two errors in a block of n fields. The factor m accounts for the decreasing field size. This formula shows that as n grows large, the probability of undetected errors will increase exponentially. The curve in Figure IV.6(b) demonstrates the point for m = n/2 and P = 0.05.

It is not our intention to continue this type of detail for each algorithm; however, it is worthwhile to note that some quick analysis can reveal interesting characteristics with respect to triangular code. Similar analysis for the other error-correcting codes may be just as revealing. Likely as not, the decision will be made to use much more powerful techniques if error correction is in fact necessary. We now investigate the even more powerful cubic and n-dimensional algorithms.

IV.3.2   Hamming Codes

At this point, error correction becomes serious business, one in which algorithms were designed specifically for error-correction powers. Although there are many such codes, we are constrained to a few of the more popular codes, which have assumed increasing significance with space and related data communications systems. The Hamming error correcting algorithm provides one such code.

Hamming codes are an attempt to find the best encoding scheme for single error correction in the presence of white noise [2]. It is an excellent error-correcting algorithm based on a syndrome that results from writing a 0 for each correct parity test and a 1 for each failure. The nature of the algorithm then allows the syndrome to identify the position of the error in the transmitted field. Thus for an n-bit syndrome, the field to be transmitted is limited to 2^n-bit positions.

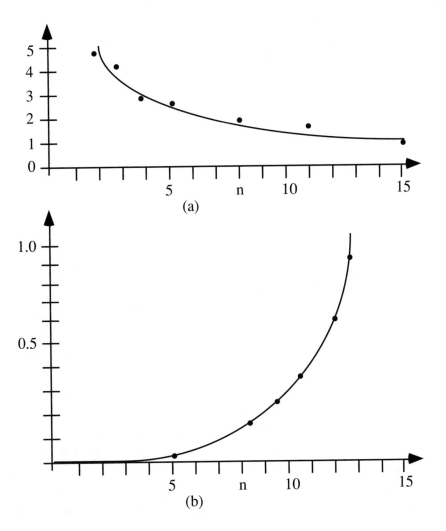

Figure IV.6 The implications of using triangular codes: (a) percent overhead; (b) probability of undetected error.

To develop the Hamming algorithm, it si first necessary to recognize certain relationships between positions that have a value of 1 for binary representation of decimal numbers. The decimal numbers are actually the positions of error in a field at the received end. Note in Figure IV.7 that one bit occurs in the right-most position at a certain interval, specifically 1, 3, 5, 7, ...

Position number (syndrome value)	Binary Representation	
1	0	0
2	0	1
3	0	1
4	1	0
5	1	0
6	1	1
7	1	1

Figure IV.7 Parity field-test patterns

The same can be said for each of the (more significant) columns resulting in 2, 3, 6, 7, ... and 4, 5, 6, 7, 12, 13, 14, 15, ..., respectively. These patterns, called the parity check fields, will be used as fields for independent parity testing. It follows then that parity bits must be strategically positioned in the transmitted field so that the syndrome can identify a position in error. Thus, bit positions 2^n in the transmitted field are reserved for parity where $0 \leq n <$ syndrome field size. For a 3-bit syndrome, bit positions 1, 2, and 4 are reserved for parity in the transmitted field. The value contained by these positions is determined by the pattern of bits in the parity check fields referred to above.

Assume a 4-bits message, 1 0 1 0, was to be transmitted (Figure IV.8). The actual field to be transmitted would consist of 7 bits with positions 1, 2, and 4 as parity, that is [_1_0 1 0]. The value assumed by these parity bits is such so as to retain an even parity in the parity check fields. The first parity check field is [_1 0 0] and thus the parity becomes 1 resulting in [1 1 0 0]. The remaining parity check fields are derived in a similar fashion resulting in [0 1 0 1] and [1 0 1 0], respectively. Combining the parities with the message produces [1 0 1 1 0 1 0].

Position:	1	2	3	4	5	6	7
Message:			1		0	1	0
Encoded:	1	0	1	1	0	1	0
Error:						X	
Received	1	0	1	1	0	0	0

Bit Position n	3	2	1
1			1
2		0	
3		1	1
4	1		
5	0		0
6	0	0	
7	0	0	
Syndrome	1 Failed	1 Failed	0 OK	= 6

| Corrected message | 1 | 0 | 1 | 1 | 0 | 1 | 0 |

Figure IV.8 Error correction in a 4-bit message

Now assume an error occurs at position 6 so that the received message is [1 0 1 1 0 0 0]. A quick analysis shows that parity check fields 2 and 3 fail, producing a syndrome of 1 1 0. Note that the syndrome identifies the failed position, which is subsequently transposed to give the correct message. The Hamming encoding procedure has a declining overhead profile; however, the possibility of error increases with increased field size. Overhead is measured as $n/2^n$; this represents a 43 percent overhead for a 4-bit message and a 96 percent overhead for a 64-bit message. Thus, there is a rise in overhead at a rate of log (base 2) in the number of information bits.

To derive the probability of an undetected error occurring is slightly more difficult.

Assume a 2^n-bit message such that the syndrome equals n bits. The number of bits in a parity check field is represented by 2^{n-1}. Given that the probability of an error is P, then the probability of an error in a parity check field is $2^{n-1}P$. An undetected error will occur when a second error occurs in a parity check field. This probability is represented by $2^{n-1})[2^{n-1}-1]P^2$. Since there are n parity check fields, there are n opportunities for this condition to occur. However, an undetected in one parity check field may also result in an undetected error in one or more adjacent parity check fields. It follows that the probability P of an undetected error is bounded by $0 < P < n\{2^{n-1}[2^{n-1} - 1]P^2\}$. Evaluating the upper bound, we see that for n = 0.01 is plotted in Figure IV.9.

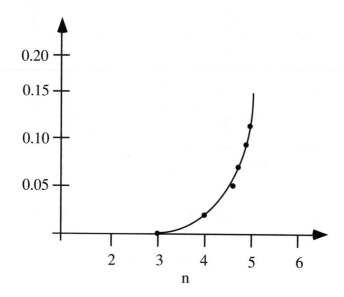

Figure IV.9 Bounding of undetected error probability, P = 0.01

One of the conclusions that can be drawn from this figure is that the probability of an undetected error occurring is relatively small for short messages. Undetected error rates can be expected to rise exponentially once the detection threshold of the Hamming code has been exceeded.

An alternative explanation of the algebraic description for multidimensional error-correcting codes is the geometric approach. The geometric description give rise to a distance function referred to as the Hamming distance. According to Hamming [2], this distance is the minimum number of sides of a cube that must be traversed to get from one point to another in communicating a message. Vertices of the cube represent specific bit values from which vectors emanate to vertices of all other possible bit configurations that may occur from a given vertex.

IV.3.3   BCH (Bose-Chaudhuri-Hocquenghem) Codes.

In contrast, BCH codes ar a class of multiple-error-correcting codes, while the Hamming codes correct only single errors. If, as in Hamming codes, n represents the length of a parity check field ($2^n - 1$), then the notation BCH (n,t) describes a set of codes that can correct t errors. BCH codes are known as cyclic or polynomial codes because of the simple feedback shift registers and modulo-2 adders that can be used for the encoding and decoding process. The key characteristic of a polynomial code is that any cyclic permutation or end-around shift of a code word will produce another code word [1]. BCH is a class of polynomial codes which possesses error-correcting powers.

We shall now trace through an example of the BCH algorithm without developing the theory [3]. Let's review the BCH (7,2) in which, from [(2^n-1, t], we determine that n = 3 and t = 2. Assume a code generation around the equation $\lambda^3 = \lambda + 1$. Table IV.1 shows the relationship of λ^i to each i. Note that in all cases the modulo-2 addition of rows (i + 3) = i + (i + 1). The object is to solve for the generator polynomial, G(x), which is defined as the minimal polynomial of the subset A = {$\lambda, \lambda^3, \lambda^5, ...\lambda^{2t-1}$}. For $\lambda^3 = \lambda + 1$, G(x) is the minimal polynomial of {$\lambda, \lambda^3, \lambda^5$). The conjugates of λ and λ^3 are {$\lambda, \lambda^2, \lambda^4$} and ($\lambda^3, \lambda^6$), respectively. Now G(x) is expressed as the product of the minimal polynomials, therefore,

$$G(x) = (x -1)(x - \lambda^2)(x - \lambda^3)(x - \lambda^4)(x - \lambda^5)$$

We can solve for G(x) in terms of x by taking advantage of the $\lambda^3 = \lambda + 1$ relationships in Table IV.1.

Table IV.1 Powers of $\lambda^3 = \lambda + 1$

i	λ^i	λ^i
0	001	000
1	010	101
2	100	111
3	011	110
4	110	011
5	111	100
6	101	010

For λ^3, G3(x) = G30 + G31 + G32x^2 which, by substitution, is equivalent to G30 [001] + G31[011] + G32[101]. Since there does not exist a modulo addition relationship between the λ^t terms, the only nontrivial solution is [G30, G31, G32] = [111]. Thus G3(x) turns out to be x^2 + x + 1. The same approach will show G1(x) to be x^3 + x + 1. Since G(x) is expressed as the modulo-2 product of minimal polynomials, we have G(x) = $(x^3 + x + 1)(x^2 + x + 1)$. Thus for BCH (7,2), G(x) = $x^5 + x^4$ + 1. To complete the BCH encoding process we need only transmit the modulo-2 product of G(x) with a polynomial whose coefficients consist of a user bit stream. The size of the user field must be constrained such that the largest exponent in the product is less than n for a BCH (n, t) encoder. Given an input vector, V=[01], the encoder bit stream is determined by simple multiplication to be C = (0110001). The one remaining step is the decoding process.

Assume that instead of C, the destination receives an incorrect bit stream R = (0110000). The receiver does not know what the original user bit stream was but will use the BCH process, in this case BCH(7,2), to decode and correct the errors. The following describes the necessary process in PL/1-oriented logic:

BCH-decode: procedure options (main);

do;

Step-1:   Call syndromes: /* so derive syndromes S(x) */

do until degree -r < t ; /* r=remainder */

Step-2:   call Euclid's algorithm (x^{2t}, S(x), t (x); /* perform Euclid's

algorithm on the generator and syndrome polynomials: returns
t (x) for j = 1, 2, ..., 2t until the degree of r < t */
end;
/* returns solutions in c(λ) */

Step-3: call polynomial solutions (t (x), c(λ));

Step-4: do i = 1 to n - 1; /* calculate error pattern */
         do j=1 to number-of-solutions;
         if λ^{-1} = c(j) then

             do;
             E(i) = 1;
             go to next i;
             end;

         else
             E(i) = 0;

Next-i: end;
         /* derive decoded field */
         /* modulo-2 subtract each E(i) from each r$\in$ R */

Step-5: D = R - E
         end;
         end BCH-decode;

Let us now demonstrate by continuing with the example. For step 1, the syndromes,
using

$$S_j = \sum_{i=0}^{n-1} R_i \lambda^{ij}, \; j = 1, 2, ..., 2t$$

are determined to be $S_j = \lambda^j + \lambda^{2j}$. Referring to Table IV.1, we decide that $S_1 = \lambda^4$, S_2
$= \lambda$, $S_3 = \lambda^4$, and $S_4 = \lambda^2$. This of course provides a solution

$$S(x) = (\lambda^2)(x^3) + (\lambda^4)(x^2) + x + (\lambda^4).$$

Results of the calculations using Euclid's algorithm is shown in Table IV.2.

Table IV.2 Results of Euclid's Algorithm on x^4 and $S(x) = (\lambda^2)$ (λ^3) +

$$(\lambda^4)\,(x^2) + x + (\lambda^4)$$

i	t_i	r_i	q_i
-1	0	x^4	—
0	1	$(\lambda^2)\,(x^3) + (\lambda^4)\,(x^2) + x + (\lambda^4)$	—
-1	*	[0,*, *, *, *]	—
0	[0]	[2, 4, 1, 4]	—
1	[5, 2]	[3, 6, 4]	[5, 0]
2	[4, 0, 5]	[1, 2]	[6, 4]

Starting values:

$t_{-1}(x) = 0$ $r_{-1}(x) = x^4$

$t_0(x) = 0$ $r_0(x) = (\lambda^2)\,(x^3) + (\lambda^4)\,(x^2) + x + (\lambda^4)$

Equations for subsequent calculations around i *

$q_i(x) = r_{t-2}(x)/r_{t-1}(x) + r_t(x)$

$r_t(x) = t_{-2}(x) - q_t(x)t_{i-1}(x)$

The upper portion of the table lists the starting values in polynomial form. However, since we are only concerned with the powers of the coefficients, the lower portion shows Euclid's derivation using brackets around the coefficient powers. The equations beneath the table are used to derive the remaining values for t_i, r_i, and q_i. The asterisk is used whenever a coefficient has assumed 0. The quotient, q_i, is of course not applicable for the first two row entries. Continuing with step 2; we select $t_i(x)$ such that the degree of $r_i < t = 2$ and set $t_i(x) = 0$. For the example, $t_i(x) = (\lambda^4)(x^2) + x + \lambda^5$. Now determine x such that $t_2(x) = 0$. We quickly see that x = $\{1, \lambda^6\}$ are solutions and that no other λ^i, $0 \le i \ne 5 \le 6$ are solutions. Using step 4 (referring again to Table IV.1), we decide E = (0000001) and C' = R - E = (0110001) which we note to be the original message. The example is now complete.

It should be obvious that BCH (n, t) for (n, t) large becomes difficult to manipulate by hand. For the computer, however, the algorithm for a small (n, t) is identical to that for a large (n, t) and it is well enough to recognize at this point that the power of the t - error-correcting algorithm is in the cyclic nature of the codes around a derived generating function. The two common features between a two-way interface is the coding/decoding algorithm and the generating function. Let us now proceed to review a related BCH algorithm, referred to as the Reed-Solomon codes.

IV.3.4   Reed-Solomon Codes

The Reed-Solomon code RS(n, t) is described as a t - error-correcting code of length n. The distinctions between the BCH and the RS codes, although minor, are in both the generating function and the decoding algorithm. For RS, the generating function is simply $G(x) = (x - \lambda)(x - \lambda^2) \dots ((x - \lambda^{2t})$ and therefore much easier to calculate for a given (n, t).

For RS(7, 2), $G(x) = (x^4) + (\lambda^3)(x^3) + (\lambda^3)$. This time, we shall borrow from McEliece [3] and use a received vector of R = $(\lambda^3, \lambda, 1, \lambda^2, 0, \lambda^3, 1)$. The previous decoding algorithm is modified to the following:

```
RS-decode:  procedure options (main);
    do;
        Step-1:  call syndromes; /* go derive syndromes S(x) */
                 do until degree-of-r < t ; /* r = remainder */
                 call Euclid's algorithm (x²ᵗ, S(x), t (x));
        Step-2:  /* perform Euclid's algorithm on the generator and
                 syndrome polynomials; returns t (x) for j = 1, 2, ..., 2t
                 until the degree of r < t */
                 end;
                 θ(x) = t (x);
                 ω(x) = r(x);
                 /* returns solutions in c(λ) */
        Step-3:  call polynomial solutions (t (x), c(λ));
                 Eᵦ = ω(β) / θ'(β); /* for each β ∈ c(λ) */
```

Step-4: do i = 1 to n - i; /*calculate error pattern */
                    do j = 1 to number-of-solutions;
                            if λ^{-i} = c(j) then
                                    do;
                                    E(i) = E_β
                                    go to next-i;
                                    end;
                            else
                                    E(i) = 0;
Next-i: end;
                    /* derive decoded field */
                    /* modulo-2 subtract each E(i) from each r ∈ R */
Step-5: C' = [r(0) - E(0), r(1) - E(1), ..., r(n-1) - E(n - 1));
                    end;
                    end RS-decode;

The formula $S_j = \sum R_j \lambda^{ij}$ is applied for deriving the syndromes, resulting in S_1 = λ^3, $S_2 = \lambda^4$, $S_3 = \lambda^4$, and $S_4 = 0$. Euclid's algorithm is again used to obtain the results of Table IV.3.

Table IV.3 Results of Euclid's Algorithm for R=(λ^3, λ, 1. λ^2, 0, λ^3, 1)

i	t_i	r_i	q_i
-1	[*]	[0, *, *, *, *]	—
0	[0]	[4, 4, 3]	—
1	[3, 3, 5]	[0, 1]	[3, 3, 5]

Step 2 of the above RS algorithm results in

$$c(x) = (\lambda^3)(x^2) + (\lambda^3)x + (\lambda^5) \text{ and } \omega(x) = x + \lambda$$

Solutions for $c(x) = 0$ are determined to be $x = (\lambda^4, \lambda^5)$. Given this, step 4 provides $E(\lambda^4) = (\lambda^4 + \lambda)/\lambda^3 = \lambda^6$ and $E(\lambda^5) = (\lambda^5 + \lambda)/\lambda^3 = \lambda^3$. The error vector is therefore determined to be $E = (0, 0, \lambda^3, \lambda^6, 0, 0, 0)$ and thus $C' = R + E = (\lambda^3, \lambda, \lambda, 1, 0, \lambda^3, 1)$ which is accepted as the original (transmitted) vector.

From the results of the above procedure, it is possible to conclude that certain Reed-Solomon encoding schemes have great potential for burst-error corrections. It hardly needs saying that this type of forward error correction lends itself well to counter natural noise such as static bursts caused by lightning. It is also being widely used for communications through jamming, which tends to be bursty in nature.

References

1   Ralston, A., and C.L. Meek, "Error-Correcting Code." Encyclopedia of Computer Science. New York: Petrocelli/Charter, 1976.

2   Hamming, R. W., Coding and Information Theory. Englewood Cliffs, N.J.: Prentice-Hall, 1980.

3.   McEliece, R.J., *The Theory of Information and Coding,* Reading, MA: Addison-Wesley, 1977.

4.   Fitzgerald, J., and T.S. Eason, *Fundamentals of Data Communications,* New York: John Wiley & Sons, 1978.

5.   Housley, T., *Data Communications and Teleprocessing systems.* Englewood Cliffs, N.J.: Prentice-Hall, 1979.

6.   Daivs, D.W., D.L. A. Barber, W.L. Price, and C.M. Solomonides, *Computer Networks and Their Protocols.* New York: John Wiley & Sons, 1979.

7.   Doll, D.R., *Data Communications: Facilities, Networks, and Systems Design,* New York: John Wiley & Sons, 1978.

Appendix V

GLOSSARY

ACK. Acknowledgement character.

Acknowledge. To respond to addressing or polling.

Acknowledge character. A communications control character transmitted by a receiver as an affirmative response to a sender.

Acknowledgement. The act of sending a response to polling or addressing (i.e., the character sequence of comprising the response).

Acoustic coupler. A device for audibly coupling a data terminal to a standard telephone set.

Adapter. A device designed to provide a compatible connection between a unit under use and the interface.

Address. To condition a terminal for receiving data; the coded representation of the destination of a message.

Addressing. The means whereby the originator or control station selects the unit to which it is going to send a message.

Alphanumeric. A combination of alphabetic and numeric characters.

Alternate frequency. Frequency assigned to use at a certain time to supplement or replace the normally used frequency.

Alternate route. A secondary communications route used to reach a destination if the primary route is unavailable.

Amplitude. The magnitude of a wave. It is the largest deviation measured from the average value.

Amplitude modulation. Variations of a carrier signal's strength (amplitude), as a function of an information signal.

Analog-to-digital. A translation of a continuously varying parameter into a digital format.

Analog signals. Signals that can assume continuous values during any specified time.

Answer back. The response of a terminal to remote-control signals.

Answering station. The station responding to a dialed call; opposite of originating station.

ASCII. American Standard Code for Information Interchange. This is the code established as an American Standard by the American Standards Association.

ASR. Automatic send/receive.

Asynchronous. Random start/stop data. Requires special start/stop information in each character.

Asynchronous transmission. Transmission in which each information character is individually synchronized, usually by the use of start and stop elements.

Attenuation. A general term used to denote a decrease in magnitude in transmission from one point to another.

Audio. Within the range of frequencies that can be heard by the human ear (15 to 20,000 Hz).

Auto answer. The facility of an answering station to respond automatically to a call.

Auto call. The facility of an originating station to initiate a call automatically.

Background processing. The automatic execution of lower-priority programs when higher-priority programs are not using the system resources.

Band. (1) The range of frequencies. (2) The frequency spectrum between two defined limits. (3) A group of channels.

Bandwidth. The difference between two limiting frequencies of a band (in Hz).

Baseband. In the process of modulation, the frequency band occupied by the total of the transmitted signals when first used to modulate a character.

Batch processing. Processing of a stream of data and/or group of jobs in a generally sequential manner.

Baud. A unit of signaling speed. The reciprocal of the duration, in seconds, of the shortest signaling element that a channel can accommodate.

Baudot code. A code for the transmission of data in which five bits represent one character.

BCC. Block check character. Used to designate either the LRC or CRC character.

Binary. Pertaining to a characteristic or property involving a selection or condition in which there are two possibilities.

Binary digit. A numeral in the binary scale of notation (either zero or one).

Binary synchronous communications. A line control procedure for communicating. It can be expressed in several data codes; 8-bit EBCDIC, 7-bit USASCII, or 6-bit transcode.

BI-SYNC. Binary synchronous communications.

Bit. A unit of information that is indivisible. It is the choice between two possible states, usually designated one or zero.

Bit rate. The speed at which bits are transmitted, usually expressed in bits per second.

Block. A group of records, words, or storage locations that is treated as a physical unit.

BPS. Bits per second. In serial transmission, the instantaneous bit speed within one character, as transmitted by a channel.

Broadband. Communications channel having a bandwidth greater than a voice-grade channel, and therefore capable of higher-speed data transmission.

Broadcast. The dissemination of information to a number of stations simultaneously.

Buffer. A storage device used to compensate for a difference in the rate of flow of information, or the time of occurrence of events.

Buffered network. A real-time, storage-and-forward message-switching network with computers at the switching points which act as buffers for the characters, words, blocks, or files in the system.

Byte. A sequence of adjacent binary digits operated on as a unit and usually shorter than a word.

Cable. An assembly of one or more conductors usually within an enveloping protective sheath in a structural arrangement that will permit their use separately or in groups.

Carrier. A radio-frequency wave that can be modulated (altered) to convey information.

Carrier system. A means of obtaining a number of channels over a single path by modulating each channel on a different carrier frequency and demodulating at the receiving point to restore the signals to their original form.

Channel. A path for electrical transmission between two or more points. Also called a circuit, facility, line, link, or path.

Channel, duplex. A channel capable of transmission in both directions simultaneously.

Channel, half-duplex. A channel capable of transmission in both directions, but in only one direction at a time.

Channel, simplex. A channel that permits transmission in one direction only.

Channel, voice-grade. A channel suitable for transmission of speech.

Channelizing. A process of dividing one circuit into several channels, or grouping narrow band channels into one wide band channel.

Character. The actual or coded representation of a digit, letter, or special symbol.

Character check. A character used for validity checking purposes.

Circuit. A means of two-way communication between two points (see *Channel*).

Circuit, four-wire. A two-way circuit using two paths so arranged that communication is transmitted in one direction only on one path, and in the opposite direction on the other path. The transmission path may or may not employ four wires.

Circuit switching. The temporary direct connection of two or more channels between two or more points in order to provide the user with exclusive use of an open channel with which to exchange information (also called line switching).

Coaxial cable. A cable consisting of two concentric conductors insulated from each other.

Code. A system of symbols or conditions which represent information. Also, the coded representation of a character.

Code conversion. A process for changing the bit grouping for a character in one code into the corresponding bit grouping for a character in a second code.

Code level. The number of bits used to represent a data character.

Common carrier. See *Communications carrier*.

Communications. The transfer of information from one point to another.

Communications carrier. A company recognized by an appropriate regulatory agency as having a vested interest in furnishing communications services.

Concentrator. A device that matches a large number of input channels with a fewer number of output channels.

Conditioning. The addition of equipment to a leased voice-grade channel to provide minimum values of line characteristics required for data transmission.

Contention. The condition on a multipoint communications channel when two or more locations try to transmit at the same time.

Control character. A character whose occurrence in a particular context indicates, modifies, or stops a control action.

Control mode. The state that all terminals on a line must be in to allow line disciplines, line control, or terminal selection to occur.

Conversational mode. A procedure with communication between a terminal and the computer in which each entry from the terminal elicits a response from the computer and vice versa.

Converter. A device that changes the manner of representing information from one form to another.

CRC. Cyclic redundancy check.

Crossbar switch. An electrical or electronic device having many vertical and horizontal paths, establishing times cross points or interconnections for the cross switching of data circuits consisting of signal data, power, modifiers, or monitors for the purpose of injecting, altering, monitoring, or comparing information for analysis.

Cross talk. Interference that appears in one channel but has its origins in another.

Cycle. One complete repetition of a regularly repeating electronic function is called a cycle. The number of cycles per second is called the frequency.

Cyclical redundancy check character. A character used in a modified cycle code for error detection and correction.

Cyclic checking. A method of error control employing a weighted sum of transmitted bits.

Data. Any representations, such as digital characters or analog quantities, to which meaning might be assigned.

Data link. The communications lines, modems, and communication controls of all stations connected to the line, used in the transmission of information between two or more stations.

Data communications. The transmission of information to and from data processing equipment. This includes assembly, sequencing, routing, and selection of such information as is generated at independent remote points of data origination, and the distribution of the processed information to remote output terminals or other data processing equipment.

Data phone. A term used by AT&T to describe any of a family of data set devices.

Data set. A device containing the electrical circuitry necessary to connect data processing equipment to a communications channel. Also called subset. Data Phone, modem.

Data transmission. The transmission of data-comprising digital information that is intelligible to both humans and machines.

Decibel (dB). The decibel (dB) is a unit that is defined as the ratio of output signal power to input signal power:

$$dB = 10 \log_{10} \frac{\text{output power}}{\text{input power}}$$

Demodulation. The process used to convert communications signals to a form compatible with data processing equipment.

Dial exchange. A common-carrier exchange in which all subscribers originate their calls by dialing.

Dial-up. The use of a dial or push-button telephone to initiate a station-to-station call.

Digital-to-analog. Translation of digital information into a continuously varying parameter.

Digital signals. Signals that can only assume certain discrete values.

Direct Distance Dialing (DDD). A telephone service that enables the telephone user to call other subscribers outside the local area without operator assistance.

Display unit. A terminal device that presents data visually, usually by means of a cathode ray tube (CRT).

Duplex. Transmission in either direction in a given link. Full-duplex (FDX) means simultaneous two-way capability; half-duplex (HDX) means one way at a time.

EBCDIC. Extended Binary Coded Decimal Interchange Code.

Echo. An electrical signal reflection from impedance discontinuities in a transmission line.

Echo check. Checking system in which the transmitted information if reflected back to the transmitter and compared with the original.

Echo suppressor. A line device used to prevent energy from being reflected back to the transmitter. It attenuates the transmission path in one direction while signals are being passed in the other direction.

Effective speed. Speed (less than rated) that can be sustained over a significant span of time and that reflects slowing effects of control codes, timing codes, error detection, retransmission.

Element. In electrical data transmission, the shortest period or interval of time used in the modulating signal to form an information pulse.

End of address.   Control characters separately control messages from control text (EDA).

End of block.   Control character indicating the end of a message.

End of message.   The specific characters that indicate the termination of a message or record (EDM).

End of text.   A communication control character used to indicate the end of a text (ETX).

End of transmission.   Control characters denoting the end of data transmission (EDT). It is usually sent by an originating station to signify that it is finished with the communications line.

EOB.   End of block.

EOT.   End of transmission.

Error.   Any discrepancy between a computed, observed, or measured quantity and the time, specified, or theoretically correct value of condition.

Error control.   An arrangement that will detect (and sometimes correct) the presence of errors.

Error rate.   A measure of quality of circuit or system. The number of erroneous bits or characters in a sample, frequency taken per 100,000 characters.

ETB.   End-of-transmission-block character.

ETX.   End-of-text character.

Exchange. A defined area, served by a common carrier, within which the carrier furnishes service at the exchange rate and under the regulations applicable in that area as prescribed in the carrier's filed tariffs.

Exchange service. A service permitting interconnection of two customer's telephones through the use of switching equipment.

Feedback. The return of a portion of the output of a circuit or device to its input.

Five-level code. A telegraph code that utilizes five impulses for describing a character. Start and stop elements may be added for asynchronous transmission. A common five-level code is Baudot.

FM. Frequency modulation.

Foreground job. A job in the system that communicates with the user via terminals and is generally given higher system priority.

Four-wire circuit. A communications path in which four wires (two for each direction of transmission) are presented to the station equipment.

Frequency. A rate of signal oscillation in hertz.

Frequency Division Multiplexing (FDM). The division of a transmission facility into two or more channels by splitting the frequency band transmitted by the channel into narrower bands, each of which is used to constitute a direct channel.

Frequency modulation. Variation of a carrier frequency in accordance with an information signal.

Full-duplex. In communications, pertaining to a simultaneous two-way and independent transmission in both directions.

Group addressing. A technique for addressing a group of terminals by use of a single address.

Half-duplex. Pertaining to an alternate, one way at a time, independent transmission.

Hand-shaking. A colloquial term that relates to an exchange of signals between data terminals prior to transmission of messages. Line coordination is the exchange of signals that identify and/or synchronize and/or validate information transmitted between two or more data terminals.

Header. The initial characters of a message designating addressee, routing, time or origination, etc.

Hertz (Hz). A unit of frequency equal to one cycle per second.

Heuristic. Pertaining to a trial-and-error method of obtaining solutions to problems.

Holding time. The length of time a communications channel is in use for each transmission. Includes both message time and operating time.

Home loop. An operation involving only those input and output circuits associated with the local terminal.

Information bits. Those bits generated by the data source and not used for error control by the data transmission system.

Information channel. The transmission and intervening equipment involved in the transfer of information in a given direction between two terminals.

In-line processing. Processing of input data in random order, without preliminary editing, sorting, or batching. (Contrast with *Batch processing.*)

In-plant system. A data-handling system confined to a number of buildings in one locality.

Input. (1) Information or data. (2) The state or sequence of states occurring on a specified input channel. (3) The process of transferring data from an external storage to an internal storage.

Input/output. A general term for the equipment and the data involved in a communications system.

Interactive system. A system in which the user can communicate directly with an executing program. Also called "man-made communication," or "conversational."

Interface. A common boundary between systems or parts of a single system.

Jitter. A data signal displaying rectangular pulses is said to contain jitter when the marking/spacing transitions deviate in an apparently random manner from their predicted time assignments, but not more than one-half of the basic pulse interval.

KHz. Kilohertz. One thousand cycles per second.

Laser. A transmitter that operates at optical frequencies. In communications it acts as a device with a coherent optical frequency carrier.

Leased line. A circuit leased for exclusive use - full time or during specific periods - by one subscriber, i. e., a private full-period line.

Line. Transmission path (see *Channel*).

Line adapter. A modem that is a feature of a particular device.

Line loop. An operation performed over a communications line from an input unit at one terminal to output units at a remote terminal.

Line speed. The maximum rate at which signals may be transmitted over a given channel (measured in bps).

Line switching. The switching technique of temporarily connecting two lines together so that the stations directly exchange information.

Link. Another term for channel or circuit.

Local central office. Office arranged for terminating subscriber lines and provided with trunks for establishing connections to and from other central offices.

Local channel. A loop or local distribution plant. A channel connecting a communications user to a central office.

Local loop. Portion of a connection from a central office to a subscriber.

Longitudinal Redundancy Check (LRC). Longitudinal redundancy check character. Parity is checked longitudinally along all the characters comprising a transmitted record.

Mark state. State of a communication line corresponding to an on, closed, or logic 1 condition.

Master station. A unit having control of all other terminals on a multipoint circuit for purposes of polling and/or selection.

Message. An arbitrary amount of information whose beginning and end are defined or implied. In data communications a message consists of a header, a body or text, and a trailer.

Message, format. Rules for the placement of such portions of a message as header, text, and end of message.

Message, routing. The function of selecting the route, or alternate route, by which a message will proceed to its destination.

Message, switching. The technique of receiving a message, storing it until the approximate outgoing channel is available, and then retransmitting it. The content of the message remains unaltered.

MHz. Megahertz. One million cycles per second.

Microwave. All electromagnetic waves (signals) in the radio-frequency spectrum above 890 MHz.

Modem. A device that modulates and demodulates signals transmitted over communication facilities. Contraction of modulator-demodulator.

Modulation. Process by which certain characteristics of a wave are modified in accordance with a characteristic of another wave or a signal. It is used to make terminal signals compatible with communications facilities.

Multidrop line. Line or circuit interconnecting several terminals.

Multiple address message. A message to be delivered to more than one destination.

Multiplex. To interleave or simultaneously transmit two or more wave messages on a single channel.

Multiplexing. The division of a transmission facility into two or more channels. This can be achieved by the use of FDM or TDM.

Multipoint line. A communication line interconnecting several stations.

NAK. Negative acknowledge character.

Network. A series of points interconnected by communications channel. A private-line network is a network confined to the use of one customer, while a switched network is a network of lines normally used for dialed calls.

Neutral. In machine telegraphy, unipolar signaling (i.e., singular-polarity, on/off).

Noise. Any extraneous signal not deliberately generated by the transmitting device in the data link. Noise tends to degrade signal quality.

Nonsynchronous. Having no fixed time phase within or between signaling elements, also asynchronous.

Off-line. Pertaining to equipment or devices not under direct control of the CPU. May also be used to describe terminal equipment that is not connected to a transmission line.

On-line. Pertaining to equipment or devices in direct communication with the CPU. May also be used to describe terminal equipment that is connected to a transmission line.

One-way channel. A channel that permits transmission in one direction only.

Operating time. The time required for dialing the call, waiting for the connection to be established, and coordinating the forthcoming transaction at the receiving end.

Out-plant system. A system not confined to one plant or locality.

Parallel transmission. The simultaneous transmission of a certain number of signal demands constituting the same data signal.

Parity. A mechanism to determine if an error occurred. Synonymous with parity check, odd-even check.

Parity, bit. A binary digit appended to an array of bits to make the sum of all the bits always odd or always even.

Parity, check. A test to determine whether the number of 1s or 0s in an array of binary digits is odd or even.

PCM. Pulse code modulation.

Phase modulation. An angular relationship between waves. If two signals have the same frequency but differ in the time they go through the maximum values, they are out-of-phase.

Point-to-point. Transmission of data between two points.

Polar. Having more than one polarity (bipolar). In data transmission, a signal that uses equal and opposite voltages and currents to define the marking and spacing line conditions in the data link or communications interface.

Polling. A technique by which each of the terminals sharing a communications line is periodically interrogated to determine whether it has anything to transmit.

Priority or procedure. Controlling transmission of messages in order of their designated importance.

Private line. A channel furnished a subscriber for his exclusive use.

Pulse. A signal characterized by the rise and decay in time of quantity whose value is normally constant.

Queue. A group of items awaiting processing by some facility.

Real time. Processing data rapidly enough to provide results useful in directly controlling a physical process.

Record. A group of related data items treated as a unit.

Record length. A measure of the size of a record, usually specified in such units as words or characters.

Redundancy. The portion of the total information contained in a message that can be eliminated without loss of essential information.

Redundant check. A check that uses extra bits or characters, including complete duplication, to help detect malfunctions or mistakes.

Remote access. Pertaining to communication with a data processing facility by one or more stations that are distant from that facility.

Remote terminal. A terminal connected to the computing system via communication lines.

Response. Same as acknowledgment.

Response time. The amount of time elapsed between generation of an inquiry at a data communications terminal and receipt of a response at that same terminal.

Restart. To return to a previous point in a program and to resume operation from that point (often associated with a checkpoint).

Selective calling. The ability of a transmitting station to specify which of several stations on the same line is to receive a message.

Serial transmission. A method of information transfer in which the bits composing a character are sent sequentially.

Signal. The event or phenomenon that conveys data from one point to another.

Signal converter. A device for changing a signal from one form or value to another form or value.

Signal-to-noise ratio (S/N). The ratio, expressed in decibels, of the useable signal to the noise signal present.

Simplex mode. Operation of a communication channel in one direction only, with no capability for reversing.

Single address message. A message to be delivered to only one destination.

SOH. Start-of-header character.

Space character. A normally nonprinting graphic character used to separate words.

Speed of transmission. The rate at which information is processed by a transmission facility expressed as the average rate over some significant time interval.

Square wave. A waveform that shifts abruptly from one to the other of two fixed values for equal lengths of time. The transmission time is negligible when compared with the duration time of each fixed value.

Start-stop transmission. A mode of data transmission in which each character is delimited by special control bits denoting the beginning and the end of the sequence of data bits representing the character.

Station. One of the input or output points on a communications system.

Status report. A term used to describe the automatic reports generated by a message-switching system generally covering service conditions.

Stop bit. The last element of a character in asynchronous serial transmissions, used to ensure recognition of the next start element.

Storage. A general term for any device capable of retaining information.

Store-and-forward. Process of message handling used in a message-switching system. The message is stored, then forwarded to the recipient.

STR. Synchronous transmit/receive.

STX. Start-of-text character.

Subscriber. A customer of a telegraph or telephone company served under an agreement of contract.

Subscriber's loop. Same as *local loop.*

Subset. A modulation/demodulation device designed to provide compatibility of signals between data processing equipment and communications facilities. Also called modem.

Subvoice-grade channel. A channel of bandwidth narrower than that of voice-grade channels. Such channels are usually subchannels of a voice-grade channel.

Switched telephone network. A network of telephone lines normally used for dialed telephone calls.

Switching center. An installation in a communication system in which switching equipment is used to interconnect communications circuits.

Synchronization pulses. Pulses introduced by transmitting equipment into the receiving equipment to keep the two terminals operating in step.

Synchronize. To get in step with another unit on a bit, element, character, or word basis.

Synchronous. Operating in isochronous harmony with connecting devices.

SYN character. A communications control character used by a synchronous transmission system in the absence of any other character to provide a signal from which synchronous may be achieved or retained between data terminals.

Synchronous mode. A mode of data transmission in which character synchronism is controlled by timing signals generated at the sending and receiving station.

Tariff. The published rate for a specified unit of equipment, facility or type of service provided by a communications common carrier.

Telegraph-grade circuit. A circuit suitable for transmission by teletypewriter equipment.

Telecommunication. Communication by electromagnetic systems; often used interchangeably with communications.

Telephone line. Telephone line is a general term used in communication practice in several different senses:
1. The conductors and supporting or containing structures extending between telephone stations and central offices or between central offices whether they be in the same or in different communities.
2. The conductors and circuit apparatus associated with a particular communications channel.

Telephone network. Describes a system of points interconnected by voice-grade telephone wire whereby direct point-to-point telephone communications are provided.

Teleprocessing. A form of information handling in which a data processing system utilizes communications facilities.

Teletype network. A system of points interconnected by telegraph channels, which provide hard-copy and/or telegraphic coded (five-channel) punched paper tape, as required, at both sending and receiving points.

Terminal. A point at which information can enter or leave a communications network.

Terminal unit. Equipment on a communication channel that may be used for either input or output.

Text. That part of the message containing the substansive information to be conveyed.

Thermal noise. Electromagnetic noise emitted from hot bodies. Also called Johnson noise.

Throughput. A measure of system efficiency. Also the rate at which work can be handled by a system.

Tie line. A private line communication channel of the type provided by communications common carriers for linking two or more points together.

Time-out. The time interval allotted for certain operations to occur before system operation is interrupted and must be restarted, e.g., response to polling or addressing.

Time-sharing. To interleave the use of a device or system for two or more purposes.

Traffic. Transmitted and received messages.

Transmission. The electrical transfer of information from one location to another.

Transmission, controller. A unit to interface communication lines with a computer.

Transmission, line. Lines or conductors used to carry signals from one place to another.

Transmission, link. A section of a channel between:
   1. A transmitting station and the following repeater.
   2. Two successive repeaters.
   3. A receiving station and the preceding repeater.

Transmit. To send data from one location and to receive the data at another location.

Trunk. A major communications link in a system, usually carrying many messages simultaneously by means of FDM or TDM interface techniques.

Turnaround time. The interval of time between submission of a job for processing and receipt of results. The time interval required to reverse the direction of transmission over a communication line.

Two-wire circuit. A circuit formed by two conductors insulated from each other. It is possible to use the two conductors as a one-way transmission path, a half-duplex path, or a duplex path.

USASCII. USA Standard Code for Information Interchange. The standard code, using a coded character set consisting of 7-bit coded characters (8 bits including parity), used for information interchange among data processing systems, communications systems, and associated equipment.

VF. Voice frequency (band).

Voice band. Denoting a communication channel capable of a transmission state exceeding 300 bps. A channel suitable for transmission of speech.

Voice frequency. Any frequency within that part of the audio frequency range essential for the transmission of speech of commercial quality.

Voice-grade channel. A channel suitable for transmission of speech, digital or analog data, or facsimile, generally with a frequency range of about 300 to 3000 Hz.

VRC. Vertical redundancy check. A method in which parity is checked vertically across each character in a record.

WATS. Wide Area Telephone Service. A service provided by telephone companies that permits a customer, by use of an access line, to make calls to telephones in a specific zone on a dial basis for a flat monthly charge.

White noise. Noise containing all frequencies equally. Most often applied to noise containing all frequencies equally in a given bandwidth.

Wideband. A channel wider in bandwidth than a voice-grade channel. Denoting a communications channel capable of high-speed transmission.

Word. An ordered set of characters that is the normal unit in which information may be stored, transmitted, or operated on within a computer. In communications, a word consists of six code combinations.

Appendix VI

List of Acronyms and Abbreviations

10base5	10 Mbs Baseband media
ABM	Asynchronous Balanced Mode (ADCCP)
ACF	Advanced Telecommunications Function (IBM SNA)
ACK	Acknowledgement
ADCCP	Advanced Data Communications Control Procedure (ANSI, SDLC)
AFC	Automatic Frequency Control
AGC	Automatic Gain Control
ALOHA	first Radio Packet Broadcasting Network (Hawaii)
AM	Amplitude Modulation
ANS	American National Standard
ANSI	American National Standards Institute
ARCnet	Attached Resource Computer Network
ARM	Arpanet Reference Model, Asynchronous Response Mode
ARP	Address Resolution Protocol (ARPA), Abnormal Release Provider (ISO)
ARPA	(Defense) Advanced Research Projects Agency
ARPANET	Advanced Research Projects Agency Network
ARQ	Automatic Repeat Request
ASK	Amplitude-Shift Keying
ASR	Automatic Send/Receive
AUTODIN	Automated Digital Information Network
BCC	Block Check Character
BDA	Baseband Demand Assignment
BER	Bit Error Rate
BISYNC	Binary Synchronous Communication (IBM)
BITNET	Because its Time Net

BIU	Basic Information Unit (message on layer 3, SNA), Bus Interface Unit
BNA	Burroughs Network Architecture
Bps	Bytes per sec
bps	bits per sec
BPSK	Binary PSK
BSC	Binary Synchronous Communication (IBM)
CATV	Cable Television
CBX	Computerized Branch Exchange
CCITT	International Telegraph & Telephone Consultative Committee, Comite Consultatif International Telegr. et Telephon.(ITU)
CD	Collision Detection, Capability Data
CDMA	Code Division Multiple Access
CODEC A/D	Coder-Decoder, Analog/Digital transformation
COMSAT	Communication Satellite Corp.
CONP	Connection-Oriented Network-Layer Protocol (ISO)
CONS	Connection-Oriented Network Service (ISO 8348)
CRC	Cyclic Redundancy Check (check information)
CS	Circuit Switching (ISDN), Connectivity Service (LEN)
CSMA	Carrier Sense / Multiple Access
CSMA/CA	Carrier Sense / Multiple Access Collision Avoidance
CSMA/CD	Carrier Sense / Multiple Access Collision Detection
CSMA/CE	Carrier Sense / Multiple Access Collision Elimination
CSMA/CP	Carrier Sense / Multiple Access Collision Prevention (e.g. LDDI)
CSNET	Computer Science Net
DA	Demand Assignment
DAA	Direct Access Arrangement
DAMA	Demand Assignment Multiple Access
DAP	Data Access Protocol (DECNET), Directory Access Protocol (SMAE, ISO)
DARPA	Defense Advanced Research Projects Agency
dB	decibel
DCA	Distributed Communications Architecture (Univac), Defense Communications Agency
DCE	Data Circuit-Terminating Equipment (Equipment NIU, X.21)

DCS	Distributed Computer System, Defined Context Set
DDCMP	Digital Data Comm. Message protocol (Data Link Protocol, DECNET)
DDCMP	Digital Data Communications Message Protocol
DDD	Direct Distance Dialing (MTS)
DDN	Defense Data Network (Successor Arpanet)
DDS	Dataphone Digital Services, Document Distribution Service (SNADS)
DECNET	Digital Equipm. Corp. NETwork Concept
DES	Data Encryption Standard (IBM, NBS)
DFC	Data Flow Control (Layer, SNA)
DL	Data Link Layer
DLC	Data Link Control
DLCN	Distributed Loop Computer Network
DNA	Distributed Network Architecture (DECNET, Digital)
DOA	Distributed Office Application (ECMA)
DOD	Department of Defense
DOS	Distributed Operating System
DPSK	Differentially Coherent PSK
DSU	Data Service Unit (CPE)
DT	Data Transport (LEN), Data Transfer (ISO)
DTE	Data Terminal Equipment (Equipment Host, X.21)
DTP	Data Transfer Protocols
DTS	Digital Termination System
EDD	Envelope Delay Distortion
EIA	Electronic Industries Association (RS)
EOA	End of Address
EOB	End of Block
EOM	End of Message
EOT	End of Transmission
ERN	Explicit Route Number (SNA)
ESS	Electronic Switching System
ETB	End of Transmitted Block

ETX	End of Text
FAP	File Access Protocol
FCC	Federal Communications Commission
FCS	Frame Check Sequence (HDLC)
FDDI	Fiber Distributed Data Interface (ANSI)
FDM	Frequency Division Multiplexing
FDMA	Frequency Division Multiple Access
FDX	Full Duplex
FEC	Forward Error Correction
FEP	Front End Processor
FM	Frequency Modulation
FMP	File Maintenance protocol
FSK	Frequency-Shift Keying
FTP	File Transfer Protocol
FTP	File Transfer Protocol
GFS	Gateway File System
HDLC	High-level Data Link Control (ISO variant of SDLC, LAP)
HDX	Half Duplex
HF	High Frequency
HFS	Host File System
ICMP	Internet Control Message Protocol
ICP	Initial Connection Protocol (ARPANET)
IDN	Integrated Digital Network (predecessor ISDN)
IEEE	Intermediate Frequency
IFIPS	International Federation of Information Processing Societies
IMP	Interface Message Processors
IP	Internet Protocol (DoD Standard,ARPANET), Interpersonal
IPDU	Internetwork PDU
IRS	Internetwork Routing Service
ISDN	Integrated Services Digital Network (CCITT)
ISO	International Standards Organization
ITT	International Telephone and Telegraph
LAN	Local Area Network

LAP	Link Access Procedure, later LAPB (CCITT,see SDLC, HDLC)
LAPB	Link Access Procedure Balanced (further development of LAP)
LCC	Logical Link Control
LED	Light Emitting Diodes
LLC	Logical Link Control(upper part DL, IEEE 802
LLP	Lower layer Protocol
LRC	Longitudinal Redundancy Checks
LU	Logical Unit (logical interface(Type 1-6), SNA)
MAC	Medium Access Control(part of DL IEEE 802), Message Authentication Code
MAN	Metropolitan Area Network (IEEE 802.6 Standard)
MAP	Manufacturing Automation Protocol (GM, ISO), Major Sync Point (ISO)
MAU	Media Attachment(Access) Unit (IEEE 802),Multistation Access Unit
MIL	Military, domain of ARPANET
MIL-STD	Military Standard (DoD)
MILNET	Military Network
MON	Mission-Oriented Networks
MTR	Multiple Token Ring
MUX	Multiplexer
NAK	Negative Acknowledgement
NAP	Network Access Protocol
NAU	Netwrok Addressable Unit
NBS	National Bureau of Standards
NCC	Network Control Center
NCP	Network Control Protocol
NFE	Network Front End
NFS	Network File Server, Network File Service (SUN,UNIX)
NIU	Network Interface Unit
NNMP	Network Management Protocol (OSI)
NOC	Network Operations Center (ARPA)
NOS	Network Operations System
NPDU	Network Protocol Data Unit (ISO, IP, DP)

NSDU	Network Service Data Unit (ISO)
NSF	National Science Foundation (national USA-Net)
NSP	Network Service Protocols (Layer 4-5 Protocol DECNET)
NUI	Network User Identification
NVP-2	Network Virtual Protocol version 2
NVT	Network Virtual Terminal
ODA	Office Document Architecture (ISO/OSI DP)
ODIF	Office Document Interchange Formats
ODP	Open Distributed Processing
OSI	Open System Interconnection
PABX	Private Automatic Branch Exchange
PAD	Packet Assember/Disassembler (X.3,X.28,X.29)
PAM	Pulse Amplitude Modulation
PAX	Private Automatic Exchange
PBX	Private Branch Exchange
PC	Path Control(SNA)
PCM	Pulse Code Modulation, Plug Compatible Manufactures
PCU	Packet Control Unit
PDAU	Physical Delivery Access Unit
PDM	Pulse Duration Modulation
PDU	Protocol Data Unit
PIU	Path Information Unit
PL	Presentation Layer, Physical Layer
PM	Phase Modulation
PPM	Pulse Position Modulation
PRN	Packet Radio Network
PS	Packet Switching, Presentation Service (SNA)
PSK	Phase-Shift Keying
PSN	Packet Switched Data Network, packet Switch Network
PTT	Post, Telegraph and Telephone Authority
PU	Physical Unit (Hardware connection type(Typ 1-5), SNA)
PWM	Pulse Width Modulation
QM	Quadrature Modulation

QPSK	Quadrature Phase Shift-Keying
RAN	Random Access Networks
RD	Request Disconnect(HDLC)
REJ	Reject
RF	Radio Frequency
RJE	Remote Job Entry (IBM, 2780,3780)
RJEP	Remote Job Entry Protocol
RPC	Remote Procedure Call
RTP	Real Time Protocol
RU	Request/Response Unit (part of BIU, Status information, SNA)
S/N	Signal-to-Noise ratio
SCSI	Small Computer System Interface (ANSI)
SCU	System Control Unit
SDLC	Synchronous Data Link Control
SDMA	Space Division Multiple Access
SFS	Schared File System
SL	Session Layer
SMTP	Simple Mail Transfer Protocol
SNA	Systems Network Architecture (IBM)
SSCP	System Service Control Point (Interface inside a domain, SNA)
ST	Stream Protocol
STDM	Statistical Time Division Multiplexing
STX	Start of Text
SYNC	Synchronization Characters
TC	Transmission Control (SNA), Trunk Control (DCA)
TCP	Transmission Control Protocol
TDM	Time Division Multiplexing
TDMA	Time Division Multiple Access, Time Division Multiplexing Access
TELNET	Telecommunication Network (ARPANET Virtual Terminal Protocol)
TFTP	Trivial File Transfer Protocol (ARPA, DoD)
TIP	Terminal Interface Processor (ARPANET, response PAD)
TL	Transport Layer
TLI	Transport Layer Interface

TOP	Technical and Office Product System
TSDU	Transport Service Data Unit
UART	Universal Asychnronous Receiver Transceiver
UDP	User Datagram Protocol (ARPA)
UHF	Ultra High Frequency
USRT	Universal Synchronous Receiver Transceiver
UUCP	Unix to Unix CoPy, also a network
VADS	Value-Added Data Services
VAN	Value Added Networks
VC	Virtual Circuit
VDI	Virtual Device Interface
VFS	Virtual File Server, Virtual File Store
VHF	Very High Frequency
VR	Virtual Route (VC, SNA)
VRC	Vertical Redundancy Check (check information)
VT	Virtual Terminal
VTP	Virtual Terminal Protocol (ISO)
VTS	Virtual Terminal Service (OSI)
WWMCCS	World Wide Military Command and Control System (DoD)
XNS	Xerox Network Systems
YP	Yellow Pages (NFS, Services Database)

Bibliography

Abramson, N., "The ALOHA System--Another Alternative for Computer Communications." *Proceedings of the FICC*, 1970.

Abramson, N., and Kuo, F. F. (eds.), *Computer-Communication Networks*. Englewood Cliffs, NJ: Prentice-Hall, 1973.

Abrams, M., Blanc, R. P., and Cotton, I. W., *Computer Networks: Text and References for a Tutorial*. New York, NY: IEEE Computer Society, 1976.

Aho, A. V.; Hopocroft, J. E.; and Ullman, J. D., *The Design and Analysis of Computer Algorithms*. Reading, MA: Addison-Wesley, 1974.

Ahuja, V., *Design and Analysis of Computer Communications/Networks*. New York, NY: McGraw-Hill, 1982.

Alcatel Corporation, "Leading LAN Standards." *Communications Week*, no date.

Andrews, D. W., and Schultz, G. D., " A Token-Ring Architecture for Local Area Networks: An Update." *Proceedings, COMPCON Fall 82*, IEEE, 1982.

Atkins, J., "Path Control: The Transport Network of SNA." *IEEE Trans. on Comm.*, April 1980.

AT&T Network Planning Division, *Notes on the Network*, 1980.

AT&T Technical Reference Number 54016, 1981.

Bachman, C., and Canepa, M., *The Session Control Layer of an Open System Interconnection.* International Organization for Standardization OSIC/TG 6/79-10, 1979.

Baran, P., "On Distributed Communications: An Introduction to Distributed Communications Networks." Report RM-3420-PR, Rand Corp., Santa Monica, CA, August 1964.

Bartoli, P. D., "The Application Layer of the Reference Model of Open System Interconnection." *Proceedings of the IEEE, 71,* 12, December 1983.

Bartee, T. C. (ed.), *Data Communications, Networks, and Systems.* Indianapolis, IN: Howard W. Sams & Co., Inc., 1985.

Bates, R., and Abramson, P., "You Can Use Phone Wire for Your Token Ring LAN." *Data Communications,* November 1986.

Beckenbach, E. F. (ed.), *Modern Mathematics for the Engineer.* New York, NY: McGraw-Hill, 1961.

Bell Telephone Companies, selected manuals: "Communicating and the Telephone," "How the Telephone Works," "Bell's Great Invention." Available from local Bell Operating Company offices; no date.

Bell Telephone, "Acoustic and Inductive Coupling for Data and Voice Transmission." Bell System Tech Reference No. 41803, Murray Hill, NJ, October 1972.

Bellamy, John, *Digital Telephony.* New York, NY: John Wiley and Sons, 1982.

Bell Laboratories, *Transmission Systems for Communications,* Number 500-036. Holmdel, NJ, 1982.

Bellamy, John, *Digital Telephony.* New York, NY: John Wiley and Sons, 1982.

Bertine, H. U., "Physical Level Protocols." *IEEE Trans. on. Comm.*, *28*, 4, April 1980.

Bhusri, G., "Considerations for ISDN Planning and Implementation." *IEEE Communications Magazine*, January 1984.

Binder, R.; Abramson, N; Kuo, F.; Okinaka, A.; and Wax, D., "ALOHA Packet Broadcasting - A Retrospect." *Proceedings, National Computer Conference*, 1975.

Binder, R., "Packet Protocols for Broadcast Satellites." In *Protocols and Techniques for Data Communication Networks* (ed. by F. Kuo). Englewood Cliffs, NJ: Prentice-Hall, 1981.

Black, U., "Data Link Controls: The Great Variety Calls for Wise and Careful Choices." *Data Communications*, June 1982.

Black, U., *Physical Interfaces*. Arlington, VA: Information Engineering Educational Series, 1986.

Black, U., *Computer Networks*. Englewood Cliffs, NJ: Prentice-Hall, 1987.

Black, U., *Communications: An Introduction*. Arlington, VA: Information Engineering Educational Series, 1987.

Black, U., *Computer Networks: Protocols, Standards and Interfaces*. Englewood Cliffs, NJ: Prentice-Hall, 1987.

Black, U., *Data Networks: Concepts, Theory, and Practice*. Englewood Cliffs, NJ: Prentice-Hall, 1989.

Boehm, S. P., and Baran, P., "On Distributed Communications II: Digital Simulation of Hot-Potato Routing in a Broadband Distributed Communications Network." Memo RM-3103-PR, Rand Corp., Santa Monica, CA, August 1964.

Boehm, B. W., and Mobley, R. L., "Adaptive Routing Techniques for Distributed Communications Systems." *IEEE Trans. on Comm. Tech.*, *COM-17*, 3, June 1969.

Boorstyn, R. R., and Frank, H., "Large-Scale Network Topological Optimization." *IEEE Trans. on Comm. Tech.*, *COM-25*, 1, January 1977.

Borsuk, L. M., "What You Should Know about Fiber Optics." *Digital Design*, *8*, 7, August 1978.

Bracewell, R., *The Fourier Transform and Its Applications*. New York, NY: McGraw-Hill, 1965.

Briley, B. E., *Introduction to Telephone Switching*. Reading, MA: Addison-Wesley, 1983.

Brown, J., and Glazier, E. V. D., *Telecommunications*. London: Chapman and Hall, 1974.

Brugger, R. D., "Information: Its Measure and Communications." *Computer Design*, *11*, 4, April 1973.

Buckley, J. E., "Bandwidth: Information Capacity and Throughput." *Computer Design*, *11*, 4, April 1973.

Bux, W., "Local-Area Subnetworks: A Performance Comparison." *IEEE Trans. on Comm.*, October 1981.

Bux, W.; Closs, F.; Janson, P. A.; Kummerle, K.; Miller, H. R.; and Rothauser, H., "A Local-Area Communication Network Based on a Reliable Token Ring System." *Proceedings, International Symposium on Local Computer Networks*, 1982.

Cacciamani, E. R., and Kim, K. S., "Circumventing the Problem of Propagational Delay on Satellite Data Channels." *Data Communications*, *3*, 7/8, July/August 1975.

Carlson, D. E., "Bit-Oriented Data Link Control Procedures." *IEEE Trans. on Comm.*, *COM-28*, 4, April 1980.

Callon, R., "Internetwork Protocols." *Proceedings of the IEEE*, December 1983.

Campbell, G. A., and Foster, R. M., *Fourier Integrals for Practical Applications.* Princeton, NJ: D. Van Nostrand, 1948.

Campbell, J., *The RS-232 Solution.* Berkeley, CA: Sybex, Inc., 1984.

Cerf, V., and Kristein, P. I., "Issues in Packet-Network Interconnection." *Proceedings of the IEEE*, November 1978.

Cerf, V. C., and Cain, E., "The DoD Internet Architecture Model." *Computer Networks*, no. 7, 1983.

Chandy, K., and Ramamoorthy, C., "Rollback and Recovery Strategies for Computer Programs." *IEEE Trans. on Computers*, June 1972.

Chapin, A., "Connectionless Data Transmission." *Computer Communications Review*, April 1982.

Cerny, R. A., and Hudson, M., C., "Fiberoptics for Digital Systems." *Digital Design*, 7, 7, August 1977.

Chapin, A. L., "Connections and Connectionless Data Transmission." *Proceedings of the IEEE*, *71*, 12, December 1983.

Chou, W. (ed.), *Computer Communications, vol. I: Principles.* Englewood Cliffs, NJ: Prentice-Hall, 1983.

Chou, W. (ed.), *Computer Communications, vol. II: Systems and Applications.* Englewood Cliffs, NJ: Prentice-Hall, 1985.

Churchill, R. V., *Fourier Series and Boundary Value Problems*. New York, NY: McGraw-Hill, 1963.

Chu, W. W., and Konkeim, A. G., "On The Analysis and Modeling of a Class of Computer Communications Systems." *IEEE Trans. on Comm., COM-20*, 3, June 1972.

Clark, D. D.; Pogran, K. T.; and Reed, D. P., "An Introduction to Local Area Networks." *Proceedings of the IEEE*, November 1978.

Clavieu, M. H., "Specifying Instrument Cables." *Instruments and Control Systems, 51*, 11, November 1978.

Clement, M. A., *Transmission*. Chicago, IL: Telephony Publishing Corp., no date.

Conrad, J. W., "Character-Oriented Data Link Control Protocols." *IEEE Trans. on Comm., COM-28*, 4, April 1980.

Conrad, J. W., "Services and Protocols of the Data Link Layer." *Proceedings of the IEEE, 71*, 12, December 1983.

Corrigan, M., "Defense Data Network Protocols." *Proceedings, EASCON 82*, 1982.

Cotton, I. W., "Technologies for Local Area Computer Networks." *Proceedings, Local Area Communications Network Symposium*, 1979.

Couch, L. W., *Digital and Analog Communications Systems*. New York, NY: Macmillan Publishing Co., 1983.

Couch, L. W., *Digital and Analog Communications Systems* (2nd edition). New York, NY: Macmillan Publishing Co., 1987.

Crowther, W.; Rettberg, R.; Walden, D.; Orenstein, S.; and Heart, F., "A System for Broadcast Communication: Reservation ALOHA." *Proceedings, Sixth Hawaii International System Science Conference*, 1973.

Cypser, R., *Communications Architecture for Distributed Systems*. Reading, MA: Addison-Wesley, 1978.

Dantzig, G., *Linear Programming and Extensions*. Princeton, NJ: Princeton University Press, 1963.

Davenport, W. P., *Modern Data Communication*. New York, NY: Hayden, 1971.

Davey, T., "Modems." *Proceedings of the IEEE*, November 1972.

Davies, D. W., and Barber, D. L. A., *Communications Networks for Computers*. London: John Wiley and Sons, 1973.

Davies, D. W.; Barber, D. L. A.; Price, W. L.; and Solomonides, C. M., *Computer Networks and Their Protocols*. New York, NY: John Wiley and Sons, 1979.

Day, J. D., and Zimmerman, H., "The OSI Reference Model." *Proceedings of the IEEE*, *71*, 12, December 1983.

Defense Communications Agency, *DDN Protocol Handbook*. Menlo Park, CA: DDN Network Information Center, SRI International, December 1885.

Deasington, R. J., *X.25 Explained*. Chicester, England: Halsted Press, 1985.

DECnet Digital Network Architecture, Document Number AA-X435A-TK. Maynard, MA: Digital Equipment Corporation, May 1982.

Davies, D. W., "The Control of Congestion in Packet Switching Networks." *Proceedings of the Second ACM/IEEE Symposium on the Optimization of Data Communications Systems*, Palo Alto, CA, October 1971.

DECnet Publication Number AA-N149A-TC.   Maynard, MA: Digital Equipment
    Corporation, May 1982.

Deo, N., *Graph Theory with Applications to Engineering and Computer Science.*
    Englewood Cliffs, NJ: Prentice-Hall, 1974.

Derfler, F., and Stallings, W., *A Manager's Guide to Local Networks.* Englewood Cliffs,
    NJ: Prentice-Hall/Spectrum, 1983.

Dijkstra, E., "A Note on Two Problems in Connection with Graphs." *Numerical
    Mathematics*, October 1959.

Dineson, M. A., and Picazo, J. J., "Broadband Technology Magnifies Local Network
    Capability." *Data Communications*, *8*, 2, February 1980.

Dineson, M. A., "Broadband Coaxial Local Area Networks, Part I: Concepts and
    Comparisons." *Computer Design*, *18*, 6, June 1980.

Dineson, M. A., "Broadband Coaxial Local Area Networks, Part II: Hardware."
    Computer Design, *18*, 7, July 1980.

Dixon, R. C., "Ring Network Topology for Local Data Communications." *Proceedings,
    COMPCON Fall 82*, IEEE, 1982.

Doll, D. R., "Multiplexing and Concentration." *Proceedings of the IEEE*, *60*, 11,
    November 1972.

Doll, D. R., *Data Communications: Facilities, Networks and System Design.* New
    York, NY: John Wiley and Sons, 1978.

Donnan, R., and Kersey, J., "Synchronous Data Link Control: A Perspective." *IBM
    Systems Journal*, May 1974.

Doweier, V. L., "Transmission Measurements: Part One." *Telecommunications*, *7*, 8,
    August 1973.

Doweier, V. L., "Transmission Measurements: Part Two." *Telecommunications*, 7, 9, September 1973.

Duyan, P., Jr., "Fiber Optic Interconnection." *Industrial Research/Development*, 21, 12, December 1979.

ECMA-61. HDLC, European Computer Manufacturers Association, August 1979.

Editors, "Why Voice Channels Are So Bad for Data." *The Datacomm Planner*, August 1973.

Electronic Industries Association (EIA), *Dial and Answer Systems.* EIA-366, 1966.

Ellis, R. L., *Designing Data Networks.* Englewood Cliffs, NJ: Prentice-Hall, 1986.

Emmons, W. F., and Chandler, A. S., "OSI Session Layer: Services and Protocols." *Proceedings of the IEEE*, 71, 12, December 1983.

Ennis, G.; Kaufman, D.; and Biba, K., *DoD Protocol Reference Model.* Sytek, TR-82026, September 1982.

Ennis, G., "Development of the DoD Protocol Reference Model." *Proceedings, SIGCOMM '83 Symposium*, 1983.

Falk, G., "The Structure and Function of Network Protocols." In Chou (ed.) *Computer Communications, vol I: Principles.* Englewood Cliffs, NJ: Prentice-Hall, 1983.

Faro, R. M., *The Transmission of Information.* New York, NY: John Wiley and Sons, 1961.

Fishman, G. S., "Statistical Analysis for Queueing Simulations." *Management Science*, 20, 3, November 1973.

Folts, H., "Coming of Age: A Long-Awaited Standard for Heterogenous Nets." *Data Communications*, January 1981.

Folts, H., *OSI Workbook*. Vienna, VA: OMNICOM, Inc., 1983.

Ford, L., and Fulkerson, D., *Flows in Networks*. Princeton, NJ: Princeton University Press, 1962.

Frank, H., and Chou, W., "Topological Optimization of Computer Networks." *Proceedings of the IEEE, 60*, 11, November 1972.

Franta, W., and Chlamtec, I., *Local Networks*. Lexington, MA: Lexington Books, 1981.

Freeman, R., *Telecommunication Transmission Handbook*. New York, NY: Wiley - Interscience, 1975.

Freeman, R., *Telecommunication System Engineering*. New York, NY: Wiley - Interscience, 1980.

Freeman, R., *Telecommunication Transmission Handbook*. New York, NY: John Wiley and Sons, 1981.

Fultz, G. L., and Kleinrock, L., "Adaptive Routing Techniques for Store-and-Forward Computer Communications Networks." *Proceedings of the IEEE International Conference on Communications*, June 1971.

Fultz, G. L., "Adaptive Routing Techniques for Message Switching Computer-Communications Network." Ph.D. Dissertation, University of California, Los Angeles, CA, June 1972.

Garlick, L.; Rom, R.; and Postel, J., "Reliable Host-to-Host Protocols: Problems and Techniques." *Proceedings, Fifth Data Communications Symposium*, 1972.

Geria, M., and Mason, D., "Distributed Routing in Hybrid Packet and Circuit Data Networks." *Proceedings of the IEEE COMPCON*, Fall 1978.

Gerla, M., "The Design of Store-and-Forward (S/F) Networks for Computer Communications." Report AD-758-204, NTIS, January 1973.

Gerla, M., and Kleinrock, L., "Flow Control: A Comparative Survey." *IEEE Trans. on Comm.*, April 1980.

Gerla, M., "Routing and Flow Control," in Kuo, F. (ed.), *Protocols and Techniques for Data Communication Networks*. Englewood Cliffs, NJ: Prentice-Hall, 1981.

Giallorenzi, T. G., "Optical Communications Research and Technology: Fiber Optics." *Proceedings of the IEEE*, *66*, 7, July 1978.

Greene, W. H., and Pooch, U. W., "A Review of Classification Schemes for Computer Communications Networks." *Computer*, *10*, 11, November 1977.

Green, P., "An Introduction to Network Architectures and Protocols." *IEEE Trans. on Comm.*, April 1980.

Green, J. H., "Microcomputer Programs Can Be Adapted for Data Network Designs." *Data Communications*, April 1986.

GTE Lenkurt Inc., *The Lenkurt Demodulator*, *20*, 10, San Carlos, CA, October 1971.

GTE Lenkurt Inc., "Increasing PCM Span-Line Capacity." *The Lenkurt Demodulator*, *25*, 5/6, San Carlos, CA, May/June 1976.

GTE Lenkurt Inc., "Fiber Optics in Telecommunications." *The Lenkurt Demodulator*, *27*, 11/12, San Carlos, CA, November/December 1978.

GTE Lenkurt Inc., "Satellite Communications Update, Part I." *The Lenkurt Demodulator*, *28*, 1/2, San Carlos, CA, January/February 1979.

GTE Lenkurt Inc., "Satellite Communications Update, Part II." *The Lenkurt Demodulator*, *28*, 5/6, San Carlos, CA, May/June 1979.

Halsall, F., *Data Communications, Computer Networks and OSI* (2nd edition). Reading, MA: Addison-Wesley, 1988.

Hamming, R. W., *Coding and Information Theory*. Englewood Cliffs, NJ: Prentice-Hall, 1980

Hammond, J. L., and O'Reilly, J. P., *Performance Analysis of Local Computer Networks*. Reading, MA: Addison-Wesley, 1986.

Hartwig, G., "What the New Data Satellite Will Offer." *Data Communications*, *4*, 3/4, March/April 1976.

Hasesawa; Hideo; Miyahara; Techisawara; Tuchihaa; and Yoshimi Teshigawara, "A Comparative Evaluation of Switching Methods in Computer Communications Networks." *ICC-75*, San Francisco, CA, June 16-18, 1975.

Haugdahl, J. S., "The Token-Ring Solution." *PC Tech Journal*, *5*, 1, January 1988.

Hayes, J. F., "Performance Models of an Experimental Computer Communications Network." *Bell System Technical Journal*, *53*, 2, February 1974.

Heath Company, *Electronic Communications*. Benton Harbor, MI, 1981.

Heggestad, H. M., "The Testbed for Evaluation of Network Routing and Control Techniques." *MICOM 85*, October 1985.

Hickey, J., "Wire and Cable--What's Happening?" *Instruments and Control Systems*, *53*, 8, August 1980.

Hollis, L. L., "OSI Presentation Layer Activities." *Proceedings of the IEEE*, *71*, 12, December 1983.

Honeywell Information Systems, Inc., *Distributed Systems Architecture*, CT37-01, 1982.

Hopkins, G. T., "Multimode Communications of the MITRENET." *Proceedings*, *Local Area Communications Network Symposium*, 1979.

Hopkins, G. T., and Wagner, P. E., *Multiple Access Digital Communications Systems*. U.S. Patent 4, 210, 780; July 1, 1980.

Hurley, B. R.; Seidl, C. J. R.; and Sewell, W. F., "A Survey of Dynamic Routing Methods for Circuit Switched Traffic." *IEEE Communications Magazine*, 25, 9, September 1987.

IBM Corp., *System Network Architecture: Concepts and Products*. GC30-3072, 1981.

Institute for Electrical and Electronic Engineers. *IEEE Projet 802, Local Network Standards*, 1983.

The Institute of Electrical and Electronics Engineering, "Logical Link Control." *ANSI/IEEE std. 802.2*, 1985.

The Institute of Electrical and Electronics Engineering, "Carrier Sense Multiple Access with Collision Detection (CSMA/CD) Access Method and Physical Layer Specification." *ANSI/IEEE std. 802.3*, 1985.

The Institute of Electrical and Electronics Engineering, "Token-Passing Bus Access Method and Physical Layer Specifications." *ANSI/IEEE std. 802.4*, 1985.

The Institute of Electrical and Electronics Engineering, "Token Ring Access Method and Physical Layer Specification." *ANSI/IEEE std. 802.5*, 1985.

The Institute of Electrical and Electronics Engineering, "Terrestrial Optical Fiber Systems," (special issue). *IEEE Communications Magazine*, 25, 10, October 1987.

International Organization for Standardization, "Information Processing Systems--Open Systems Interconnection--Basic Reference Model." DIS 7498, 1984.

International Organization for Standardization. *Basic Reference Model for Open Systems Interconnection*, DIS 7498, 1983.

International Organization for Standardization. *Correction Oriented Transport Protocol*, DP 8073, 1983.

ISO 8822/3. *OSI: Presentation Service/Protocol Specification*, 1985.

ISO 8326/7. *OSI: Session Service/Protocol Specification*, 1985.

International Telephone and Telegraph Corp., *Reference Data for Radio Engineers*. Indianapolis, IN: Howard W. Sams, 1975.

Jacobs, I.; Binder, R.; and Hoverston, E., "General Purpose Packet Satellite Networks." *Proceedings of the IEEE*, November 1978.

Jayant, N. S., and Noll, P., *Digital Coding of Waveforms: Principles and Applications to Speech and Video*. Englewood Cliffs, NJ: Prentice-Hall, 1984.

Jeruchim, M. C., "A Survey of Interference Problems and Applications to Geostationary Satellite Networks." *Proceedings of the IEEE*, *65*, 3, March 1977.

Johnson, S., "Architectural Evolution: Digital Unveils Its DECnet Phase III." *Data Communications*, March 1980.

Jurenko, J. A., "All About Modems and Related Topics." Huntsville, AL: Universal Data Systems, 1981.

Kahn, A. E., and Crowther, W. R., "A Study of the ARPA Computer Network Design and Performance." Report 2161; Bolt, Beranek, and Newman, Inc. Cambridge, MA, August 1971.

Kaminiski, M., "Protocols for Communicating in the Factory." *IEEE Spectrum*, April 1986.

Kaplan, W., *Advanced Calculus*. Reading, MA: Addison-Wesley, 1952.

Kennedy, G., *Electronics Communications Systems*. New York, NY: McGraw-Hill, 1970.

Kimbleton, S. F., and Schneider, M. G., "Computer Communication Networks: Approaches, Objectives, and Performance Considerations." *ACM Computing Surveys*, *7*, 3, September 1975.

Kleinrock, L., *Communications Nets: Stochastic Message Flow and Delay*. New York, NY: McGraw-Hill, 1964.

Kleinrock, L., "Analytical and Simulation Methods in Computer Network Design." *Proceedings of the AFIPS SICC*, 1970.

Kleinrock, L., and Lam., S., "Packet Switching in a Slotted Satellite Channel." *NCC, AFIPS Conference Proceedings*, vol. 42, 1973.

Kleinrock, L., "Advanced Teleprocessing Systems." Report AD-A034-111, *NTIS*, June 1976.

Kleinrock, L., "Principles and Lessons in Packet Communications." *Proceedings of the IEEE*, November 1978.

Knightson, K. G., "The Transport Layer Standardization." *Proceedings of the IEEE*, *71*, 12, December 1983.

Krechmer, K., "Integrating Medium Speed Modems into Communications Networks." *Computer Design*, *17*, 2, February 1978.

Kullstan, P., (guest ed.), (special issue), "Satellite Communications." *IEEE Communications Magazine, 22,* 3, March 1984.

Kuo, F. (ed.), *Protocols and Techniques for Data Communication Networks,* Englewood Cliffs, NJ: Prentice-Hall, 1981.

Lam, S., "Packet Broadcast Networks--A Performance Analysis of the R-ALOHA Protocol." *IEEE Trans. on Computers,* July 1980.

Lane, M. G., *Data Communications Software Design,* Boston, MA: Boyd & Fraser Publishing Co., 1985.

Laughans, R. A., and Mitchell, T. H., "Linking the Satellite to a Data Communications Net." *Data Communications, 8,* 2, February 1980.

Levine, S. T., "Focus on Modems and Multiplexers." *Electronics Design, 27,* October 25, 1979.

Li, T., "Optical Fiber Communication--The State of the Art." *IEEE Trans. Comm., COM-26,* 7, July 1978.

Linnell, D., *SNA Concepts Design and Implementation.* McLean, VA: Gate Technology, 1987.

Linnington, P. F., "The Virtual Filestore Concept." *Computer Networks,* February 1984.

Lippman, R., "New Routing and Preemption Algorithms for Circuit-Switched Mixed Media Networks." *MILCOM 85,* October 1985.

Liu, M. T., "Distributed Loop Computer Networks." In *Advances in Computers,* Vol. 17 (ed. M. C. Yovits). New York, NY: Academic Press, 1978.

Liu, M. T.; Hilal, W.; and Groomes, B. H., " Performance Evaluation of Channel Access Protocols for Local Computer Networks." *Proceedings, COMPCON Fall 82,* 1982.

Luczak, E. C., "Global Bus Computer Communication Techniques." *Proceedings, Computer Network Symposium,* 1978.

Lyon, D., "How to Evaluate a High-Speed Modem." *Telecommunications, 9,* 10, October 1975.

Markov, J. D., and Strole, N. C., "Token-Ring Local Area Networks: A Perspective." *Proceedings, COMPCON Fall 82,* IEEE, 1982.

Markley, R. W., *Data Communications and Interoperability.* Englewood Cliffs, NJ: Prentice-Hall, 1970.

Martin, J., *Teleprocessing Network Organization.* Englewood Cliffs, NJ: Prentice-Hall, 1970.

Martin, J., *Systems Analysis for Data Transmission.* Englewood Cliffs, NJ: Prentice-Hall, 1972.

Martin, J., *Telecommunications and the Computer.* Englewood Cliffs, NJ: Prentice-Hall, 1977.

Martin, J., *Future Developments in Telecommunications.* Englewood Cliffs, NJ: Prentice-Hall, 1977.

Martin, J., *Communications Satellite Systems.* Englewood Cliffs, NJ: Prentice-Hall, 1978.

Martin, J., *Computer Networks and Distributed Processing.* Englewood Cliffs, NJ: Prentice-Hall, 1981.

Martin, J., and Kavanaugh, C. K., *SNA: IBM's Networking Solution.* Englewood
    Cliffs, NJ: Prentice-Hall, 1987.

McCaskill, R. C., "Fiber Optics: The Connection of the Future." *Data
    Communications*, 7, 1, January 1979.

McClelland, F. M., "Services and Protocols of the Physical Layer." *Proceedings of the
    IEEE*, *71*, 12, December 1983.

McFarland, R., "Protocols in a Computer Internetworking Environment." *Proceedings,
    EASCON 79*, 1979.

McHale, J., "Answering one of Connectivity's Interesting Challenges." *LAN Times*,
    March 1988.

McNamara, J. E., *Technical Aspects of Data Communication.* Bedford, MA: Digital
    Press, 1982.

McQuillan, J., "Adaptive Routing Algorithms for Distributed Computer Networks."
    Report AD-781-467, *NTIS*, May 1974.

McQuillan, J. M., and Cerf, V. G., *A Practical View of Computer Communications
    Protocols.* Washington, DC: IEEE Computer Society Press, 1978.

McShane, T. J., "Acoustic Coupling for Data Transmission." *Digital Design*, *10*, 6,
    June 1980.

Metcalfe, R. M., and Boggs, D. R., "Ethernet: Distributed Packet Switching for Local
    Computer Networks." *Proceedings of the ACM*, 1976.

Mier, E., "Bell Shines New Light on Digital Transmission Specification." *Data
    Communications*, April 1983.

Miller, C. K., and Thompson, D. M., "Making a Case for Token Passing in Local Networks." *Data Communications*, March 1982.

Mokhoff, N., "Communications: Fiber Optics." *IEEE Spectrum*, January 1981.

Morrison, R., "Answers to Grounding and Shielding Problems." *Instruments and Control Systems*, *52*, 6, June 1979.

Myers, W., "Toward a Local Network Standard." *IEEE Micro*, August 1982.

National Bureau of Standards. *Features of Internetwork Protocols*, ICST/HLNP-80-8, July 1980.

National Bureau of Standards. *Features of the Transport and Session Protocols*, ICST/HLNP-80-1, March 1980.

National Bureau of Standards. *Specification of a Transport Protocol for Computer Communications*, ICST/HLNP-83-1 to ICST/HLNP-83-5, January 1983.

Nelson, J., "802: A Progress Report." *Datamation*, September 1983.

Nelson, K. C., "Understanding Station Carrier." *Lee's ABC of the Telephone*, Geneva, IL, 1975.

Neumann, J., "OSI Transport and Session Layers: Services and Protocol." *Proceedings*, *INFOCOM 83*, 1983.

Noguchi, T.; Davido, Y.; and Nossek, J. A., "Modulation Techniques for Microwave Digital Radio." *IEEE Communications Magazine*, *24*, 10, October 1986.
Nording, K. I., "Taking a Fresh Look at Voice-Grade Line Conditioning." *Data Communications*, *3*, 5/6, May/June 1975.

Novell, Inc., *LAN Evaluation Report*. Provo, UT: Novell, Inc., 1986.

Padlipsky, M., "A Perspective on the ARPANET Reference Model." *Proceedings, INFOCOM 83*, 1983.

Pake, G. E., "Research at Xerox PARC: a Founder's Assessment." *IEEE Spectrum*, October 1985.

Papoulis, A., *The Fourier Integral and Its Applications*. New York, NY: McGraw-Hill, 1962.

Parker, R., and Shapiro, S., "Untangling Local Area Networks." *Computer Design*, March 1983.

Penny, B. K., and Baghdadi, A. A., "A Survey of Computer Communications Loop Networks." *Computer Communications*, August and October, 1979.

Personick, S. D., "Fiber Optic Communication." *IEEE Communications Society Magazine*, *16*, 3, March 1978.

Pickens, R., "Wideband Transmission Media I: Radio Communications." In Kuo, F. (ed.), *Computer Communications, Vol. I: Principles*. Englewood Cliffs, NJ: Prentice-Hall, 1983.

Pickens, R., "Wideband Transmission Media II: Satellite Communications." In Chou, W. (ed.), *Computer Communications, Vol. I: Principles*. Englewood Cliffs, NJ: Prentice-Hall, 1983.

Pickholtz, R. L. (ed.), *Local Area and Multiple Access Networks*. Rockville, MD: Computer Science Press, 1986.

Pooch, U. W.; Greene, W. H.; and Moss, G. G., *Telecommunications and Networking*. Boston, MA: Little, Brown, and Company, 1983.

Postel, J. B.; Sunshine, C. A.; and Ciheu, D., "The ARPA Internet Protocol." *Computer Networks*, 1981.

Pouzin, L., and Zimmerman, H., "A Tutorial on Protocols." *Proceedings of the IEEE*, November 1978.

Pouzin, L., "Methods, Tools, and Observations on Flow Control in Packet-Switched Data Networks." *IEEE Trans. on Comm.*, April 1981.

Pritchard, W., "The History and Future of Commercial Satellite Communications." *IEEE Communications Magazine*, May 1984.

Prosser, R. T., "Routing Procedures in Communications Networks--Part I: Random Procedures" and, "Routing Procedures in Communications Networks--Part I: Directory Procedures." *IRE Transcripts on Communication Systems*, December 1962.

Rauch-Hindin, W., "IBM's Local Network Scheme." *Data Communications*, May 1982.

Rauch-Hindin, W., "Upper-Level Network Protocols." *Electronic Design*, March 3, 1983.

Rey, R. F. (ed.), *Engineering and Operations in the Bell Systems*, (2nd edition). Murray Hill, NJ: AT&T Laboratories, 1983.

Riley, E. W., and Acuma, V. E., "Transmission Systems." *Lee's ABC of the Telephone*, Geneva, IL, 1976.

Roberts, L., and Wessler, B., "Computer Network Development to Achieve Resource Sharing." *Proceedings, Spring Joint Computer Conference*, 1970.

Roberts, L., "Dynamic Allocation of Satellite Capacity Through Packet Reservation." *Proceedings, National Computer Conference*, 1973.

Roberts, L., "ALOHA Packet System With and Without Slots and Capture." *Computer Communications Review*, April 1975.

Rocher, E., "Taking a Fresh Look at Local Data Distribution." *Data Communications*, May 1979.

Roden, M., *Digital and Data Communication Systems*. Englewood Cliffs, NJ: Prentice-Hall, 1982.

Roman, G. S., "The Design of Broadband Coaxial Cable Networks for Multimode Communications." The MITRE Corp., Report No. MTR-3527, November 1977.

Rosenthal, R. (ed.), *The Selection of Local Area Computer Networks*. National Bureau of Standards Special Publication 500-96, November 1982.

Rosner, R., *Packet Switching: Tomorrow's Communications Today*. Belmont, CA: Lifetime Learning, 1982.

Roux, E., "OSI's Final Frontier: The Application Layer." *Data Communications*, January 1988.

Rudin, H., "On Routing and Delta Routing: A Taxonomy of Techniques for Packet-Switched Networks." Report RZ-701, IBM Research, Zurich, Switzerland, June 1975.

Rudin, H., "A Performance Comparison of Routing Techniques for Packet-Switched Networks." Report RZ-702, IBM Research, Zurich, Switzerland, June 1975.

Rudin, H., "On Routing and Delta Routing: A Taxonomy and Performance Comparison of Techniques for Packet-Switched Networks." *IEEE Trans. on Comm.*, January 1976.

Rush, J. R., "Microwave Links Add Flexibility to Local Networks." *Electronics*, January 13, 1982.

Rustin, R. (ed.), *Computer Networks*. Englewood Cliffs, NJ: Prentice-Hall, 1972.

Salomon, J., "Satellite Communications Systems." *Telecommunications*, *13*, 5, May 1979.

Saltzer, J. H., and Pogran, K. T., "A Star-Shaped Ring Network with High Maintainability." *Proceedings*, *Local Area Communications Network Symposium*, 1979.

Sastry, A. R. K., "Performance Objectives for ISDN's." *IEEE Communications Magazine*, 22, 1, January 1984.

Scarcella, T., and Abbott, R., "Orbital Efficiency Through Satellite Digital Switching." *IEEE Communications Magazine*, May 1983.

Schutt, T. E., et. al., "Message-Handling Systems Based on the CCITT X.400 Recommendations." *IBM Systems Journal*, 26, 3, 1987.

Schwartz, M.; Bennet, W. R.; and Stein, S., *Communication Systems and Techniques*. New York, NY: McGraw-Hill, 1966.

Schwartz, M., *Computer-Communication Networks Design and Analysis*. Englewood Cliffs, NJ: Prentice-Hall, 1977.

Schwartz, M., and Stern, T. E., "Routing Techniques Used in Computer Communications Networks." *IEEE Trans. on Comm.*, April 1980.

Schwartz, M., "Optical Fiber Transmission--From Conception to Prominence in 20 Years." *IEEE Communications Magazine*, May 1984.

Schwartz, M., *Telecommunication Networks, Protocols, Modeling and Analysis*. Reading, MA: Addison-Wesley, 1987.

Selvaggi, P., "The Department of Defense Data Protocol Standardization Program." *Proceedings*, *EASCON 82*, 1982.

Seyer, M. D., *RS-232 Made Easy*. Englewood Cliffs, NJ: Prentice-Hall, 1984.

Shannon, C. E., "Communication in the Presence of Noise." *Proceedings of IRE*, January 1949.

Shannon, C. E., and Weaver, W., *The Mathematical Theory of Communication*. Urbana, IL: University of Illinois Press, 1949.

Sherman, K., *Data Communications: A User's Guide*, (2nd edition). Reston, VA: Reston Publishing Company, Inc., 1985.

Sherman, K., *Data Communications: A User's Guide*. Reston, VA: Reston Publishing Company, Inc., 1985.

Shotwell, R. E. (ed.), *The Ethernet Sourcebook*. Amsterdam, The Netherlands: Elsevier Science Publishing, 1985.

Sippl, C. J., *Data Communications Dictionary*. Princeton, NJ: D. Van Nostrand Reinhold, 1976.

SMC Corporation, "Programming the COM 9026." Hauppauge, NY: SMC Corporation, 1983.

Systems Network Architecture, Technical Overview, GC30-3073-0. IBM, 1982.

Sneddon, I. A., *Fourier Transforms*. New York, NY: McGraw-Hill, 1951.

Sondak, N. E., "Line-Sharing System Multiplexing and Concentrating." *Telecommunications*, *12*, 4, April 1978.

Spilker, J., *Digital Communications by Satellite*. Englewood Cliffs, NJ: Prentice-Hall, 1977.

Stallings, W., *Tutorial: Local Network Technology.* Silver Spring, MD: IEEE Computer Society Press, 1983.

Stallings, W., "Local Network Overview." *Signal Magazine*, January 1983.

Stallings, W., "The Integrated Services Digital Network." *Datamation*, December 1984.

Stallings, W., *Local Networks: An Introduction.* New York, NY: Macmillan Publishing Company, 1984.

Stallings, W., "Local Networks." *Scientific American*, 1984.

Stallings, W., "IEEE Project 802: Setting Standards for Local-Area Networks." *Computerworld*, February 13, 1984.

Stallings, W., "Local Networks." *Computing Surveys*, March 1984.

Stallings, W., *Data and Computer Communications.* New York, NY: Macmillan Publishing Company, 1985.

Stallings, W., *Tutorial: Computer Communications Architectures, Protocols, and Standards.* Silver Spring, MD: IEEE Computer Society Press, 1985.

Stallings, W., "Here is One Way to Get a Close Estimate of a Data Link's Efficiency." *Data Communications*, October 1986.

Stallings, W., *Handbook of Computer Communications Standards*, Vol. 2. New York, NY: MacMillan Publishing Company, 1987.

Stallings, W., *Handbook of Computer Communications Standards*, Vol. 1. New York, NY: MacMillan Publishing Company, 1987.

Stallings, W., *Handbook of Computer Communications Standards*, Vol. 2. New York, NY: MacMillan Publishing Company, 1987.

Stallings, W., *Handbook of Computer Communications Standards*, Vol. 3. New York, NY: MacMillan Publishing Company, 1987.

Stewart, A., "A User's Guide to ISDN Standards." *Telecommunications*, May 1988.

Stieglitz, M., "Local Network Access Tradeoffs." *Computer Design*, October 1981.

Stuck, B., "Which Local Net Bus Access is Most Sensitive to Congestion?" *Data Communications*, January 1983.

Stuck, B., "Calculating the Maximum Mean Data Rate in Local Area Networks." *Computer*, May 1983.

Suda, T.; Miyahara, H.; and Hasegawa, T., "Performance Evaluation of an Integrated Access Scheme in a Satellite Communication Channel." *IEEE Journal on Selected Areas in Communications*, January 1983.

Sunshine, C., "Transport Protocols for Computer Networks." In Kuo, F., *Protocols and Techniques for Data Communication Networks*. Englewood Cliffs, NJ: Prentice-Hall, 1981.

Sy, K. K.; Shiobara, M. O.; Yamagushi, M.; Kobayashi, Y.; Shukuya, S.; and Tomatsu, T., "OSI-SNA Interconnections." *IBM Systems Journal*, 26, 2, 1987.

Talley, D., *Basic Telephone Switching Systems*. Rochelle Park, NJ: Hayden Book Company, Inc., 1987.

Tanenbaum, A. S., *Computer Networks*. Englewood Cliffs, NJ: Prentice-Hall, 1981.

Tanenbaum, A. S., "Network Protocols." *Computing Surveys*, December 1981.

Tanenbaum, A. S., *Computer Networks* (2nd edition). Englewood Cliffs, NJ: Prentice-Hall, 1988.

Tobagi, F. A., "Multiaccess Protocols in Packet Communications Systems." *IEEE Trans. on Comm.*, April 1980.

Tropper, C., *Local Computer Network Technologies*. New York, NY: Academic Press, 1981.

Unsoy, M., and Shanahan, T., "X.75 Internetworking of Datapac and Telenet." *Proceedings, Seventh Data Communication Symposium*, 1981.

Walker, S., "Department of Defense Data Network." *Signal*, October 1982.

Ware, C., "The OSI Network Layer: Standards to Cope with the Real World." *Proceedings of the IEEE, 71*, 12, December 1983.

Webster's New Collegiate Dictionary (8th edition). Springfield, MA: G. and C. Merriam Company, 1977.

Wecker, S., "DNA: The Digital Network Architecture." *IEEE Trans. on Comm., COM-28*, 4, April 1980.

Weissler, R.; Binder, R.; Bressler, R.; Rettberg, R.; and Walden, D., "Synchronization and Multiple Access Protocols in the Initial Satellite IMP." *Proceedings, COMPCON Fall 78*, 1978.

Wilkes, M. V., and Wheeler, D. J., "The Cambridge Digital Communications Ring." *Proceedings, Local Area Communications Network Symposium*, 1979.

Withers, D. J., "Effective Utilization of the Geostationary Orbit for Satellite Communication." *Proceedings of the IEEE, 65*, 3, March 1977.

Wood, D. C., "Local Networks." In Chou, W. (ed.), *Computer Communications, Vol. I: Principles*. Englewood Cliffs, NJ: Prentice-Hall, 1984.

Yeh, L. P., "Telecommunication Transmission Media." *Telecommunications*, *10*, 4, April 1976.

Yeh, L. P., "Fiber-Optic Communications Systems." *Telecommunications*, *12*, 9, September 1978.

Ziemer, R. E., and Tranter, W. H., *Principles of Communications*. Boston, MA: Houghton Mifflin, 1976.

Ziemer, R.; Trauter, W.; and Fannin, D., *Signals and Systems: Continuous and Discrete*. New York, NY: Macmillan Publishing Company, 1983.

Zimmermann, H., "OSI-Reference Model-The ISO Model of Architecture for Open System Interconnection." *IEEE Trans. on Comm.*, April 1980.

Index